"This book is a landmark in the process i [...]
'quest for identity'; its imagining of a co[...] ...., ... iounu a
worthy chronicler and analyst in Amitav Acharya."

Anthony Reid
Emeritus Professor,
Australian National University

"extremely insightful, timely, and instructive"

Harvard Asia Quarterly

"... this is a thought-provoking book, loaded with valuable observations
and insights. It also provides a needed corrective to orientalist perspective
and to the sometimes tunnel vision of international relations scholars.
It is highly recommended, and should be added to the reading lists of
every Southeast Asia international relations course."

Contemporary Southeast Asia

"The book succeeds on a number of levels. For one thing, it pays close
attention to the notion of 'region' rather than simply examining the
various individual parts that constitute the area we now regard as
Southeast Asia. In doing so it stakes out new ground not only in theoretical
terms but practical ones as well. Moreover, because the development
of a regional identity has been consumed with efforts to create a unity
amongst its members, the charting of its successes, its failures, its hopes
and prospects is a worthwhile task in itself. The author is not simply
content to lay out the history of these in analytical fashion but rather
seeks to go beyond in assessing the way in which regionalism has affected
how they see themselves in terms of regional identity."

International Affairs

"... an excellent and compelling historical overview of regional relations
and regionalism in Southeast Asia. One of Acharya's stated objectives
in writing the book is to address a lack of historical analysis among
political scientists when it comes to examining Southeast Asia ... This
is an important book, which makes a valuable contribution towards the
study of Southeast Asian regionalism by opening new areas for discussion
and debate about this concept."

Canadian Council for Asia Pacific Security (CANCAPS) Bulletin

"In his comparative approach, ... [Acharya] challenges the 'gap' between discipline-based approach and the country-specific approach adopted by many area specialists ... While dealing with great complexity, Acharya is able to present his ideas clearly and concisely ..."

Journal of Contemporary Asia

"The book ... is timely in its attempt to discern the conceptual meaning of Southeast Asia's efforts to forge its own identity ... *The Quest for Identity* will be a welcome source for newcomers to the field. With its easy-to-read and subtle presentation of major topics, readers should be tempted into a deeper exploration of the field of Southeast Asian international relations."

International Relations of the Asia-Pacific

"... numerous insights and important but neglected facts to be learned from this account ..."

Australian Journal of International Affairs

"a perceptive study ... Southeast Asia is different from Europe, South Asia or the Middle East ... If ... ASEAN's core countries managed heroically to imagine themselves in Benedict Anderson's sense to be an entity, it was mainly because of the Cold War and the conflict in Vietnam. In the process, they developed cohesion, confidence and a sense of purpose. Acharya also exposes the hype ..."

Times Higher Education Supplement

THE MAKING OF
SOUTHEAST ASIA

A volume in the series

Cornell Studies in Political Economy

edited by Peter J. Katzenstein

A list of titles in this series is available at www.cornellpress.cornell.edu.

The **Institute of Southeast Asian Studies (ISEAS)** was established as an autonomous organization in 1968. It is a regional research centre dedicated to the study of socio-political, security and economic trends and developments in Southeast Asia and its wider geostrategic and economic environment. The Institute's research programmes are the Regional Economic Studies (RES, including ASEAN and APEC), Regional Strategic and Political Studies (RSPS), and Regional Social and Cultural Studies (RSCS).

ISEAS Publishing, an established academic press, has issued more than 2,000 books and journals. It is the largest scholarly publisher of research about Southeast Asia from within the region. ISEAS Publishing works with many other academic and trade publishers and distributors to disseminate important research and analyses from and about Southeast Asia to the rest of the world.

THE MAKING OF
SOUTHEAST ASIA

INTERNATIONAL RELATIONS OF A REGION

AMITAV ACHARYA

CORNELL UNIVERSITY PRESS
Ithaca and London

INSTITUTE OF SOUTHEAST ASIAN STUDIES
Singapore

Copyright © 2012 Institute of Southeast Asian Studies,
Singapore

First edition published in Singapore in 2000 by
Oxford University Press

New expanded edition published in Singapore in 2012 by
ISEAS Publishing
Institute of Southeast Asian Studies
30 Heng Mui Keng Terrace
Pasir Panjang
Singapore 119614

This reprint edition is a complete reproduction of the Singapore
edition, specially authorized by the original publisher, Institute
of Southeast Asian Studies, for publication and sale only in the
North American and European markets.

First printing, Cornell Paperbacks, 2013

ISBN 978-0-8014-7736-2 (paper : alk. paper)

Typeset by International Typesetters Pte Ltd

Librarians: A CIP catalog record for this book is available from
the Library of Congress.

Cornell University Press strives to use environmentally responsible suppliers and materials to the fullest extent possible in the
publishing of its books. Such materials include vegetable-based,
low-VOC inks and acid-free papers that are recycled, totally
chlorine-free, or partly composed of nonwood fibers. For further
information visit our website at www.cornellpress.cornell.edu.

Paperback printing   10   9   8   7   6   5   4   3   2   1

Cover photos: The images of the tall buildings and the battleship
are from Shutterstock; the map of Southeast Asia is by Getty
Images.

Dedication

The late Ananda Rajah, a social anthropologist and close personal friend, was a steadfast enthusiast behind my attempts to imagine and interpret Southeast Asia and live the region for a dozen years. It is to his beloved memory that this book is dedicated.

Contents

Preface

In 1999, when I first discussed with Oxford University Press in Singapore the idea of writing a book on Southeast Asia, the commissioning editor asked for a manuscript that could be used as a text for university courses on the international relations of Southeast Asia. What turned out, however, was not as much a "textbook" (in the sense of being a comprehensive narrative of major issues and developments), but an argument about how Southeast Asia's international relations should be understood and analysed. The book's narrative on Southeast Asia's modern international relations was structured around a central thesis: that regions are socially constructed, and that regionalist ideas, a desire for regional identity and intraregional patterns of interaction are crucial factors in the making of Southeast Asia as a region. Hence, they should be given as much attention as the role of external powers and the balance-of-power dynamics stressed in the traditional literature on the region. It is this argument about the imagination and social construction of the region that would make *The Quest for Identity: International Relations of Southeast Asia* provocative reading and generate a lively debate among the scholarly and policy community interested in Southeast Asian affairs. In this sense, the book's major purpose has been accomplished.

The *Making of Southeast Asia* incorporates and significantly expands on *The Quest for Identity*. Among other changes, it contains two new chapters. Chapter 2 presents the perspective and analytical framework of the book, drawing upon recent writings on regions and regional identity in the scholarly literature as well as some of the commentary, both positive and critical, that the first edition generated. Chapter 8 examines the challenges facing Southeast Asia's regional concept since the onset of the Asian economic crisis in 1997. The book also provides important new material on the contribution of Southeast Asian studies to the regional concept. Chapter 3 adds to the discussion of the precolonial state systems that introduces more variations among them, and provides an expanded evaluation of alternative historiographical perspectives that reinforce or challenge the claim of Southeast Asia to be a region. Chapter 3 adds new material on Southeast Asian nationalist ideas of regionalism. A rich collection of photographs has been added to illustrate and supplement the text throughout the book.

A key purpose of *The Making of Southeast Asia* is to build a dialogue between area studies and disciplinary (international relations) approaches to the study of Southeast Asia. Despite the growing sophistication of "Southeast Asian studies" in general, including "a diversification of authors, [and] a corollary diversification of their intellectual debts and inclinations", (Don Emmerson's words),[1] as well as growing "indigenization" (Ben Anderson's term)[2] of scholarship on Southeast Asia, one still gets the sense that discipline-based specialists and traditional area studies scholars of Southeast Asia do not communicate very well with each other, despite some recent efforts to bridge the gap.[3] Their pathways have diverged significantly since the growing visibility (sometimes to the chagrin of some area specialists) of international relations as a discipline unto itself. This is unfortunate, especially for those who have devoted significant parts of their careers to living and working in the region, and to studying its international relations. Moreover, it is unrealistic to speak of the indigenization of scholarship on the region without taking into account its international relations, because a good and growing volume of indigenous scholarship on the region concerns its regionalism (ASEAN in particular).

To a certain degree, this book is inspired by theoretical developments in the discipline of international relations and the debates between rationalist and social constructivist approaches. At the same time, I have benefited immersely from my interactions with those from disciplines other than political science who are also interested in investigating Southeast Asia's emergence and claim to be a region. While writings and debates about Southeast Asia's regionness are not rare among historians and other area specialists, this book is the first attempt undertaken by a discipline-based scholar to incorporate insights from that literature into a study of the international relations of the region. I am thus particularly fortunate to have the encouragement of the leading historians of the region, Anthony Reid and Anthony Milner and a highly gifted anthropologist, the late Ananda Rajah. This is thus by no means a book drawing upon primary historical sources, but it uses, especially in the initial chapters, the classic writings of area specialists as its "primary" material with which to draw a picture of how "Southeast Asia" emerged, and what it means.

I am indebted to several outstanding scholars of Southeast Asia, especially Don Emmerson, Kevin Hewison, Carlyle Thayer, Richard Stubbs, Donald Crone and Diane Mauzy, for their support and constructive critiques of the first edition and suggestions for further improvement. *The Making of Southeast Asia* would not have seen the light of the day but for a generous Visiting Professorial Fellowship offered to me by the Institute of Southeast Asian Studies (ISEAS) in Singapore. My sincere thanks goes to the then Director of ISEAS, Ambassador K. Kesavapany for this invaluable opportunity. The Managing Editor of ISEAS, Mrs Triena Ong, deserves my special gratitude for taking on this project. At ISEAS, Sheryl Sin provided excellent editorial support while Mark Tallara helped with the collection of photos. I acknowledge the crucial assistance of a young Indian scholar of Southeast Asia, M.V. Malla Prasad, who offered valuable suggestions for improving the draft and retyped the entire manuscript. Tan Kwoh Jack provided excellent research assistance for Chapter 8 and updated the bibliography. And the inimitable Roger Haydon of Cornell University Press embraced this project with his usual enthusiasm and critical eye, proving once again why he is so widely regarded as one of the outstanding publishers and editors among scholarly presses.

The photos in this book, presented in three sections, are intended to be supplementary, rather than merely illustrative of the text. Photos are not necessarily presented in a chronological sequence, but generally relate to the themes of the different chapters. Each of the three sections speak to the previous chapters, except Section A, which also speaks to the themes of Chapter 4.

Amitav Acharya
Washington, D.C.
February 2012

NOTES

1   Donald K. Emmerson, "Beyond Western Surprise: Thoughts on the Evolution of Southeast Asian Studies", in *Southeast Asian Studies: Options for the Future*, edited by Ronald A. Morse (Lanham, MD: University Press of America, 1984), p. 57.

2   Benedict Anderson, "Politics and their Study in Southeast Asia", ibid., pp. 49–50.

3   A particularly admirable recent effort to integrate theories and concepts in comparative politics with Southeast Asia area studies is Erik Kuhonta, Dan Slater and Tuong Vu, *Southeast Asia in Political Science* (Stanford: Stanford University Press, 2008). A similar effort to bridge international relations theory and Southeast Asian studies can be found in Amitav Acharya and Richard Stubbs, *Theorizing Southeast Asian Relations* (London: Routledge, 2009).

List of Abbreviations

ACCI	ASEAN Chambers of Commerce and Industry
ACFTA	ASEAN-China Free Trade Area
ACSC	ASEAN Civil Society Conference
ADB	Asian Development Bank
AEC	ASEAN Economic Community
AFFMA	ASEAN Federation of Furniture Manufacturers Association
AFTA	ASEAN Free Trade Area
AIJV	ASEAN Industrial Joint Venture
ALTSEAN-Burma	Alternative ASEAN Network on Burma
AMDA	Anglo-Malayan Defence Agreement
AMIA	ASEAN Music Industry Association
AMP	Asiatic Mode of Production
ANS	Armee Nationale Sihanoukist
APCET	Asia-Pacific Coalition for East Timor
APEC	Asia-Pacific Economic Cooperation
APF	ASEAN People's Forum
APSC	ASEAN Political-Security Community
APT	ASEAN Plus Three
ARF	ASEAN Regional Forum
ASA	Association of Southeast Asia
ASCC	ASEAN Socio-Cultural Community
ASEAN	Association of Southeast Asian Nations
ASEAN-ISIS	ASEAN Institutes for Strategic and International Studies
ASEANTA	ASEAN Tourism Association
ASEM	Asia-Europe Meeting
AUSC	ASEAN University Sports Council

CGDK	Coalition Government of Democratic Kampuchea
CMI	Chiang Mai Initiative
COMECON	Council for Mutual Economic Assistance
CPM	Communist Party of Malaya
CSCAP	Council for Security Cooperation in the Asia Pacific
DPJ	Democratic Party of Japan
DRV	Democratic Republic of Vietnam
EAC	East Asian Community
EAEC	East Asian Economic Caucus
EAEG	East Asian Economic Grouping
EASG	East Asia Study Group
EAVG	East Asia Vision Group
EAGA	East ASEAN Growth Area
EAMF	East Asian Monetary Fund
EAS	East Asian Summit
EEC	European Economic Community
EEPSEA	Economy and Environment Program for Southeast Asia
EFEO	École française d'Extrême-Orient
EOI	export-oriented industrialization
EPG	Eminent Persons' Group
ESCAP	Economic and Social Commission for Asia and the Pacific
EU	European Union
FAO	UN Food and Agriculture Organization
FDI	foreign direct investment
FPDA	Five Power Defence Arrangement
GATT	General Agreement on Tariffs and Trade
GDP	gross domestic product
GNP	gross national product
ICK	International Conference on Kampuchea
IISS	International Institute for Strategic Studies
IMF	International Monetary Fund
IMT-GT	Indonesia-Malaysia-Thailand Growth Triangle
ISI	import-substituting industrialization

JIM   Jakarta Informal Meetings

KPNLF   Khmer People's National Liberation Front

NATO   North Atlantic Treaty Organization
NEP   New Economic Policy
NGO   non-governmental organization
NIC   newly industrializing country

OAS   Organization of American States
OAU   Organization of African Unity
ODA   official development assistance

PECC   Pacific Economic Cooperation Conference
PKI   Partai Komunis Indonesia (Indonesian Communist
                       Party)
PRK   People's Republic of Kampuchea
PTA   Preferential Trading Arrangements
PUPJI   Pedoman Umum Perjuangan Jama'ah Islamiyah
                       (General Guidelines for the Jemaah Islamiyah
                       Struggle)

SEAC   Southeast Asia Command
SEAMEO   Southeast Asia Ministers of Education Organization
SEATO   Southeast Asian Treaty Organization
SIJORI   Singapore-Johor-Riau growth triangle

UN   United Nations

ZOPFAN   Zone of Peace, Freedom and Neutrality

List of Tables

TABLE 1
Selected Basic Indicators of Southeast Asian Countries
As of 15 February 2011

Country	Total land area km² 2009	Total population[1/] thousand 2009	Population density[1/] persons per km² 2009	Gross domestic product[2/] at current prices US$ million 2009	Gross domestic product per capita at current prices US$[2/] 2009	Gross domestic product per capita at current prices US$ PPP[3/] 2009	Year of Independence	Year of joining ASEAN
Brunei Darussalam	5,765	406.2	70	10,758.6	26,486.0	36,177.4	1984	1984
Cambodia	181,035	14,957.8	83	10,359.2	692.6	1,787.6	1953	1999
Indonesia	1,860,360	231,369.5	124	546,864.6	2,363.6	4,371.2	1945	1967
Lao PDR	236,800	5,922.1	25	5,579.2	910.5	2,250.0	1949	1997
Malaysia	330,252	28,306.0	86	193,107.7	6,822.0	12,353.3	1957	1967
Myanmar	676,577	59,534.3	88	24,972.8	419.5	1,138.1	1948	1997
The Philippines	300,000	92,226.6	307	161,357.6	1,749.6	3,591.8	1898/1946	1967
Singapore	710	4,987.6	7,023	182,701.7	36,631.2	52,871.8	1965	1967
Thailand	513,120	66,903.0	130	264,322.8	3,950.8	7,943.5	1967	1967
Vietnam	331,212	87,228.4	263	96,317.1	1,119.6	3,123.8	1945	1995
ASEAN	4,435,830	591,841.0	133	1,496,341.3	2,532.5	4,872.9		

Sources: ASEAN Finance and Macro-economic Surveillance Unit Database, ASEAN Merchandise Trade Statistics Database, ASEAN Foreign Direct Investment Statistics Database (compiled/computed from data submission, publications and/or websites of ASEAN Member States' national statistics offices, central banks and relevant government agencies, and from international sources)

Symbols used

– not available as of publication time

n.a. not applicable/not available/not compiled

Data in *italics* are the latest updated/revised figures from previous posting.

[p/] preliminary

Notes

[1/] Refers to/based on mid-year total population based on country projections, 2009 is preliminary figures

[2/] 2009 annual figures for Lao PDR and Myanmar are taken from the IMF WEO Database April 2010.

[3/] Computed based on IMF WEO Database October 2009 estimates and the latest actual country data

[4/] 1898 (independence proclaimed from Spain); 1946 (independence recognized by the US)

1

Introduction:
Region, Regionalism and Regional Identity in the Making of Southeast Asia

A central concern of this book is to explore the issue of "identity" in the international relations of Southeast Asia. The term "identity" is understood here as "regional identity", and is examined with specific reference to two basic propositions. The first holds that the international relations of Southeast Asia have much to do with conscious attempts by the region's leaders (with some help from outside scholars and policy-makers) to "imagine", delineate, and organize its political, economic, social and strategic space. In this sense, politics among the states of Southeast Asia may be understood as a quest for common identity in the face of the region's immense diversity and myriad countervailing forces, including the ever-present danger of intraregional conflict and the divisive impact of extraregional actors and events. The second proposition holds that regional cooperation, in various conceptions and guises, has played a central role in shaping the modern Southeast Asian identity. By seeking to limit external influences and by developing a regulatory framework for managing interstate relations, regional cooperation has made the crucial difference between the forces of conflict and harmony that lie at the core of the international relations of Southeast Asia.

By emphasizing the idea of "region", this book seeks to overcome what John Legge once described as "the almost universal tendency of historians to focus on the constituent parts of Southeast Asia rather than to develop a perception of the region as a whole as a suitable object of study."[1] While some historians have now overcome this tendency (notably Anthony Reid in his two-volume *Southeast Asia in the Age of Commerce* and Nicholas Tarling in his *Nations and States in Southeast Asia*),[2] regional perspectives on Southeast Asian politics and international relations remain scarce. Scholarly works on the foreign policies of individual Southeast Asian states, as well as studies of regional security and regional political economy, are often undertaken without regard to the question of what constitutes the region and its identity. Through the analysis of the international relations of Southeast Asia, this book seeks to ascertain whether there are regional patterns and characteristics that could validate or negate Southeast Asia's claim to be a region.

It is important to bear in mind that many scholars who made important contributions to the development of Southeast Asian studies in the post-war era did not find it worthwhile to adopt a regional perspective. As Victor Lieberman notes in a review of the historiography of Southeast Asia, the earlier "externalist" historiography of Southeast Asia, with the exception of Coedès (who defined Southeast Asia mainly in terms of Indic influence), "had no vision of Southeast Asia as a coherent region", and "the criteria for regional identity, potential or actual, were not discussed".[3] Similarly, several important post-war texts "devoted to 'Southeast Asia' consist of chapters on individual countries", and pay "little attention to the region as a whole".[4] D.G.E. Hall, a doyen of Southeast Asian history and author of one of the earliest and most influential books on Southeast Asian history, devoted a mere paragraph to the controversy surrounding the emergence and usage of the term.[5] Characterizing the area as "chaos of races and languages",[6] Hall observed that the term "South-East Asia" only "came into general use during the Second World War to describe the territories of the eastern Asiatic mainland forming the Indo-Chinese peninsula and the immense archipelago which includes Indonesia and the Philippines". Hall did note the various spellings of the term. These included "South-East Asia" (used by the British Royal Navy); "South East Asia" (used by the Southeast Asia Command most of the time but not always); and "Southeast Asia" (preferred by many American writers). But he found "no valid reason" why the last should be considered better than the others. For him, all these were terms of convenience and, like many other large areas, open to objections. Yet further discussion of these controversies, Hall contended, would be "unnecessary, since our use of the term is dictated solely by convenience".[7] Hall was not alone in choosing to ignore the controversies surrounding the definition of the region. One of the most important post-war collections of essays on the politics of the region, *Governments and Politics of Southeast Asia*, published by the Cornell University Press in 1964, consisted of country studies and contained no attempt to develop a regional or comparative (cross-country) perspective involving more than one Southeast Asian state.[8]

Recent scholarship on Southeast Asia has increasingly acknowledged the importance of studying Southeast Asia from a regional perspective. Commenting on a special issue of the *Southeast Asian Journal of Social Science* that served as a precursor to this volume, Hans-Dieter Evers notes, "As the field of Southeast Asian studies is dominated by empirical studies on individual communities, villages, towns and nation-states it is refreshing to read the papers in this volume that take on the region as a whole."[9] A primary catalyst of this interest in regional affairs is the emergence of Southeast Asian regionalism. By emphasizing the role of "regionalism", this book highlights one of the defining features of the international relations of Southeast Asia in the post-World War II period. The history of Southeast Asia's international relations is, to a great extent, a history of attempts to forge regional unity — and of the success and failure of these attempts. Yet most studies of Southeast Asian regionalism have dealt with the political, strategic and economic aspects of regional cooperation without attempting to assess their cumulative impact on regional identity. A specific aim of this book is to investigate the impact of regionalism on the idea of regional identity.

The task of rethinking Southeast Asia in terms of the categories of region and regionalism has assumed a new importance in view of several developments. First, intraregional linkages within Southeast Asia have been transformed. For the first time in its history, there is a regional organization that claims to represent the "entire" region of Southeast Asia. The political division of Southeast Asia — based on the relative intensity of nationalism and competing ideological orientations of regimes that characterized intraregional relations after the end of World War II — has come to an end. Notwithstanding differences among Southeast Asian states in terms of their openness to the global economy, their domestic social and political organization, and their relationship with outside powers, Southeast Asia today arguably displays far more homogeneity and convergence than at any other time in the modern era.

Second, there has been a shift from external, imperial and orientalist constructions of Southeast Asia to internal, indigenous and regional constructions. As John Legge points out, much of the pre-war study of Southeast Asia (largely done by outside observers) saw "events [in the region] being shaped by external influences".[10] This is not surprising for a region where outsiders have, since the classical period, played a dominant role in defining its regional space. Indeed, the main terms of reference to the area now regarded as Southeast Asia were coined by outsiders, for instance the term *Suvarnabhumi* (covering areas east of the Bay of Bengal) found in Indian Buddhist writings, or the Chinese concept of *Nanyang* (the Southern Ocean) or *Nanhai* (the Southern Sea), an area extending roughly in the west from the port of Fuzhou to Palembang, and in the east from Taiwan to the west coast of Borneo.[11] In the past, scholars of Southeast Asia have been justly accused of being "interested ... primarily in external stimuli, to the detriment of the study of indigenous institutions".[12] Today, there is a greater sense that the affairs of Southeast Asia, including its international relations, are to a larger extent being shaped by local actors and processes of interaction. The shift is from a simplistic Cold War geopolitical view of Southeast Asia prevailing in the West to a regionalist conception of Southeast Asia as a region-for-itself, constructed by the collective political imagination of, and political interactions among, its own inhabitants.

Looking at the main forces of continuity and change in Southeast Asia, I have been struck by the way in which debates about "regionness" and regional identity have lurked beneath the surface of major issues in the foreign policy and international relations of Southeast Asian states. This is true of the principal geostrategic events, such as the end of the Vietnam War, the Vietnamese invasion of Cambodia, or the establishment of the Association of Southeast Asian Nations (ASEAN), which have shaped Southeast Asian history since World War II. It is also true of the way in which economic and political issues, be they economic globalization or contemporary debates over human rights and democracy, have been perceived and debated within the region. In all these cases, questions such as "Where is Southeast Asia?", "Who is a Southeast Asian?" and "What is the typical and appropriate Southeast

Asian way of doing things?" have been crucial factors influencing both Southeast Asia's intraregional international relations and its relationship with the outside world. Thus, no serious study of Southeast Asia's international relations can afford to ignore the question of regional identity.

Unity in Diversity

But what makes Southeast Asia a "region"? Any scholar writing a book on Southeast Asia is immediately confronted with this difficult question. Any generalizations about the region run the risk of oversimplification. A principal reason for this has to be the sheer diversity — geographical, ethnosocial, political and so on — of the region. Clark Neher, a political scientist, argues that the diversity of Southeast Asia is the main reason why there have been so few scholars who attempted to study the region systematically.[13] But diversity can be a unifying theme as well. One could even argue that it is this very diversity that underlies Southeast Asia's claim to be a distinctive region.

Wang Gungwu, the noted historian of Southeast Asia, raises such a possibility in his preface to a famous volume on Southeast Asian history during the period between the ninth and fourteenth centuries. During this era, Wang notes, the boundaries of Southeast Asia were not so clearly defined. Moreover, "local peoples during this period showed little consciousness of strong cultural commonalities". As a result, "[t]here was no sense of belonging to a region, and it is probably anachronistic to expect such feelings". But then he wonders, "[w]as that very lack of consciousness of boundaries itself a major common trait that distinguished the region from others?"[14]

From this perspective, one could argue that diversity is what gives Southeast Asia its distinctiveness and makes Southeast Asian studies interesting and worthwhile. Certainly, diversity is not a deterrent to applying the label of "region" to Southeast Asia. Indeed, the sociologist Hans-Dieter Evers suggests that diversity provides a useful focus for studying the region:

> There is, undoubtedly, some unity ranging from a certain 'South-East Asianism' in culture and social organization to a commonality of political interest expressed in the recent formation of ASEAN. But there is no need ... to deny the obvious diversity in the South-East Asian region. In fact, this diversity should be recognized and analysed.[15]

While some may dismiss it as a mere "academic" question, the "regionness" of Southeast Asia is a matter of considerable significance for its states and societies. It is a crucial issue for those who want to study the international relations of the region, including, as with this author, those assessing not only the pattern of conflict and cooperation within the region but also the relationship between the region and the outside world.

In addressing the question of the regionness of Southeast Asia, scholars writing on the region have usually begun with a "unity in diversity" approach, which relies heavily on a consideration of the geographical and cultural elements common to the states and societies inhabiting the general area. This approach assumes the existence of a region despite conceding important differences between the states and societies comprising it. Thus, Donald McCloud, one of the pioneers of a regional approach to Southeast Asian affairs, notes: "an understanding of Southeast Asia must begin with the balancing of ... often divergent and overlapping characteristics".[16] In a similar vein, Milton Osborne describes "South-east Asia" as "an immensely varied region marked by some notable unities and containing great diversity".[17]

Foremost among the sources of diversity in Southeast Asia is the division between mainland and maritime or archipelagic segments. This division has been important to studies of the classical interstate relations of Southeast Asia. Mainland Southeast Asia consists of a series of mountain chains enclosing major depressions — the Mekong Valley, the Central Plain of Thailand and the Irrawaddy Basin. Interestingly, each of these depressions has been at the heart of major polities. While the mountains are not high enough to have offered a serious barrier to communication (only the Arakan Yoma exceeds 3,000 metres), they create a sufficient enclosure to allow for the consolidation of political systems. These core areas fostered imperial states that dominated much of the mainland as well as parts of maritime Southeast Asia. Indeed, the very first major classical state of Southeast Asia, Funan, provides a good example: reaching its height at the end of the fifth century, it extended control over much of the Malay Peninsula.[18]

Maritime Southeast Asia presents a different (although how different is a matter of debate) and more complex picture. Here the river valleys are not as large, and the alluvial lowland areas (except for eastern Sumatra and Kalimantan) are also relatively small in size. This means that the agricultural resources available to early states were limited. It also explains why political systems in maritime Southeast Asia were much more fragmented and volatile than in the mainland, and why it was only through the control of sea routes that small states could transform themselves into larger empires. The rise of the port city-state of Srivijaya between the seventh and thirteenth centuries attests to this. Command over the sea route between India and China, especially the Straits of Malacca, was the basis of its strength and prominence. Srivijaya's example would be followed in later periods by Malacca, Aceh, Penang, and Singapore, all port city-states.[19]

Among other writers, Victor Lieberman has done much to challenge the conception of Southeast Asian unity by stressing the mainland-maritime divide. Lieberman emphasizes not so much the geographical, linguistic or cultural differences between the two but the divergent trajectories of state-formation and consolidation experienced by them. In his view, "the Indonesian-Malay world as a whole did not experience political integration comparable to that on the mainland."[20] This view, as will be discussed in Chapter 3, challenges Anthony Reid's "Age of Commerce" thesis, which in Lieberman's view is guilty of using the "Malay-Indonesian kingdoms as a template for the entire region".[21]

Other sources of Southeast Asia's diversity are well known and range from the religious (represented by Islam, Buddhism, Hinduism and Confucianism) and the ethnic (mainland Southeast Asia is home to more than 150 distinct ethnic groups; Indonesia alone has some twenty-five major languages and 250 dialects) to assorted, non-ethnic factors such as agricultural practices (upland versus lowland), habits of domicile, belief systems and communications patterns. On the other hand, linguistic diversity is now thought to have been overstated, as scholars sympathetic to the notion of Southeast Asia as a distinctive region like to point out. This is evident not just from the fact that the Malay language is spoken, with expected variations, in Malaysia, Indonesia, Brunei, southern Philippines and the southern coastal regions of Thailand, Cambodia and Vietnam. Recent research has led to the discovery of a common ancestry among mainland languages, including the modern Vietnamese and Khmer languages, as well. Vietnamese and the Tai (comprising Thai, Lao, Shan and others),[22] once thought to belong to the Sino-Tibetan school, are now understood to be closer to the Austro-Asiatic school, which is related to the Mon-Khmer languages spoken in Pegu and Cambodia (as well as other parts of mainland Southeast Asia) in older times. Clearly, if a common language were to be the basis of political structures, then the modern "national" boundaries of Southeast Asia would appear to be very artificial indeed.

While language may provide a clear example of the "unity in diversity" approach, other elements are no less important. Anthony Reid, for example, points to water and forest as the "dominant elements" in the physical environment of Southeast Asia. Rice, fish and betel are quintessentially Southeast Asian, while meat and milk products are not. Of the human element, Reid writes that while the "bewildering" range of languages, cultures and religions in Southeast Asia as well as exposure to commerce from outside the region may make it difficult to generalize about the region, there exists a greater similarity and congruence of human characteristics at the level of "popular beliefs and social practices of ordinary Southeast Asians".[23] Recent historical and archaeological research suggests that cultural and political interactions took place within and across the continental and maritime domains long before the colonial era. These interactions range from the distribution of pre-Indic Dong Son artefacts (jars and bells that may have symbolized political authority) in Vietnam, Thailand and Malaysia to the overlapping (in both time and space) system of *mandalas*, a term of reference for the loosely territorialized and hierarchical polities in classical Southeast Asia that were based on the Indic model, such as Funan, Champa, Srivijaya, Pagan, Angkor, Ayutthaya, Ava, Majapahit and Malacca. (Malacca had started as a Hindu polity and, even after its rulers embraced Islam, remained true to some extent to the idea of an Indic *mandala*.) A synthesis of research on the early civilizations of Southeast Asia by the archaeologist Dougald J.W. O'Reilly contends that the appearance of Dong Son drums and jars "in many diverse parts of mainland and island Southeast Asia provides evidence [not only] of a sophisticated exchange network ... at an early time" (meaning pre-Indic) but also of political connections, as the drums "probably served as symbols of authority, conferred upon other regional chiefdoms as emblems of power".[24] Moreover, the subsequent flow of "Indian cultural styles allowed the [Southeast Asian] elite to share a 'cultural vocabulary' which underpinned a regional political and economic order."[25]

Even more directly concerned with Southeast Asia's regional characteristics was Charles A. Fisher, who in his 1964 book, *South-East Asia: A Social, Economic and Political Geography*, found it important to discuss "The Personality of South-east Asia", and to distinguish it from that of neighbouring civilizations. Fisher characterized "South-east Asia" as a "collective name for the series of peninsulas and islands which lie to the east of India and Pakistan and to the south of China". Before the advent of European colonialism, Fisher noted, the region had been overshadowed by the cultural and civilizational influences of India and China, receiving recognition as a distinctive region only after World War II.[26] Fisher highlighted the two older terms for this geographical region, "Further India" and "Far Eastern Tropics", the former connoting "an eastward extension of India" and the latter "a tropical appendage of the Far East proper".[27]

Justifying a regional concept, Fisher spoke of the double unity of Southeast Asia. The first kind of unity, "the inherent geographical unity of South-east Asia", had always been negative in character.[28] He identified three ways in which the area can be differentiated from the rest of Asia. The first is the fact that Southeast Asia straddles the Equator and lies wholly within the humid tropics, while only part of the Indian subcontinent is strictly tropical and the whole of the Far East is within the temperate zone. The second is the remoteness of the region from human settlements in the vast continental interior of Asia and the related fact of its location as a maritime crossroads exposed to repeated seaborne invasions. The third is the geographical and geological complexity of Southeast Asia when compared to India and China. Southeast Asia is a region "deeply interpenetrated by arms and gulfs of the sea, and further broken up topographically by its intricate and rugged relief".[29]

Apart from the geographical unity of Southeast Asia, Fisher also referred to the "underlying cultural unity" of its lowland peoples, which constitute the majority of the populations of all the states of the region. In his view, the "most important common denominator within the region" was similarities in their "folklore, traditional architectural styles, methods of cultivation, and social and political organization".[30] These were supplemented by the similarity in physical and mental characteristics of the region's peoples, including the Burmans, Thais, Cambodians, Vietnamese, Malays, most Indonesians and Filipinos. These peoples were described as being of "the same predominantly Mongoloid cast of countenance, yellow-brown skin colour, and rather short stature, as well as a natural elegance of bearing and an apparently innate cheerfulness and good humour".[31]

Like many Southeast Asianists of the period, Fisher cautioned against overemphasizing the historical influences of India and China in shaping the culture and civilization of Southeast Asia (this point will be discussed in greater detail in Chapter 1).[32] He concluded that Southeast Asia ought to be regarded as "a distinctive region within the larger unity of the Monsoon Lands as a whole, and worthy to be ranked as an intelligible field of study on its own account".[33] As he summed up, "tropical and maritime, focal but fragmented, ethnically and culturally diverse, plural alike in economy and society, and demographically a low-pressure area in an otherwise congested continent, South-east Asia clearly possesses a distinctive personality of its own and is more than a mere indeterminate borderland between India and China."[34]

While some scholars have responded to the diversity of the region by identifying common elements, others have drawn from it to formulate new analytic concepts and theories. Evers point to a number of concepts developed by Southeast Asian studies scholars that provided the basis not just for the comparative study of Southeast Asian countries but that also came to be used for social research elsewhere, becoming "standard concepts of textbook social science".[35] Among the examples he cites are J.S. Furnivall's "plural societies" and J.H. Boeke's "dual organization" or "dual economy".[36] Other concepts and approaches also mattered. Robert Heine-Geldern's 1942 study, "Conception of State and Kingship in Southeast Asia", which identified the "exemplary entre" in Hindu-Buddhist societies, "helped attach the label of 'Southeast Asia'", because the Austrian scholar viewed the area as a region.[37]

While not necessarily applicable to the whole of Southeast Asia as we understand it today, these concepts nonetheless provided the impetus to view the economic and institutional structure of the region systematically. As such, they transcended country-specific perspectives while helping to bring out Southeast Asia's distinctiveness *vis-à-vis* other regions.

Despite its wide acceptance by scholars, the "unity in diversity" approach is ultimately an inconclusive effort to establish Southeast Asia as a regional unit. Apart from a lingering question over whether it overstates the geographical and sociocultural similarities among its constituent units, this approach provides only a static conception of the region. The purpose of this book is not to dismiss the contribution of the "unity in diversity" approach but to look beyond it, by identifying and studying the dynamic and interactive and ideational factors that create a region.

Interactions and Identity

Historical works on Southeast Asia were not totally incognizant of such understanding. While for Fisher, Southeast Asia's regionness was a matter of geographical location and geostrategic vulnerabilities,[38] for O.W. Wolters, constructing a regional history of Southeast Asia meant investigating not just "cultural communalities", but also "intra-regional relationships".[39] Anthony Reid has done more than most scholars to highlight the pattern of pre-colonial commercial linkages in the regional construction of Southeast Asia.[40] Recent scholarship on Southeast Asia itself points to a growing recognition of the importance of regional identity. Leonard Andaya contends that "region may be defined as an area incorporating ethnonations and nation-states which perceive or 'imagine' common bonds that unite them and distinguish them from others."[41] Applying this definition to Southeast Asia, he concludes, "'Southeast Asia' is no longer simply a term of convenience. Southeast Asians themselves now think regionally."[42]

Political scientists studying Southeast Asia have also come to recognize the importance of regionalism in the making of Southeast Asia. Illustrative of this is Michael Leifer's contention, as cited at the outset, that Southeast Asia's growing "measure of coherence is a direct result of the imaginative initiative taken in August 1967 by the five founding governments of Association of South-east Asian Nations (ASEAN)".[43] How much coherence Southeast Asia enjoys today and what impact regional identity has on regional order would be of course be matters of debate.[44] And despite his rejection of a regional understanding of Southeast Asia, Donald Weatherbee would write, five years after *The Quest for Identity* was first published, in terms that support the approach of this book:

> What we might call the Southeast Asian 'virtual' or 'imagined' region is a product of a process of regionalism that is as much ideational as structural on both sides of the regional boundary … [regionalism in Southeast Asia] originates not from natural circumstances, but in the political will of Southeast Asian policy elites. Very importantly, this proclaimed Southeast Asian regional identity has been accepted by members of the global international system.[45]

The need for rethinking the "unity in diversity" perspective and taking cognizance of social and ideational forces in the making of Southeast Asia is also necessitated by developments in the wider social sciences and humanities, where a variety of new approaches to defining "regionness" have emerged. As discussed in Chapter 2, traditional conceptions of regions as geographical or geopolitical entities, as well the "scientific" or positivist approaches that "measured" regionness by using concrete empirical indicators, have been challenged by efforts that view regions as primarily "imagined communities" and socially constructed entities.

For the purposes of this book, one of the main catalysts of the evolution of Southeast Asia as a region can be found in intraregional perceptions and interactions. While scholars like Wolters and Reid analysed the role of intraregional interactions, mainly cultural and economic respectively, the approach of this book in defining the regional concept of Southeast Asia in pre-colonial times is more explicitly focused on political, strategic and economic interactions in the post-war period.

In exploring the regional concept of Southeast Asia, the book argues that regions are socially constructed rather than geographically or ethnosocially preordained. Southeast Asia's regionness cannot be established simply by looking at its geographical proximity or shared cultural attributes. Regions, like nation-states, are imagined communities. This by itself is no longer a novel argument, although few people have provided a systematic, historical study of the construction of Southeast Asia's regional identity. That is attempted here, based on the belief that such an approach can be useful in understanding the international relations of Southeast Asia. Southeast Asia's international relations represent a quest for regional identity. Success or failure in developing this identity explains a great deal of the patterns of conflict and cooperation among countries professing to be part of the region.

In developing this book, I have been conscious of the need to borrow insights from other disciplines. A recent collection of essays on the regional concept of Southeast Asia combines insights from comparative politics, international relations, history and anthropology, thereby explicitly acknowledging the need for cross-disciplinary perspectives.[46] I am also conscious of the need to trace the historical evolution of the regional concept by identifying stages at which different factors — domestic politics, academic scholarship and extraregional developments — may have been most influential. A good example of this approach comes from Russell Fifield, who identified five steps in the evolution of Southeast Asia as a regional entity, namely, the creation of the Southeast Asia Command (SEAC); the development of Southeast

Asian studies, especially in the United States during the 1940s and 1950s; the First and Second Indochina Wars and the articulation of the "domino theory" by successive U.S. administrations; the decolonization process; and the acceptance and development of the regional concept by the region's governing elites.[47]

Structure of the Book

The book is divided into nine chapters. After Chapter 1 outlines the changing understanding of Southeast Asia, Chapter 2, newly written for this edition, presents a conceptual and discursive framework for understanding regions, drawing upon both the emergent social science perspectives on regions and the area studies literature on Southeast Asia. I have decided to add this chapter to address and clarify some of the conceptual issues raised in the course of the debate over the first edition and in the interest of offering a more comparative framework for studying regional identity, for scholars of comparative politics and international relations. Chapter 3 follows by first discussing, in broad historical terms, some of the key features of the pre-colonial pattern of interstate relations within the area that is roughly considered to be Southeast Asia today. The analysis centres on the insights of a few scholars — none of them political scientists — who have discerned patterns of statehood and interactions within varied historical and geopolitical settings. The key patterns include Oliver William Wolters' concept of the *mandala* state, Clifford Geertz's notion of the "theatre state", and Stanley Tambiah's concept of the "galactic polity". While selectively time-specific, these "imagined" frameworks do provide an immensely useful base upon which to begin a study of the modern interstate and international relations of Southeast Asia. The chapter then looks at the impact of commerce and colonialism on the regional concept of Southeast Asia, and the regional pattern of interstate relations that developed during the classical period. It ends by examining the factors that contributed to a "resurrection" of the Southeast Asia concept and pattern in the aftermath of World War II.

Chapter 4 looks critically at the interrelationship between nationalism, regionalism and the Cold War international order in Southeast Asia and its contribution to the idea of region. The main historical force examined here is nationalism. Regionalism played only a secondary role, although it was clearly an ascendant force. Moreover, the concept of region and regionalism that best described the relations among the new nation-states of Southeast Asia was Asia-wide, rather than Southeast Asian. Nonetheless the convergence and divergence among nationalist movements, the debates about the appropriate form of regional organization, and the impact of Cold War alignments on these concepts were influential in shaping Southeast Asia's claim to be a region.

Chapter 5 deals with an era in which the forces of nationalism outside of Indochina and Myanmar were yielding slowly to a new regional consciousness born out of common fears of communism and a pragmatic concern with economic development. This was the period of the birth of ASEAN, after earlier experiments in regional unity had faltered. The chapter looks at the circumstances surrounding the emergence of ASEAN, the development of its political, security and economic cooperation, geared to management of intraregional relations, as well as the relationship between Southeast Asia and the outside powers.

While the emergence of ASEAN gave a powerful boost to the concept of Southeast Asia, it did not solve the problem of regional unity and integration. The Vietnamese invasion of Cambodia and ASEAN's efforts to resist and roll it back — the defining events of Southeast Asian international relations through the 1980s — had paradoxical effects on regional identity. While confirming the polarization of the region into two ideologically competing blocs, it also gave Southeast Asia greater international recognition. By creating a common purpose among the ASEAN regimes, the Cambodian conflict helped to accelerate the process of socialization and norm-setting in the region. While Vietnam remained isolated and excluded from this process, these norms and the "ASEAN Way" of socialization would constitute the basis of regional reconciliation during the following decade. Chapter 6, which focuses on the ASEAN-Indochina divide, concludes by discussing the domestic, intraregional and international forces that ended the polarization of Southeast Asia.

Chapter 7 examines the international relations of Southeast Asia from the end of the Cold War and the Paris Peace Agreement on Cambodia (1991) until the outbreak of the Asian financial crisis in 1997. The decade of the 1990s saw dramatic twists in the fortunes of Southeast Asia. It began on a highly optimistic note: the end of superpower rivalry, the political settlement of the Cambodian conflict and the surge of global recognition for, and confidence in, ASEAN's ability to manage regional order. The idea of region seemed triumphant. The dream of "One

Southeast Asia", comprising the ten states that are officially recognized as Southeast Asian, was reinvented and pursued. But the region also faced new perils threatening to undermine its unity and coherence. Some of these came from interstate conflicts that had been "swept under the carpet" during the Cold War and were now brought to the surface with the lifting of the superpowers' strategic blanket. But the problems facing the region resulted also from the forces of globalization, which had dominated the economic and political landscape of Southeast Asia. These forces included economic linkages that tied the fate of Southeast Asian economies to those of the wider Asia-Pacific, and new regional production structures and multilateral institutions that went beyond the Southeast Asian interstate system. In building a regional identity, ASEAN had clearly underestimated the burdens imposed by the "One Southeast Asia" concept.

Chapter 8, a new chapter for this edition, examines some of the most pressing challenges to the regional concept of Southeast Asia since the Asian economic crisis that began in mid-1997. The crisis brought to the fore many of the latent contradictions and tensions in the regional concept of Southeast Asia that were brought about by economic globalization. The crisis posed a critical test of regionalism in shaping international relations of the region in competition with wider regional and global trends. But this was by no means the only challenge. Southeast Asia has seen a succession of crises, such as the terrorist attacks on Bali in October 2002, the Severe Acute Respiratory Syndrome (SARS) outbreak in 2003 and the Indian Ocean tsunami in December 2004. The future of the idea of Southeast Asia as a region depends very much on how it survives and overcomes these transnational challenges, which along with the rise of China and the emergence of China-centred East Asian regional institutions have called into question the coherence and integrity of Southeast Asia as a region. Chapter 9 presents the conclusions of this study, focusing on the rise and decline of the regional concept and the fluidity and uncertainty that the regionalist imagination of Southeast Asia faces today.

Although the chapters follow a rough historical sequence, I have avoided dividing them into distinct periods or phases. Any attempt to divide Southeast Asian history is bound to be arbitrary. Some of the chapters in the book clearly overlap with one another. For example, Chapter 3 ends with a look at post-war efforts to intellectually recon-struct Southeast Asia as a region, while Chapter 4 discusses the more material relationships between nationalism, regionalism and Cold War geopolitics during roughly the same period. Similarly, Chapter 4 begins with a discussion of the emergence of Southeast Asian regional organizations (ASA and Maphilindo) in the early 1960s, although this period is also previewed in Chapter 3, which contains discussions of mostly pan-Asian (as opposed to Southeast Asian) conceptions of regional unity. Because ASA and Maphilindo were direct precursors to ASEAN, it is more useful to discuss them in the chapter that deals primarily with ASEAN's formation and early evolution. On the whole, the chapters are organized on the basis of a thematic rather than strictly chronological approach. Thus, the main theme of Chapter 3 is the intellectual reconstruction of the Southeast Asian state system and regional identity from a historical perspective; Chapter 4 focuses on the impact of nationalism on regionalism; Chapter 5 on the evolution of Southeast Asian regionalism; Chapter 6 on the ASEAN-Indochina divide; Chapter 7 on the prospects for regional order in Southeast Asia in the immediate post-Cold War period; and Chapter 8 on Southeast Asia's regional identity since the 1997 Asian financial crisis.

Before we turn to the chapters, it is important to state what this book does not seek to accomplish. It is not a political history of Southeast Asia. Nor does it intend to provide a comprehensive historical narrative on the evolution of regionalism or the various frameworks of regional organization, although these are important and continuous themes of the book. It is also important that this is a book about the international relations *of* the region, in contrast to other works that analyse the international relations *in* the region. It offers a historical analysis of the broad political, economic and strategic forces that have influenced the international relations of Southeast Asia *at the intraregional level*. I do not claim to describe the place and role of Southeast Asia in the international system. That would require a much more detailed analysis of great-power policies and the impact of global events on regional relationships. This book adopts a bottom-up approach, focusing on the evolution of intraregional interactions that determine how external actors and events are perceived in the region, and which shape their impact on the region as a whole.[48]

I do not think great powers made Southeast Asia. They did have a major influence on the region but, in the ultimate analysis, Southeast Asia is what its peoples and societies have made it to be.

NOTES

[1] John D. Legge, "The Writing of Southeast Asian History", in *The Cambridge History of Southeast Asia*, vol. 1, edited by Nicholas Tarling (Cambridge: Cambridge University Press, 1992), pp. 4–5.

[2] Anthony Reid, *Southeast Asia in the Age of Commerce 1450–1680*, 2 vols. (New Haven: Yale University Press, 1988 and 1993); Nicholas Tarling, *Nations and States in Southeast Asia* (Cambridge: Cambridge University Press, 1998). In subsequent years, studies assuming a region of Southeast Asia have appeared. The introduction to a recent collection of essays on the regional concept of Southeast Asia noted a move from an "area studies" approach to what it called a "regional studies" approach to Southeast Asian studies. This was helped by the work of scholars who had looked *reflexively* at a "region" of Southeast Asia. Amitav Acharya and Ananda Rajah, "Introduction: Reconceptualising Southeast Asia", special issue of *Southeast Asian Journal of Social Science* 27, no. 1 (1999), p. 1.

[3] Victor Lieberman, *Strange Parallels: Southeast Asia in Global Context, c. 800–1830* (Cambridge: Cambridge University Press, 2003), p. 9.

[4] Paul Kratoska, Remeo Raben and Henk Schulte Nordholt, "Locating Southeast Asia", in *Locating Southeast Asia: Geographies of Knowledge and Politics of Space*, edited by Paul Kratoska, Remeo Raben and Henk Schulte Nordholt (Singapore: Singapore University Press/Athens: Ohio University Press, 2005), p. 5.

[5] D.G.E. Hall, *A History of South East Asia* (London: Macmillan, 1968), p. 3.

[6] Ibid., p. 5.

[7] Ibid., p. 3.

[8] George McTurnan Kahin, *Governments and Politics of Southeast Asia* (Ithaca, NY: Cornell University Press, 1964). Another book that did take a regional view at this period was John Bastin and Harry J. Benda, *A History of Modern Southeast Asia: Colonialism, Nationalism and Decolonization* (Englewood Cliffs, NJ: Prentice Hall, 1968).

[9] Hans-Dieter Evers, "Review of 'Reconceptualizing Southeast Asia'", *International Quarterly for Asian Studies* 30, nos. 3–4 (1999), p. 414.

[10] Legge, "Writing of Southeast Asian History", p. 6.

[11] The same is true of terms "Golden Khersonese" ("golden peninsula") and "the lands below the winds". Michael Aung-Thwin, "The 'Classical' in Southeast Asia: The Present in the Past", *Journal of Southeast Asian Studies* 26, no. 1 (1995), p. 81.

[12] David Joel Steinberg, ed., *In Search of Southeast Asia: A Modern History*, rev. ed. (Honolulu: University of Hawaii Press, 1987), p. 1.

[13] Clark D. Neher, "The Social Sciences", in *Southeast Asian Studies: Options for the Future*, edited by Ronald A. Morse (Lanham, MD: University Press of America, 1984), p. 130.

[14] Wang Gungwu, "Introduction", in *Southeast Asia in the 9th to 14th Centuries*, edited by David Marr and Anthony Crothers Milner (Singapore: Institute of Southeast Asian Studies, 1986), p. xviii.

[15] Hans-Dieter Evers, "The Challenge of Diversity: Basic Concepts and Theories in the Study of South-East Asian Societies", in *Sociology of South-East Asia*, edited by Hans-Dieter Evers (Kuala Lumpur: Oxford University Press, 1980), p. 2.

[16] Donald G. McCloud, *System and Process in Southeast Asia: The Evolution of a Region* (Boulder, CO: Westview Press, 1986), p. 5. This book reappeared in a revised edition in 1995 under the title *Southeast Asia: Tradition and Modernity in the Contemporary World*.

[17] Milton Osborne, *Southeast Asia: An Illustrated Introductory History*, 5th ed. (St. Leonards, NSW: Allen and Unwin, 1990), p. 13.

[18] Chris Dixon, *South East Asia in the World-Economy: A Regional Geography* (London: Cambridge University Press, 1991), p. 36.

[19] The only exception to sea-based political strength can be found in east-central Java, where states could achieve centralization and authority similar to that in the mainland states by exploiting highly fertile river basins to produce resources like in the mainland states. Martin J. Murray, *The Development of Capitalism in Colonial Indochina, 1870–1940* (Los Angeles: University of California Press, 1980); Joseph E. Spencer, *Oriental Asia: Themes Toward a Geography* (Englewood Cliffs, NJ: Prentice Hall, 1973); Charles A. Fisher, *South East Asia: A Social, Economic and Political Geography* (London: Methuen, 1964); Brian Harrison, *South East Asia: A Short History* (London: Macmillan, 1963); B.W. Andaya and L.Y. Andaya, *A History of Malaysia* (London: Macmillan, 1982); J.C. van Leur, *Indonesian Trade and Society* (The Hague: van Hoeve, 1955).

[20] Lieberman, *Strange Parallels*, p. 22.

[21] Ibid., p. 18.

[22] The Tai language is spoken with dialectal variations in Thailand, southern China, Vietnam, the Shan states of Myanmar, Laos, Cambodia (in the west and northeast) and to a lesser extent in the northern parts of peninsular Malaysia. Osborne, *Southeast Asia*, pp. 7–8.

[23] Anthony Reid, *Southeast Asia in the Age of Commerce 1450–1680*, vol. 1, *The Lands Below the Winds* (New Haven: Yale University Press, 1988), p. 3.

[24] Dougald J.W. O'Reilly, *Early Civilizations of Southeast Asia* (Lanham, MD: Rowman and Littlefield, 2007), pp. 39–40.

[25] Ibid., p. 190

[26] Fisher, *South-East Asia: A Social, Economic and Political Geography*, p. 3.

[27] Ibid.

[28] Ibid.

[29] Ibid., p. 5.

[30] Ibid., p. 7.

[31]   Ibid.
[32]   Ibid., p. 9.
[33]   Ibid., p. 5.
[34]   Ibid., p. 9.
[35]   Evers, "Challenge of Diversity", pp. 2–7.
[36]   Ibid. J.S. Furnivall's "plural societies", outlined in a work published in 1939, described a distinct Southeast Asian form of social organization that had developed in Myanmar, Malaya, and the Netherlands Indies towards the end of colonial rule. This organization consisted of three social orders — the natives, the Chinese and the Europeans — that coexisted and interacted in the material and economic spheres while maintaining their cultural distinctiveness; see J.S. Furnivall, *Colonial Policy and Practice: A Comparative Study of Burma and Netherlands India* (New York: New York University Press, 1956). Another concept was J.H. Boeke's "dualistic economies" or "dual organization". Originally published in 1940, his book presented a model describing how capitalist economic development under colonial rule, including the influx of mass products from the metropolitan countries, had produced an economic duality in which the lower stratum of society sank into greater poverty while the upper stratum became richer, urbanized and Westernized; see J.H. Boeke, *Economics and Economic Policy of Dual Societies as Exemplified by Indonesia* (New York: Institute of Pacific Relations, 1953). Other concepts include Geertz's "agricultural involution" (comparing Javanese social development with that of Japan) and John Embree's "loosely structured social systems" (contrasting Japanese and Thai rural societies).
[37]   The quote is from Lauriston Sharp, a student of Heine-Geldern. Cited in Russell H. Fifield, "Southeast Asian Studies: Origins, Development, Future", *Journal of Southeast Asian Studies* 7, no. 2 (1976), p. 152. Heine-Geldern's essay was later revised and republished by the Cornell Southeast Asia Program. Robert Heine-Geldern, *Conceptions of State and Kingship in Southeast Asia*, Data Paper no. 18, Southeast Asia Program, Cornell University, April 1956.
[38]   Fisher, *South-East Asia: A Social, Economic and Political Geography*.
[39]   O.W. Wolters, *History, Culture and Region in Southeast Asian Perspectives* (Singapore: Institute of Southeast Asian Studies, 1982), p. x. A revised and expanded edition of this book was jointly published in 1999 by the Cornell University Southeast Asia Program and the Institute of Southeast Asian Studies.
[40]   Reid, *Southeast Asia in the Age of Commerce*.
[41]   Leonard Y. Andaya, "Ethnonation, Nation-State and Regionalism in Southeast Asia", in *Proceedings of the International Symposium, "Southeast Asia: Global Area Studies for the 21st Century"*, organized by Project Team: An Integrated Approach to Global Area Studies (funded by Monbusho Grant-in-Aid for Scientific Research on Priority Areas) and the Center for Southeast Asian

Studies, Kyoto University, Kyoto International Community House, 18–22
October 1996, p. 131.

[42] Ibid., p. 135.

[43] Michael Leifer, "International Dynamics of One Southeast Asia: Political and
Security Contexts", in *One Southeast Asia: In a New Regional and International
Setting*, edited by Hadi Soesastro (Jakarta: Centre for Strategic and International
Studies, 1997).

[44] For a review of this debate, see Amitav Acharya, "Do Norms and Identity
Matter? Community and Power in Southeast Asia's Regional Order", *Pacific
Review* 18, no. 1 (2005): 95–118.

[45] Donald Weatherbee et al., *International Relations in Southeast Asia: The Struggle
for Autonomy* (Lanham, MD: Rowman and Littlefield, 2005), pp. 15–16. The
quotes are from the introductory chapter written by Weatherbee himself.

[46] See Acharya and Rajah, "Introduction: Reconceptualising Southeast Asia".

[47] Russell Fifield, "'Southeast Asia' and 'ASEAN' as Regional Concepts", in
Morse, *Southeast Asian Studies: Options for the Future*, pp. 125–26.

[48] In this crucial respect, the approach of my book contrasts with that of Donald
Weatherbee et al. (see note 45). Another difference between our approaches
is that *International Relations in Southeast Asia* self-consciously "seeks to bring
the state as the primary actor in international relations in Southeast Asia
back into focus to balance the … attention … to … the collective framework
for intra-regional and international interactions" (p. xv), the latter being my
focus. I do agree, however, that the two approaches need not be contradictory,
but may instead be complementary.

2

Imagined Communities and Socially Constructed Regions

Defining Regionness

What are regions? What and who make them? How do they emerge and perish? These questions remain heavily contested in the literature on international relations. There are a variety of ways in which the concept of region has been studied. But no single attempt has proven, or is likely to prove, definitive and universally acceptable.

What is clear, however, is that the study of regions has evolved considerably in the scholarly literature on international relations. Regions are no longer viewed as "natural" or "physical constants". Traditional conceptions of regions focus on relatively fixed variables, such as geographic proximity, shared cultural and linguistic features, and a common heritage. They seek to determine what is common among the peoples and political units that inhabit a given geographical and geopolitical space. In the 1960s, there emerged behavioural perspectives in which regions were "not to be identified by the traditional geopolitical criteria, but to be discovered by inductive, quantitative methods".[1] A classic study published in 1970 by Cantori and Spiegel on "regional sub-systems" (a code word for regions among international relations scholars of that period) identified geographical proximity, international interaction, common bonds (including ethnic, cultural, social and historical) and a sense of regional identity that may be enhanced by attitude and the role of external actors.[2] Another well-known study by Russett suggested five criteria: social and cultural homogeneity, political attitudes or external behaviour, political institutions, economic interdependence, and geographical proximity.[3] A survey of the work of twenty-two scholars on regions by William Thompson found three clusters of necessary and sufficient attributes of "regional sub-systems": general geographical proximity, regularity and intensity of interactions, and shared perceptions of the regional subsystem as a distinct theatre of operations.[4] But none of these studies laid to rest the ambiguities surrounding the concept of region. Nor did they resolve tensions between the geographical and the perceptual, the fixed and the dynamic, and the rationalistic and the discursive elements that shape regionness.

Recent approaches to the study of regions have moved beyond geographical and geopolitical views of regionness and behavioural approaches to measuring it.[5] For example, a political economy perspective conceptualizes regions as by-products of the process of globalization. In this view, location and linkages within the global economy and transnational production structures determine regionness.[6] Another perspective stresses the central role of hegemonic powers in region formation.[7] Yet another approach defines regionness in terms of patterns of conflict and cooperation. In this view, the existence of intense regional conflicts may be as important to regionness as other factors.[8] The literature on regions also increasingly recognizes the role of interactions and socialization. Regions are no longer conceptualized "in terms of geographic contiguity, but rather in terms of purposeful social, political, cultural, and economic interaction among states which often (but not always) inhabit the same geographic space".[9] Yet another way of studying regions has been to view them as clusters of shared identity, as perceived both by self and by others. In this view, regionness depends as much on representation as on "reality".[10]

These new and emerging perspectives on regions tend to coalesce around social constructivist approaches to international relations, although they can also be found in a variety of other fields, such as geography, history and sociology. Thus, Adler holds that "socially constructed 'cognitive regions' ... [are those] whose people imagine that ... borders run, more or less, where shared understandings and common identities end".[11] Arguing that regions "are socially constructed rather than natural entities", Jayasurya explains, "The critical point of difference between these perspectives is that ... The constructionist (sic) perspective ... demands greater sensitivity to the contingent nature of regional projects."[12] In the words of Katzenstein, whose work on the world of regions has been seminal, "regions are not simply physical constants or ideological constructs; they express changing human practices".[13] And outside of international relations scholarship, Murphy argues, "As social constructions, regions are necessarily ideological and no explanation of their individuality or character can be complete without explicit consideration of the types of ideas that are developed and sustained in connection with the regionalization process."[14]

A key argument of this book is that, as with nation-states, regions may be "imagined" and "socially constructed".[15] The term "imagined" can be misunderstood. Alex Bellamy reminds us that "to say that a group or community is imagined is not to say that it is 'false', 'fabricated', or 'invented'".[16] By "imagined", I mean that territorial proximity and functional interactions are by themselves inadequate to constitute a region in the absence of an "idea of the region", whether conceived from inside or out. By "socially constructed", I imply that regional coherence and identity are not givens, but result primarily from self-conscious socialization among the leaders and peoples of a region. As Michael Banks puts it, "regions are what politicians and peoples want them to be".[17]

To say that regions are imagined communities is not to accept that "questions about the identity of Southeast Asia are implicitly questions about whether Southeast Asia is or can be a nation writ large".[18] Regions are different from nations or nation-states. Although there may be some parallels, the process of imagining the region is not necessarily the same as the process of imagining the nation. The nation-state is imagined as a sovereign political entity; the region in many if not all cases as a community of sovereign states (at least in the first instance). Moreover, accepting the view of regions as "nations writ large" does not necessarily clarify the relationship between national identities and regional identity. This book argues that a clash between the two is by no means inevitable. As Peter Katzenstein argues in his recent comparative study of Asia and Europe, "regional identities complement, rather than replace, evolving state and national identities".[19] This supports a central claim of this book, that an evolving sense of regional identity need not be negated by the persistence of national identities.

What follows is the elaboration of my analytic framework for studying regionness from an ideational, interactionist and social constructivist perspective. It has five key elements:

- Regionalist ideas and identities that move the study of regions beyond purely materialist understandings
- A regional (as opposed to mainly country-specific) perspective based on a marriage between disciplinary and area studies approaches
- The historical understanding of regions, going beyond contemporary policy issues
- The internal construction of regions, stressing the role of local agency, as opposed to external stimuli or the naming of regions by external powers
- The fluidity, "porosity" and transience of regions.

My intention is not to supplant materialist perspectives but to expand their horizons. This approach reflects and draws upon both international relations theory and area studies. I also draw upon the insights from the emerging social science literature on regions, and from the varied, contested and changing understanding of Southeast Asia in area studies literature, to develop a conceptual framework for studying regional identity in world politics. Although applied here to the study of Southeast Asia's international relations, I do hope that my approach might constitute the basis of a broader comparative framework for investigating the emergence and decline of regions and regional identities in world politics.

Material and Ideational Perspectives

Most analysts of regions stress material variables, including geographical location, power or economic linkages and interdependence. These are important, but this book argues that regions are also and to an even more important degree social entities, born out of imagination, discourse and socialization. A region is conceived as an ideational as well as a material construct, existing and acting as a social entity, having its own rules of inclusion and exclusion, with its identity defined in relation to the perceived characteristics of other regions. This view challenges the exclusively materialist conception of regions defined in terms of geography, geopolitics or market forces.

Alexander Murphy contends that the study of regions "requires a social theory in which regional settings are not treated simply as abstractions or as prior spatial givens, but instead are seen as the results of social processes that reflect and shape particular ideas about how the world is or should be organized."[20] Among the ideational forces shaping regions are thus regionalist ideas, or conceptions held by people about how a region originated, what sort of distinctive values and characteristics it represents, and what its future evolution ought to be. The core element of this book's approach, to use Donald Crone's terms, is the "'constructive' (as well as 'constitutive') relationship between the idea of a Southeast Asia region and its institutional manifestations and strength over time".[21] Some of the regionalist imagination is necessarily ideological and "idealistic", which may seem to fit uneasily with contemporary realities. Yet this is not unique to Southeast Asia. As Andrew Hurrell notes, although the idea of regions such as Europe, the Americas or Asia are "framed by historically deep-rooted arguments about the definition of the region and the values and purposes that it represents", there is, "as with nationalism ... a good deal of historical rediscovery, myth-making, and invented traditions".[22]

As important as the ideational element of regionness is the shared identity of its constituents. In a commentary appearing for the Thai newspaper *The Nation*, Pavin Chachavalpongpun argues that regional identity reflects "a certain level of organisational achievement, common values and ethical beliefs among members, a striving for international stature and, most importantly, political commitment" to the region-building project.[23] I accept this formulation, but would also add insights from recent work on questions about "identity" in international relations.[24]

Identity can draw upon domestic attributes, such as cultural, historical, religious and civilizational features shared among states, but it is fundamentally a relational view of a group's position and role. Since "identities of political actors are tied to those outside the boundaries of the community and the territory respectively",[25] identity-building occurs when a given unit or group of units (the Self) begins to define its character in relation to Others. In Southeast Asia, an identity-based approach would investigate how a group of states (ASEAN) defined their character and role in regional order in relation to others within (e.g., Vietnam) and outside the region, and how these states developed a "we" feeling that challenged the assumptions of anarchy commonplace in realist narratives of Southeast Asia. Actors may start an identity-building project by "imagining" themselves to be part of a collective entity, or a region, by making use of shared attributes and experiences, both historical and contemporary, but not necessarily to be limited by them. Efforts at identity-building may start initially on normative assumptions about the need for, and desirability of, unity, despite the presence of many structural disparities and differences.

The identity-based approach underlying this book also stresses the importance of socialization. The notion of regional identity of which this book speaks is not a geographical or cultural given, but something constructed out of self-conscious social interaction among the region's elite. Regionalism, as noted in Chapter 1, plays a key role here. Just as the nation-state cannot be viable without a sense of nationalism, regions cannot be regions without a sense of regionalism.

As such, a central theme of this book is regionalism. Regionalism, defined here broadly to include intraregional interdependence, institution-building and regional identity involving the states and peoples of a given area, can shape the idea of region in a variety of ways.[26] It may reduce diversity and accentuate homogeneity, especially in the political, economic and social spheres, even as the geographical parameters and cultural matrices of regions stay unchanged. This process of homogenization can be achieved through a diffusion of norms, policies and practices of regional organizations and associations, formal and informal. For example, regional organizations can promote common ideologies and political values, adopt convergent development policies and facilitate their implementation, and take steps to reduce inequity among members. This could produce greater homogeneity and commonality — traits that are essential to regional identity.

In addition, intraregional interactions help to manage differences and conflicts among states and contribute to greater regional cohesion, an important aspect of regionness. The perception of regionness can be strengthened through the peaceful management of intramural conflicts and disputes over territorial, political and economic issues. Furthermore, regionalism can contribute to the idea of a region by enhancing the commitment on the part of countries of a given geographical area to present a unified front *vis-à-vis* the outside world. Such a quest for regional autonomy is often revealed through policies of inclusion and exclusion, and by the adoption of common policies that secure the interests and identity of the region from larger global forces.

Unlike some traditional approaches to international relations, such as neorealism and neoliberalism, social theories do not treat identity as a given or as fixed, but as being a constant state of "process".[27] It is through socialization that states develop collective identities that ameliorate the security dilemma. Socialization processes may start even when the participating units lack significant structural commonalities, such as shared cultural heritage, similar political systems or a common language. Collective identities are "imagined" during, and as a result of, an actor's or group of actors' interaction within an institutional context.

As such, the approach of this book goes beyond a simple estimation of the structural similarities and differences among the states and societies of Southeast Asia, which, as discussed in Chapter 1, is known as the "unity in diversity" approach. Instead, it discusses two types of discursive imagination and social construction of region. The first is the imagination of Southeast Asia's past, mainly, but not exclusively, by its historians. The second is the imagination of a Southeast Asian political present and future by its contemporary elites. In short, the book investigates the international relations of Southeast Asia by looking not just at what is common between and among its constituent units, but at how the countries of the region, especially the elite elements engaged in a process of socialization within the institutional context of ASEAN, have "imagined" themselves to be part of a distinctive region.

The concept of regional identity as used in this book is not treated as a given, but rather as a "peg" on which to hang a core analytic perspective in investigating the international relations of Southeast Asia.[28] I also make a further and more crucial distinction between regional identity as an accomplished fact ("region-in-being") and as a quest ("region-in-making"),[29] hence the term *Quest* was in the title of the previous edition of this book. As Hettne and Soderbaum note, "Mostly when we speak of regions we actually mean regions in the making."[30] This book does not take "as its basic premise the tautology of South-east Asia as a coherent region".[31] It does not assume, a priori, a region of Southeast Asia, but investigates such a possibility. Just as from a Braudelian perspective, the unity of the Mediterranean could not be assumed but needed to be investigated (hence Braudel's warning, in the opening pages of his classic, "Woe betide the historian who thinks that this preliminary interrogation is unnecessary, that the Mediterranean as an entity needs no definition because it has been clearly defined ..."),[32] I do not assume but I do investigate Southeast Asia's claim to be a region, and I do so by going beyond contemporary, event-driven narratives, concentrating instead on historical, long-term trends.

Nor do I claim that Southeast Asia has completed its region-building project and has achieved the kind of regional identity that would survive the test of time. The only claim made in the book is that Southeast Asia is a region in the making and that this largely owes to a significant and self-conscious effort at regional identity-building, especially since the formation of ASEAN in 1967.

More importantly, the book argues that it is the relative successes and limitations of this effort, rather than the material forces and circumstances facing the region (such as shifting patterns of great-power rivalry) that explain many significant aspects of the international relations of Southeast Asia. Instead of being presented as a given, regional identity should be seen as an evolving phenomenon, something that is aspired to and striven for by a group of states and societies. And it is these efforts towards identity that are the key force shaping the international relations of Southeast Asia. The fact that an act of imagination does not always coincide with reality does not negate the importance of the former as a causal force.

Whole and Parts

A region is more than the sum total of its constituent territorial and political units; a regional approach offers insights into the international relations of states not available from country-specific perspectives on the foreign policies of states.

The whole-or-parts question is highly contentious. Commenting on D.G.E. Hall's monumental *A History of South East Asia*, Victor Lieberman notes that the notion of Southeast Asia in the book "remained smaller than the sum of its parts" because for the most part it was "a collection of country histories, without interest in synthesis or regional themes".[33] Michael Leifer warns that a regional perspective leads one to concentrate "on the wood of the region to the neglect of the trees of the foreign policies of the resident states".[34] But Diane Mauzy welcomes an approach that "pays close attention to the notion of 'region' rather than simply examining the various individual parts that constitute the area we now regard as Southeast Asia".[35] From the perspective of this author, while national histories that incorporate the foreign relations of Southeast Asian countries are not uncommon, they do not offer an adequate picture of the international relations of the region that is larger than the sum of its parts.

Barry Buzan has told us why the regional level of analysis matters. "In the absence of any developed sense of region", he writes, our understanding of international political and security issues "tends to polarise between the global system level on the one hand, and the national ... level of individual states on the other". Such a perspective "swings between an overemphasis on the dominant role of the great powers within the global system, and an overemphasis on the internal dynamics and perspectives of individual states".[36] The regional perspective has become even more important in recent years. David Lake and Patrick Morgan argue that "the importance of regional relations has expanded with the end of the Cold War", and that regions are now "a substantially more important venue of conflict and cooperation than in the past".[37] While these comments were made in specific relation to security affairs, they have a broader resonance to the study of international relations as a whole.

A wood is rarely the sum total of its trees. Intellectual trekking through the nation-states, villages and communities of Southeast Asia does require a holistic regional perspective. Country-specific approaches to Southeast Asia have considerable merit. But there is also an attendant risk of accentuating national particularities and overstating intraregional differences. They create the false impression that the nation-state remains the only meaningful unit of international relations, and that it is not significantly affected by the forces of economic globalization and regionalization, as well as the changing global normative and ideational environment within which it operates. To be sure, neither approach may be sufficient, but there is no reason to believe that looking at the trees without having a sense of the wood yields a more accurate understanding of reality than the converse. Furthermore, as noted at the outset of this chapter, accepting a "regional" view, and recognizing regional identity or the cognitive personality of regions, does not mean ignoring the continuing importance of national or state identities, since the two are not mutually exclusive but coexist and may complement one another.

The disagreement between country-specific and regional perspectives often reflects an underlying tension between those who approach

Southeast Asia from an area studies perspective and those who do so from a disciplinary perspective.[38] The latter are more likely to be interested in regionalism, regional orders and the forces of regionalization and globalization as they affect Southeast Asia. Area specialists have been wary of the "intrusion" of disciplinary scholars and their thematic concerns. The tension between area studies and disciplinary social science approaches is not new or unique to the study of Southeast Asia and underlies larger issues of methodology and approach.[39] Robert Bates, a major critic of area studies in the past, has highlighted the difference between the two approaches: discipline-based scholars "do not seek to master the literature on a region, but rather to master the literature of a discipline".[40] Discipline-based scholars have criticized area specialists for being "'real estate agents' with a stake in a plot of land rather than an intellectual theory", and for being "cameras", rather than "thinkers".[41] Area studies scholars, on the other hand, proud of their lifelong devotion to studying a nation or a region, are disdainful of what they see as the tendency of disciplinary scholars to "parachute" into the region and focus on issues with short-term "policy" significance. For them, a major danger of purely disciplinary approaches, to borrow James Scott's words, is the failure to illuminate "real societies and the conduct of historically situated human agents".[42]

Turning to the specific question of Southeast Asia, Sanjay Subrahmanyam has argued that "area studies can very rapidly become parochialism, and we often see an insistence, taken to the limits of the absurd, concerning the unity of 'Southeast Asia', 'South Asia' or whatever one happens to study."[43] Taking issue with Anthony Reid's approach, which leans more to the unity approach, he contends: "it is salutary to bear in mind that any Vietnamese voyager who found himself in Arakan in the late seventeenth century would have been as much at a loss as he would in Hughli, whereas many a Bengali notable found a comfortable living in the Magh court."[44]

But as we have seen, not all area specialists on Southeast Asia accept the regional framework, nor does area studies have the monopoly over the regional perspective. My main disagreement is not with area studies (far from it), but with approaches that reflexively privilege the part (country) over the whole (region). In this book, I discuss and demonstrate how international relations scholars use the regional approach and why it matters or should matter in the study of Southeast Asia. Interestingly, Subrahmanyam critiques both Reid's area studies approach for exaggerating the regional coherence of Southeast Asia (especially the extent of intraregional similarities and interactions) and Lieberman's "comparative history" approach[45] for (1) ignoring the links between mainland Southeast Asia and the Bay of Bengal littoral of modern-day India, (2) accepting modern-day national units like Vietnam, Myanmar and Siam as a historical given, and (3) overgeneralizing about state formation in the cases included in his study (Vietnam, Myanmar, Siam, Japan, France, Russia) while ignoring similar processes in those excluded (such as India in the Mughal period). Yet, ultimately, Subrahmanyam notes, somewhat ambivalently, that the works of both area specialists (such as Reid and Denys Lombard, who argued for including coastal southeastern China in the regional concept of Southeast Asia) and comparative historians (such as Lieberman) have helped to project Southeast Asian history "on a world stage".[46] The contribution of area specialists is important to my approach, which intends to place Southeast Asia's international relations within a wider international and theoretical context. It should also be noted that Lieberman, despite his comparative history approach, was also exploring a regional idea: "Eurasia" as an alternative to Reid's "Southeast Asia". And Subrahmanyam, who advocates a "connected history" approach that focuses on the circulation of ideas, elites and materials across conventionally understood regions, is not beyond indicating a regional concept (the Bay of Bengal, which subverts Reid's notion of an internally coherent Southeast Asia). In other words, ideas and debates about how to define, locate and challenge regional boundaries have been central to the development of Southeast Asia's historiography. So should they be to the study of Southeast Asia's international relations.

To the extent that these debates suggest the essentially contested nature of any regional construction, a key objection to "Southeast Asia", that regions must be coherent physical or cultural entities, or products of deep and continuous interactions, is hard to sustain. Instead, as this book assumes, regions are by definition fluid and uncertain constructs. In order to be meaningful, they have to be imagined, at least partly. And such imaginations, which occur frequently in history, are not always trivial, but have serious academic and policy implications.

Moreover, while acknowledging the tension between the whole versus the parts, between area studies and comparative history, I argue that regions are best studied through a combination of both discipline-based and area studies approaches. My purpose is to bridge the artificial divide between international relations scholars interested in Southeast Asia and those who are specialists in "Southeast Asian studies". For long, debates about the regional coherence of Southeast Asia have been the exclusive preserve of area specialists.[47] This book is an attempt to study regional definition from an international relations disciplinary perspective. One purpose of this effort is to take the study of Southeast Asian international relations beyond "a strict international relations paradigm" and to demonstrate a relevance to "historians, political scientists and Southeast Asia area specialists".[48] At the same time, this book seeks to alert disciplinary scholars of international relations to the substantial insights they could derive by paying closer attention to the contributions of area specialists, especially Southeast Asianists from non-political science and social science disciplines and the humanities. My objective is to urge disciplinary international relations scholars to make use of the abundance of "local knowledge" and "knowledge about the locality" of Southeast Asia produced by area specialists from within and without the region. In this way, this book seeks to extend some of the core concerns of area specialists into the international relations domain. In so doing, it also seeks to offer insights that, though derived from a Southeast Asian context, can be used as a framework for studying the international politics of regions elsewhere.

Past and Present

Regions are historically specific entities, rising and falling through historical time; regional status cannot be evaluated simply by analysing contemporary events. History, including discourses about the historical origins of regions and historical memories, is a major source of regional identity. In this book, I self-consciously address the undue neglect of long-term historical processes that go into the making of international and regional orders. It is hardly surprising that a good deal of scholarship on Southeast Asian international relations is ahistorical, or "event-driven", rather than based on a careful appraisal of long-term trends. This tendency is not confined to policy-oriented scholarship, which is frequently accused of short-term perspectives. Nor is it surprising that the most powerful support for an identity-based approach to Southeast Asia, including its international relations, comes from historians.[49] In contrast, political scientists, including scholars of Southeast Asian international relations, have spent little time dealing with pre-colonial events, even though many of them (especially realists) tend to present, implicitly or explicitly, some of the region's rivalries as primordial and intractable. In Southeast Asian studies scholarship, none have been more ahistorical than the political scientists focusing on international relations and security studies. For them, the international relations of Southeast Asia begin with the end of World War II.

Against this backdrop, this book's investigation into Southeast Asia's pre-colonial past assumes importance. But its use of history is admittedly qualified and limited, as noted in Chapter 1, to "the broad political, economic and strategic forces which have influenced the international relations of Southeast Asia *at the intraregional level*". Providing a comprehensive narrative of Southeast Asian international relations is not the intention of this book. But even the limited use of history may provoke disagreements and criticisms. Critics may ask, was there ever an *actual* historical region of Southeast Asia? What sort of evidence is out there to prove its existence? Furthermore, even if there was such a region in the pre-colonial era, can we use it as a model or construct with which to analyse and explain the modern conception of Southeast Asia as a region?

It is important to respond to these criticisms at the outset. First, in invoking the "regional past" of Southeast Asia, I refer mainly to a "region-wide pattern" of interactions, rather than to a region in its modern sense. I do not argue that ancient Southeast Asians imagined themselves to be part of a region. That sense of identity developed much later, with the emergence of Southeast Asian regionalism.

Second, my reliance on the historian's imagination of classical Southeast Asia in this book might be faulted for interpreting Southeast Asia's present in terms of its past, or at least in terms of constructs derived from the analysis of its past. Is this the kind of historicism that Karl Popper critiqued? Popper defines historicism as an approach that assumes that one could discover "'rhythms' or the 'patterns', the 'laws' or the 'trends' that underlie the evolution of history".[50] I make no such claim in this book. But I argue that there are good reasons to use historical examples of state systems as the basis for imagining a regional concept of Southeast Asia. Looking at modern political institutions in Southeast Asia, McCloud observes, "Elements of the traditional system have important explanatory value in regard to contemporary politics ... in order to explain much of the current activity at both the national and regional system levels."[51] These insights from the study of domestic politics are relevant for the study of regional identity and institutions.

But it is not my intention to argue that the current international politics of Southeast Asia can be likened to the *mandala* system first described by Wolters.[52] This would be a fundamental misreading of this book's approach. It is important also to note that a good deal of "history" in this book is actually historiography. Historiography is "a discourse about, but different from, the past".[53] The point about this book's use of historiography is not to say that the contemporary international relations of Southeast Asia is nothing but a reproduction of the politics associated with the age of the *mandalas*, the *theatre states* and the *galactic polities*. I use such constructs chiefly to show how Southeast Asia was "imagined", in this case by historians from the West, who preceded or complemented the nationalist imaginings of Southeast Asia as a region. This also explains my reliance on "secondary" sources, for example, the writings of such scholars, to investigate the evolution of Southeast Asia's regionness. In a historiographical study, the so-called secondary sources, especially those written by eminent scholars of Southeast Asia, become primary material. It is they who imagined "regionness", delineated (however artificially) its outer limits and defended the usage of the regional concept. Reliance on such writings is thus mainly an interpretative and discursive approach, and may sometimes replicate biases present in the original text. But the approach is legitimate, even if it results in findings at variance with studies drawing on archival research and with "official" histories written with the consent of those who were directly engaged in policy-making.

As Chapter 3 shows, the concept of regional identity employed in the book is based on an analysis of the work of scholars such as O.W. Wolters and Stanley Tambiah, who found it necessary and important to imagine a historical region made up of pre-colonial polities. In describing how Southeast Asia's regional identity evolved, the book "relies heavily on attempts to 'imagine' Southeast Asia's pre-colonial past featuring regional patterns of statehood and inter-state relations".[54] The long "historical relationships" that underlie some of the more recent claims about the regional identity of Southeast Asia are not my own discoveries or claims, but were extrapolated from the work of prominent Southeast Asianists. It is the work of these scholars, and the discourses of regional identity surrounding the concepts they invented, that the book identifies and analyses as my primary source in developing a "historical" basis for Southeast Asia's claim to be a region. Despite, or because of, the absence of definitive archaeological evidence, historiographical discourses about Southeast Asian political forms from a distant past played a crucial role in the making of a regional identity. Without the contribution of these scholars and their constructs, the regional concept of Southeast Asia would not have emerged in its present form.

To sum up, my use of history in tracing the evolution of Southeast Asia's regionness, including my references to historical state systems such as the *mandala*, is not to make the argument that the past can be or is being reproduced in the present. I share Wang Gungwu's belief that "history never really repeats itself and every event when closely examined is different."[55] Nor do I accept without qualification the commonplace proposition that we must understand the past in order to make sense of the present. But I accept Wang's assertion that "history can teach us about [an] important kind of reality". I also agree with his view that "when enough of the historical is knowable, that might go some way in preparing ourselves for what individuals and societies might do in the future."[56] The purpose of using history and historiography in this book is to identify and discuss the various ways in which the regional imagining of Southeast Asia has been undertaken, rather than to assert that classical patterns are now resurfacing or reproducing themselves.

Inside and Outside

Regions are now more likely to be imagined and constructed from within than to emerge as convenient labels by outside observers reflecting primarily external strategic or economic interests. As noted at the outset, some of the new literature on regions stresses the role of outside agents, such as great powers or a hegemonic actor. Traditional studies of regional dynamics have been dominated by "hegemonic regionalism, with its major empirical referents being the Cold War regional alliances sponsored by the US and the Soviet Union, such as NATO, SEATO, CENTO and the Warsaw Pact".[57] But a major limitation of regionalism "imposed from outside and 'from above'" is that it "led to few, if any, links among its members and were of little use in intra-regional and intra-state conflict resolution".[58] As Iver Neumann argues, to portray a region as an "imagined communit[y]" is to present it as a "cognitive construct shared by persons in the region themselves".[59]

Who constructed Southeast Asia? Clark Neher argues that "the notion of 'Southeast Asia' is more a result of American and European professors looking for a convenient way to study a geographic region than it is a meaningful term for an area that systematically shares commonalities."[60] This is to some extent true. As mentioned in the previous section and discussed in detail in Chapter 3, Western scholars, especially historians, were instrumental in imagining a shared Southeast Asian regional past. Tony Reid refers to the "turning away" tendency of Western historians and scholars located at the peripheries of Southeast Asia, such as India for Myanmar, China for Vietnam and America for the Philippines. For example, D.G.E. Hall at Rangoon University in the 1920s and 1930s, at a time when Myanmar was still part of British India, became convinced that "Burma's history was separate from India's and belonged with its eastern neighbours."[61]

But the real question about Neher's perspective is not whether the term "Southeast Asia" is an invention, but whose invention it is. The answer should be fairly obvious to students of modern Southeast Asia. If the term Southeast Asia originated from the scholarly musings of American and European professors, it was much less from the musings of *political scientists* than from the musings of historians and archaeologists. The latter tend to be far more sensitive to culture and identity than political scientists, even those working in the area studies tradition. And this in itself is telling. Moreover, it is the historians who have led the call for giving primacy to local Southeast Asian agency, and to the importance of local elements shaping foreign influences on the region, which is very germane to the question "Who made Southeast Asia?" This is evident in the debate over the "Indianization" thesis (to be discussed in Chapter 3), proposed most prominently by French historian Georges Coedès, which revolves around the idea that, until the fourteenth century, pervasive Indian cultural, religious and ideational influences defined much of what we know today as Southeast Asia and might even have given some unity and coherence to an otherwise diverse geographical space.[62] Yet the result of the Indianization debate was to stress the role of Southeast Asians in selectively borrowing and localizing foreign ideas, whether Indian, Chinese or other, thereby establishing their own agency. As Michael Aung-Thwin writes, "After a generation or two of objecting to his [Coedès'] 'Indianization' theory, we have increasingly realized not that the conceptualization was wrong, but that we can discern more precisely the extent and quality of Indian influences in a better informed context of *indigenization*."[63]

Moreover, this is not the only type of regional imagination and construction that led to the emergence of Southeast Asia as a distinctive concept. A second, and perhaps more important and enduring type of imagination and social construction, was that by its contemporary elites. This populist, if not popular, imagining of Southeast Asia as a shared political and cultural space was, as will be discussed in Chapter 4, crucial to the development of ASEAN regionalism and to the crystallization of Southeast Asia as a region.

Region-naming is different from region-building. While the *naming* of Southeast Asia may have been accomplished by Allied powers and Cold War geopolitics, the fact of Southeast Asia as a region with shared features and continuous interactions has its basis in a prior history and cultural matrix. And an awareness of this heritage could be considerable, if contested, rationale for contemporary Southeast Asian regionalism.[64] But this does not mean history and culture are sufficient explanation for Southeast Asian regionalism. Culture has been incorporated into what has essentially been a regionalism dominated by political considerations. Culture-based regional identity has been made and remade by regionalist-biased elite politics. In short, the cultural basis of Southeast Asian regional identity is contingent upon a particular kind of interaction and socialization, undertaken through a contemporary and modernist regional organization.

Hence, argues Nicholas Tarling, "'Southeast Asia' was once a term used by outsiders far more than by those living in the region; but now it is becoming something of an economic and political reality, and its leaders themselves are moving to make ASEAN an organisation of and for the region, instead of an organisation designed to add to the security of some of its states vis-à-vis others."[65] Such understandings of regional identity constitute an important point of departure for the book, which makes a conscious effort to examine the question of regional identity in terms of local thinking and approaches, especially of Southeast Asia's nationalist elite. In so doing, the book recognizes the "shift from external, imperial, and orientalist constructions of Southeast Asia to internal constructions, as a reaction to the simplistic Cold War geopolitical view of Southeast Asia".[66]

Like their counterparts in other parts of the developing world, Southeast Asian elites saw that colonialism not only imposed artificial boundaries on nations, but also on regions. Thus, post-colonial Asian elites could see in the end of colonialism both an imperative and opportunity for reconstituting lost regional linkages and identities. But other external forces, especially the Cold War, continued to shape the boundaries of region, sometimes against the spirit of the regional inhabitants themselves. That Cold War alliance, the Southeast Asian Treaty Organization (SEATO), was one example of an externally imposed regional construct. Yet the importance of external forces, including imaginative forces, in the making of the Southeast Asia can be overstated, even in the case of such turning points as World War II and the Southeast Asia Command (SEAC). Fifield argues that while the SEAC helped to make Southeast Asia a "fixed and practical term even in the United States", he would concede that the regional concept of Southeast Asia "would have emerged, though much more slowly, without the benefit of the highly stressed Southeast Asia Command".[67]

External forces, such as transnational production networks, different forms of the "new" regionalism and great-power intervention, remained important throughout the Cold War as determinants of regional boundaries. But with the end of the colonial period, regions throughout the world have shown an increasing capacity for self-construction. The regional concept of Southeast Asia has become progressively more developed through such processes of internal construction. By internal construction, I mean that intraregional forces and actors now drive the regional concept, sometimes if not always to a greater extent that external forces. To be sure, this shift was initially helped by the work of Western professors seeking an "autonomous" history of Southeast Asia, which called for moving beyond the colonial history of the region to the "general domestic history of the area",[68] and for the development of "a study of the past which was not dominated by the tale of progress through European contact, colonial domination, and the emergence of westernized elites to the creation of the modern nation-state".[69] It's not a big leap from "autonomous history" to "autonomous region" and "autonomous regionalism", the latter being a term used to differentiate Southeast Asian regionalism from the hegemonic construction of regions, or "hegemonic regionalism".[70] Hence, the purpose and significance of the approach of my book, as Eric Thomson puts it, "is to undermine the overbearing Washington, Moscow, or Beijing reading of the region as a theater in which their own passion play was performed, with local petty lords as bit players". Instead, it "reads the field ... from the point of view of the motives, desires, and activities of local actors, with Cold War geopolitics, the retreat of Europe, and the rise of America, China, and the Soviet Union a backdrop".[71]

The idea of internal construction is not limited to the discovery of Southeast Asia's "cultural autonomy" or of the crucial role played in region-building by material and ideational forces internal to the region; it also implies the active participation of scholars from within the region in generating scholarship *on* the region, including the discourse of region-building. And here, striking changes have taken place. As James Scott notes, "There was a time not long ago when many Southeast Asianists in Europe and North America lived in an intellectual world confined largely to their own nation or metropolitan language. Now, however, virtually every nation in Southeast Asia has a vibrant, creative scholarly community which, if anything, is producing the bulk of path-breaking work."[72] While this might be overstating the case, it is also no longer justified to view the regional concept of Southeast Asia as exclusively generated through Western academic scholarship.

Internal construction also implies, as already alluded to, the self-conscious and political desire of its elites to view Southeast Asia as a region distinct from China and India, and interactions among them to promote the idea of Southeast Asia. Chapter 3 documents the efforts by nationalist leaders such as Aung San and others to develop a Southeast Asian regional entity separate from broader Asian regionalist discourses and frameworks, while Chapters 4 and 5 discuss the more successful project by ASEAN since 1967 to develop the notion of "One Southeast Asia". Academic scholarship within the region has paralleled these developments, thereby challenging the view that the development of a "region" of Southeast Asia is but "the result of American and European professors looking for a convenient way to study a geographic region".

Permanence and Transience

"Nations come and go, why not regions?" asks Don Emmerson.[73] Regions are fluid entities, with no permanent boundaries. Any theory of regional identity should account for its emergence, transformation and decline or demise. The decline may result from both material and ideational forces, both internal and external to the region. Chapters 6 and 7 discuss a range of contributing factors, such as globalization and the

Asian economic crisis, the burdens imposed on ASEAN by membership expansion, the emergence of wider conceptions of regionalism driven by market integration, the challenge from a non-official regionalism to ASEAN's elitist brand, and the intramural differences within ASEAN over the basic norms of sovereignty and non-interference in dealing with transnational issues. True to the book's analytic framework, I pay attention to the relationship between these forces and the question of identity. My analysis fully accounts for ideational forces and the effects of these and material variables on the quality of socialization.

The literature on regions is divided between perspectives that stress their insularity on the one hand and those that emphasize their "porosity" on the other. In their theory of regional security complexes, Buzan and Wæver posit that, while regions are relatively autonomous units and exclusive to each other, there can be expansion or contraction of their boundaries (a "regional security complex"), leading to changes in the power structure and the pattern of conflict and cooperation within.[74] Peter Katzenstein argues that regions are made porous mainly by two processes: globalization and internationalization. Globalization is a transnational process with a transformative impact on world politics. It is driven by technology and marked by the "emergence of new actors and novel relations", while internationalization is about the old nation-state politics, or the "continued relevance of existing actors and the intensifications of existing relations". The former captures non-territorial actors and processes, such as multilateral corporations and non-governmental organizations, while the latter is about territorially based exchanges, where national sovereignty is "bargained away", rather than transcended.[75]

No region is immune to these processes. While regions may enjoy *relative* autonomy from external influences, they will not have absolute autonomy. Nor can there be permanent regions. Regional boundaries can also change in response to changing conflict patterns and economic forces.

Such a perspective leads to the consideration of another important aspect of studying regionness: the rise and decline (or demise) of regions. Aside from the rise of new external power centres and the porosity induced by globalization, regional boundaries and definitions can change in response to internal dynamics. Because regions are fundamentally social constructs, changing patterns of socialization could affect their domain. The expansion of ASEAN membership to include all the ten countries of Southeast Asia had paradoxical effects on regional identity. On the one hand, it adds to the political diversity of ASEAN as a regional organization. On the other hand, it makes Southeast Asia look like a single, "coherent" region.

One of the challenges facing regional identity would indeed be the rise of powerful new actors beyond the region. The outward strategic, sociocultural and economic influences of a rising power can blur regional boundaries and affect the identity of neighbouring regions. China's economic and military rise is already having a major impact on the concept of Southeast Asia as a region. There has been growing talk about *East* Asia, rather than Southeast Asia, as the relevant region or as the dominant regional concept encompassing Southeast Asian states. With the rise of India, the sense of regional definition may be changing again. The simultaneous rise of China and India on Southeast Asia's frontiers has fuelled speculation about a return to Southeast Asia's classical past, when India and China acted as the two big trading neighbours and sources of cultural and political ideas for Southeast Asia.

On the other hand, given that identity is often defined negatively in relation to the "other", if the influence-seeking by outside powers becomes too intrusive, then it may trigger a greater sense of solidarity among the regional actors and enhance their sense of common identity. In other words, if either China or India tries to dominate Southeast Asia, either individually or through their mutual competition, it may lead to solidarity among regional actors, which would be a positive factor influencing Southeast Asian regional identity. The impact of China's influence may turn out to be a more important factor than the United States' role in redefining Southeast Asia's identity.

Regional boundaries may also be altered by increased socialization with neighbouring countries, leading to changing conceptions of regional identity. The emergence of new regional institutions could trigger changes in the conception of regional boundaries and limits. There is a challenge for the integrity of Southeast Asia with the rise of Asia-Pacific regional institutions, such as the ASEAN Regional Forum (ARF) or East Asian institutions (such as the ASEAN Plus Three, East Asia Summit, or the proposed East Asian Community).

In sum, growing interaction with China and India as major centres of economic and political power, and the emergence of wider regional organizations such as APEC, ARF and now the EAS could challenge Southeast Asia's claim to be a distinctive region because it fuses Southeast

Asia with the larger East Asian and Asia-Pacific concepts of regionalism. As T.J. Pempel writes, "The outer boundaries of any Asian regionalism shift with issues, institutions, and advocates."[76]

It is important not to gloss over the limitations of Southeast Asian regionalism and identity-building efforts. While highlighting how regional countries "developed cohesion, confidence and a sense of purpose", the book "also exposes the hype".[77] Instead, as Michael Leifer noted, my discussion of the international politics of Southeast Asia "fully accounts for" the challenges that the regional identity of Southeast Asia faces today.[78] This draws attention to "The Making and Unmaking of Southeast Asia as a Region", as per the subtitle of the original paper on which the book was based,[79] or "The Making and Possible Unmaking of Southeast Asia", which is the title of its concluding chapter. A good deal of the book is concerned about identifying and explaining obstacles to regionalism and identity-building.

Summary of the Argument

Although the chapters of the book deal with a wide range of themes and periods, they seek to capture, to varying degrees, the following:

1. The similarities and differences among the states and societies in the region in terms of their physical attributes, sociocultural characteristics, domestic political and economic systems and approaches, and material capabilities;

2. The nature and impact of regionalist ideas, and shared and conflicting attitudes toward regionalist projects, such as free trade, defence cooperation, normative instruments, etc.;

3. Patterns of interaction and socialization among key regional actors aimed at reducing intraregional diversity and conflict and enhancing regional solidarity and identity;

4. The regional actors' perception of external powers and forces and approaches to the reduction of their vulnerability to external influences.

5. Discourses about regional identity and the nature and limitation of efforts to construct such an identity.

I do not claim that ideas, social construction and identity-building are the only factors that make up Southeast Asia's international relations, but they are crucial factors. Such an approach might be criticized for underplaying the role of great-power politics in the making of regions. This is certainly not the case with the narrative that follows. It pays considerable attention to international power relations and material forces such as economic interdependence (see Chapter 3 for imperialism, Chapters 4 and 5 for U.S. intervention and the Cold War, and subsequent chapters for the role of economic forces, including investment). But it refuses to assign them causal monopoly or primacy.

For realist scholars of international relations, ideas, institutions and identities are epiphenomenal. The international relations of regions is shaped mostly by shifts in the balances of material power. In the context of Southeast Asia, realist perspectives link the fortunes of Southeast Asian regionalism to international power dynamics. Michael Leifer has written that ASEAN's "political heyday" as a regional institution was the by-product of "a unique pattern of international alignments, distinguished, above all, by a strategic partnership between the United States and China".[80] The centrality of the balance of power also permeates the thinking of some of the region's leaders, such as Singapore's Lee Kuan Yew, who has attributed East Asian stability and economic growth to the balance of power maintained by the U.S. military presence in the region.[81]

But there are at least two major problems with this view. The U.S.-led balance of power might have deterred war between the major powers such as the United States and China or the United States and the Soviet Union. But it could not prevent local or regional conflicts, such as those between Indonesia and Malaysia in the 1960s, and between Vietnam and ASEAN in the 1970s and 1980s. Such regional conflicts, the most likely threats to regional stability,[82] had to be managed through regional efforts. A second problem with the balance-of-power perspective is that what is called "balance" in Asia is actually a fig leaf for U.S. strategic preponderance. American hegemony has been a constant feature of Asia's post-war strategic environment, yet the condition of peace and stability in Southeast Asia has fluctuated. In fact, Asia was quite unstable at the height of U.S. dominance, as in the early post-war period. Hence something other than U.S. power balancing would have mattered, and this brings into consideration the role of regional norms, socialization and identity-building.

I do not dismiss the relevance of power or realism in the international relations of Southeast Asia.[83] But this book takes the study of Southeast Asia beyond static, power-centric and externalist perspectives. I reject the view that regional order in Southeast Asia rests predominantly on external power dynamics. My approach, to borrow Lieberman's phrase, is aimed at "denying exclusive agency to foreign actors" in the making of Southeast Asia, and dispelling the notion that "without external stimuli, Southeast Asian states existed in space, but not in time".[84] At the same time, my purpose is not to *advocate* a regional identity for Southeast Asia. Nor is it my intention to celebrate Southeast Asia as a timeless regional entity. The book's main concern is to highlight the evolution of this region as an imagined community, which, while not bereft of conflict and limitations (as happens with the other imagined communities that are nation-states), is substantially the product of a process of regionalist social construction. This dynamic has seldom been recognized, not to mention conceptualized and studied in detail, by the scholars of the international relations of Southeast Asia. It is the central theme of this book.

NOTES

[1]   Charles Pentland, "The Regionalization of World Politics: Concepts and Evidence", *International Journal* 30, no. 4 (1974–5), p. 615.

[2]   Louis J. Cantori and Steven L. Spiegel, eds., *The International Politics of Regions: A Comparative Approach* (Englewood Cliffs, NJ: Prentice Hall, 1970).

[3]   Bruce Martin Russett, *International Regions and the International System: A Study in Political Ecology* (Chicago: Rand McNally, 1967), and "Delineating International Regions", in *Quantitative International Politics: Insights and Evidence*, edited by Joel David Singer (New York: Free Press, 1968), pp. 317–52.

[4]   William R. Thompson, "The Regional Subsystem: A Conceptual Explication and a Propositional Inventory", *International Studies Quarterly* 17, no. 1 (1973): 89–117.

[5]   Peter J. Katzenstein, *A World of Regions: Asia and Europe in the American Imperium* (Ithaca, NY: Cornell University Press, 2005), pp. 6–13.

[6]   See for example, Mitchell Bernard, "Regions in the Global Political Economy: Beyond the Local-Global Divide in the Formation of the Eastern Asian Region", *New Political Economy* 1, no. 3 (1996): 335–53. See also Richard Stubbs and Geoffrey R.D. Underhill, eds., *Political Economy and the Changing Global Order*, 2nd ed. (Toronto: Oxford University Press, 1999).

[7]   For example, Peter Katzenstein argues that "the United States plays the central role in a world of regions", and "actions that the United States took in the late 1940s were crucial in bringing about the regional institutional orders that have characterized Asia and Europe for the past half century".

Katzenstein, *A World of Regions*, p. 43. See also Hari Singh, "Hegemonic Construction of Regions: Southeast Asia as a Case Study", in *The State and Identity Construction in International Relations*, edited by Sarah Owen (London: Macmillan, 1999).

8   An influential formulation is Barry Buzan's notion of "regional security complexes". See Barry Buzan, *People, States, and Fear: An Agenda for International Security Studies in the Post-Cold War Era* (Boulder, CO: Lynne Rienner, 1990) and Barry Buzan and Ole Wæver, *Regions and Powers: The Structure of International Security* (Cambridge: Cambridge University Press, 2003). See also David Lake and Patrick Morgan, eds., *Regional Orders: Building Security in a Modern World* (University Park: Pennsylvania State University Press, 1997).

9   Emanuel Adler and Beverly Crawford, "Constructing a Mediterranean Region: A Cultural Approach", paper presented at the conference on "The Convergence of Civilizations? Constructing a Mediterranean Region", Lisbon, Portugal, 6–9 June 2002, p. 3.

10   See Arif Dirlik, "The Asia-Pacific Region: Reality and Representation in the Invention of the Regional Structure", *Journal of World History* 3, no. 1 (1992): 55–79; O. Wæver, "Culture and Identity in the Baltic Sea Region", in *Cooperation in the Baltic Sea Region*, edited by Pertti Joenniemi (London: Taylor and Francis, 1993), pp. 23–48.

11   Emanuel Adler, "Imagined (Security) Communities: Cognitive Regions in International Relations", *Millennium: Journal of International Studies* 26, no. 2 (1997), p. 250.

12   Kanishka Jayasuriya, "Singapore: The Politics of Regional Definition", *The Pacific Review* 7, no. 4 (1994): 411–20.

13   Katzenstein, *A World of Regions*, p. 12.

14   Alexander B. Murphy, "Regions as Social Constructs: The Gap Between Theory and Practice", *Progress in Human Geography* 15, no. 1 (1991), p. 30.

15   Benedict Anderson, *Imagined Communities: Reflections on the Origin and Spread of Nationalism*, rev. ed. (London: Verso, 1991); Adler, "Imagined (Security) Communities", pp. 249–77.

16   Alex J. Bellamy, *Security Communities and Their Neighbours: Regional Fortresses or Global Integrators?* (London: Palgrave Macmillan, 2004), p. 32.

17   Michael Banks, "Systems Analysis and the Study of Regions", *International Studies Quarterly* 13, no. 4 (1969), p. 338.

18   Paul Kratoska, Remeo Raben and Henk Schulte Nordholt, "Locating Southeast Asia", in *Locating Southeast Asia: Geographies of Knowledge and Politics of Space*, edited by Paul Kratoska, Remeo Raben and Henk Schulte Nordholt (Singapore: Singapore University Press / Athens: Ohio University Press, 2005), p. 11. I do, however, share the general ethos of this outstanding collection of essays, especially that found in Heather Sutherland's chapter, which rejects "essentialist" approaches to the regional concept of Southeast Asia, arguing

instead that "geographic entities should be treated as contingent devices, not as fixed categories". Heather Sutherland, "Contingent Devices", in Kratoska et al., *Locating Southeast Asia*, p. 13.

[19] Katzenstein, *A World of Regions*, p. 77.

[20] Murphy, "Regions as Social Constructs", p. 24.

[21] Donald Crone, "Review of *The Quest for Identity: International Relations of Southeast Asia*", *Pacific Affairs* 75, no. 2 (2002), p. 320.

[22] Andrew Hurrell, "Explaining the Resurgence of Regionalism in World Politics", *Review of International Studies* 21, no. 4 (1995), p. 336.

[23] Pavin Chachavalpongpun, "In Search of an Asean Identity", *The Nation*, 4 May 2006 <http://www.nationmultimedia.com/2006/05/04/opinion/opinion_30003161.php> (accessed 21 June 2006).

[24] Alexander Wendt, "Collective Identity and the International State", *American Political Science Review* 88 (1994): 384–96, and *Social Theory of International Politics* (Cambridge: Cambridge University Press, 1999); Peter Katzenstein, ed., *The Culture of National Security: Norms and Identity in World Politics* (New York: Columbia University Press, 1996).

[25] Emanuel Adler and Michael Barnett, "A Framework for the Study of Security Communities", in *Security Communities*, edited by Emanuel Adler and Michael Barnett (Cambridge: Cambridge University Press, 1998), p. 47.

[26] For an extensive discussion of the meaning and dimensions of regionalism, see Hurrell, "Explaining the Resurgence of Regionalism in World Politics", *Review of International Studies* 21, no. 4 (1995), p. 336.

[27] Adler and Barnett, "A Framework for the Study of Security Communities", p. 47.

[28] Sunanda K. Datta-Ray, "Tying Together a Rope of Sand", *Times Higher Education Supplement*, 16 February 2001.

[29] Recognizing this distinction, Diane Mauzy refers to my approach as "centering on the efforts to construct a regional identity". Diane Mauzy, "Review of *The Quest for Identity: International Relations of Southeast Asia*", *Contemporary Southeast Asia* 22, no. 3 (2000), p. 613.

[30] Bjorn Hettne and Frederik Soderbaum, "Theorising the Rise of Regionness", in *New Regionalisms in the Global Political Economy*, edited by Shaun Breslin, Christopher W. Hughes, Nicola Phillips and Ben Rosamond (London and New York: Routledge, 2002), p. 39.

[31] John T. Sidel, "Review of *The Quest for Identity: International Relations of Southeast Asia*", *Survival* 43, no. 4 (2002), p. 162.

[32] Fernand Braudel, *The Mediterranean and the Mediterranean World in the Age of Philip II*, vol. 1 (Berkeley: University of California Press, 1995), p. 17.

[33] Victor Lieberman, *Strange Parallels: Southeast Asia in Global Context, c. 800–1830* (Cambridge: Cambridge University Press, 2003), p. 9.

34 Michael Leifer, "Review of *The Quest for Identity: International Relations of Southeast Asia*", *Pacific Review* 14, no. 3 (2001), p. 484.

35 Kenneth Christie, "Review of the Quest for Identity: International Relations of Southeast Asia", *International Affairs* 77, no. 2 (2001), p. 470.

36 Barry Buzan, "A Framework for Regional Security Analysis", in *South Asian Insecurity and the Great Powers*, edited by Barry Buzan and Gowher Rizvi (London: Croom Helm, 1986), p. 4.

37 David A. Lake and Patrick M. Morgan, "The New Regionalism in Security Affairs", in *Regional Orders: Building Security in a New World*, edited by David A. Lake and Patrick M. Morgan (Philadelphia: Pennsylvania State University Press, 1997), p. 7.

38 Some of the discussion below draws from Amitav Acharya, "Identity Without Exceptionalism: Challenges for Asian Political and International Studies", keynote address to the inaugural workshop of the Asian Political and International Studies Association (APISA), Kuala Lumpur, Malaysia, 1–2 November 2001.

39 David Ludden, "Area Studies in the Age of Globalization", University of Pennsylvania, 1998, p. 1 <http://www.sas.upenn.edu/~dludden/areast2.htm>.

40 Robert H. Bates, "Area Studies and the Discipline: A Useful Controversy?" *PS: Political Science and Politics* 30, no. 2 (1997), p. 166.

41 Christopher Shea, "Political Scientists Clash Over Value of Area Studies", *Chronicle of Higher Education*, January 1997, pp. A12–13.

42 Association of Asian Studies, "The Future of Asian Studies", *Viewpoints* 1997 (Contributions from James Scott, Bruce Cummings, Elizabeth Perry, Harry Harootunian, Arjun Appadurai, Andrew Gordon, Thongchai Winichakul), p. 2.

43 Sanjay Subrahmanyam, "Connected Histories: Notes Towards A Reconfiguration of Early Modern Eurasia", *Modern Asian Studies* 31, no. 3 (1997), p. 742.

44 Ibid., p. 743. See also, Sanjay Subrahmanyam, "Notes on Circulation and Asymmetry in Two Mediterraneans", in *From the Mediterranean to the China Sea: Miscellaneous Notes*, edited by Claude Guillott et al. (Wiesebaden: Harrassowitz, 1998), pp. 21–44.

45 Lieberman's approach finds "strange parallels" in the state-building trajectories of Siam, Myanmar, Vietnam, Japan, Russia and France, thereby not only refuting Reid's alleged treatment of mainland and maritime Southeast Asia as a single unit, but also challenging the notion of Southeast Asia (as opposed to Eurasia) as a meaningful regional concept. Lieberman, *Strange Parallels*.

46 Subrahmanyam, "Connected Histories", p. 742.

47 A useful survey of this literature can be found in Kratoska, Raben and

Nordholt, "Locating Southeast Asia".

[48] Diane Mauzy, "Review of *The Quest for Identity: International Relations of Southeast Asia*", pp. 613–15; Clark Neher, "Review of *The Quest for Identity: International Relations of Southeast Asia*", *Journal of Asian Studies* 61, no. 3 (2002): 1101–3.

[49] See, for example, D.G.E. Hall, "Looking at Southeast Asian History", *Journal of Asian Studies* 19, no. 3 (1960): 243–53; John R. Smail, "On the Possibility of an Autonomous History of Modern Southeast Asia", *Journal of Southeast Asian History* 2, no. 2 (1961): 72–102; Anthony Reid, "A Saucer Model of Southeast Asian Identity", *Southeast Asian Journal of Social Science* 27, no. 1 (1999): 7–24, and *Charting the Shape of Early Modern Southeast Asia* (Chiang Mai: Silkworm Books, 1999).

[50] Karl Popper, *The Poverty of Historicism* (Boston: The Beacon Press, 1957).

[51] Donald G. McCloud, *Southeast Asia: Tradition and Modernity in the Contemporary World* (Boulder, CO: Westview Press, 1995), pp. 18–19.

[52] O.W. Wolters, *History, Culture and Region in Southeast Asian Perspectives* (Singapore: Institute of Southeast Asian Studies, 1982).

[53] Alun Munslow, *The Routledge Companion to Historical Studies* (London: Routledge, 2000), p. 133.

[54] Amitav Acharya, *The Quest for Identity: International Relations of Southeast Asia* (Oxford: Oxford University Press, 2000), p. 37.

[55] Wang Gungwu, "The Universal and the Historical: My Faith in History", Fourth Daisaku Ikeda Annual Lecture, Singapore Soka Association, 2005, p. 6.

[56] Ibid.

[57] Amitav Acharya, "Regional Military-Security Cooperation in the Third World: A Conceptual Analysis of the Association of Southeast Asian Nations", *Journal of Peace Research* 29, no. 1 (1991): 7–21.

[58] Bjorn Hettne and Abdras Inotai, *The New Regionalism* (Tokyo: United Nations University, World Institute for Developmental Economics Research, 1994), p. 6.

[59] Iver B. Neumann, "A Region-Building Approach to Northern Europe", *Review of International Studies* 20, no. 1 (1994), p. 57.

[60] Neher, "Review of *The Quest for Identity*".

[61] Reid, "A Saucer Model of Southeast Asian Identity", pp. 14–15.

[62] Georges Coèdes, *The Indianised States of Southeast Asia*, edited by Walter Vella and translated by Susan Brown (Honolulu: East-West Center Press, 1968), pp. 3–4; Wolters, *History, Culture and Region*, pp. 43–44.

[63] Michael Aung-Thwin, "The 'Classical' in Southeast Asia: The Present in the Past", *Journal of Southeast Asian Studies* 26, no. 1 (1995), p. 76.

[64] O.W. Wolters, *History, Culture and Region in Southeast Asian Perspectives*,

2nd ed. (Singapore: Institute of Southeast Asian Studies, 1999).

[65] Nicholas Tarling, *Nations and States in Southeast Asia* (Cambridge: Cambridge University Press, 1998), p. viii.

[66] Amitav Acharya and Ananda Rajah, "Introduction: Reconceptualizing Southeast Asia", *Southeast Asian Journal of Social Science* 27, no. 1 (1999), p. 3.

[67] Russell Fifield, "The Southeast Asian Command", in *The ASEAN Reader*, edited by Kernial Singh Sandhu (Singapore: Institute of Southeast Asian Studies, 1992), p. 23.

[68] Smail, "Autonomous History", pp. 100–2.

[69] Ruth McVey, "Change and Continuity in Southeast Asian Studies", *Journal of Southeast Asian Studies* 26, no. 1 (1995), p. 8.

[70] Acharya, "Regional Military-Security Cooperation in the Third World".

[71] Eric C. Thompson, "Southeast Asia", in *International Encyclopedia of Human Geography*, vol. 1, edited by R. Kitchin and N. Thrift (Oxford: Elsevier, 2009), p. 253.

[72] Association of Asian Studies, "The Future of Asian Studies", p. 1.

[73] Donald K. Emmerson, "Southeast Asia: What's in a Name?" *Journal of Southeast Asian Studies* 15, no. 1 (1984), p. 20.

[74] Barry Buzan and Ole Wæver, *Regions and Powers: The Structure of International Security* (Cambridge: Cambridge University Press, 2003), p. 53.

[75] Katzenstein, *A World of Regions*, pp. 13 and 16.

[76] T.J. Pempel, "Conclusion: Tenativeness and Tensions in the Construction of an East Asian Region", in *Remapping East Asia: The Construction of a Region*, edited by T.J. Pempel (Ithaca, NY: Cornell University Press, 2005), p. 268.

[77] Datta-Ray, "Tying Together a Rope of Sand"; see also Sorpong Peou, "Realism and Constructivism in Southeast Asian Security Studies Today", *The Pacific Review* 15, no. 1 (2002), p. 16.

[78] Leifer, "Review of *The Quest for Identity*".

[79] Amitav Acharya, "Imagined Proximities: The Making and Unmaking of Southeast Asia as a Region", *Southeast Asian Journal of Social Science* 27, no. 1 (1999): 55–76.

[80] Leifer, "Review of *The Quest for Identity*".

[81] For an extended discussion of this claim, see Amitav Acharya and See Seng Tan, "Betwixt Balance and Community: America, ASEAN, and the Security of Southeast Asia", *International Relations of the Asia-Pacific* 6, no. 1 (2005): 37–59.

[82] Leifer downplays ASEAN's record in the peaceful management of disputes by arguing that there was never a genuine *casus belli* among the ASEAN states since the Indonesia-Malaysia *Konfrontasi* that might have put ASEAN regionalism to a genuine test. Leifer, "Review of *The Quest for Identity*". But as Peou notes, the fact that there had been no major *casus belli* among the ASEAN states itself contradicts realist predictions and attests to the pacific

impact of regionalism. Peou, "Realism and Constructivism", p. 15.

[83] Diane Mauzy described my approach as one that "ventures beyond, but wisely does not completely reject, the now unfashionable realist school, while attempting a 'bottom-up approach' ... centering on the efforts to construct a regional 'identity'". Mauzy, "Review of *The Quest for Identity*".

[84] Lieberman, *Strange Parallels*, pp. 9 and 21.

3

Imagining Southeast Asia

Introduction

For most students of the "international relations" of Southeast Asia, the starting point of investigation is often the end of World War II. This is also the beginning of the international recognition of Southeast Asia as a distinctive region. Political scientists examining the international relations of Southeast Asia have paid little attention to its pre-colonial interstate system. The latter has largely been left to historians and, to a lesser extent, anthropologists. And it is the historians who account for much of the scholarship on the diplomatic interactions and interstate relations of the pre-colonial period.

To some extent, this reflects a general bias in the literature of international relations, much of which sees the roots of the modern international system as lying in the European political order that emerged from the Peace of Westphalia in 1648. From this perspective, the modern state system in Southeast Asia is but an extension of the Westphalian model of sovereign, equal and territorial nation-states, scarcely modified by any indigenous political tradition and institutional framework that might have existed before the advent of European colonialism. The long period of European colonial rule saw not only the erosion of traditional polities but, at the time of their departure, the colonial powers also ensured that the newly created polities would at least possess the nominal attributes of the "nation-state", which had become the centrepiece of the modern international order. Since the concept of the nation-state in Southeast Asia is very much a post-World War II phenomenon, it seems therefore proper to begin one's understanding of the "international relations" of the region from the post-1945 period.

But the tendency to ignore the pre-colonial interstate system of Southeast Asia has three unfortunate consequences for scholarship on the region's international relations. The first is to ignore the possibility that an indigenous and "regional" pattern of interstate relations did exist in Southeast Asia before the advent of colonialism. This possibility in itself is enough to challenge the view that those seeking to study the idea of Southeast Asia need not look before the Southeast Asia Command (SEAC), established in 1943. The second is to miss an opportunity to remedy the essentially Euro- and Americanocentric nature of contemporary international relations theories and concepts. The third consequence is to be unable or unwilling (as most international relations scholars are) to use the past to understand the present. As Wolters tells us, anyone who seeks to understand the sources and patterns of conflict and cooperation (the staple of international relations studies) in Southeast Asia can benefit from insights available from its pre-colonial state system.[1]

The Southeast Asian States and State System in the Pre-Colonial Era

But is it possible to think in terms of a regional state system in pre-colonial Southeast Asia? Lucian Pye, the noted American political scientist, categorically denies such a possibility. In his view, "there was never a Southeast Asian system of inter-state relations" before the colonial period.[2] The idea of a state system implies a certain degree of similarity among the major political units of a given period as well as a certain level of interaction among them, based on mutually recognized patterns of statecraft. But "the story of Southeast Asia before the Europeans arrived", argues Pye, "was one of the rise and fall of kingdoms and dynastic wars of conquest between separate and isolated kingdoms".[3]

MAP 1
Selected Pre-Colonial States of Southeast Asia
(See Table 3.1)

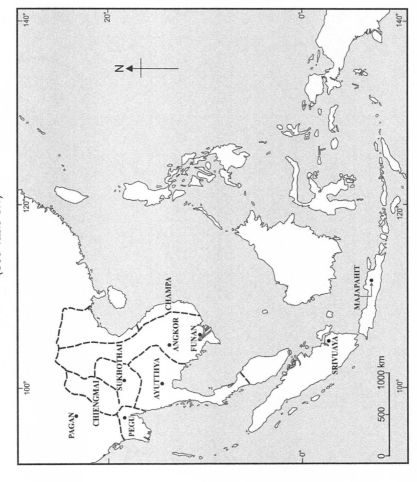

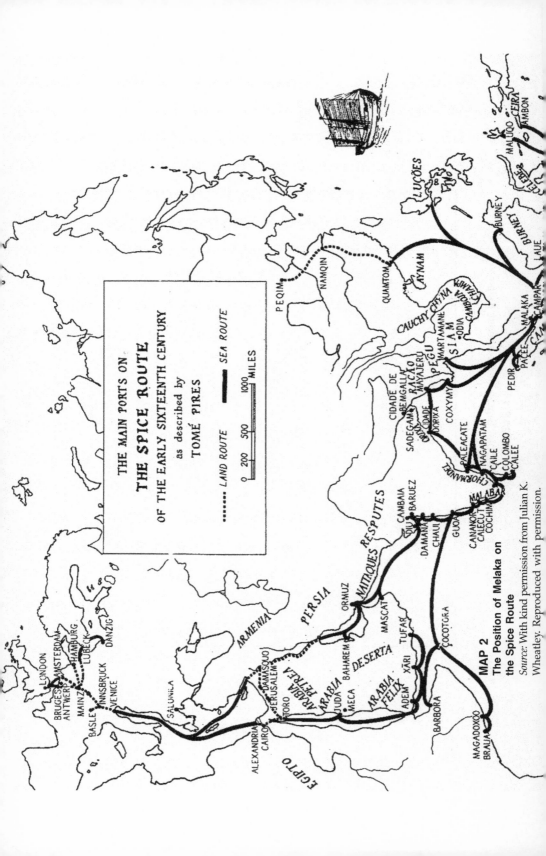

THE MAIN PORTS ON
THE SPICE ROUTE
OF THE EARLY SIXTEENTH CENTURY

as described by

TOMÉ PIRES

······ LAND ROUTE   ── SEA ROUTE

0   200   500   1000
           MILES

MAP 2
The Position of Melaka on
the Spice Route

Source: With kind permission from Julian K.
Wheatley. Reproduced with permission.

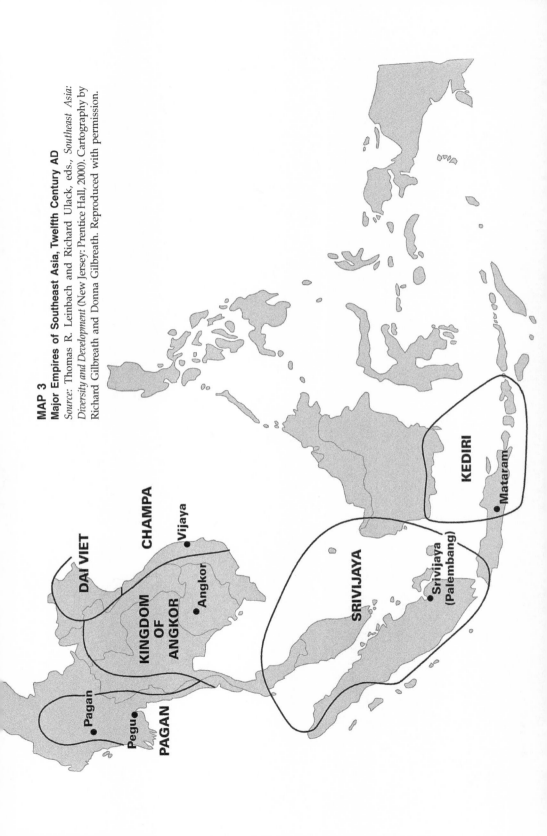

MAP 3
Major Empires of Southeast Asia, Twelfth Century AD
Source: Thomas R. Leinbach and Richard Ulack, eds., *Southeast Asia: Diversity and Development* (New Jersey: Prentice Hall, 2000). Cartography by Richard Gilbreath and Donna Gilbreath. Reproduced with permission.

DAI VIET

CHAMPA

•Vijaya

KINGDOM
OF
ANGKOR

•Angkor

Pagan•

Pegu•

PAGAN

SRIVIJAYA

Srivijaya
(Palembang)•

KEDIRI

•Mataram

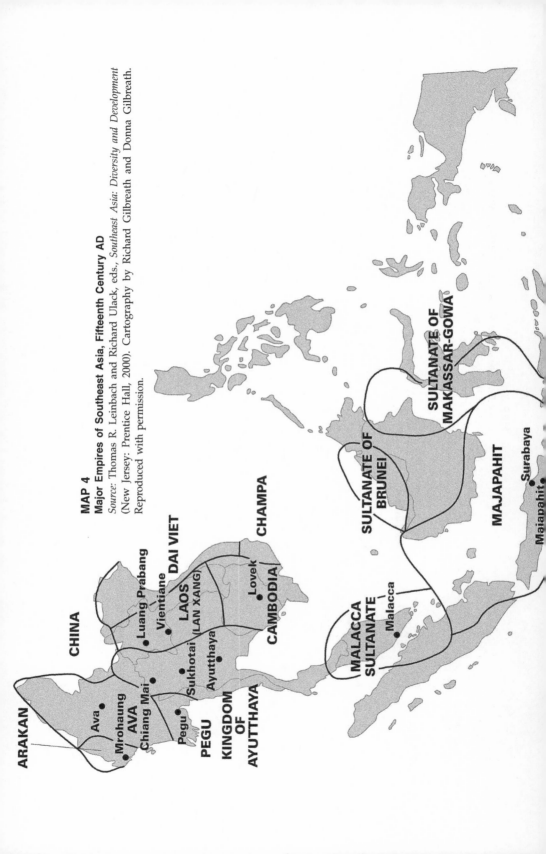

MAP 4
Major Empires of Southeast Asia, Fifteenth Century AD
Source: Thomas R. Leinbach and Richard Ulack, eds., *Southeast Asia: Diversity and Development* (New Jersey: Prentice Hall, 2000). Cartography by Richard Gilbreath and Donna Gilbreath. Reproduced with permission.

CHINA

ARAKAN

Ava
AVA
Mrohaung
Chiang Mai

DAI VIET

Luang Prabang

Vientiane
LAOS
(LAN XANG)

Sukhotai
Pegu
PEGU
Ayutthaya
KINGDOM
OF
AYUTTHAYA

CHAMPA

Lovek
CAMBODIA

MALACCA
SULTANATE
Malacca

SULTANATE OF
BRUNEI

SULTANATE OF
MAKASSAR-GOWA

MAJAPAHIT
Surabaya
Majapahit

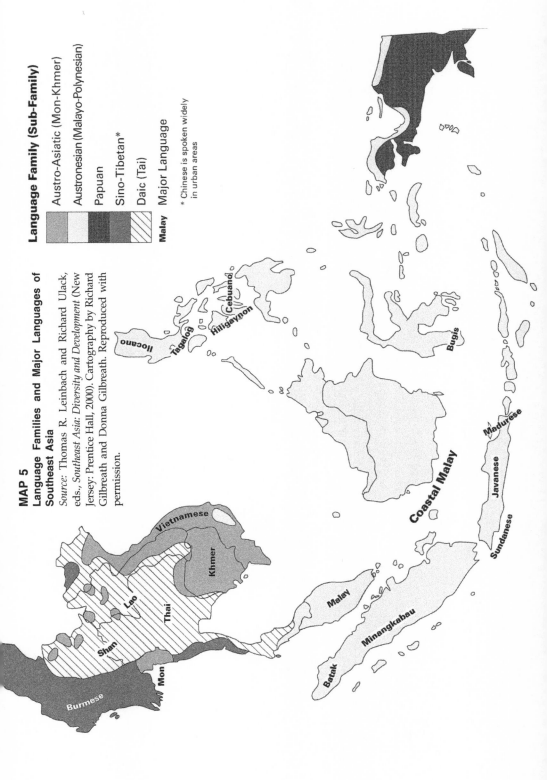

MAP 5
Language Families and Major Languages of Southeast Asia

Source: Thomas R. Leinbach and Richard Ulack, eds., *Southeast Asia: Diversity and Development* (New Jersey: Prentice Hall, 2000). Cartography by Richard Gilbreath and Donna Gilbreath. Reproduced with permission.

Language Family (Sub-Family)

- Austro-Asiatic (Mon-Khmer)
- Austronesian (Malayo-Polynesian)
- Papuan
- Sino-Tibetan*
- Daic (Tai)

Malay — Major Language

* Chinese is spoken widely in urban areas

TABLE 3.1

Selected Pre-Colonial States of Southeast Asia

Empire	Time Period	Geographical Scope
Funan	1st–6th centuries	The Mekong delta, the greater part of modern Cambodia, the lower Menam area and the coastal regions of the Malay Peninsula.
Champa	2nd–17th centuries	Central and southern coastal region of Vietnam.
Pagan	1044–1287	Irrawaddy River region. The Pagan empire extended its influence over a region roughly the size of modern Myanmar.
Srivijaya	7th–13th centuries	Maritime empire with hegemony over Bangka, Sumatra, and the Malay Peninsula.
Angkor	9th–15th centuries	Extended from the tip of the Indochinese peninsula northward to Yunnan and from Vietnam westward to the Bay of Bengal.
Majapahit	13th–16th centuries	Mainly East Java and Bali with lesser influence over Sumatra and the Malay Peninsula, Borneo and the Lesser Sunda Islands, the Celebes and the Moluccas.
Sukhothai	1238–1350	North central Thailand. The Sukhothai kingdom was the first independent Tai state in Thailand's central plain and its hegemony extended north into Laos, west to the Andaman Sea and south to the Malay Peninsula.
Ayutthya	1350–1767	Most of modern Thailand, the Menam basin, and a substantial part of the Malay Peninsula.

Adding to the difficulty of identifying a pre-colonial state system in Southeast Asia is the sheer diversity among the classical Southeast Asian polities identified by historians. While external cultural influences, such as "Indianization" and "Sinicization", brought about a degree of cultural unity to the area east of India and south of China, they also entrenched broader cultural-political divisions between the Indianized and Sinicized parts, with the Philippines, relatively untouched by either force, constituting a distinctive third segment.[4] Trade, as the chief medium of the transmission of Indian and Chinese cultural influences, was polarizing as well. Among other things, it was responsible for the division of Southeast Asia's political economy into an inland, agrarian "hydraulic" segment (Angkor and the early Mataram) and a riparian or coastal commercial segment (Srivijaya being the most important example).

Yet, other scholars of Southeast Asia disagree with Pye (whose point of reference for comparing pre-colonial Southeast Asian polities, it may be noted, was the far more developed Chinese state system and political order) in acknowledging the possibility of a regional framework of interstate relations. In rejecting the popular Western view that the recognition of Southeast Asia as a distinctive region began with the establishment of the Southeast Asia Command during World War II, Milton Osborne has argued that, as early as in the 1920s and 1930s, historians and anthropologists had already begun to take note of similarities among the states and societies of what is now called Southeast Asia. Among these were not only similarities in rituals and family structure, but also evidence of a "regional pattern of international relations within Southeast Asia from its earliest historical periods".[5] This interstate system of Southeast Asia was loosely defined (I use the term "interstate" system instead of Osborne's "international relations" to reflect the fact that the latter is a modern construct that connotes the existence of "nation-states"), and its constituent units and boundaries shifted almost continuously. But it did cover, at various points of the pre-colonial era, much of what we call Southeast Asia in the post-colonial period.

In looking for the outline, however vague, of a pre-colonial interstate system in Southeast Asia, one can turn to the work of some of the most noted Southeast Asianists of our time. Of particular importance here is the contribution of the historian O.W. Wolters and the anthropologist Stanley Tambiah.[6]

Wolters' concept of the *mandala* (covering both maritime and mainland Southeast Asia)[7] and Tambiah's notion of the "galactic polity" (derived mainly from mainland Southeast Asian history) are among the most serious attempts by Southeast Asianists to "construct" a regional pattern of statehood and interstate relations during the pre-colonial period. These constructs draw our attention not only to the shared politico-cultural attributes among the units, but also to the meaningful levels of interaction and interdependence among them. The anthropologist Clifford Geertz's "theatre state" in Bali is another relevant construct, notwithstanding the fact that it describes the politics and interstate relations of nineteenth-century Bali, as compared to the late "classical" period of Southeast Asian history (roughly the ninth to the fourteenth centuries)[8] featured in the works of Wolters and Tambiah. Indeed, the close affinities between the theatre state and the *mandala* have been noted by C. Reynolds, who argues that both represent "indigenous, culturally-oriented" models of state that ought to be differentiated from "the Marxian and Weberian notions of the state with fixed boundaries and the rule of law over a given territory".[9]

Common to the three constructs[10] is the idea of loosely organized states existing side by side without clearly defined territorial limits. The central political authority exercised by the king generally permitted a considerable amount of autonomy to vassals and lower kings, especially those not in the immediate vicinity of the capital. This is the core of Wolters' formulation of the *mandala* (literally, "circle") state. A *mandala* system consists of overlapping "circles of kings" in which the king, "identified with divine and universal authority" and defined as the conqueror, could claim personal hegemony over his allies and vassals.[11] The important feature of this system is that the authority of the king over the latter is rarely direct and absolute. Thus, each *mandala* is itself composed of concentric circles, describing centre-periphery relations. The capital and the region of the king's direct control form the centre. This is surrounded by a circle of provinces ruled by princes or governors appointed by the king. These again are surrounded by a third circle comprising tributary polities.[12] Those in the outer circle remain more or less independent kingdoms; while acknowledging the overlordship of the centre, they escape the direct political control of the latter.[13]

Within a *mandala*, statehood was defined not by its "territorial scale", but by sets of "socially definable loyalties that could be mobilized for common purposes".[14] Wolters provides a number of examples of *mandalas* between the seventh and fourteenth centuries, the most prominent examples being Srivijaya, Angkor, Ayutthaya and Majapahit. Of these, the *mandala's* lack of fixed territorial limit is best exemplified by Srivijaya, distinguished by the "notorious uncertainty about its geographical span and political identity".[15] It may be instructive to note that the concept of statehood underlying the *mandala* system was markedly different from the Chinese conception of state, featuring fixed boundaries and strict rules of dynastic succession.[16] This, especially the boundary system, was not to be found anywhere in Southeast Asia except Vietnam.

In describing the modern international system, political scientists, especially those identifying with the realist school, often use the "billiard ball" metaphor. In this concept, units (states) of similar characteristics relate to one another while maintaining their independent and distinctive existence on the basis of the twin attributes of sovereignty and territoriality. The *mandala*, on the other hand, has been likened to the light of a torch radiating outward from the centre, "gradually fading into the distance and merging imperceptibly with the ascending power of a neighboring sovereign".[17] For Wolters, the state system of early Southeast Asian history is akin not to a table full of billiard balls, but to a "patchwork of often overlapping *mandalas*". Because of the vagueness of his territory and the uncertain political loyalties of his vassals, the ruler in the *mandala* system could make no clear distinction between the purpose and conduct of "internal" and "external" relations.[18] The *mandala* thus "represented a particular and often unstable situation in a vaguely definable geographic area without fixed boundaries and where smaller centers tended to look in all directions for security". They would expand and contract in an almost continuous manner as vassals and tributary rulers shifted their loyalties from ruler to ruler as opportunity presented itself.[19]

Weak territoriality and loose central political authority are also key features of Tambiah's construction of the "galactic polity". Drawing on examples such as the kingdoms of Pegu, Pagan, Chiang Mai, Sukhothai, Ayutthaya, Laos and Cambodia,[20] the concept of "galactic polity" refers to the domain of a universal king (*chakravartin* in Sanskrit) who rules not as an absolute monarch, but rather as a "king of kings". Within his domain are numerous lesser kings who are permitted to remain autonomous after having submitted to the centre. Just as a *mandala* consists of concentric circles of authority, the galactic polity is "a center-oriented arrangement". The satellite principalities and provinces that exist within this arrangement "reproduced the features of the center on a decreasing scale in a system of graduated autonomies".[21] In describing the interstate system, Tambiah highlights the "pulsating nature" of the galactic polity:

> It was part of a large field of coexisting galaxies which mutually inflected one another, and thus expanded or shrank their outer frontiers according to their success in attracting, and then keeping, the outermost satellites within their orbits.[22]

As a region of galactic polities, mainland Southeast Asia consisted of "several core domains and satellite regions that continually changed their affiliation according to the fortunes of war and diplomacy".[23]

Geertz develops a similar conception of interstate relations in his study of the "theatre state" (*negara*) in Bali. Analysing politics in nineteenth-century Bali and relations among the major states — Den Pasar, Tabanan, Badung, Karengasem and Klungkung — Geertz found that no single state possessed the power to exercise hegemony over the others. Moreover, the major states had to live with "dozens of independent, semi-independent, and quarter-independent rulers" within and beyond their domain.[24] In such a situation, rulers resorted to the use of ceremony and ritual as tools of power and authority. While Geertz's emphasis on ritual reflects the distinctive situation in Bali and sets his work apart from that of Wolters and Tambiah, in essence it conjures up the same image of states with limited hierarchical organization, weak internal political and administrative control, and blurred and overlapping territorial domains. In these states, boundaries were not "clearly defined lines but zones of mutual interest". They did not insulate states but served as transition areas "through which 'neighboring' power systems interpenetrated in a dynamic manner". The rulers could not practise "ritualized formal relations across standardized borders".[25] Instead, through exemplary state ritual, they sought to command the loyalty of their subjects and unify their domain, even as their state's political and territorial structure remained highly centrifugal. Rulers competed for prestige rather than property, for people rather than land.[26] Disagreements and conflicts were seldom over territory, but over "delicate questions of mutual status, of appropriate politesse". Rulers fought over their right to "mobilize particular bodies of men" for state ritual rather than warfare, although as Geertz notes, the two objectives often converged.[27]

Assuming that the *mandala*, the galactic polity, and the theatre state constituted accurate, if somewhat crude, representations of statehood in Southeast Asia before the advent of the nation-state, one could imagine a *regional pattern* of interstate relations in classical Southeast Asia based on essentially similar political forms. But what about the political and cultural interaction and transmission among these units that would have been essential to the creation of a *regional identity*? That this too occurred is a crucial claim of Wolters, who argues that the *mandala* system helped to establish a common pattern of intraregional authority in a region that was "demographically fragmented", politically "multicentered", and socially "characterized by stubborn small-scale sub-regional identities".[28] For Wolters, the overlapping physical, political and cultural space of the *mandalas* assumes crucial importance:

> Sometimes … a *mandala* would only comprise a group of states on the island of Java, but a *mandala* could also be geographically extensive and comprise peoples whose descendants live today in separate nation-states. The Malay rulers of Srivijaya exercised some kind of authority in Sumatra and the Malay Peninsula from the seventh to at least the eleventh century. The Angkorian kings at intervals during the eleventh and twelfth centuries had similar authority in the Chao Phraya basin and the Malay Peninsula and also in parts of what is today southern Vietnam. The *mandala* of the Thai state of Ayudhya was, to some extent, the same *mandala* that the Khmer rulers had once claimed to control but with the overlord in a new center. The Javanese *mandala* of Majapahit in the fourteenth century comprised Java, much of Sumatra, and no doubt other Indonesian islands.[29]

Wolters highlights the impact of overlapping *mandalas* in increasing the flow of communications between contiguous areas and reducing the cultural cleavages of the earlier period:

> A glance at some of the famous *mandalas* which adorn the textbooks on earlier Southeast Asian history shows that each of them increased the flow of communications between some of the many centers in different parts of the region. We may too often tend to strike contrasts between these earlier states and the modern states as though great men in the past made exciting impressions in their own day but left nothing behind them of consequence. But there were some enduring consequences which helped to reduce the multicentric character of earlier Southeast Asia.[30]

Elaborating on how the *mandala* system might have contributed to the regional coherence and unity of Southeast Asia, Andaya observes:

Communities large and small retained their independent existence, while acknowledging the superior political and spiritual talents of a wo/man [sic] of prowess. In a mutually beneficial arrangement, the wo/man of prowess offered economic favors, spiritual knowledge and protection to subordinate rulers in return for local products and human resources in times of warfare or crisis. The looseness of the political arrangement was nevertheless reinforced by the general adherence by all to a supralocal religion from India or China in which the *mandala* ruler was equated with the supralocal deity of the new religion. But while individual communities were now becoming incorporated, though loosely, within the larger *mandalas*, there were no centralized institutions of reinforcement of central values and no fixed boundaries. Common cultural values were forged through interaction within and among the *mandalas*, thus preparing the way for the growth of nation-states and the concept of a Southeast Asian region.[31]

While the imperial kingdoms differed from the *mandalas* in terms of their size and power, they too contributed to a greater homogeneity within Southeast Asia. The *mandala* system created intraregional homogeneity by virtue of their being "overlapping circles or spheres of influence". The imperial kingdoms emerged through and fostered a continuous process of interlocal or interregional integration.[32]

Attempts to develop a regional concept of statehood and interstate relations by using such categories as the *mandala*, the theatre state, or the galactic polity do invite considerable scepticism. One obvious question is whether the *mandala* pattern marked the entirety of what we call Southeast Asia today. Some critics have argued that the *mandala* system was a phenomenon of lowland Southeast Asia, not found in the uplands, such as in large parts of Myanmar, Laos and northern Thailand.[33] Vietnam and the Philippines raise major problems in the use of the *mandala* concept as the basis of a regional interstate system.[34] Vietnam, under Chinese rule for the first thousand years of the first millennium AD, has been described as a centralized bureaucratic state, in contrast to the loosely integrated Indic states of other parts of Southeast Asia. The Chinese-style polity in Vietnam made for a political order that was less volatile and more centralized than that which characterized the *mandala* system.[35] One must, however, bear in mind that parts of the south were physically located within the Angkorian *mandala*,[36] and Vietnamese rulers, despite adopting Chinese-style diplomatic practices, retained an essentially "Southeast Asian" way of relating to people with the "tolerance and closeness" that were characteristic of the *mandala* polity.[37] In the case of the Philippines, Wolters identifies Mindoro on the Luzon coast as one of the earliest examples of a Philippine *mandala* that emerged around the second half of the tenth century. After it disappeared, another *mandala* began to take shape on the Luzon coast as an extension of the Islamic *mandala* in Brunei. Thus, half a century before the arrival of the Spanish, the spread of Islam to the southern Philippines areas of Sulu and Mindanao was beginning to extend the *mandala* pattern there.[38] But others challenge this view. In pre-colonial Philippines, political authority rested with too many small chiefs, and the central figure of a king around which a *mandala* could be constructed was lacking. As a political form, the Philippines *barangay* consisted of villages with a chief whose status and authority were almost entirely locally determined, without being linked to a source from above or from another realm, as with the god-king in the *mandala* system. These villages were politically autonomous units until they were incorporated into the colonial state apparatus. The *barangay* may be the main reason why the Philippines could not fit into the pre-modern regional concept of Southeast Asia.

Other problems confront the concept of *mandala* as the basis of the classical Southeast Asian polity and interstate system.[39] The *mandalas* were not always culturally or ethnically homogeneous. For example, in Sukhothai, the *mandala* was comprised almost entirely of Tais, but the Pagan *mandala* consisted of Burmans, Shans and Mons.[40] The *mandalas* may have increased the flow of communication within particular subregions, and reduced the "multicentric" character of the region.[41] But this effect was countered by the fact that, while the *mandalas* overlapped in terms of space, they did so less in terms of time. They arose more or less in succession. For example, the Srivijaya *mandala* lasted from the seventh to the eleventh century, while the Angkorian *mandala* extended to Lopburi in Thailand only periodically during the eleventh and twelfth centuries, and the Ayutthaya *mandala* (like the Majapahit) was founded in the mid-fourteenth century. Since the political influence of the *mandalas* did not last for very long, it is not certain that the cultural commonalities they generated could be enduring.[42]

Looking at the *mandala*, the galactic polity, and the theatre state, one may get the impression that the early states of Southeast Asia were not in a position to consolidate their domains and expand their political and territorial reach. What then explains the emergence of several powerful states such as Angkor and Ayutthaya that conquered many of their neighbours and controlled vast territories? This phenomenon has led some scholars to question the historical validity of the *mandala* concept, even if states like Angkor and Ayutthaya continued to exhibit considerable centrifugal tendencies as well as uncertain and overlapping territorial jurisdictions *vis-à-vis* neighbouring powers. Kulke argues that while the *mandala* may describe interstate relations before 1000 AD, the later states of Southeast Asia were more centralized. Based on research into state formation in Java and the modern eastern Indian state of Orissa (which, under its ancient name of Kalinga, had extensive maritime links with Southeast Asia and might hence have possessed a political system similar to that of Southeast Asian kingdoms), Kulke presents an evolutionary model of state formation in Southeast Asia, thereby challenging the essentially static nature of the *mandala*. He traces the evolution of the Southeast Asian state from the "local" to the "regional" and then finally to the "imperial" (or "nuclear areas", "early kingdom", and "imperial kingdom"). It is the second type that most resembles the *mandala,* in the sense of being characterized by "a 'multiplicity' of local political centres and shifting loyalties of their leaders, particularly at the periphery of their system".[43] But beginning with Angkor in the early ninth century, there emerged in Southeast Asia a trend towards a small number of "supra-regional" powers, which was to become a dominant feature of continental Southeast Asia from the eleventh century onwards. After the decline of Angkor, the Thai kingdom of Ayutthaya took over the role of imperial kingdom in continental Southeast Asia. The kingdom of Pagan also covered vast areas of western continental Southeast Asia from the middle of the eleventh century to the end of thirteenth century, while Java saw the emergence of a similar entity in the form of Majapahit in the fourteenth century.

Victor Lieberman's work on state formation in Southeast Asia highlights major variations in the respective polities of maritime and mainland areas and raises the possibility of the mainland states acquiring much greater levels of centralization and institutionalization than the loose nature of the *mandala* would permit. Lieberman accepts Tambiah's notion of a galactic polity, but renames it as "solar polity", which in his view has more descriptive accuracy insofar as it "connotes provincial 'planets' revolved around a sun whose 'gravitational pull' diminished with distance".[44] While such polities marked mainland Southeast Asia until 1600, thereafter they gave way to consolidated and centralized states. Lieberman's thesis about the emergence of stronger polities in the mainland is not unlike Kulke's tracing of the evolution of mainland polities from "nuclear areas" to "imperial kingdoms". But a major difference is that the former was talking mainly about the internal consolidation and coercive ability of states, while the latter's "imperial kingdom", as the very term implies, directs attention to the external physical power of the state.

Lieberman traces the trajectories of mainland polities in four historical (although slightly overlapping) patterns. The first pattern, lasting from 900 to 1450 AD, are represented by the "Charter Administrations" found in Pagan, Angkor, early Ava, Champa and early Dai Viet. The second pattern of the "Decentralized Indic Administration" characterized polities in all of the western and central mainland to 1600, and the Khmer, Malay and weaker Tai states to 1840. The third pattern, that of "Centralized Indic Administration", could be found in Siam and Myanmar and to a lesser degree Cambodia and Lan Sang between 1600 and 1840. The fourth pattern was the "Chinese-style Administration" (1460–1840), which could be found in Dong Kinh until 1831, and thereafter in the rest of Vietnam. These patterns represented an evolutionary, if not entirely linear, form of institutionalization and consolidation. The charter administration period consisted of solar polities, semi-independent tributaries and autonomous religious institutions that performed extensive social and economic roles. A reduction of the authority and functions of religious institutions marked the Decentralized Indic Administration period, during which political structures nonetheless remained solar polities, with little centralized administrative and manpower control. This changed during the Centralized Indic Administration, which grew more efficient at tax collection and at securing services rendered to the government around the capital cities, and which also exercised tighter control over their tributaries. The Chinese-style Administration was the most centralized, adopting civil service examinations, developing nominally bureaucratic supervisory and tax procedures, and standardizing its provincial administration.[45]

Implicit in the historiographical constructions of the *mandala*, the *theatre state*, or the *galactic polity* is a desire to distinguish between the historical trajectories of the respective state systems in Southeast Asia and in Europe. While the solar or galactic polities were states in the minimalist Tillyan sense, as "coercion-welding organizations that are distinct from households and kinship groups and exercise clear priority in some respects over all other organizations within substantial territories",[46] they were not European "absolutist" or "Weberian" states. Comparing European and Southeast Asian state formation processes, Anthony Day observes:

> The features that made European states "absolutist" — that is, the concept of "sovereignty" as a "co-ordinated system of administrative rule"; the theories about how kings and fathers mirrored one another and reinforced each other's claims to absolute authority; the bounded, territorial form of the state; diplomatic training; intelligence gathering; international congresses; the "balance of power" concept; mastery of the seas; the legal concept of private ownership; the administrative and fiscal reforms brought about through the constant waging of war; the appearance of "incarceration" as a mode of social control; and the new mode of anonymous and disciplined armies — do not have parallels or echoes in Southeast Asia that are strong enough to be meaningful.[47]

This statement generally rings true, but should be used with three caveats. First, Day is seemingly using European concepts of sovereignty and balance of power, to take two of the main concepts associated with the modern state system, as the ideal type against which Asian political concepts and practices are to be judged. This is not to say that he is implying the Asian forms to be "inferior" to Europe's, but that he is simply reflecting a familiar and nearly universal assumption among political scientists, that Europe provides the standard of a modern state system, and that in order to be considered a "proper" state system, a regional order must resemble the political units and behaviour established in and associated with Europe. Second, the differences between Europe and Asia identified by Day can be overstated, at least in some areas. Interstate relations in Southeast Asia did feature espionage, administrative centralization as a result of war, and mutual recognition of each other's absolute authority. The record of seafaring (if not mastery of the seas) by some Southeast Asian states was not unlike that in European maritime nations before the latter's colonial expansion. And, as Day himself notes, the downplaying of the "role of territoriality and space in the history of the premodern Southeast Asian state" needs to be "reexamined".[48] This leads to the third caveat about Day's sharp differentiation between Europe and Southeast Asia: some of the above features of political Europe in the age of the absolutist state, such as the territorial integrity norm, international congresses and the systematic exercise of "balance of power" as a tool of interstate relations, became regular and significant features of the European geopolitical landscape only after the Peace of Westphalia in 1648. This is about the time when the indigenous Asian state system went into sharp decline, or was "overlaid" by colonialism. What might have happened to Southeast Asian political structures and statecraft had there been no colonial takeover is anybody's guess, but it is at least worth speculating whether, without colonialism, Southeast Asian states might have developed some of the so-called "European" features of polity and gone through even greater administrative centralization. Similarly, for Tambiah, the galactic polity with its "exemplary center pulling together and holding in balance the surrounding polity" might seem "a far cry from a bureaucratic hierarchy in the Weberian sense".[49] But it must be borne in mind that the two polities are not comparable. The galactic polity (which is similar to the *mandala*) resembles the European state of the pre-Westphalian period, while the Weberian state is mostly a post-Westphalian construct.

An even more controversial claim about the "distinctiveness" of the pre-colonial Southeast Asian state system concerns the place of warfare. The work of Wolters and Geertz plays down the role of warfare and violence in the exercise of political authority and the management of interstate relations.[50] Moreover, these scholars also suggest that, while the classical state system of Southeast Asia was not entirely free from war, there was less coercion of the vanquished. Thus, Wolters argues that "victories rarely, if ever, led to the permanent obliteration of local centers either by colonization or through the influence of centralized institutions of government."[51] The reason why the *mandala* system, with few exceptions, did not expand into large imperial states through conquest may be that the system of *mandala* rule was relaxed, not coercive. As Wolters puts it, the "*mandala* rulers coerced as well as wooed".[52] Citing the case of Majapahit, Wolters points out that its vassals offered tribute and sought investiture. If they ignored the ruler, punishment was mild as long as they all acknowledged the overlordship of Majapahit. Wolters suggests that this loose relationship between lord and vassal was a prime example of an interstate system and intraregional relations in "old" Southeast Asia based on a minimal use of force.

Wolters also contrasts the value placed upon consensus in Southeast Asia's pre-colonial interstate system with the frequent occurrence of coercion and conflict in European interstate relations. To be sure, as noted earlier, the *mandala* system of overlapping sovereignty, patrimonial authority, and vaguely definable and continuously shifting territorial boundaries was not unlike the European state system before Westphalia. But the possibility of conflict resolution represented a key difference between the two. Wolters claims that "confrontations between the *mandalas* are unlikely to have brought persisting prejudices in their wake comparable with those associated with the history of European nationalisms."[53] Southeast Asia, in his view, was not prone to the internecine warfare that characterized the European continent both before and after Westphalia. Moreover, Wolters' earlier work implies that inheriting a pacific tradition might have been a big help in Southeast Asia's quest for regional unity in the post-colonial period. In Southeast Asia's case, "nothing prefigures a European-style contrast between a past that bristled with 'national' rivalries and a present that is groping toward regional consensus."[54] Thanks at least in part to the *mandala* system, differences among Southeast Asian cultures in the past were not significant enough to preclude the development in modern times of a regional consciousness and regional cooperation.

Geertz's generalizations about the theatre state in nineteenth-century Bali provides a somewhat more ambiguous basis for considering a pacific tradition in Southeast Asia. In the theatre state, what mattered in the hierarchical organization of the state system was not the relative preponderance of material power, military or economic, but relative claims of ritualistic and symbolic authority, and "the scale on which those pronouncements [about divine representation] could be mounted". The struggle for power was but a "competitive display" of ritual and symbol, not an accumulation of the instruments of warfare.[55] When the ruler faced centrifugal tendencies, he resorted to ritual and symbol to hold the state together instead of carrying out a military expedition. He also reduced the need to use force for maintaining unity through highly decentralized local administrative structures. As Wolters argues, "What was high centralization representationally was enormous dispersion institutionally, so that an intensely competitive politics, rising from the specificities of landscape, custom, and local history, took place in an idiom of static order emerging from the universalizing symbology of myth, rite and political dream."[56]

The use of ritual and symbol, rather than force and coercion, may be seen as representing a fundamentally different view of the state and the interstate system than that found in the Western political tradition.[57] However, such claims about the pre-colonial Southeast Asian interstate system can be overstated. Angkorian kings such as Jayavarman II and Suryavarman II were able to wage massive warfare. This belies the impression that they shunned force because their executive power in day-to-day government was limited to the role of umpire, securing material resources for themselves and their religious establishments. The *mandala* ruler was not just an umpire who communicated with divinity, ruling by example and ritual through the possession of divine knowledge and the representation of god. He was also able to mobilize massive resources from his network of loyalties, resources that could be used to prepare for major wars.[58] Tambiah contrasts the idyllic picture of Geertz's *negara* with the "perennial warfare, interregional conflicts, and litigious treaties"[59] among the Balinese states that emerges from other parts of Geertz's account.[60] And historical evidence points to warfare as a fairly common mode of interaction between the mainland Buddhist states, including the twenty-four wars waged by Siam and Myanmar between 1539 and 1767 that are recorded in Prince Damrong's classic account of rivalry.[61] As Anthony Day observes, although Southeast Asian states did not become "Weberian", they still engaged in massive warfare. Day is right to question the "silencing" of violence in the theatre state and *mandala* models of Geertz and Wolters respectively; "The fact that wars were waged to capture manpower ... does not mean that they were not brutal and destructive."[62]

While agreeing with the broad relevance of the *mandala* concept for the study of Thai history, the Thai historian Sunait Chutintaranond argues that the *mandala* concept does not denote a state structure per se, but "networks of personal connections among rulers, all of whom aspired to the highest leadership". Hence, the concept has a competitive geopolitical significance, whereby a ruler could use both diplomatic and military means to incorporate neighbouring states into his own domain. Sunait applies this understanding to explain the centralization of medieval Ayutthaya, as well as the policy of the Burmese monarchs of the Toungoo dynasty, Tabinshwehti (1531–50) and Bayinnaung (1551–81) in attacking Ayutthaya.[63] Craig Reynolds questions the picture of the *mandala* as a non-coercive cultural form of authority. Such constructions, Reynolds maintains, perpetuate "an exotic, idealist, Orientalist construction of the Southeast Asian past".[64] As he sees it, "the historian's desire to return to a past as yet untrammeled by European intervention may have resulted in an overly benign view of early Southeast Asia, a time in which the region is not seen as conflictual, as warlike, nor as ridden by social, economic, and environmental problems as in more modern periods."[65] But despite having questioned Wolters' tendency to claim a Southeast Asian past free from European-style conflict or warfare, Day ironically

TABLE 3.2
Summary of Prince Damrong's Twenty-Four Wars

War	Date	Summary of Events
1. Chiang Kran	1539	Border skirmish on Mae Lamao route.
2. Suriyothai	1548	Burmese probe during Ayutthayan dynastic fight. Invasion via Three Pagodas. Retreat.
3. White Elephants	1563	Invasion by Burmese dynast. Ayutthaya besieged. Surrenders. Indemnity.
4. First sack	1568–69	Burmese expansion to north. Ayutthaya falls to siege. Booty. Dependent status.
5. Ban Khraeng	1584	Naresuan "declares independence", drives Burmese out of northern provinces.
6. Suphanburi	1584	Hongsawadi sends two armies. Naresuan repels in Suphanburi and Phromburi.
7. Ban Saket	1585	Hongsawadi sends generals from Lanna. Naresuan repels north of city.
8. Ayutthaya siege	1586	Hongsawadi king leads invasion via Lanna. Ayutthaya besieged but holds.
9. Kanchanaburi	1590	Hongsawadi sends dependents via Three Pagodas. Naresuan repels in Kanchanaburi.
10. Nong Sarai	1592	Three-army attack. Naresuan kills Burmese Uparat in elephant duel.
11. Peninsula 1	1592	Naresuan sends disgraced generals to take Tavoy and Tenasserim.
12. Peninsula 2	1594	Ayutthaya's influence extended north up the coast to Moulmein and Martaban.

TABLE 3.2 *(Cont'd)*

War	Date	Summary of Events
13. Hongsawadi siege	1595	Naresuan continues through Mon country, besieges Hongwasadi, retreats.
14. Toungoo siege	1599	Naresuan quells Mon revolt, besieges Toungoo, retreats when supplies fail.
15. Shan states	1604	Naresuan dies en route to invade Shan states via Lanna.
16. Tavoy	1613	Burmese briefly take Tavoy and Tenasserim, but Ayutthaya recovers.
17. Chiang Mai	1614	Burmese besiege and take Chiang Mai.
18. Tavoy	1622	Burmese take Tavoy.
19. Chiang Mai	1662	Narai sends Kosa Lek to besiege and take Chiang Mai while Ava attacked by Ho.
20. Sai yok	1663	Burmese army through Three Pagodas, repelled in Khwae valley.
21. Pagan	1664	Narai mounts three-army attack, takes Martaban, besieges Pagan retreats.
22. Alaungpaya	1759	New Burmese dynast takes Mon ports, besieges Ayutthaya, dies in accident.
23. Peninsula	1764	Burmese retake Mon ports, then follow through and maraud down the peninsula.
24. Second sack	1767	Burmese armies from Lanna and Tavoy besiege, sack and burn Ayutthaya.

Source: Extracted from Prince Damrong Rajanubhab, *Our Wars with the Burmese: Thai-Burmese conflict 1539–1767*, translated by Phra Phraison Salarak and Thein Subindu, edited by Chris Baker (Bangkok: White Lotus, 2001), pp. xxii–xxiii.

also stresses several differences between Southeast Asia and Europe concerning the relationship between war and state formation. While European rulers waged war for "legitimation", their counterparts in Southeast Asian used war for "glory, out of rage, or in revenge".[66] War in Southeast Asia was romanticized as ritual and used to maintain and express an "aesthetic of state 'beauty'".[67] While violence in Europe was controlled and directed outwards, violence in Southeast Asia remained uncontrolled and was directed inwards to maintain internal discipline and prevent defection, as in the case of the restored Toungoo kings. In Europe, rulers centralized the military in the state capital; in Southeast Asia, especially in seventeenth- and eighteenth-century Myanmar, Siam and Java, rulers dispersed military power out of the capital in order to diffuse potential threats to the ruler.[68] Such juxtapositions, in the view of this author, have their limits. Southeast Asian violence was not always inward-looking, as would be evident from the numerous wars involving Siam, Myanmar, Dai Viet, Champa and Cambodia. Buddhist rulers in mainland Southeast Asia did wage war for legitimation and not just for glory, although in most cases they did it for both. (Glory, after all, has been a major motivation for warfare through the ages, and was cited as such by Thucydides in his classic account of the Peloponnesian War.) Prince Damrong's "explanation of the causes of war between the Siamese and the Burmese" views it as a spillover of the rivalry between the Burmese and the Mons, which itself was an outgrowth of geo-economic factors rather than glory, rage or revenge. Consider the following passage:

> The country of the Burmese was situated in the upper reaches of the Arawadi (Irrawaddy) river and the Satong (Sittaung) river and that of the Mons was situated at the mouth of these rivers. The Kingdom of the Burmese was not so prosperous as the Kingdom of the Mons. To travel to and trade with other countries by sea, the Burmese had to depend on the Mons and had to pass through the Kingdom of the Mons. Because of this physical difference there was constant hostility between them. Therefore when the Burmese and the Mons were both powerful, there were wars between them almost always ... Sometimes there arose among the Burmese a man of outstanding ability who was able to conquer neighbouring countries and hold sway over them. Then the boundary of the Burmese kingdom adjoined that of Siam. When this happened, war with Siam occurred as a consequence. Because the Burmese had the opportunity of amassing a great force and of obtaining the country of the Mons as their base, they came and encroached on Siamese territory.[69]

Apart from the overlapping physical structures of the *mandalas* and their shared characteristics as non-Weberian polities (presumed but admittedly "questionable"), other forces might have engendered commonality and homogeneity in classical Southeast Asia. The advent of Buddhism and various rulers' zeal in establishing their polities as leading centres for Buddhist learning (as in the Thai kingdom of Ayutthaya, founded in 1350) brought about a sense of commonality in advance of institutional centralization, which did not occur until the end of the eighteenth century.[70] Another homogenizing agent (the transmission of which was facilitated by commerce) was Indian literature, which according to Wolters engendered a certain "catholicity of outlook" in Southeast Asia. Indian literary models, such as the *Arthasastra*, used in Java by King Erlangga in the eleventh century, brought Southeast Asia "closer to an intra-regional communality of outlook" among the rulers.[71] Perhaps one of the most crucial factors was the sea, which provided "an obvious geographic framework for discussing possibilities of region-wide historical themes".[72] Maritime commerce helped to increase the material resources and geographical reach of at least some of the *mandala* rulers, thereby enabling them to spread the values and political structures associated with the *mandala* system. And it is to the impact of commerce in creating a regional pattern of interaction that we turn in the following section.

Commerce, Colonialism and the Regional Concept

The pattern of intraregional relations that was characteristic of the *mandala* system was transformed by two factors. The first of these was commerce, which had a mixed impact insofar as Southeast Asia's regionness was concerned. The second force, with a more destructive implication for the region, was colonialism.

The importance of trade in the making of Southeast Asia has not always received scholarly attention. Attempts to examine Southeast Asia's political economy, including the once influential "Asiatic Mode of Production" (AMP) school, did not view trade as an important aspect of the domestic economy in classical states. The latter were seen as autarkic, without any significant marketing system. They either produced their needs locally or produced them through fixed reciprocal exchange rates and redistributive relationships, despite the existence of the "bazaar" states of the archipelago.

Yet, there is now substantial evidence to suggest that trade played a major role in creating the state in Southeast Asia. The earliest Southeast Asian states were established along trade routes between India and China.[73] These included third-century states in the lower Mekong area and on the isthmus of the Thai-Malay peninsula. In the sixth century, other states emerged in Sumatra and west Java on the maritime route between India and China. In his study of trade relationships from the early Christian era to the beginning of the fifteenth century, K.R. Hall found substantial linkages between maritime trade and early state formation. Control over sources of export products was generally a key feature of coastal states except south-central Java, and the ability to benefit from maritime trade was critical to the fortunes of even the so-called "agrarian" kingdoms such as Pagan, Champa, Sukhothai, Ayutthaya, Majapahit and Vietnam.[74]

In Southeast Asia, trade created states in many ways. It provided new resources such as arms and weapons and luxury goods for redistribution. Just as importantly, it gave rulers new ideas of political organization and legitimacy, which they used to expand their authority and control. Control over trade routes was a crucial basis of political organization. On the Malay Peninsula, states came to be organized on the basin of a large river or groups of rivers, with their capital strategically located at the point where the river met the sea. Positioned in such a manner, the ruler could control the movement of persons and goods, defend from external attack, and levy taxes on imports and exports.

Trade helped to transform Southeast Asia by producing unprecedented commercial prosperity, cultural cosmopolitanism and trends towards centralized polities. Southeast Asian traders (especially Malays) were major players. Unlike in the later period of rapid urbanization and economic transformation, a significant proportion of the rural population became dependent on international trade. This process was accompanied by religious revolution, with the expansion of Islam and Christianity creating "more precise religious boundaries, a portable, universally-applicable textual authority, and a predictable moral universe".[75] The political impact of commerce was equally far-reaching, and included a shift in the political centre of gravity from interior to coastal areas in Cambodia, Indonesia, Thailand and Myanmar. State revenues became the preoccupation of states, with the emergence of trade monopolies and more effective local administrative structures.

According to Anthony Reid, trade created not only states but also the region. Developing the notion of "the Age of Commerce" between the fifteenth and seventeenth centuries, Reid suggests a high degree of commercial intercourse connecting the great maritime cities of Southeast Asia, such as Malacca, Pasai, Johor, Patani, Aceh and Brunei. The consequences of increased intraregional trade included, among other things, reduction of cultural barriers and the spread of the Malay language as the language of commerce. Reid also makes the more far-reaching claim that, until the advent of the Dutch East India Company in the seventeenth century, the "trading links within the region continued to be more influential than those beyond it":[76]

> [M]aritime intercourse continued to link the peoples of Southeast Asia more tightly to one another than to outside influences down to the seventeenth century. The fact that Chinese and Indian influences came to most of the region by maritime trade, not by conquest or colonization, appeared to ensure that Southeast Asia retained its distinctiveness even while borrowing numerous elements from these larger centres. What did *not* happen (with the partial exception of Vietnam) was that any part of the region established closer relations with China or India than with its neighbours in Southeast Asia.[77] [emphasis original]

By creating a picture of how intraregional trade links contributed to cultural and other linkages in pre-colonial Southeast Asia, Reid's historical research helps us understand the extent to which colonialism disrupted Southeast Asia's evolution as a region. It made various parts of the region more interdependent with (or dependent upon) the outside Western world (especially the colonial powers), at the expense of mutual dependence within the region itself. But trade was a double-edged sword insofar as the creation of a regional concept of Southeast Asia is concerned. The trade networks cited by Reid were pan-Asian rather than intra-Southeast Asian, with India and China serving as important nodal points. Moreover, the impact of trade conforms to what Wolters has described as the uniting as well as dividing role of the sea in Southeast Asian history. On the one hand, the "single ocean" concept, with its trading connections linking opposite ends of maritime Asia, created "a fundamental unity of communications".[78] It also created the basis of an intraregional cultural framework based on Indian textual models, thereby supplying "an enduring shape to 'Southeast Asian history'".[79] But trade did not necessarily create in Southeast Asia a commercial class with region-wide economic interests.[80] Instead, accessibility to the sea more likely served as a source of localization, as it allowed the emergence of a multitude of landfalls able independently to thrive by taking advantage of both local and foreign trade.[81] Within such a milieu, "each locality saw itself as belonging to a microcosm of the world", rather than as part of a broader regional system.[82]

Reid's emphasis on maritime interactions in the making of Southeast Asia has invited criticism. The most direct challenge comes from Victor Lieberman, who, along with his criticism of Reid's failure to distinguish "between mainland trajectories and those in the archipelago as well as between various patterns on the mainland", refuses "to grant automatic priority to maritime factors" in the making of Southeast Asia in general.[83] Instead, he regards maritime influence as but one of several dynamics.[84] Lieberman thus issues a twofold challenge to Reid's conception of Southeast Asia as a region. First, he "disaggregates Southeast Asia" by contrasting, as discussed earlier, the greater consolidation and centralization of continental Southeast Asian states as compared to those in the maritime domain.[85] Second, he recognizes "the critical impact of global currents"[86] by drawing "strange parallels" between state formation in mainland Southeast Asia and that in Russia, Japan, France and the Islands. To the extent that "in terms of linear-cum-cyclic trajectories, chronology, and dynamics, the mainland [Southeast Asia] resembled much of Europe and Japan, but diverged significantly from South Asia and island Southeast Asia", it is thus problematic, from Lieberman's point of view, to consider Southeast Asia as a coherent region, at least in terms of Reid's "Age of Commerce" thesis.[87]

It is important, however, to bear in mind that, while disaggregating Southeast Asia, Lieberman is as prone to generalizations across regions as Reid is within the region. Moreover, Lieberman's contention that Reid's "Age of Commerce" thesis has moved the historiography of Southeast Asia's closer to the "externalist" position[88] is unsustainable. As Lieberman himself points out, the externalist position not only denied Southeast Asian agency but also Southeast Asian regional coherence. Reid, through his emphasis on the maritime influences and especially on European colonialism (among other forces) as the major reason for bringing the "Age of Commerce" to an end, might have questioned Southeast Asian agency. But his focus on the intraregional concentration of trade and his attempt to develop the "Age of Commerce" as a "template for the entire region" would be consistent with the "autonomous" view of Southeast Asian history, as it highlights not just Southeast Asian interdependence (as in Wolters though in the economic sense) but also coherence.

Apart from the contrasting positions of Reid and Lieberman on the imagination of Southeast Asia as a region, it is also useful to contrast the perspectives of Wolters and Reid on the evolution of Southeast Asia as a region. Unlike Reid, Wolters views maritime linkages as less significant in moulding Southeast Asia into a regional unit, focusing instead on the importance of the cultural and political space created by the *mandala* system. But it is evident that the two are dealing with rather different stages of Southeast Asian history: Wolters deals primarily, but not exclusively, with the classical period, Reid with the post-*mandala*, immediately pre-colonial period. In this sense, their perspectives may actually be complementary. The "Age of Commerce" took up where the *mandala* system had left off in the region, until colonialism undermined the homogenizing influence of both.

A related point of contention in the imagination of Southeast Asia as a region is the "Mediterranean analogy",[89] which had been invoked in various contexts by several historians of the region. Georges Coedès, who directed France's prestigious École française d'Extrême-Orient (EFEO) from 1929 to 1946, referred to the Southeast Asian waters enclosed by the South China Sea, the Gulf of Siam and the Java Sea as a "veritable Mediterranean" and a "unifying factor" for the peoples in the region.[90] He did not include the Bay of Bengal in this conception of the Asian Mediterranean, although Wolters interpreted him to include all Southeast Asian waters in general. A Franco-German conference organized in 1997 — by French scholar Denys Lombard (director of EFEO from 1993 to 1998), who regarded coastal south China as part of Southeast Asia, and German scholar Roderich Ptak (from the University of Munich) — considered the idea of an Asian Mediterranean.[91] In the preface to his own two-volume *Southeast Asia in the Age of Commerce*, Reid acknowledges that Braudel's work on the Mediterranean was "a great inspiration" to him. He singles out the Braudel's multidisciplinary approach as being especially important in highlighting the "'collective destinies' of a broad region".[92] Historians such as Reid and Lombard were "inspired" and "fascinated" by Braudel's classic study of the Mediterranean,[93] not just because of its multidisciplinary approach and focus on the sea but also because, as Sutherland put it, "seeking parallels between Southeast Asia and the civilizations of the Mediterranean seemed to offer a solution to nagging doubts regarding Southeast Asian identity and agency".[94]

But the Mediterranean analogy is controversial. Critics point to the "dangers of Eurocentric model-making", and argue that "the history of the Asian seas could be rewritten from an entirely Asian perspective", and that Braudel himself "tended to see the Mediterranean from the 'north'; that should be avoided when dealing with other 'Mediterranean' scenarios such as the Southeast Asian seas".[95] Furthermore, Braudel himself could not assume the unity of the Mediterranean, viewing it "not so much a single entity as a 'complex of seas'".[96] How could one then be so sure of "the coherence and authenticity of Southeast Asia as a region"?[97]

In the end, notwithstanding scepticism regarding its validity, the utility of the Mediterranean analogy as a tool of historical analysis in looking beyond the nation-state model has been acknowledged, even by some critics.[98] Moreover, criticism of the Mediterranean analogy as "Eurocentric model-making" actually reinforces the importance of and need for indigenous perspectives in conceptualizing Southeast Asia. And as Lieberman notes, the dismissal of the Mediterranean analogy need not "invalidate Southeast Asia as a unit of study, whose integrity one can justify in terms of underlying cultural commonalities, classical and colonial parallels, current interactions, or simply geographic convenience".[99]

The Mediterranean analogy and other analytic frameworks for studying Southeast Asia's past — whether the *mandala* management of political and territorial space or the "Age of Commerce" thesis — may not amount to an authentic and enduring basis for a regional notion of Southeast Asia; yet with the advent of European colonialism, much of the commonality and shared consciousness implied by these metaphors was disrupted and, in some cases, severely eroded. Colonialism dealt the decisive blow to the classical interstate system of Southeast Asia. Among its chief effects was the severe disruption and eventual disintegration of the Asian trade network. This proved to be one of the most significant effects of the Portuguese conquest of Malacca.[100] The growth of European influence after 1825 directly inhibited contacts between Southeast Asian societies and polities, as each colony became progressively more linked to the metropolitan area. Moreover, the response of Southeast Asian societies to the colonial expansion was marked by so much diversity that there could be little scope for a sense of common destiny or a community of experience to serve as the basis of regional identity and cooperation.[101] European writings and intellectual thought also overshadowed Southeast Asian cultural and political traditions.[102] A further blow to Southeast Asia's historical intraregional ties was the colonial authorities' lack of interest in developing a regional diplomatic framework. For example, there are no recorded meetings between the American governor-general of the Philippines and his British, French or Dutch counterparts.[103]

Adding to these forces of fragmentation was the long-range communication system driven by colonial imperatives. One of the clearest examples of this was the Spanish occupation of the Philippines during the period between the 1660s and the mid-nineteenth century. As Spain strove to defend its possession against the Dutch, the Portuguese and Muslims, it relied heavily on the trans-Pacific link to Mexico as a kind of lifeline. This broke up the traditional maritime routes binding Southeast Asia together and linking it as a whole to the outside world. Spanish rule also introduced a new and important religious division into classical Southeast Asia, already fragmented by the advent of Islam.

The drawing of artificial boundaries under colonialism also had a disintegrating impact on the regional interstate system. This was done on the basis of the geographical location of particular peoples rather than their ethnic spread or loyalties. Since there were few clearly defined geographical boundaries already existing, they had to be drawn arbitrarily, without regard to the network of overlapping hierarchies and personal allegiances existing in Southeast Asia. The colonial powers imposed frontiers on a landscape where the concept of territoriality had not been well established. Thus, the idea of a "national" frontier in Southeast Asia was applied despite the absence of the essential attributes of nationhood.[104] The newly drawn boundaries bore little resemblance to national frontiers in Europe, which had been drawn over a long period of time, through centuries of warfare, conquest and the centralization of loyalty to the state. The Europeanization of the international relations of Southeast Asia through the drawing of these boundaries was primarily intended to prevent disputes among the colonial powers. It helped to settle their disputes in Europe as much as to facilitate governance within a particular geographical area. But the territorial limits did not match ethnic, social, political or economic realities. Indeed, they often reflected the accidental nature of colonial takeovers. Many were consciously designed for the sake of administrative and economic efficiency, or to satisfy the strategic interests of the colonial powers in Europe. The result of the boundary-drawing was the creation of what J.S. Furnivall would call "plural societies", that is, a single state containing a multitude of racial and ethnic groups or a single ethnic group divided across many states.[105]

The impact of colonialism in the destruction of Southeast Asia's regional character was to become a part of the nationalist thinking in Southeast Asia. Indeed, in the aftermath of colonialism, some Southeast Asian elites would see the task of post-colonial region-building as a matter of restoring the pre-colonial integrity of the region; "The isolation of centuries had to be breached; lost ties had to be restored."[106] But European colonialism did have significant homogenizing influences as well. While the response of the various colonial units to Westernization differed, the clash between Western political, cultural and economic pressures and indigenous traditions also produced similar changes[107] and led to an increased degree of commonality in social and political structures throughout colonial Southeast Asia. While the delineation and protection of national frontiers was detrimental to regional identity, the influence of Westernization helped to blur the historical differences between the Indianized, Sinicized and Philippine segments of Southeast Asia.[108] Moreover, the colonial heritage and post-colonial developments formed a key part of the basis for thinking about Southeast Asia in regional terms. While the shared experience of colonial rule (with the exception of Thailand) had been offset by differences among colonial regimes and the divergent patterns of retreat by colonial powers, the diversity was moderated by a common sense of nationalism, the common task of nation-building, and efforts towards modernization. These, as Neher argues, would provide "a general framework for studying Southeast Asia as an entity".[109]

After the War: (Re)inventing the Region

If most international relations scholars tend to view the concept of Southeast Asia as a post-World War II construct, the origins of this construct must be traced to two defining features of the war itself. The first was the relatively brief era of Japanese colonialism. This period in Southeast Asian history must be regarded as qualitatively different from that of European domination in terms of its implications for regional identity. The impact of the Japanese victory in encouraging Southeast Asian nationalists has been widely noted. But this was not its only unintended political effect. It also stoked a regional consciousness in several ways. This was the first time that "the region had ever known one common ruler".[110] Japanese rule destroyed the "colonial partition" of Southeast Asia among the various Western powers. It also introduced various Southeast Asian nationalist leaders to one another. For example, President Jose P. Laurel of the Philippines, Prime Minister Ba Maw of Myanmar and Prince Wan Waithayakon of Thailand, representing Premier Phibul, all attended the Assembly of Greater East Asiatic Nations held in Tokyo in November 1943, the first meeting of three such prominent Southeast Asian political leaders.[111]

To some extent, Japanese policy accorded a greater recognition to the distinctiveness of Southeast Asia. Southeast Asia enjoyed a greater prominence in Japan's concept of a Greater East Asian Co-Prosperity Sphere than in Japan's earlier framework of Pan-Asianism. The latter, as Tarling points out, had focused on China and was inspired by a desire to prevent western powers from exercising domination over East Asia. Its aim was to bring China under Japanese hegemony, since in Japan's view an independent China, even with Japanese assistance, lacked the strength to stand up to the Western powers. The idea of the Greater East Asian Co-Prosperity Sphere, on the other hand, placed more emphasis on Southeast Asia, not just because of Japan's concerns about access to resources, but also because of Japan's frustrations in dealing with China.[112]

While Japanese occupation may have created an incipient basis for a Southeast Asian regional order, it was the powers challenging Japanese hegemony that gave Southeast Asia its name. Of particular emphasis here is the impact of World War II and the Southeast Asia Command (SEAC). According to Hall, SEAC gave the area an "identity, which it previously lacked, and by coming into current use, [the term South East Asia] ... accentuated the inappropriateness of names such as the Indian Archipelago, Indonesia, Indo-Chinese Peninsula, Greater India, Little China, or the Nanyang ..."[113] In Fifield's view, SEAC helped to make Southeast Asia a "fixed and practical term even in the United States" during World War II.[114] SEAC was created in 1943, embracing Myanmar, Malaya, Singapore and Thailand, and with its headquarters in Kandy, Ceylon (Sri Lanka). Its frontiers were extended to southern Indochina and much of Indonesia after the Japanese surrender, and its headquarters moved to Singapore. While SEAC was intended to serve as a means of accepting the Japanese surrender, repatriating Japanese personnel and restoring order in the formerly occupied areas (including restoration of colonial rule until the determination of their final status), it was forced in this process to become involved in regional politics. Since, with the exception of Britain, the former colonial powers were utterly dependent upon the United States in Southeast Asia, SEAC soon came to represent the total Allied response to regional security and politics.[115]

While SEAC put Southeast Asia in the international spotlight, what contributed to a "rediscovery" of Southeast Asia's regional coherence was the role of academic scholarship, inspired by World War II as well as the advent of the Cold War immediately thereafter. To be sure, as Fifield argues, a regional concept of Southeast Asia might have emerged, albeit at a slower pace, had there been no Southeast Asia Command. The concept of Southeast Asia had slowly been emerging in academic and policy discourses before the advent of the SEAC or even before the outbreak of World War II.[116] But there is little doubt that the outbreak of the Cold War gave a major impetus to academic interest on Southeast Asia. Southeast Asia — with its proliferation of communist insurgencies — became a focal point of the new global geopolitics. As Western policy-makers concerned with the threat of communist expansionism began to look at the Southeast Asian situation with greater concern, academic interest in the region increased.

The outcome was a virtual reinvention of the Southeast Asian concept, by imagining it to be a "culturally independent region".[117] Post-war scholarship on Southeast Asia marked the onset of an intellectual endeavour (which continues today) that challenged the historical links between Southeast Asia and the "great" Asian civilizations. Dominated by Sinologists and Indologists or "Sanskritists", Southeast Asianists had seen the region as a "lesser version" of China and India and as a receptacle for cultural ideas from the two.[118] The new scholarship focused on exposing the overemphasis on Indian and Chinese influences and on dismissing the notion of this region as a mere cultural hybrid. This may have seemed ironic, since, as noted earlier, some works that had portrayed the region as a "weaker and inferior"[119] extension of the great civilizations of India and China also had a major influence in creating a regional understanding of Southeast Asia. The ideas about Indianization and Sinicization did provide a generalized framework for linking toget-her the diverse cultures of Southeast Asia, and had enabled scholars to "assert the unity of the region" by drawing attention to the "shared ideas of statecraft, architecture and religion through their common link to India and China".[120] Yet a great deal of post-war scholarship (while still being undertaken by Westerners) was concerned with identifying and articulating the differences among Southeast Asian societies vis-à-vis the two neighbouring civilizations and establishing what were regarded as distinctive Southeast Asian cultural traits.[121] New research, archaeological discoveries and intellectual discourses among Western and local scholars produced a tendency towards "recovering" the region's "autonomous" past. Historians pointed not only to Southeast Asia's distinctive civilizational traits pre-dating Indian, Chinese and Islamic influences but also to the resilience of its indigenous cultural, social and political traditions, which had survived foreign influences of all kinds. The emphasis was less on how Southeast Asian societies had adopted Indic or Sinic artistic, religious and political concepts and practices and more on how they had "adapted these foreign ideas to suit their own needs and values".[122] For example, such perspectives pointed to how the use of Sanskrit, once widespread in government and religion, slowly waned as Southeast Asians used Indian scripts to develop written forms of their own languages. Once regarded in terms of their Indian heritage, the region's symbolic and organizational features were now seen to be "merely redefinitions of indigenous institutions".[123] Southeast Asians were not to be "regarded as recipients (or victims) of history, but as makers of it".[124] A major turning point was the work of Dutch economic historian Van Leur, who described all foreign influences on Indonesia, including Hindu-Buddhism and Islam, as "only a thin, easily *flaking glaze* on the massive body of indigenous civilization".[125]

Scholars pointed to important variations between the original Indian and Chinese ideas and practices and those found in Southeast Asia. Examples ranged from Southeast Asia's rejection or modification of the Indian caste system (the kings used the Indian caste system to describe themselves, but the caste system did not catch on in societies by and large) and the nature of Buddha images in Thailand (as they differed from Indian images) to the distinctive character of temple art in the Hindu-Buddhist kingdoms of Pagan, Angkor and Java.[126] Similarly, Tambiah argues that Indian Buddhist notions of kingship, including that of the *Chakravartin,* took a deep hold in Southeast Asia, assuming "an effective and enduring organizing role in the constitution of emergent societies", yet this was not a matter of wholesale and unaltered transmission imposed by Indian rulers or merchants but a development that was "sought, appropriated, and transformed to suit a Southeast Asian context and milieu".[127]

The new preoccupation of historians of Southeast Asia was to show how Indian culture and political ideas were "absorbed by the local population and joined to their existing cultural patterns".[128] In sum, "Southeast Asians ... borrowed but they also adapted. In some very important cases they did not need to borrow at all."[129] The historiography of Southeast Asia became a project to demonstrate how the region had "adopted the alien cultural traits without in the process losing its identity".[130] Out of this body of work emerged a number of key concepts that must be counted as major contributions to the scholarship on the transmission of ideas and culture in international relations.[131] These include Van Leur's "idea of local initiative", or the argument that Indian religious and political ideas were not imposed on or brought into Southeast Asia by conquest or even commerce, but by the voluntary initiative of Southeast Asian rulers who "called upon Indian civilization to the east in a bid to use them for spiritual and political legitimation".[132] A similar concept is "local genius" — developed by H.G. Quaritch Wales to signify the role of local Southeast Asian artists, sculptures and builders in "guiding the evolution of the Indianized civilization itself" — which explained the variations in the design of sculpture and architecture between India and Southeast Asia (despite Indian influence on the latter), and between different Southeast Asian cultures, for example, Cham and Khmer, both of which had been subject to Indian influence.[133] Wolters' concept of "localization" and "relocalization" also spoke to a similar dynamic, with localization defined as a "local statement ... into which foreign elements have retreated".[134] The Indian "cultural ideas" discussed covered a broad range, including religion, art, architecture, statecraft, concepts of power, authority, and legitimacy, ideas about political stratification, territorial organization, political institutionalization, diplomatic practice and law.[135] A number of secular Indian legal, political and diplomatic texts made their way into the ancient Southeast Asian political landscape. These included the *Manusmrti* (Code of Manu), the *Dharmasastras* (legal treatises) and the *Arthasastra*, the most famous Indian classic on statecraft, all of which were "widely revered" in classical Southeast Asia.[136]

It is not too much of an exaggeration to say that the new understanding of Southeast Asia and the attendant quest for an "autonomous history"[137] also supported the quest for an "indigenous" framework of regional international politics. It coincided with a redrawing of the boundaries of the region itself. No longer were India and China included in the region; no longer was Southeast Asia considered part of South Asia or East Asia.[138] Moreover, the immediate post-war period saw what Reid has called the "turning away" tendency in states with the closest proximity to larger powers, that is, Myanmar and Vietnam (as well as the Philippines in relation to the United States). Thus, for the elite in Myanmar and Vietnam, knowing themselves to be part of an ancient Southeast Asian cultural matrix was an immensely useful way to claim a distinctive national identity *vis-à-vis* the feared Indian and Chinese neighbours. For the Philippines, imagining a pre-Hispanic past with pan-Malay linkages helped overcome the sense of being an American appendage. Thus, academic claims about a Southeast Asian cultural identity distinct from that of India or China supported a quest for regional order focusing on a common Southeast Asian political identity.

But whatever positive feelings about the prospects for regional order that the discovery of Southeast Asia's cultural unity might have generated were offset by the emergence of "nation-states" in the political landscape of Southeast Asia. Expectations of conflict and disorder in this nation-state system exceeded those of peace and harmony. Apart from the conflicts associated with the decolonization process itself, including anti-colonial wars in Myanmar, Indonesia and Vietnam, the pessimism about Southeast Asia's future stemmed from the very artificial nature of colonially imposed boundaries. Nothing illustrated this pessimism more starkly than the designation of Southeast Asia as "the Balkans of the Orient", which came to feature in a great deal of Western thinking about the region in the early post-war period. The scholar who contributed most to this analogy, C.A. Fisher (whose argument for considering Southeast Asia as coherent region is discussed in the Introduction), suggested that Southeast Asia, like the Balkans, was located in a "cultural and political fault zone". Both formed a border region between two greater civilizations. Moreover, both regions were characterized by "geographical fragmentation, an area broken up into peninsulas and islands, a characteristically mountainous region, where lowlands are the exception rather than the rule".[139] This topography, as in the Balkans, would make it difficult to maintain internal stability and invite frequent foreign invasions and attempts by foreign powers to control the sea lanes and straits. Regional disorder would be compounded by pervasive minority strife, caused by weaker ethnic groups seeking refuge in the mountains to protect themselves from attack by stronger plains-people. Finally, Fisher predicted, in both regions local memories about past conflicts, abundant in folklore, would render the prospects for cooperation among its countries remote.[140]

The Contribution of "Southeast Asian Studies"

The debates over Southeast Asian identity did not occur in an institutional vacuum. The emergence of "Southeast Asian studies" in the post-war period in the United States, Europe, Australia, Japan and within the region itself contributed greatly to the perception of Southeast Asia as a region. European scholars were key to the debate over Southeast Asia's cultural matrix and autonomy (Coedès, Van Leur, Lombard and others, although some Europeans such as Wolters and Heine-Geldern made their academic careers in the United States).[141] The creation of the Chair of South East Asian History at the School of Oriental and African Studies in 1949 (its first holder being D.G.E. Hall) contributed to the further advancement of Southeast Asian studies. European scholars also contributed to the conceptual repertoire of Southeast Asian studies (e.g., Boeke's "dual economy" and Furnivall's "plural society"). But during the 1950s and 1960s at least, notes Ruth McVey, "the centre of this new field [of Southeast Asia] was undoubtedly the United States".[142] McVey calls it the "coincidence between Southeast Asia's birth as a concept and the triumph of world power".[143] In the United States, the first and second Indochinese wars had a major influence in advancing Southeast Asia both as a concept and as a field of study.[144] This was reflected in the establishment of a number of Southeast Asian studies centres: Yale in 1947, followed by Cornell in 1951, UC Berkeley in 1960 (although it was merged into the Center for South Asia Studies in 1969) and Michigan (Center for South and Southeast Asian Studies) in 1960. Subsequently, Southeast Asian centres were established at Hawaii, Ohio and Northern Illinois universities respectively. A brochure issued by the Southeast Asia Regional Council in 1972 listed Southeast Asia programmes at fourteen universities: apart from the universities mentioned above, the list included American University, Chicago, Columbia, Kansas, Southern Illinois, Washington and Wisconsin.[145]

But by the 1980s, the state of Southeast Asian studies in the United States aroused decidedly mixed feelings. The field had done well in terms of numbers. As a paper presented at the 1984 "Conference on Southeast Asian Studies: Options for the Future", organized by the Woodrow Wilson Center in Washington, D.C., noted, the number of specialists on the region grew from about fifty in 1940 to an estimated 500 "who are now actively studying and producing knowledge on the region", with an additional 500 "serious observers who keep up with events in the region".[146] Yet, the conference also highlighted the limitations of American-led Southeast Asian studies, especially in terms of quality. Benedict Anderson, a participant at the Wilson Center conference, lamented that the number of scholars studying the politics of the region numbered some 100–130 persons, and out of those only about a quarter were active scholars "publishing with any regularity or distinction". These numbers were "not very impressive for the country of the size, wealth and power of the United States".[147] He was even harsher on quality, describing the "academic study of the politics of Southeast Asia in North America" as "feeble and fragile". (Note that he was referring specifically to the politics of Southeast Asia and its states, not Southeast Asian studies more broadly).[148] Among the reasons he identified for this state of affairs was lack of interest and recognition from the U.S. government and fluctuation "in Washington's concern with that region". "Most of us recognize the bitter irony that the heyday of Southeast Asian studies in the widest sense was the era of the Vietnam War."[149] The consequence of "political marginality", combined with "disciplinary marginality", encouraged "journalistic moonlighting" and "a deepseated lack of sense of purpose" among the scholars of Southeast Asia.[150]

While Anderson blamed lack of official interest and assistance in the United States as a major reason behind the decline of Southeast Asian studies, he might not have approved of the consequences of such official patronage. Indeed, the "general sentiment of the conference" was that the decline of U.S. government funding to Southeast Asian studies had "had a salutary effect on Southeast Asian studies", because the cycles of federal interest in funding, closely tied as it had been to the U.S. foreign policy agenda in the region, had created a "roller-coaster" uncertainty, and skewed the content and direction of research.[151] Anderson found the situation with regard to indigenous scholarship on Southeast Asia to be exactly the reverse when it came to "the distance between university people (teachers and students alike) and their governments". This distance, he contended, was "quite narrow".[152] Yet, it did not preclude what he would call the "indigenization" of Southeast Asian studies, a trend featuring a wide range of contributors, from academics to activists.

The issue of "indigenization" is of course vital to the ability of Southeast Asian studies to endure and acquire a durable measure of autonomy. Anderson observed that, although indigenization was taking hold in scholarship on the politics of Southeast Asia, the evidence for this trend was not to be found in the traditional halls of academia but also in a variety of other fora, and in people from a great variety of backgrounds and perspectives. He cited the example of speeches made by student demonstrators in 1974 and 1978, where "in almost every case the defense rests on detailed and critical analysis of contemporary Indonesian political and economic conditions".[153] Another type of indigenization was highlighted by the director of Singapore's Institute of Southeast Asian studies, who pointed to "indigenous Southeast Asian scholars ... trying to develop their own approaches to regional and local issues".[154] The issue of indigenization is not unrelated, as a paper by Reid and Diokono argued, to the fact that many pioneering Western scholars, such as D.G.E. Hall, J.S. Furnivall, George Louis Finot, George Coedès and Louis-Charles Damais, had actually been based within the region for significant periods of time. The EFEO conducted its most significant project, the restoration of Angkor, from its headquarters in Saigon and later in Hanoi, and it also maintained a Jakarta office. Coedès was director of the Thai Royal Museum for several years. He wrote his classic integrated history of Southeast Asia (Indianized kingdoms) at his EFEO headquarters in Hanoi was therefore "no accident".[155] Moreover, if one defines "indigenization" to include academic institutions and programmes focusing on the region, one cannot ignore the major role played by the Institute of Southeast Asian Studies, established in Singapore in 1968, which took a whole as well as parts approach to the region, co-publishing, among others, Wolters' influential *History, Culture and Region in Southeast Asian Perspective* (jointly with the Cornell Southeast Asia Program) and Marr and Milner's edited collection, *Southeast Asia in the 9th to 14th Centuries*, a book that was inspired by Wolters' work.[156] Also important was the development of Southeast Asian studies at the Rangoon University, the University of the Philippines and the University of Malaya (later the University of Singapore and still later the National University of Singapore). The contribution of these institutions cannot be ignored. Later, institutes focusing on Southeast Asia were set up in Vietnam and China.

These developments seemed to respond to the hopes of Donald Emmerson, another notable participant at the conference, that conceptual innovation from Southeast Asian studies would finally overcome its ethnocentric tendency towards "Western surprise".[157] According to

Emmerson, the central questions and agenda of Southeast Asian studies had for long been shaped by the Western observers' puzzlement or "creative surprise" at the lack of fit between Western norms and experiences of domestic stability, integration and development and those in the Southeast Asian context. These perceived anomalies aroused the curiosity of scholars and drove conceptual innovation, resulting in such concepts as Boeke's "dual economy" in the Netherlands Indies, Furnivall's "plural society", Riggs' "bureaucratic polity" (in Thailand), Anderson's "Javanese concept of power", Heine-Geldern's "exemplary centre", Feith's "decline of constitutional democracy" (in Indonesia), Lende' s "patron-client" model of politics in the Philippines and James Scott's "moral economy". Yet, as Emmerson saw it, Southeast Asian studies could progress by becoming "less negative and less conditioned by alien experience: not 'Why can't Southeast Asia be more like the West?' but 'Why is Southeast Asia the way it is?'"[158] And in contrast to Anderson's pessimism, Emmerson, looking not just at U.S. but Western scholarship more generally, noted "encouraging trends ...: a diversification of authors, [and] a corollary diversification of their intellectual debts and inclinations".[159] Kernial Sandhu, one of the region's representatives at the conference and a long-time director of the Institute of Southeast Asian Studies, challenged the pessimism about the state of Southeast Asian studies, both in scale and quality. He argued that "given the dynamism of the region and given the obvious academic attention to research on Southeast Asia, we are actually doing quite well". As proof, he told the audience, "Institutions dedicated to Southeast Asia are springing up around the world ... People who have ignored the region for hundreds of years are now trying to catch up."[160]

If progress was indeed taking place (and Sandhu's optimism was as much debatable as Anderson's pessimism), it did not mean the study of the whole was taking hold relative to that of its parts. An *International Biographical Directory of Southeast Asian Specialists*, compiled by Professor Robert Tillman in 1969, found that out of 660 researched and a total of 941 specialists, no one self-identified under the category "region" or "multi-country".[161] In the Ness and Morrow survey presented at the Wilson Center Conference in 1984, among the 959 specialists on Southeast Asia (called "producers of knowledge about Southeast Asia") during 1975–80, only 128 were classified as "regional" as opposed to country-specific specialists (all except Brunei among the ASEAN-10 members were included in the survey). And only 176, or eighteen per cent, of the total number of specialists surveyed focused on "supra-national systems" (covering regional organizations, world political position and international organizations, international trade, international alliances, diplomacy, imperialism and colonialism).[162] Yet these are the topics that lend themselves more easily to regional analysis.

Moreover, scholars studying the politics or society of more than one country remained scarce. Anderson had been a notable exception; barred from Indonesia, he turned to Thai and Philippine studies, as his presentation at the Wilson Center conference, marshalling the evidence for his "indigenization" thesis, so superbly demonstrated.[163] Although the diversity of Southeast Asia meant greater scope for comparative studies among the countries of the region, the same diversity imposed a "major constraint on scholars who attempt to analyze the region as a whole" and wished "to deal holistically with the area".[164] As a result, "rather than attempting to deal with Southeast Asia as a whole, Western social scientists have instead become country specialists".[165] Moreover, the "constraints of diversity" were "as great for indigenous scholars as for foreign scholars".[166] Indeed, the "indigenization" of Southeast Asian studies did not mean, at least by the early 1980s, adequate "knowledge and communication among the various scholars and research organizations" across national boundaries in the region itself.[167] I will return to this theme in the final chapter.

Conclusion

This chapter has sketched an outline of the interstate system in Southeast Asia before the advent of the nation-state. This outline relies heavily on attempts to "imagine" Southeast Asia's pre-colonial past in terms of regional patterns of statehood and interstate relations. It also provides an examination of the historical forces that made and unmade the region, including the seemingly contradictory effects of pre-colonial commerce and colonial rule on the regional system. The major themes of the chapter — including the nature of the state system associated with the *mandala* and similar constructs; the impact of colonialism in disrupting Southeast Asia's traditional political, cultural and commercial linkages; the emergence of a geopolitical notion of Southeast Asia during and in the immediate aftermath of World War II; and the early post-war attempts by regional specialists to "imagine" and delineate a region of Southeast Asia — would have an important bearing on the international relations of the region in subsequent periods. They provide the necessary backdrop to considering the relationship between nationalism and regionalism, the impact of the Cold War international order on intraregional relations, and the evolution of regional organization geared to the management of regional conflict.

At the beginning of the post-war period, while efforts to restore Southeast Asia's cultural unity and regional coherence had begun, its political future as a region appeared highly uncertain. The Japanese conquest of Southeast Asia and entities such as the SEAC attracted international attention to the region and laid the basis for a regional geopolitical framework that had never existed during the colonial period. The advent of the Cold War furthered the development of this framework. But such sources of regional international order in Southeast Asia were inspired largely by external events and forces. There was little in the form of an *internal making* of Southeast Asia. To make matters worse, initial efforts to create a Southeast Asian regional identity through cooperation were minimal and unsuccessful.

NOTES

[1]   See O.W. Wolters, *History, Culture and Region in Southeast Asian Perspectives*, rev. ed. (Ithaca, NY: Cornell University Southeast Asia Program, 1999), postscript, p. vi.

[2]   Lucian Pye, *International Relations in Asia: Culture, Nation and State*, Sigur Center Asia Papers no. 1 (Washington, D.C.: Sigur Center for Asian Studies, George Washington University, 1998), p. 6.

[3]   Ibid.

[4]   Harry J. Benda, "The Structure of Southeast Asian History: Some Preliminary Observations", *Journal of Southeast Asian History* 3, no. 1 (1962): 106–38.

[5]   Milton Osborne, *Southeast Asia: An Illustrated Introductory History*, 5th ed. (St. Leonards, NSW: Allen and Unwin, 1990), p. 5.

[6]   Another possible claimant is the term *Suvarnabhumi*, which points to an era when "polities of Southeast Asia, such as Angkor, Pagan, Ayutthaya, Srivijaya, as well as a multitude of smaller entities were culturally interrelated through the Sanskrit lingua franca which carried with it a loosely integrated set of political and cosmological beliefs related to Brahmanic traditions ..." Excluding the Philippines and the Red River Delta, this was a "region stretching from the Cham principalities of what is now south and central Vietnam to the Indian subcontinent and through the Indonesian archipelago and mainland Tai, Khmer, and Bamar polities (where Thailand, Laos,

Cambodia, and Myanmar are now located)". Eric C. Thompson, "Southeast Asia", in *International Encyclopedia of Human Geography*, vol. 1, edited by R. Kitchin and N. Thrift (Oxford: Elsevier, 2009), p. 251.

[7] Wolters, *History, Culture and Region*, pp. 27–40.

[8] Historians differ on what constitutes the "classical" period in Southeast Asian history. For Benda it spans from the fourth century BC to the fourteenth century AD, while for Aung-Thwin it "usually" means roughly between the ninth and fourteenth centuries AD. Most agree that the classical period ended with the collapse of the region's "Indian period". Benda, "The Structure of Southeast Asian History"; Michael Aung-Thwin, "The 'Classical' in Southeast Asia: The Present in the Past", *Journal of Southeast Asian Studies* 26, no. 1 (1995), p. 75; Leonard Y. Andaya and Barbara Watson Andaya, "Southeast Asia in the Early Modern Period: Twenty-Five Years on", *Journal of Southeast Asian Studies* 26, no. 1 (1995), pp. 92–93.

[9] Craig Reynolds, "A New Look at Old Southeast Asia", *Journal of Asian Studies* 54, no. 2 (1995), p. 426.

[10] A recent discussion of the *mandala*, "theatre state" and "galactic polity" concepts can be found in Craig J. Reynolds, *Seditious Histories: Contesting Thai and Southeast Asian Pasts* (Seattle: University of Washington Press, 2006), Chapter 2, "Paradigms of the Premodern State".

[11] Wolters, *History, Culture and Region*, p. 16. Lockard defines *mandala* as "fluctuating zones of power and influence emanating in concentric circles from a central court which attempted, with varying success, to dominate economic and human resources in outlying areas through a combination of diplomacy and military might". Craig A. Lockard, "Integrating Southeast Asia into the Framework of World History: The Period before 1500", *The History Teacher* 29, no. 1 (1995): 7–35.

[12] I have relied on Stanley J. Tambiah in describing these features of O.W. Wolters' notion of *mandala*. See Stanley J. Tambiah, *Culture, Thought, and Social Action: An Anthropological Perspective* (Cambridge, MA: Harvard University Press, 1985), p. 260.

[13] Ibid., p. 261.

[14] Wolters, *History, Culture and Region*, p. 25.

[15] Ibid., p. 32.

[16] Ibid., p. 24.

[17] Benedict Anderson, "The Idea of Power in Javanese Culture", in *Culture and Politics in Indonesia*, edited by C. Holt (Ithaca, NY: Cornell University Press, 1972), p. 28.

[18] Wolters, *History, Culture and Region*, p. 29.

[19] Ibid., pp. 27–28.

[20] Tambiah, *Culture, Thought, and Social Action*, p. 324.

[21] Tambiah, *Culture, Thought, and Social Action*, p. 323.

[22] Ibid., p. 324.

[23] Ibid.

[24] Clifford Geertz, *Negara: The Theatre State in Nineteenth-Century Bali* (Princeton, NJ: Princeton University Press, 1980), pp. 18–19.

[25] Ibid., p. 24.

[26] Ibid.

[27] Ibid.

[28] O.W. Wolters, "Culture, History and Region in Southeast Asian Perspectives", in *ASEAN: Identity, Development and Culture*, edited by Ram Prakash Anand and Purificacion Valera Quisumbing (Quezon City: University of the Philippines Law Center/Honolulu: East-West Center, Culture Learning Institute, 1981), p. 3.

[29] Ibid., p. 9.

[30] Ibid., p. 12. But Wolters took a more cautious view of the homogenizing effects of *mandalas* in his revised monograph. See Wolters, *History, Culture and Region*, p. 31.

[31] Leonard Y. Andaya, *Ethnonation, Nation-State and Regionalism in Southeast Asia*, in Proceedings of the International Symposium, "Southeast Asia: Global Area Studies for the 21st Century", organized by Project Team: An Integrated Approach to Global Area Studies (funded by Monbusho Grant-in-Aid for Scientific Research on Priority Areas) and Center for Southeast Asian Studies, Kyoto University, Kyoto International Community House, 18–22 October 1996, p. 137.

[32] Hermann Kulke, "The Early and Imperial Kingdom in Southeast Asian History", in *Southeast Asia in the 9th to 14th Centuries*, edited by David G. Marr and Anthony Crothers Milner (Singapore: Institute of Southeast Asian Studies/Canberra: Australian National University, Research School of Pacific Studies, 1986), p. 17.

[33] Wolters, *History, Culture and Region*, p. 39.

[34] This problem also has to do with the debate over whether and to what extent these two countries could be regarded as part of Southeast Asia. D.G.E. Hall himself did not include Philippines in the first edition of his book *A History of South-East Asia*. Later, he did reconsider it, after his Filipino students protested: "They made it quite clear that they regarded themselves as Southeast Asians; and they could point to important connections between their country and Southeast Asia. It has felt in some way they said the influence of India upon its early culture. There were those who claimed that the Philippines had come within the scope of Srivijaya's far flung commercial activities. The Islamization of the Malay world had indeed had a powerful effect upon the southern islands of the group, and had the Spaniards not appeared at Manila precisely when they did, it would certainly have been brought into the Muslim fold, and with it presumably the remainder of the Philippines."

D.G.E. Hall, "The Integrity of Southeast Asian History", *Journal of Southeast Asian History* 4, no. 2 (1973), p. 166. On Vietnam, there is a debate over its Sinic and pre-Sinic culture and identity (see note 36). Grant Evans regards Vietnam to be politically part of Southeast Asia, but culturally of East Asia. See Grant Evans, "Between the Global and the Local There are Regions, Cultural Areas, and National States", review of *History, Culture and Region in Southeast Asian Perspectives*, by O. W. Wolters, *Journal of Southeast Asian Studies* 33, no. 1 (2002): 147–61.

[35] Charles Higham, *The Archeology of Mainland Southeast Asia from 10,000 B.C. to the Fall of Angkor* (Cambridge: Cambridge University Press, 1989), Chapters 5–6.

[36] Ibid., p. 111.

[37] Vietnam scholars warn against analysing the pre-colonial Vietnamese state entirely in terms of Chinese principles. As Keith Taylor contends in his study of the Ly Dynasty in eleventh-century Vietnam, while the state adopted the Chinese model of centralization and emulated Chinese diplomatic practices, questions of authority and legitimacy were decided on the basis of "patterns of thought shared with other Southeast Asian peoples". Keith Taylor, "Authority and Legitimacy in 11th Century Vietnam", in Marr and Milner, *Southeast Asia in the 9th to 14th Centuries*, p. 141. Wolters contends that the similarities between Vietnam and the rest of Southeast Asia, despite the Sinic polity of the former, are striking, and confirm the relative uniqueness of Southeast Asian polity. While Vietnam's polity was based on the Chinese model of a powerful and permanent centre within a fixed territorial space, the Vietnamese rulers were also very un-Sinic and more Southeast Asian in their high degree of tolerance and closeness to the people, and the simple and informal court customs. Wolters, *History, Culture and Region*, p. 37.

[38] Ibid., pp. 33–34.

[39] While the concept of *mandala* may be one of the most far-reaching attempts to think of Southeast Asia in terms of an "indigenous" regional system, it is ironically also Indic in origin and hence of limited utility as a tool for differentiating Southeast Asia from other societies.

[40] Andaya, *Ethnonation, Nation-State and Regionalism in Southeast Asia*, p. 136.

[41] Wolters, *History, Culture and Region*, p. 31.

[42] Ibid., pp. 31–32.

[43] Kulke, "The Early and Imperial Kingdom", p. 7.

[44] Victor Lieberman, *Strange Parallels: Southeast Asia in Global Context, c. 800–1830* (Cambridge: Cambridge University Press, 2003), p. 33.

[45] Ibid., p. 35.

[46] Charles Tilly, *Coercion, Capital, and European States: AD 990–1990* (Cambridge: Cambridge University Press, 1990), p. 1, cited in Lieberman, *Strange Parallels*, p. 33.

[47] Anthony Day, *Fluid Iron: State Formation in Southeast Asia* (Honolulu: University of Hawaii Press, 2002), p. 23.

[48] Day, *Fluid Iron*, p. 231.

[49] Tambiah, *Culture, Thought, and Social Action*, p. 266.

[50] Reynolds, "A New Look at Old Southeast Asia", p. 427.

[51] Wolters, *History, Culture and Region*, p. 28.

[52] Ibid., p. 34.

[53] Ibid., p. 36.

[54] Ibid.

[55] Geertz, *Negara: The Theatre State in Nineteenth-Century Bali*, p. 125.

[56] Ibid., p. 132.

[57] Wolters, "Culture, History and Region", p. 97.

[58] Wolters, *History, Culture and Region*, p. 34.

[59] Tambiah, *Culture, Thought, and Social Action*, p. 324.

[60] Geertz, *Negara: The Theatre State in Nineteenth-Century Bali*, p. 43.

[61] Prince Damrong Rajanubhab, *The Chronicle of Our Wars with the Burmese: Hostilities Between Siamese and Burmese When Ayutthaya was the Capital of Siam* (Bangkok: White Lotus Press, 2001). The book, first published in 1917, is considered to be Thailand's "most famous history book", and "the first Thai book in the Western sense of an analytical work based on a range of documentary sources", according to the preface by the editor, Chris Baker. Although as a half-brother of King Chulalongkorn and a senior official in his court the author shows some obvious biases in favour of the Thai, this book narrative may also be regarded as a rare non-Western account of war, albeit one that has received no attention in the "causes of war" literature in international relations.

[62] Day, *Fluid Iron*, p. 231.

[63] Sunait Chutintaranond, "*Mandala*, 'Segmentary State' and Politics of Centralization in Medieval Ayudhya", *Journal of the Siam Society* 78, no. 1 (1990), pp. 90–91.

[64] Reynolds, "A New Look at Old Southeast Asia", p. 427.

[65] Ibid., p. 422.

[66] Day, *Fluid Iron*, p. 231.

[67] Ibid., p. 289.

[68] Ibid., p. 231.

[69] Prince Damrong, *The Chronicle of Our Wars with the Burmese*, p. 5.

[70] Wolters, *History, Culture and Region*, p. 31.

[71] Ibid., p. 47.

[72] Ibid., p. 42.

[73] Jan Wisseman Christie, "Negara, *Mandala*, and Despotic State: Images of Early Java", in Marr and Milner, *Southeast Asia in the 9th to 14th Centuries*, p. 69.

[74] Kenneth R. Hall, *Maritime Trade and State Development in Early Southeast Asia* (Honolulu: University of Hawaii Press, 1985).

[75] Victor Lieberman, "An Age of Commerce in Southeast Asia? Problems of Regional Coherence", *Journal of Asian Studies* 54, no. 3 (1995), p. 797.

[76] Anthony Reid, *Southeast Asia in the Age of Commerce 1450-1680*, vol. 1, *The Lands Below the Winds* (New Haven, CT: Yale University Press, 1988), p. 7.

[77] Ibid., p. 6.

[78] Wolters, *History, Culture and Region*, pp. 44–45.

[79] Wolters, "Culture, History and Region", p. 27.

[80] Ibid., p. 21.

[81] Ibid.

[82] Ibid., p. 33.

[83] Lieberman, *Strange Parallels*, pp. 22–23 and 46.

[84] Ibid., p. 21.

[85] Ibid., p. 46.

[86] Ibid.

[87] Ibid., p. xx.

[88] Ibid., p. 16. It should be pointed out that Lieberman divides Southeast Asian historiography into four categories: "externalist", "autonomous", "Age of Commerce" and his own "strange parallels", which "seeks to connect diverse changes in local structure to global patterns". Ibid., pp. 6–23.

[89] Heather Sutherland, "Southeast Asian History and the Mediterranean Analogy", *Journal of Southeast Asian Studies* 34, no. 1 (2003): 1–20.

[90] Georges Coedès, *The Indianised States of Southeast Asia*, edited by Walter Vella and translated by Susan Brown (Honolulu: East-West Center Press, 1968), pp. 3–4; Wolters, *History, Culture and Region*, pp. 43–44.

[91] Roderich Ptak, "International Symposium on the 'Asian Mediterranean' (Paris, 3–5 March 1997)", *Archipel* 55 (1998): 11–14, and "In Memoriam Denys Lombard (1938–1998)", *IIAS Newsletter* 16 (Summer 1998) <http://www.iias.nl/iiasn/16/general/gen11.html> (accessed 12 March 2010).

[92] Reid, *Southeast Asia in the Age of Commerce, 1450–1680*, vol. 1, p. xiv.

[93] Fernand Braudel, *The Mediterranean and the Mediterranean World in the Age of Philip II*, vols. 1 and 2 (Berkeley: University of California Press, 1995).

[94] Sutherland, "Southeast Asian History and the Mediterranean Analogy", p. 13.

[95] Ptak, "International Symposium on the 'Asian Mediterranean'", p. 13.

[96] Braudel, *The Mediterranean*, vol. 1, p. 23.

[97] Sutherland, "Southeast Asian History and the Mediterranean Analogy", p. 14.

[98] Sanjay Subrahmanyam, "Notes on Circulation and Asymmetry in Two Mediterraneans", in *From the Mediterranean to the China Sea: Miscellaneous Notes*, edited by Claude Guillot et al. (Wiesbaden: Harrassowitz, 1998), p. 42.

[99] Victor Lieberman, "Local Integration and Euroasian Analogies: Structuring Southeast Asian History c. 1350–c. 1830", *Modern Asian Studies* 27, no. 3 (1993): 475–572.

[100] Merle Calvin Ricklefs, *A History of Modern Indonesia Since c.1300*, 2nd ed. (Stanford, CA: Stanford University Press, 1993), p. 26.

[101] David J. Steinberg, ed., *In Search of Southeast Asia: A Modern History*, rev. ed. (Honolulu: University of Hawaii Press, 1987), p. 100. While colonialism created greater diversity within Southeast Asia, the colonial period constituted a small part of Southeast Asian history. This raises questions as to whether one should pay too much attention to its impact in moving the countries of Southeast Asia in different political and administrative directions. Osborne, *Southeast Asia*, p. 12.

[102] Donald G. McCloud, *System and Process in Southeast Asia: The Evolution of a Region* (Boulder, CO: Westview Press, 1986), p. 5.

[103] Russell Fifield, "'Southeast Asia' and 'ASEAN' as Regional Concepts", in *Southeast Asian Studies: Options for the Future*, edited by Ronald A. Morse (Lanham, MD: University Press of America, 1984), p. 126.

[104] Nicholas Tarling describes the differences between the drawing of frontiers in Europe and in Southeast Asia in the following terms: "In the drawing of the frontiers there was something of a paradox. In Europe the concept dealt with subjects and citizens in terms of their geographical locality rather than their personal allegiance; and the state laid claim to their taxes and imposed its obligations on an impersonal basis. That contrasted with much of previous Southeast Asian practice, especially in the archipelago where, insofar as geographical frontiers existed, they might be only vaguely defined. Often more important within states, even within some of the larger ones, were personal allegiances, client-patron relations, differential connections between court and core, court and periphery; often more important among states were overlapping hierarchies, dual loyalties. Such structures better reflected the conditions of the Southeast Asian past. But the concept that the Europeans sought to apply in Southeast Asia also contrasted with the European present. In Europe frontiers had been created over a long period of time, often as a result of struggle, and within them new loyalties had been built up. Increasing loyalty was to the state itself, as representing the nation in whose name, it had come to be accepted, its government ruled. No such ideology could apply to the colonial territories; nor was there a clear substitute for it. The colonial powers were utilizing a concept not only drawn from a system of international relations that differed but from one which they themselves were not in fact applying." Nicholas Tarling, ed., *The Cambridge History of Southeast Asia*, vol. 2, *The Nineteenth and Twentieth Centuries* (Cambridge: Cambridge University Press, 1992), pp. 6–8.

[105] Carl A. Trocki, "Political Structures in the Nineteenth and Early Twentieth Centuries", ibid., p. 85.

[106] A. Melchor, Jr., "Security Issues in Southeast Asia", in *Regionalism in Southeast Asia* (Jakarta: Centre for Strategic and International Studies, 1975), pp. 46–47.

[107] Benda, "The Structure of Southeast Asian History", p. 35.

[108] Ibid.

[109] Clark D. Neher, "The Social Sciences", in Morse, *Southeast Asian Studies: Options for the Future*, p. 129.

[110] Amry Vandenbosch and Richard Butwell, *The Changing Face of Southeast Asia* (Lexington: University of Kentucky Press, 1966), p. 340.

[111] Ibid.

[112] Nicholas Tarling, *Nations and States in Southeast Asia* (Cambridge: Cambridge University Press, 1998), pp. 82–83.

[113] D.G.E. Hall, "Looking at Southeast Asian History", *Journal of Asian Studies* 19, no. 3 (1960), p. 243.

[114] Russell Fifield, "The Southeast Asia Command", in *The ASEAN Reader,* edited by Kernial Singh Sandhu et al. (Singapore: Institute of Southeast Asian Studies, 1992), p. 21.

[115] Ibid., pp. 20–23.

[116] Ibid., p. 23.

[117] Osborne, *Southeast Asia*, p. 5.

[118] Andaya, *Ethnonation, Nation-State and Regionalism in Southeast Asia*, p. 133. Since Indian cultural influence was seen as the greater and more extensive geographically of the two, there is a great deal more writing among historians on the possibility and limits of "Indianization". See Konrad Bekker, "Historical Patterns of Cultural Contact in Southeast Asia", *Far Eastern Quarterly* 9, no. 1 (1951): 3–15; Lawrence Palmer Briggs, "The Hinduized States of Southeast Asia: A Review", *Far Eastern Quarterly* 7, no. 4 (1948): 376–93; George Coedès, "Some Problems in the Ancient History of the Hinduized States of Southeast Asia", *Journal of Southeast Asian History* 5 (1964): 1–14; and *The Indianized States of Southeast Asia* (Honolulu: University of Hawaii Press, 1968); I.W. Mabbett, "The 'Indianization' of Southeast Asia: Reflections on the Prehistoric Sources", *Journal of Southeast Asian Studies* 8, no. 1 (1976): 1–14; and "The 'Indianization' of Southeast Asia: Reflections on the Historical Sources", *Journal of Southeast Asian Studies* 8, no. 2 (1976): 143–61; R.C. Majumdar, *Greater India*, 2nd ed. (Bombay: National Information and Publications, 1948); R.C. Majumdar, Hemchandra Raychaudhuri and Kalikinkar Datta, *An Advanced History of India* (London: Macmillan, 1948); Justus M. van der Kroef, "The Hinduization of Indonesia Reconsidered", *Far Eastern Quarterly* 9, no. 1 (1951): 17–30; J.C. van Leur, "On Early Asian Trade", in *Indonesian Trade and Society: Essays in Asian Social and Economic History* (The Hague:

W. van Hoeve, 1955); H.G. Quaritch Wales, *The Making of Greater India*, 2nd ed. (London: Bernard Quaritch, 1951); W.F. Wertheim, "Early Asian Trade: An Appreciation of J.C. van Leur", *Far Eastern Quarterly* 13, no. 2 (1954): 167–73; Paul Wheatley, "Desultory Remarks on the Ancient History of the Malay Peninsula", in *Malayan and Indonesian Studies*, edited by John Bastin and Roelof Roolvink (Oxford: Clarendon Press, 1964), pp. 33–75; P. Wheatley, "Comments on the Dynamics of the Process of Indianization", in *Early Malaysia*, edited by Kernial Singh Sandhu (Singapore: Singapore Education Press, 1973), pp. 37–49; and "Presidential Address: India Beyond the Ganges — Desultory Reflections on the Origins of Civilization in Southeast Asia", *Journal of Asian Studies* 42, no. 1 (1982): 13–28; Wolters, *History, Culture and Region*.

[119] Andaya, *Ethnonation, Nation-State and Regionalism in Southeast Asia*, p. 134.

[120] Ibid.

[121] Some scholars have cited the absence of the Hindu caste system in Southeast Asia as an example of how the region differed from India. Among the distinctive "Southeast Asian" cultural traits that Southeast Asianists have used to differentiate it from China and India are "the concept of spirit or 'soul stuff' animating living things, prominence of women in descent, ritual matters, marketing and agriculture, and the importance of debt as a determinant of social obligations". Reid, *Southeast Asia in the Age of Commerce 1450–1680*, vol. 1, p. 6. Osborne highlights the contrast between the Indian emphasis on extended family and the Southeast Asian concept of the nuclear or individual family, and the differences between Thai and Indian Buddha images. In Vietnam, he argues, the impact of Chinese political and cultural traditions was more salient at the level of the court than at societal levels, attesting to the strength of indigenous Vietnamese traditions, which were more Southeast Asian rather than Sinic in nature. Osborne, *Southeast Asia*, pp. 5–6.

[122] Ibid., p. 5. One prominent example of how Southeast Asia adapted, rather than adopted, foreign cultures concerns Islam, an interesting example since it is not associated with either Indic or Sinic civilizations. Islam came to Southeast Asia as an alien culture, but from the sixteenth century onwards it had become a mass culture, expressing itself in Malay and taking on a "self-conscious" Southeast Asian character. The Islamic people of Southeast Asia, including the Acehnese, Javanese, Makassarese, Filipinos, southern Tais and Chams, distinguished themselves from the rest of the Islamic world. They were recognized at the religious centres of Islam as a distinctive group (as seen from the fact that they were put in the same hostels when they went on pilgrimage). Anthony Reid, "A Saucer Model of Southeast Asian Identity", special issue of *Southeast Asian Journal of Social Science* 27, no. 1 (1999), pp. 12–13.

[123] Wheatley, "Presidential Address", p. 27.

[124] G. Carter Bentley, "Indigenous States of Southeast Asia", *Annual Review of Anthropology* 76 (1985), p. 299. In evaluating the debate over the extent of the Indianization of Southeast Asia, it is useful to bear in mind George Coedès' observation, that scholars with specialization in Indian culture (Indologists and Sanskritists) usually stressed the deep civilizing role of Indian culture, while those trained in social sciences put more emphasis on indigenous initiative and response. Coedès, *Indianized States of Southeast Asia*.

[125] Van Leur, *Indonesian Trade and Society*, p. 169.

[126] Other examples of cultural variation included the salience of the nuclear family in Southeast Asia, as opposed to the extended family in India, and the important role of women in the traditional peasant society of Southeast Asia, which was in sharp contrast to China or India.

[127] Stanley J. Tambiah, *World Conqueror and World Renouncer: A Study of Buddhism and Polity in Thailand Against a Historical Background* (Cambridge: Cambridge University Press, 1976), p. 74.

[128] Osborne, *Southeast Asia*, p. 24.

[129] Ibid., p. 25.

[130] D.R. Sardesai, *Southeast Asia: Past and Present* (Boulder, CO: Westview Press, 1994), p. 16.

[131] Amitav Acharya, "How Ideas Spread: Whose Norms Matter? Norm Localization and Institutional Change in Asian Regionalism", *International Organization* 58, no. 2 (2004): 239–75.

[132] Van Leur, *Indonesian Trade and Society*, p. 98.

[133] Wales, *The Making of Greater India*, pp. 42, 183 and 195.

[134] Wolters, *History, Culture and Region*, p. 57.

[135] Moreover, these aspects were closely interrelated; "art, religion and government are inseparable phenomena in earlier Southeast Asia". Wolters, "Culture, History and Region", p. 43.

[136] John F. Cady, *Southeast Asia: Its Historical Development* (New York: McGraw-Hill, 1964), p. 45. The *Arthasastra*, according to D.G.E. Hall, "for centuries was almost the nature of a prescribed textbook at South-East Asian courts". The text prescribed ideas and norms for both domestic governance and interstate relations, covering areas such as the pacification of newly acquired territories; prescriptions regarding maintenance of good customs and abrogation of bad ones; procedures for settling lawsuits; the uses of spies; and principles for the levying and collection of revenues. D.G.E. Hall, *A History of Southeast Asia*, 4th ed. (London: Macmillan, 1981), p. 250. Other Indian influences included writing systems in Southeast Asia, which with the exception of those of Muslim Malays and the Vietnamese were based on the Indian alphabet, and the terminologies for law and administration.

"Even where the Indian governmental system was not fully introduced, as among the Bugenese and the eastern Indonesian islanders, Hindu influences were reflected at the higher levels of social stratification." Cady, *Southeast Asia: Its Historical Development*, p. 45.

[137] John R.W. Smail, "On the Possibility of an Autonomous History of Modern Southeast Asia", *Journal of Southeast Asian History* 2, no. 2 (1961): 72–102. See also Benda, "The Structure of Southeast Asian History"; D.G.E. Hall, "Looking at Southeast Asian History", *Journal of Asian Studies* 19, no. 3 (1960): 243–53.

[138] Donald K. Emmerson, "Southeast Asia: What's in a Name?" *Journal of Southeast Asian Studies* 15, no. 1 (1984), p. 8.

[139] Charles A. Fisher, "Southeast Asia: The Balkans of the Orient? A Study in Continuity and Change", *Geography* 47 (1962), p. 347.

[140] Ibid., p. 9.

[141] Donald K. Emmerson, "Beyond Western Surprise: Thoughts on the Evolution of Southeast Asian Studies", in Morse, *Southeast Asian Studies: Options for the Future*, pp. 52–59.

[142] Ruth McVey, "Change and Continuity in Southeast Asian Studies", *Journal of Southeast Asian Studies* 26, no. 1 (1995), p. 1.

[143] Ibid., p. 2.

[144] Russell H. Fifield, "Southeast Asian Studies: Origins, Development, Future", *Journal of Southeast Asian Studies* 7, no. 2 (1976), p. 151.

[145] Ibid., p. 154. I rely heavily on Fifield's detailed account of the growth of Southeast Asian studies in the United States and outside.

[146] Garry Ness and Martha Morrow, "Assessing U.S. Scholarly Resources on Southeast Asia", in Morse, ed., *Southeast Asian Studies in the United States*, p. 25.

[147] Benedict Anderson, "Politics and their Study in Southeast Asia", in Morse, *Southeast Asian Studies in the United States*, p. 40.

[148] Ibid., p. 43.

[149] Ibid. Another reason for the allegedly poor state of Southeast Asian studies in the United States might have to do with the fact that Southeast Asian studies lacked institutional autonomy; see Van Neil's 1964 observation, that "Much American scholarship on Southeast Asia is produced by college or university staff members from institutions with only a peripheral interest in Southeast Asia, and some of it by persons whose academic tasks have no association with any sort of organized program even remotely related to Southeast Asia." Robert Van Neil, "Southeast Asian Studies in the U.S.A.", *Journal of Southeast Asian History* 5, no. 1 (1964), p. 194. This state of affairs remained true to the 1980s, and one might dare say even to this day, both in the United States and worldwide.

[150] Anderson, "Politics and their Study in Southeast Asia", p. 43.

151 Ronald A. Morse and David B.J. Adams, "Establishing a New Agenda for Southeast Asian Studies in America", in Morse, *Southeast Asian Studies: Options for the Future.*

152 Ibid., p. 44.

153 Ibid., pp. 49–50.

154 Kernial S. Sandhu, "Comment", in Morse, ed., *Southeast Asian Studies in the United States*, p. 60.

155 Anthony Reid and Maria Serena Diokno, "Completing the Circle: Southeast Asian Studies in Southeast Asia", in *Southeast Asian Studies: Pacific Perspectives*, edited by Anthony Reid (Tempe: Arizona State University, Program for Southeast Asian Studies, 2003), p. 98.

156 Marr and Milner, *Southeast Asia in the 9th to 14th Centuries*, pp. 49–63.

157 Emmerson, "Beyond Western Surprise", pp. 52–59.

158 Ibid., p. 55

159 Ibid., p. 57.

160 Sandhu, "Comment", p. 60.

161 Cited in Ness and Morrow, "Assessing U.S. Scholarly Resources on Southeast Asia", p. 30.

162 Ibid., p. 38.

163 Anderson, "Politics and their Study in Southeast Asia". See also Benedict Anderson, *The Spectre of Comparisons: Nationalism, Southeast Asia, and the World* (New York: Verso, 1998).

164 Neher, "The Social Sciences", pp. 129 and 131.

165 Ibid., p. 131.

166 Ibid., p. 130.

167 Morse and Adams, "Establishing a New Agenda for Southeast Asian Studies in America".

Section A

1. Bagan

Bagan (formerly Pagan), Myanmar, was the cultural and political centre of one of the "imperial kingdoms" of Southeast Asia, from the eleventh century till the thirteenth century.

Source: Photo taken by the author.

2. Champa

The Po Nagar Tower in Nha Tranh, Vietnam. Champa was one of the early classical states of Southeast Asia, covering central and southern Vietnam, although its territorial extent and power varied considerably with time. Some argue that there was not a single Champa, but several domains with that name, consistent with the fluid territorial and political contours of the *mandala* concept.

Source: Photo taken by the author.

3. Borobudur

Built around ninth century AD by the Sailendra dynasty in central Java, the Borobudur is the largest Buddhist temple in the world.

Source: Photo taken by the author.

4. Angkor

The Bayon, built in the late twelfth or early thirteenth century by King Jayavarman VII, is a majestic symbol of the Angkoran *mandala*, one of the most extensive and powerful kingdoms of Southeast Asia, covering at its height the Mekong delta, modern Cambodia, and parts of central and northeastern Thailand.

Source: Photo taken by the author.

5. Srivijayan Temple, Chaiya, Thailand

Centred in Palembang, Sumatra, the Srivijayan empire at one point controlled commerce in the Malacca Straits and extended its jurisdiction over the Malayan peninsula and southern Thailand, including Chaiya and Nakhon Si Thammarat.

Source: Photo taken by the author.

6. Malacca

Porta de Santiago, the surviving gatehouse of A Famosa, a fortress built by the Portugese shortly after their capture of the Malay Sultanate of Malacca in 1511. The fall of Malacca ushered in the era of European colonialism in Southeast Asia.

Source: Photo taken by the author.

7. Malacca

A sixteenth-century caravel (a small, highly manoeuvrable Portugese sailing ship) fires a salute as it anchors off Malacca.

Source: Artwork by Hervey Garret Smith/National Geographic/Getty Images.

8. First Filipino Jose Rizal
The statue of the Philippine hero Jose Rizal, one of Asia's earliest and foremost nationalist leaders.

Source: Photo by Jack Birns/Time Life Pictures/Getty Images.

9. The Fall of Singapore

World War II, 15 February 1942: some of the 120,000 British, Australian, Indian and Chinese forces captured by the Japanese forces, stand before their Japanese guards.

Source: Photo by Paul Popper/Popperfoto/ Getty Images.

10. Greater East Asia Co-Prosperity Sphere

Leaders attending the Greater East Asia Conference in Tokyo, 5 November 1943. Left to right: Premier Ba Maw of Myanmar, President Chang Ching-hui of Manchukuo (Manchuria), Premier Wang Ching-wei of the Nanking government, Premier Tojo of Japan, Prince Wan Waithayakon of Thailand, President Jose Paciano Laurel of the Philippines and Premier Subhas Chandra Bose of the Free State of India. The Japanese victory over European colonial powers stoked nationalist sentiments in Southeast Asia, destroyed the Western "colonial partition" of Southeast Asia, gave various parts of Southeast Asia "a common ruler" for the first time, and implied a greater recognition of the distinctiveness of Southeast Asia.

Source: Courtesy of The Mainichi Newspapers Co., Japan.

11. The Liberation of the Philippines
9 January 1945: General Douglas MacArthur (C) and General Richard Sutherland (L) &
Col. Lloyd Lehrbas wading ashore during American landing at Lindgayen Gulf.

Source: Photo by Carl Mydans/Time & Life Pictures/Getty Images.

12. Japanese surrender
12 September 1945: Mountbatten's wartime Southeast Asia Command (SEAC) helped
popularize the idea of Southeast Asia as a region. Opposite is Japanese General Itagaki
Seishiro signing the surrender document.

Source: Netherlands Institute for War Documentation, National Archives of Singapore.

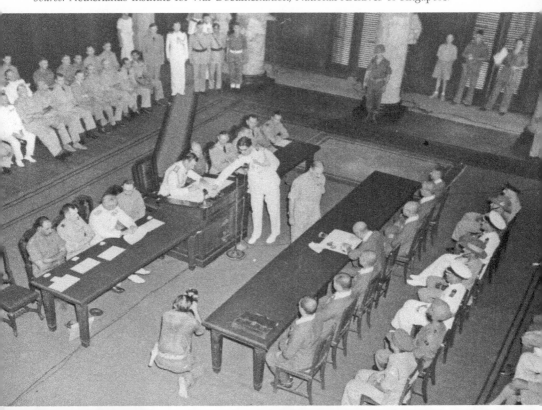

13. Aung San of Myanmar
Aung San, leader of the Myanmar's Anti-Fascist People's Freedom League (seen here arriving in London in January 1947 for talks with the British government on Myanmar's future), had a regionalist imagination, calling for an "entente" of countries and regions neighbouring Myanmar, including Yunnan, and India's Northeast region, and imagined an "Asiatic Federation".

Source: Photo by George W. Hales/Getty Images.

14. Asian Relations Conference, New Delhi, India, 23 March–2 April 1947
Organized by India's Prime Minister Jawaharlal Nehru, this was the first post-World War II congress (albeit unofficial) of Asian nations. Worried about Indian and Chinese dominance, Southeast Asian delegates to this conference from Indonesia, Myanmar, Thailand, Vietnam, the Philippines and Malaya "debated ... a Southeast Asian Association ... even dreamt of a 'greater Southeast Asia, a federation'".

Source: Photo by Volkmar K. Wentzel/National Geographic/Getty Images.

15. A Triumph of Indonesian Nationalism
Queen Juliana of the Netherlands at the ceremony of Transfer of Sovereignity of Indonesia, 27 December 1949 at the Royal Palace in Amsterdam. The cause of Indonesian independence was helped by the anti-colonial sentiments expressed at the Second Asian Relations Conference organized by Nehru in New Delhi in January 1949.

Source: Photo by Keystone/Getty Images.

16. French Defeat in Dien Bien Phu
Battle in Dien Bien Phu, Vietnam, May 1954. Vietminh troops taking prisoners away after their victory. The French defeat led the United States to be more interested in the creation of a regional defence pact to counter communism in Southeast Asia.

Source: Photo by Collection Jean-Claude Labbe/Gamma-Rapho via Getty Images.

17. Birth of SEATO

U.S. Secretary of State John Foster Dulles (L) during the Manila conference (8 September 1954) where he signed the Treaty (Manila Treaty) establishing the Southeast Asian Treaty Organization (SEATO). SEATO proved to be a divisive factor in Asian and Southeast Asian regionalism, with Myanmar and Indonesia (along with India and Ceylon), refusing the invitation to join the alliance, as Thailand, the Philippines and Pakistan had done.

Source: Photo by Howard Sochurek/Time Life Pictures/Getty Images.

| M. U Nu | P.M. Sir John Kotelawala | P.M. Nehru | P.M. Ali Sastroamidjojo | P.M. Ali |
| Burma | Sailan | India | Indonesia | Pakistan |

18. Asia-Africa Conference, Bandung, 1955

A postcard showing the five official sponsors of the Asia-Africa Conference held in Bandung Indonesia during 18–24 April 1955. They were collectively and formally known as the Conference of South-East Asian Prime Ministers, or the Colombo Powers, suggesting that the boundary between what was then "South-East Asia" and what later came to be known as "South Asia" was not clear.

Source: Author's own collection.

19. Asia-Africa Conference, Bandung, 1955
Delegates at Bandung. Prominent is the newly anointed leader of Egypt, Gamel Abdel Nasser. At this stage, there were no concrete effort to develop a "Southeast Asian regionalism", and Bandung did not create any permanent regional or cross-regional grouping of Asian and African nations, although it paved the way tor the subsequent emergence of the global Non-Aligned Movement.

Source: Author's own collection.

20. Asia-Africa Conference, Bandung, 1955
Premier U Nu (L) of Myanmar, Jawaharlal Nehru of India and Indonesian Prime Minister Ali Sastroamidjojo conversing during the Bandung Conference. Nehru played a central role in early post-war Asian regionalist efforts, organizing two Asian Relations Conferences in New Delhi (in 1947 and 1949), and being a co-sponsor of the Bandung Conference. Nehru enjoyed close personal ties with several nationalist leaders in Southeast Asia, especially Myanmar and Indonesia. At that time India was seen as an inspirational, if not overbearing diplomatic actor in the region that would later develop a more distinctive identity as Southeast Asia.

Source: Photo by Howard Sochurek/Time Life Pictures/Getty Images.

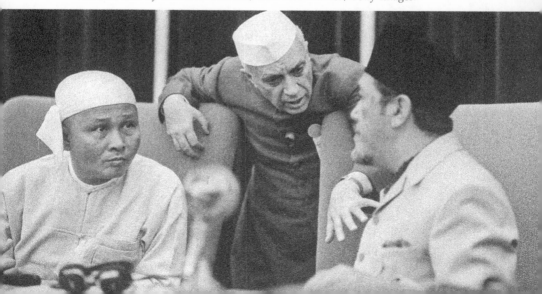

4

Nationalism, Regionalism and the Cold War Order

The aftermath of World War II was a period of profound change in Southeast Asia. The main historical forces shaping Southeast Asia's destiny were nationalism and decolonization, and the struggle of the newly independent states to create stable political systems and viable national economies. In the international arena, Southeast Asia became progressively drawn into the Cold War between the United States and the Soviet Union. A key feature of this period was the close nexus between domestic politics (including nationalism, national integration and democracy), prospects for regionalism and international relations. The Cold War helped to polarize the region, and influenced the domestic politics of Southeast Asian states. It contributed to the rise of authoritarianism in the non-communist states of Southeast Asia. At the same time, domestic problems, including weak national integration and regime survival concerns, had major consequences for the foreign policy orientation of the non-communist Southeast Asian states, especially their attitude toward regionalism. The early post-war period saw the first articulation of ideas about regional unity by Southeast Asia's nationalist leaders. Yet most of these were not concerned with a Southeast Asian identity, but instead focused on larger pan-Asian or Afro-Asian unity. And a range of domestic and international factors ensured the non-fulfilment of these aspirations.

The Nationalist Vision of Regionalism

In her diplomatic history of post-war Southeast Asia, C.M. Turnbull points out that "the two most important factors affecting regionalism and international relations in the immediate postwar years were the decolonization process itself, and the problems of creating national identity within the (often artificial) former colonial boundaries."[1] Nationalism was the major political force in Southeast Asia during the first two decades of the post-war era. But it had a mixed impact on regionalism. On the one hand, Southeast Asian nationalists recognized regionalism as an inevitable trend; something that was "bound to come" as a way of undoing the artificial divisions and separations among Southeast Asian peoples and territories brought about by colonial rule. Nationalist leaders such as Aung San of Myanmar and Elpidio Quirino of the Philippines were among the first people to lament that Southeast Asian countries maintained much closer economic, cultural and political links with their metropolitan powers than with each other. Even in the Philippines, despite its relative geographical isolation and different colonial heritage, the discourse of nationalism was not devoid of a regional context. While there was little connection between nationalist movements in the Philippines and in other Southeast Asian countries, references by the Filipino nationalist José Rizal to the Filipinos as "Malays" did invoke a regional identity.[2] But it was soon evident that shared nationalism was not an adequate basis for reinventing a notion of Southeast Asia. Regionalism was constrained by differing circumstances of decolonization, the greater appeal of pan-Asianism and Afro-Asianism as regionalist frameworks, and the tendency among Southeast Asian leaders to use regionalism as a tool of partisan ideology rather than of collective identity.

The decolonization process in Southeast Asia was unexpectedly sudden and marked by wide variations. Thailand, the only state not to experience colonial rule, used the post-war American ascendancy to break free from the Anglo-French hold, especially as a way of escaping possible retribution from the latter for its wartime collaboration with Japan. Elsewhere in the region, the colonial powers took different approaches to their Southeast Asian possessions. The United States fulfilled its pledge to give independence to the Philippines while maintaining close economic and military links with it. France and the Netherlands sought to give their colonies equal status in a French or Dutch union. But these did not match the aspirations of the Vietnamese and Indonesian nationalists, who took up armed struggle as the means of national liberation. The British were in a different position, much stronger in their colonies than the French or the Dutch. Britain came back to its colonies pledging self-government for them. Churchill, like the French and the Dutch, wanted a reimposition of colonial rule, but Britain had allowed independence movements to appear and grow legitimately and to pursue a more peaceful, constitutional path to independence. The concept of the British Commonwealth, already tested in the case of the old dominions, helped to persuade the nationalists to seek independence while retaining links with Britain. It also made it easier for Britain to transfer power to the newly independent states. British economic links and defence responsibilities continued to play an important role in the affairs of the new states.

In general, Britain found it easier to carry out an orderly and more "voluntary" transfer of power than the Dutch or the French. In Myanmar, the British War Cabinet had promised the colony independence with full Commonwealth membership as soon as it was ready. The popularity of Aung San's Anti-Fascist People's Freedom League forced Britain to quicken the process of independence even in the absence of safeguards for Myanmar's minorities. Notwithstanding the assassination of Aung San in July 1947, Britain granted Myanmar independence in January 1948, although this "premature" move plunged Myanmar into a civil war situation. The decolonization process in the Malay Peninsula evolved relatively smoothly. In 1946, Singapore was separated as a Crown Colony. The Malay Peninsula was organized into a Malayan Union. In 1948, this became the Federation of Malaya. Later, Sarawak and North Borneo were placed under direct colonial rule, while Brunei remained as a protectorate. In contrast, the Netherlands' attempts to incorporate its colonies into a Netherlands Union and undermine the Republic of Indonesia formed by the Indonesian nationalists failed. In Indochina, the French did not recognize the independent regimes created by Japan and re-established control in Cambodia and Laos in 1946. But its attempt to do so in Vietnam soon led to war.

The contrasting circumstances under which decolonization proceeded contributed to the differing attitudes of Southeast Asian countries towards regionalism. The initial appeal of regionalism was as an instrument of national liberation. Certainly, Ho Chi Minh was keen to use regional cooperation to further the cause of Vietnamese independence.[3] In September 1945, he mentioned to a U.S. official his interest in the creation of a "pan-Asiatic community", comprising Vietnam, Cambodia, Laos, Thailand, Malaya, Myanmar, India, Indonesia and the Philippines. (China, Japan and Korea were not included in Ho's vision of an Asiatic community.) His ostensible goal at this stage was to foster political and economic cooperation among these countries while maintaining good relations with the United States, France and Britain. This was a time when Ho still hoped that the colonial powers, exhausted by war, would voluntarily speed up the process of decolonization. But when this proved to be a false hope, Ho and other Southeast Asian nationalist leaders began considering the use of regional cooperation to oppose the return of European colonialism. This was clearly evident in Ho's November 1946 letter to the Indonesian Prime Minister, Sutan Sjahrir, urging cooperation between the two countries to advance their common struggle for freedom. In this letter, Ho asked Indonesia to join him in getting India, Myanmar and Malaya to develop initiatives towards a "Federation of Free Peoples of Southern Asia". But Indonesian leaders responded coolly to this idea, apparently worried that cooperating with the Vietnamese communists would give the Dutch an opportunity to use the fear of communism to delay Indonesia's own independence. This incident showed how differences among nationalist strategies in Southeast Asia served as impediments to regional cooperation.

But the Vietnamese communists would continue to see regionalism as a means of advancing their goal of national liberation. While direct cooperation with their Vietnamese counterparts was troublesome to Indonesian nationalists, cooperation within a larger pan-Asian framework could be politically more useful. It was in this context that Southeast Asian nationalists saw as a welcome opportunity efforts by India under Nehru to develop a pan-Asian framework to foster decolonization and regional cooperation. Apart from the Democratic Republic of Vietnam (DRV) under Ho and the Indonesian nationalists, support for the idea of using regionalism to advance the cause of national liberation came from the Philippines, where Carlos P. Romulo, then the Philippines delegate to the UN, endorsed the forthcoming Asian Relations Conference in New Delhi as a way of giving encouragement to anti-colonial struggles in Asia.

The unofficial Asian Relations Conference, held in New Delhi in 1947, saw all the Southeast Asian states represented among the thirty-one delegations. The tone of the conference was anti-European, pro-liberation and pro-neutrality. The meeting provided a platform for subsequent action by the regionalists in protesting against the second Dutch police action against Indonesia in 1948. But it did not lead to the establishment of regional machinery and organization. A more explicit call for a regional organization was made by the Indian Prime Minister, Nehru, at another conference of Asian countries in January 1949 (known as the second Asian Relations Conference). At this conference, whose ostensible goal was to support Indonesian independence, Nehru urged the participants to emulate emerging trends towards regionalism in Europe and the Americas: it would be "natural that the free countries of Asia should begin to think of some more permanent arrangement than this Conference for effective mutual consultation and concerted effort in the pursuit of common aims".[4] But prospects for a pan-Asian grouping were plagued by differences among the pro-communist, pro-Western and neutrality-minded delegations. They had little to agree upon apart from the end to direct colonial rule. Moreover, some Southeast Asian leaders viewed the prospects for a pan-Asian community with some unease, fearing its domination by China or India. As one Myanmar leader put it, "It was terrible to be ruled by a Western power, but it was even more so to be ruled by an Asian power."[5]

Southeast Asian nationalists were disappointed at Nehru's mild approach to the colonial powers and India's refusal to provide more than "moral" support to the anti-colonial struggles in the region. This also convinced them of the need for an entirely Southeast Asian sub-grouping. Abu Hanifa, one of the Indonesian representatives to the 1947 New Delhi Conference, wrote later that the idea of a wholly Southeast Asian grouping was conceived at the conference in response to the belief among the Southeast Asian delegates that the larger states, India and China, could not be expected to support their nationalist cause. At the meeting, delegates from Indonesia, Myanmar, Thailand, Vietnam, the Philippines and Malaya "debated, talked, [and] planned a Southeast Asian Association closely cooperating first in cultural and economic matters. Later, there could be perhaps be a more closely knit political cooperation. Some of us even dreamt of a Greater Southeast Asia, a federation."[6]

The idea of a Southeast Asian grouping also received support from nationalist leaders in Myanmar and Vietnam. It was part of the pan-

Asian thinking of Aung San of Myanmar. Aung San's regionalist vision deserves special attention, as it represents perhaps the strongest example of how Asian leaders sought to reconcile nationalism, regionalism and internationalism. Aung San's vision of Myanmar's role in international affairs was not one of isolationism but engagement. He believed in Asia's underlying cultural unity and championed Asian, East Asian and Southeast Asian cooperation. He believed that regional cooperation could compensate for Myanmar's weaknesses in the defence and economic spheres. He called for a permanent regional organization of Myanmar and her neighbours as well as for ad hoc forms of collaboration from time to time on specific issues of common concern. He felt that Myanmar's destiny lay within the community of Southeast Asian and Asian nations with whom it shared deep and historical bonds.

Aung San's conception of a new Asian order was founded upon a recognition that Asia was resurgent after centuries of colonialism: "Asia has been rejuvenated and is progressively coming into world politics. Asia can no longer be ignored in international councils. Its voice grows louder and louder. You can hear it in Indonesia, you can hear it in Indo-China, you can harken to it in Burma and India and elsewhere."[7] In an All-India Radio broadcast in 1947, he advocated the task of Asian reintegration: "we can [and] will have such tasks as peculiar to Asia only, such as reintegration and reorientation of Asian culture, so that we might rediscover our Asian destiny, and thus contribute further to the enrichment of world culture and civilisation."[8]

Aung San was a believer in regional and international interdependence: "The one fact from which no nation, big or small, can escape is the increasing universal interdependence of nations. A free and independent Burma is quite ready to enter into any arrangement with other nations for common welfare and security etc."[9] Perhaps his most important contribution was to reconcile nationalism with regionalism and internationalism: "I recognise both the virtues and limitations of pure nationalism, I love its virtues, I don't allow myself to be blinded by its limitations, though I knew that it is not easy for the great majority of any nation to get over these limitations."[10] Aung San's nationalism could support regional and international cooperation.

His idea of how regional cooperation should be organized evolved in keeping with his political circumstances in leading Myanmar's struggle against colonialism. In 1941, while seeking Japan's help in fighting British rule, Aung San had endorsed Japan's idea of a Greater East Asia Co-

Prosperity Sphere. In an essay, "Blue Print for Burma", he argued that "Burma shall be responsible for the western defence of the Greater East Asia Co-prosperity Sphere while Japan will guard over the East Asiatic Bloc from the last side"[11] and sought a "common defence policy for all East Asia with mutual cooperation and not with mutual suspicion".[12] In the same essay, he would "look forward to a time when we co-operate not merely in limited spheres such as economics and defence but in a more compact union like one brotherhood of nations".[13] But he also insisted that "a common defence policy in East Asia as the best guarantee for the maintenance of the Greater East Asia Co-prosperity Sphere"[14] should also be accompanied by "only one foreign policy in all East Asia" and that policy "must be evolved by mutual consultation and cooperation".[15]

Disillusionment with Japan soon led him to abandon support for an exclusionary regional organization under a dominant power. Hence, "a new Asian order ... will not and must not be one like the Co-prosperity Sphere of militarist Japan, nor should it be another Asiatic Monroe doctrine, nor imperial preference or currency bloc".[16] He rejected regional blocs that practised discrimination: "We of course must oppose attempts to form economic blocs and preferences. We stand for free, mutual economic co-operation and transaction with any nation or nations. For that is what the world and our country need at the moment. But British imperialism does not feel like agreeing to such free and multi-lateral economic co-operation in the international field. Even some so-called Socialists in Britain appear to be opposed to such free economic internationalism."[17]

He also rejected hegemonic forms of regionalism and international cooperation founded upon the principles of power politics. Regional cooperation must not be involuntary. Wondering how one might "reconcile" "universal interdependence of nations with that of national independence for Burma",[18] he argued that while "a greater union or commonwealth or bloc"[19] may seem a desirable option for Myanmar, it must be a "voluntary affair and not imposed from above".[20] It must not be "the kind like the United States of Europe".[21] Nor should it be "conceived in the narrow spirit of the classic balance of power"[22] of the kind "Mr. Churchill once suggested obviously as a check against any advancing influence of the Soviet Union."[23]

A new Asian order, Aung San held, "should not be one imposed on us, separate or altogether, in which one race or the other can come to dominate and dicate [sic] and wire-pull. At any rate, we must see that it does not become camouflaged balkanisation of Asia where some people from outside can come in and play one against the other."[24] This was a rejection of the regional military alliances that the superpowers would advocate as instruments of their Cold War geopolitical rivalry. Instead of exclusionary regionalism, he preferred to cast regionalism as "the Asiatic branch of the world family organisation, formed for the purpose of Asian unity and cooperation to win not only Asia's but also all the world's freedom, security and progress and peace."[25] At the same time, "it should not permit of any exclusionism in any sphere within the walls of ethnic and geographical limits, though no doubt we must set before us the primary and practical task of putting our own home in order first ..."[26]

Aung San's concept of regionalism was integrative and broad in scope. He argued that Asia could form "interim joint arrangements to face common problems of the immediate present" before "we can have that bigger concept" of Asian integration.[27] In a paper, "Defence of Burma", dated 1945, he argued that the defence of Myanmar required a helping hand from neighbours: "As an entity unto herself also, Burma must be strong in her defence and will need the helping hand of one or more of her neighbours at least — an entente of Burma, Indo-China, Thailand, Malaya, Philippines, East Indies, Yunnan, and Eastern India on this side of the Brahmaputra."[28] At various times, Aung San advocated wider Asian unity as well as a subregional unity of Southeast Asia. After breaking with imperial Japan, he continued to see Myanmar "as a unit of East Asia, Burma shall of course benefit from the joint contribution of all East Asia, and at the same time she will have to share out her own contribution to others as well. She has got to be strong not merely for herself but for East Asia also, as its western or westernmost gate or at any rate as a vital strategic link between the two biggest countries on earth."[29] Later, he would advocate Asian and Southeast Asian cooperation. In a speech to welcome Mr. Sarat Bose, brother of Subhas Chandra Bose, at the City Hall of Rangoon on 24 July 1946, he stated that Myanmar would "stand for an Asiatic Federation in a not very, very remote future, we stand for immediate mutual understanding and joint action, wherever and whenever possible, from now for our mutual interests and for the freedom of India, Burma and indeed all Asia".[30] At the same time, he recognized that "some day it may be proved necessary and possible for us to have, say, something like the United States of Indo-China comprising French Indo-China, Thailand,

Malaya, Indonesia, and our country."[31] In his view, "while India should be one entity and China another, Southeast Asia as a whole should form an entity — then, finally, we should come together in a bigger union with the participation of other parts of Asia as well."[32]

Aung San's assassination in July 1947 ended Myanmar's quest for regional cooperation.[33] After unsuccessfully seeking a pan-Asian platform, the Vietnamese communists also began thinking in terms of a Southeast Asian grouping. They were urging Thailand, because of its independent status and its geographical location, to take the lead in organizing such a group, to be modelled after the principles of the UN charter, and to resist the reimposition of European rule.

Discussions about the usefulness of regionalism during the early post-war period highlighted the smallness of Southeast Asian countries and their inability to achieve self-reliance without collective efforts. Vietnamese commentators, juxtaposing a "united and free" posture on the part of Southeast Asian states with the colonial powers' "divide and rule" strategies, also stressed that, without regional unity, Southeast Asia would become nothing more than "slaves" of colonial powers producing raw materials for them and buying their expensive manufacturing products.[34] The ethnic and sociocultural similarities and ties among Southeast Asian countries were stressed. Their location between China and India, the existence of common interests in addressing domestic problems, and the importance of mutual support in anti-colonial struggles were cited as rationales for regional unity. A regional grouping, according to the *Bangkok Post* newspaper, need not be a "tightly cohesive federation" but a forum for the exchange of policies on agriculture, communications and trade. The *Malayan Tribune* saw regionalism among Southeast Asian countries, including Myanmar, Thailand, Indochina, Malaya and Indonesia, as a way of safeguarding the "tremendous potential and great riches" of Southeast Asia, which might otherwise "tempt the powerful".[35]

Thailand, which had been seen as a potential leader of a Southeast Asian grouping, found a reason to get involved when it failed to win back disputed territories in French-ruled Laos and Cambodia. An offshoot of this was the Thai support (including by such leaders as Pridi Phanomyong and Thamrong Nawasawat) in sponsoring the creation of the Southeast Asian League on 8 September 1947, with representatives from Vietnam, Laos, Cambodia, Indonesia, Thailand and Malaya (there were no Burmese and Filipino delegates). This was intended to be an "unofficial" and provisional organization that could later develop into an official body once it had secured recognition from the national governments of the region. But the group failed to take off. Delegates from Indonesia and Malaya were worried that their participation would jeopardize their own negotiations with the Dutch and the British concerning the transition to independence, especially given the radical undertone of the grouping and the involvement of the DRV government. This in itself illustrates how differing nationalisms and pathways to independence may have undermined the prospects for regionalism in Southeast Asia. Although it had attracted support from upper-echelon Thais,[36] the Southeast Asian League came to be seen as primarily a support mechanism for communist movements, since one of its activities was gun-running for the Vietminh. Among the league's active members was Prince Souphanouvong, who became a leader of the Laotian communists under the Pathet Lao.

For many Southeast Asian nationalists, enthusiasm for regional organization depended on the extent to which it could be seen to support the nationalist cause. Thus, after their initial efforts to use regionalism to advance the cause of national liberation proved abortive, Vietnamese nationalists not only lost interest in a Southeast Asian grouping but also harshly criticized efforts by moderate nations such as Malaya, Thailand, the Philippines and Indonesia under Soeharto to build a Southeast Asian regional organization. Hanoi then pursued unity among the Indochinese states, based largely on strategic and ideological considerations. The interest of the nationalist leaders in Indonesia and Malaya in a Southeast Asian grouping that included the DRV was countered by the fear that it could delay their own struggle for independence. This divergence planted the seeds of the future ideological and political polarization of Southeast Asia.

In this context, Vietnam's vision of Indochina as "one strategic unit", outlined by General Giap in February 1950, merits attention. In a speech before the sixth All-Country Military Meeting in February 1950, Giap stated:

> The war of liberation of the three peoples of Vietnam-Laos-Cambodia cannot be separated; that is: Indochina is one strategic unit, it is one battlefield. That is also why in military terms, the Indochinese battlefield constitutes one block in the enemy's aggressive and defensive projects. For these reasons, and above all for geo-strategic ones, we cannot consider Vietnam to be entirely independent as long as Cambodia and Laos are still ruled by imperialism.[37]

These fateful words would acquire a singular notoriety in the capitals of the non-communist Southeast Asian states as the justification for Vietnamese expansionism and hegemonism. This was especially so in the aftermath of the Vietnamese invasion of Cambodia in 1978, after Hanoi had criticized ASEAN as a tool of Western imperialism. But to consider Giap's notion as an alternative regional or subregional framework under Vietnamese hegemony would be a mistake. His concept of Indochina as one strategic unit was context-dependent (Vietnam's struggle against the French) and time-bound ("as long as Cambodia and Laos are still ruled by imperialism"). But the concept did move from being the basis of Vietnam's anti-colonial struggle to being the organizational framework of its revolutionary regional politics. And while not amounting to an alternative regional framework, it remained a powerful barrier to the development of a single regional identity for Southeast Asia. It was not until the 1990s (through the Vietnamese withdrawal from Cambodia in 1989, the Paris Peace Agreement of 1991 and Vietnamese membership in ASEAN in 1995) that Vietnam came to re-embrace the regional concept of Southeast Asia.

In commenting on the relationship between nationalism and regionalism, Wang Gungwu has argued, "the main obstacle in the way of Southeast Asian regionalism is not so much nationalism itself as the two different types of postwar nationalism."[38] Wang sees the roots of intraregional discord in Southeast Asia in terms of the radically different conceptions of the region held by moderate and revolutionary nationalists. The revolutionaries rejected the idea of a region dominated by Western powers, while the moderates had more to fear from a region dominated by China. While the revolutionaries hoped for a confederated region, the moderates would only accept regional cooperation based on the principles of equality and sovereignty. The moderates desired a region freely and multilaterally linked to the outside world, while the revolutionaries would accept this only if the communist powers were integral to this external linkage.[39] It is important to note that the framework of regionalism that proved viable in Southeast Asia in the end was the one promoted by the moderate camp, led by Thailand, Malaysia and Soeharto's Indonesia, the last being a significantly more "moderate nationalist" regime than its predecessor.

When nationalist leaders in Southeast Asia expressed interest in regional unity, they also acknowledged that their ties to former colonial powers were often much stronger than those to their own neighbours.

Nationalists such as Aung San of Myanmar and Elpidio Quirino of the Philippines recognized the existence of strong pre-colonial ties,[40] but when they called for regional cooperation, they were not calling for a recreation of pre-colonial geographical and political entities but for the realization of a pan-Asian consciousness.[41] While Aung San's regionalist ideas went beyond Southeast Asia and the Vietnamese view of regionalism was somewhat tactical, geared to securing regional support for communist-dominated national liberation, Indonesia under Sukarno's stewardship had little interest in the idea of Southeast Asia as a region. While earlier Indonesian nationalists had been reluctant to embrace a Southeast Asian regional organization out of fear that it would undermine their negotiations with the Dutch, even after achieving independence, Indonesia made little effort to bring together Southeast Asian countries under one grouping. Independent Indonesia saw itself as a leader of the region (thereby supplanting Thailand, which had earlier been seen as a regional leader, and Myanmar, which after Aung San's assassination was too preoccupied with its domestic troubles). But Sukarno's foreign-policy beliefs were too grandiose to fit into a Southeast Asian framework. His vision was for a grouping of the "new emerging forces" to oppose the "old established forces" — a global rather than regional movement. Moreover, among those whom Sukarno considered to be "old established forces" and therefore a target of Indonesia's dislike and opposition was a fellow Southeast Asian country with which it had substantial ethnic ties, Malaysia. If Sukarno was interested in any regional cooperation, it was well beyond Southeast Asian in scope. Indonesia had derived considerable support for its independence struggle from anti-colonial elements in Asia and Africa (especially from India under Nehru's leadership), and naturally saw regionalism covering the newly independent countries in Asia and Africa as a more important instrument of nationalism than what the idea of Southeast Asia could offer.

Sukarno's approach became evident when he became involved in a grouping known as the Colombo Powers (not to be confused with the Commonwealth-inspired Colombo Plan) that met in Ceylon in 1954 to commit itself to opposing the polarization of the world into competing blocs. One of the most interesting aspects of this group was its official nomenclature: "Conference of the South-East Asian Prime Ministers". This indicates that the notion of Southeast Asia, excluding Pakistan, India and Sri Lanka (which would later be classified as belonging to "South Asia") was not yet complete, at least in the political and diplomatic arena. The grouping itself achieved little but put forward a proposal for an Afro-Asian Conference in Bandung the following year. As at the Asian Relations Conference, Southeast Asian participation at Bandung was quite extensive, with only Malaya and British Borneo absent (present were delegates from Myanmar, Thailand, Cambodia, Laos, the State of Vietnam, the Democratic Republic of Vietnam (DRV) and the Philippines). Yet, no single "Southeast Asian view" could be detected at Bandung. Instead, one of the most pronounced splits at Bandung involved Southeast Asians — the Philippines and Thailand on the one hand and Indonesia and to a lesser extent Myanmar on the other. The former believed that their independence and security were threatened by the communist menace and that entering into military pacts with the United States was essential to protect their national interests. Indonesia, on the other hand, believed that an "independent foreign policy", which meant not entering into rigid military alliances with either of the two superpowers, was the only way for the newly independent states to safeguard their sovereignty. Given its status as the largest country in Southeast Asia in terms of size and population, even mere indifference on the part of Jakarta was a major obstacle to the prospects for regionalism in Southeast Asia. Sukarno pursued a foreign policy that was nationalist in motivation and internationalist in scope, missing the regional level where cooperation and unity-building were seen to be unimportant (to the internationalist agenda) at best and detrimental (to the nationalist cause) at worst.

As may be seen from the foregoing discussion, many of the ideas concerning regionalism during this period were made in the context of decolonization and of political and ideological considerations linked to the Cold War. The pan-Asian and Afro-Asian frameworks, despite being largely stillborn, did make a contribution to Southeast Asian regionalism. They introduced the concept of regional cooperation and created opportunities for the region's leaders to meet one another. These would prove important steps towards Southeast Asian regionalism in subsequent periods. For the time being, however, a Southeast Asian community remained a distant concept. There were a number of obstacles to its development even among the moderate nationalist countries, which were more inclined to accept Southeast Asian regionalism that was identity-based (as espoused by Aung San of Myanmar) as opposed to ideology-based (as with Vietnam on the one hand and Thailand and the

Philippines on the other). Two sets of obstacles are especially noteworthy. The first had to do with the domestic conditions of the Southeast Asian states, where the main problems were communist rebellion and ethnic separatism, problems that the governments of the day sought to address through differing mixes of economic development and political control. The second set of obstacles stemmed from the international security environment, where Cold War geopolitics constrained the willingness and ability of Southeast Asian governments to undertake effective regional cooperation.

Development, Legitimacy and Regional (Dis)order

With the departure of the colonial powers from the region, the new governments of Southeast Asia faced a serious challenge in ensuring domestic stability and regime legitimacy. To cope, nationalist elites throughout the region emphasized growth and development, and all favoured rapid industrialization. For them, primary production and import of manufactured goods were associated with colonialism, while industrialization was seen as the symbol of, and passport to, economic independence. Economic nationalism contributed to efforts to boost national self-sufficiency and reduce foreign influence. But the focus on domestic economic development left little scope for attention to regional economic cooperation. During the colonial era, the economies of Southeast Asian countries were heavily dependent on tropical products. In 1950, manufacturing accounted for 12 per cent of the Philippines' GDP, and 5 to 10 per cent or less elsewhere in the region.[42] As a result, these economies were competitive, not complementary, a factor inhibiting the motive for regional cooperation.

Moreover, significant differences marked the development policies of Southeast Asian states in the post-colonial era. One area of divergence was openness to the global economy. Singapore was the most open and was the first to develop export-oriented industrialization (EOI). This reflected Singapore's unique circumstances: a small population, no natural resources and no hope for economic self-sufficiency. The island also sought to capitalize on its strategic location, its bureaucratic efficiency, absence of corruption and well-disciplined labour force. Singapore served as a financial centre and took advantage of its modern banking system and stock market, helped by overseas Chinese financial networks, while also looking to serve international markets. None of the other Southeast

Asian countries adopted Singapore's approach. Malaysia, for example, focused on primary production, with its dependence on the two major exports of rubber and tin continuing for two decades after World War II. The oil and timber of Sabah and Sarawak also benefited growth.

Malaysia (in the 1950s), the Philippines and Thailand were among the regional economies to try import-substituting industrialization (ISI). The Philippines was the first country in Southeast Asia to try ISI. For the first decade and a half after World War II, the Philippines posted the best economic growth in Southeast Asia, helped by a combination of U.S. aid, a well-educated population and relatively good institutional infrastructure. However, despite the clear problems of overprotection, slowing demand, falling commodity prices and high population growth rates, domestic vested interests in ISI prevented a switch to EOI. The contrasting policies and experiences of Singapore and the Philippines are striking, although both were founding members of ASEAN and thus subscribed to ASEAN's common "free market" orientation.

In addition, Southeast Asian governments adopted different attitudes towards property rights. Here, a threefold classification has been proposed by Norman Owen.[43] The governments of the Philippines, Singapore, Malaysia and Thailand preferred economic systems based on respect for private property throughout the post-war period. South Vietnam (1954–75), the Khmer Republic under Lon Nol (1970–75) and Indonesia under Soeharto also fell into this category. On the opposite side were the governments of Democratic Kampuchea (1975–78), North Vietnam after 1954, Myanmar after 1962, South Vietnam after 1975 and Laos after 1975. A somewhat middle course was taken by Myanmar under U Nu (1948–62), Indonesia under Sukarno (particularly the Guided Democracy period of 1957–65) and Cambodia under Norodom Sihanouk (1953–70). Thailand under Pridi Phanomyong (1945–47) and Laos in the 1950s and 1960s may also be included in this category, which had a socialist orientation although it did little to actually redistribute wealth.

The differing economic philosophies of the Southeast Asian countries were reflected in their stand on foreign companies. Vietnam, Laos and Kampuchea expropriated all foreign firms, while under Guided Democracy Indonesia nationalized all Dutch holdings and threatened to do so with respect to other foreign holdings, a policy not reversed until 1965. In the 1960s and 1970s, Malaysia and the Philippines adopted laws to develop a higher indigenous stake in the corporate sector, which resulted in foreign firms selling out to locals or the government. Singapore, Thailand and

Brunei were the only states not to have tried systematically to curb or diminish foreign investment.

The problems of considering Southeast Asia as a coherent economic region in the immediate aftermath of decolonization were perhaps best captured by an important study by Burmese economist Hla Myint. The book, entitled *Southeast Asia's Economy: Development Policies in the 1970s*, was the product of an early attempt to develop a regional or subregional perspective on Southeast Asia's economic development. In April 1969, the Fourth Ministerial Conference for the Economic Development of Southeast Asia, held in Bangkok, requested the Asian Development Bank (ADB) to carry out a study of Southeast Asia's economy in the 1970s. (The report was first published by ADB in 1971 and published as a book by Praeger in 1972.) While pointing to differences, the book also laid the basis for a regional perspective on development.[44]

The aim of the study was "to analyse the nature of the major problems which confront the nations in the region in the seventies and explore the possibilities of individual and cooperative action by governments to effect their solution".[45] It sought to provide a "general background of the economic development of the region", highlighting what it called the "colonial pattern of economic development that prevailed before World War II, based on expansion of primary exports and import of cheap consumer goods".[46] Generalizing about the region during the post-war period before the 1970s, it identified two key variables: "the importance of exports in the economic development of Southeast Asia, and the importance of appropriate domestic economic policies and improvements in internal organization in enabling these countries to take better advantage of their external economic opportunities".[47]

The study pointed to the diversity of Southeast Asia's economic development patterns, conditioned by historical circumstances as well as the political and psychological attitudes of the ruling elite.[48] Historical circumstances played a big part in the Indochinese countries, Vietnam, Cambodia and Laos, where war and instability impeded economic recovery. But even in the rest of the region, economic performance varied due to differing degrees of economic nationalism. The "moderately minded" countries, such as the Philippines, Thailand and Malaya, enjoyed speedy post-war economic recovery, rapid export expansion and high growth rates, while in Indonesia and Myanmar, which pursued stronger nationalist policies, recovery was slow and growth modest. Thus, the level of aggregate real income in 1960 as a percentage of the pre-war level for the Philippines, Thailand and Malaya was 201, 191 and 164 per cent respectively, while for both Indonesia and Myanmar, it was a lowly 111 per cent.[49] The result was "the division of Southeast Asia into two groups of countries", one comprising the Indochinese countries as well as Indonesia and Myanmar, and the other consisting of the "moderately minded" nations of Malaya, the Philippines and Thailand, all of which achieved growth rates of 5 to 7 per cent in contrast to the essentially stagnant economies of the former.[50]

The study was not only one of the first attempts to present a regional analysis of development patterns and policies, it was also among the first to seriously advocate regional economic cooperation in order to overcome the smallness of domestic markets. The manufacturing sectors in various Southeast Asian countries, noted the report, were producing a similar range of products and were offering similar tariffs and tax concessions to foreign multinationals. Against this backdrop, "there would seem to be a considerable scope for increasing the efficiency of the manufacturing industries if the Southeast Asian countries can be persuaded to open their markets to the manufactured exports of each other."[51] Pointing to the "considerable scope for mutual gain if the Southeast Asian countries can moderate their 'economic nationalism' against each other", the study argued:

> The gains from such regional cooperation arise from two sources. Firstly, even among the Southeast Asian countries, local conditions vary considerably and there is scope for intra-regional division of labour in manufacturing. Secondly, the access to the wider markets will enable these more efficient industries to attain their full economies of scale.[52]

The study drew a close linkage between regional identity and regionalism: "A friend of Southeast Asia cannot but hope that her distinctive ways of life and culture which already create a sense of unity in the countries of the region may be preserved and strengthened by a movement towards closer regional economic cooperation."[53]

Despite the urging of economic regionalism, the economic divide in post-colonial Southeast Asia meant little prospect for regional governments to develop the necessary political will for mutual economic cooperation. The only possibility for such cooperation would be on a subregional basis, such as among the more "moderately minded" governments, but this had to await the stabilization of domestic changes in Indonesia.

While nationalism delivered Southeast Asia from the colonial yoke, it did not remove the problems of national integration or regime legitimacy.

Southeast Asian states were typical "weak states", suffering from the problems of ethnic divisions, separatism and challenges to regime survival that could not be managed through Western-style democratic frameworks. These factors tended to inhibit regionalism by forcing governments to be inward-looking (and in the case of Myanmar, even isolationist) in their political and security outlook. Differing national responses to domestic challenges and interstate tensions caused by transborder movements of communist and separatist insurgents also undermined the basis of regional unity. Yet, over the long term, these very domestic weaknesses would produce a convergence of political, economic and security predicaments among a group of Southeast Asian states that would view regional cooperation as a necessary means of coping with internal as well as external vulnerabilities. As in the economic arena, the domestic political and security challenges facing Southeast Asian states would facilitate cooperation only on a subregional basis.

Among the most serious domestic challenges facing several Southeast Asian rulers were the twin threats of communism and ethnic separatism. Communist movements, which proliferated throughout Southeast Asia even before the French defeat in Indochina (leading to the establishment of the first communist regime in Southeast Asia, North Vietnam) derived support from China and Russia. But they also depended on cross-border sanctuaries in neighbouring states. For example, the survivors of the Communist Party of Malaya (CPM) retreated into Thai territory. The Vietcong's ability to survive depended critically on sanctuaries in Cambodia. North Vietnam's support of the Pathet Lao and the Khmer Rouge in Cambodia was a major source of interstate tensions in Indochina before the communist victories in all three states in 1975. Separatist movements lacked significant extra-regional backing, but derived some support from neighbouring Southeast Asian countries. Examples include the support for Muslim separatists in southern Thailand from elements in Malaysia, similar Malaysian support for Islamic groups in Mindanao and Thai sanctuaries for ethnic rebels in Myanmar. The impact of these in creating serious friction was evident in Malaysia-Thailand and Myanmar-Thailand relations.

Moreover, internal challenges undermined regionalism by creating a continuous pattern of dependency by Southeast Asian states on external military aid. This dependence lessened their interest in regional cooperation as a means of addressing domestic challenges. While the

TABLE 4.1
Selected Communist Movements and Parties in Southeast Asia, 1946–76

Country	Movement
Burma	Burma Communist Party (1948–)
Cambodia	Khmer Rouge (1970–75)
Indonesia	Madium Communist Rebellion (1948) Partai Kommunist Indonesia
Laos	Pathet Lao (1951–75)
Malaysia	Communist Party of Malaya (CPM) (1948–) North Kalimantan Communist Party (1950s–)
Philippines	New People's Army (1969–) Huk Trbrllion (1946–54)
Singapore	none (The CPM operated in Singapore before its separation from Malaysia in 1965)
Thailand	Communist Party of Thailand (1965–)*
Vietnam	National Liberation Front (1958–75)

* Approximate year of origin
Source: Adapted from Sukhumbhand Paribatra and Chai-Anan Samudavanija, "Internal Dimensions of Regional Security in Southeast Asia", in *Regional Security in the Third World*, edited by Mohammed Ayoob (London: Croom Helm Ltd., 1986), p. 61.

TABLE 4.2
Selected Separatist Movements in Southeast Asia, 1946–76

State	Armed Rebellion
Burma	Ethnically related armed rebellions (1948–)
Indonesia	Darul Islam (1948–62) PRRI Permesta (1958–61) Organisasi Papua Merdeka (1963–) Aceh Merdeka (1976–)* Fretilin (1974–)†
Laos	Le Ligue de Resistance Meo (1946–75)
Philippines	Moro National Liberation Front (1972–)‡ Moro Islamic Liberation Front (1984–)‡
Thailand	Pattani United Liberation Organization (1967–) Barisan Nasional Pembebasan Patani (1971–)

* The Indonesian Government and the Free Aceh Movement signed a peace deal in August 2005.
† East Timor gained independence from Indonesia in 1999. Fretilin won elections to the constituent assembly held in August 2001.
‡ Approximate year of origin.
Source: Adapted from Sukhumbhand Paribatra and Chai-Anan Samudavanija, "Internal Dimensions of Regional Security in Southeast Asia", in *Regional Security in the Third World*, edited by Mohammed Ayoob (London: Croom Helm Ltd., 1986), p. 61.

TABLE 4.3
Ethnic Composition of Southeast Asian States, 1976

State	Ethnolinguistic Groups	Percentage of Population
Burma	Burman	75
	Karen	10
	Shan	6
	Indian-Pakistani	3
	Chinese	1
	Kachin	1
	Chin	1
Cambodia	Khmer	90
	Chinese	6
	Cham	1
	Mon-Khmer tribes	1
Indonesia	Javanese	45
	Sundanese	14
	Madurese	8
	Chinese	2
Laos	Lao	67
	Mon-Khmer tribes	19
	Tai (other than Lao)	5
	Meo	4
	Chinese	3
North Vietnam*	Vietnamese	85
	Tho	3
	Muong	2
	Tai	2
	Nung	2
	Chinese	1
	Meo	1
	Yao	1
South Vietnam	Vietnamese	87
	Chinese	5
	Khmer	3
	Mountain chain tribes	3
	Mon-Khmer tribes	1
Malaysia	Malay	44
	Chinese	35
	Indian	11

TABLE 4.3 (*Cont'd*)

State	Ethnolinguistic Groups	Percentage of Population
Philippines	Cebuano	24
	Tagalog	21
	Ilocano	12
	Hiligaynon	10
	Bicol	8
	Sumar-Leyte	6
	Pampangan	3
	Pangasinan	3
Singapore	Chinese	77
	Malay	14
	Indian	7
	Others	2
Thailand	Thai	60
	Lao	25
	Chinese	10
	Malay	3
	Meo, Khmer and others	2

* Vietnam was unified in 1975 as a result of the Communist takeover of the South.
Source: Adapted from Sukhumbhand Paribatra and Chai-Anan Samudavanija, "Internal Dimensions of Regional Security in Southeast Asia", in *Regional Security in the Third World*, edited by Mohammed Ayoob (London: Croom Helm Ltd., 1986), pp. 63–64.

U.S. intervention in South Vietnam and the British role in the Malayan Emergency were examples of direct external intervention, other regimes, in Thailand and the Philippines, also relied on external security support. It was only after the U.S. failure in Vietnam caused governments to realize that seeking foreign support against domestic opponents could prove counter-productive that they turned to regional cooperation. This included a common respect for the doctrine of non-interference as a more effective strategy for dealing with domestic insurgencies.

Throughout Southeast Asia in the 1950s and 1960s, preoccupation with domestic problems diminished foreign policy capacity, including capacity for regional cooperation ventures and institutions. It also led to a tendency to create foreign diversions to shift attention from domestic problems, as the case of Sukarno's *Konfrontasi* showed.

The ways and approaches employed by Southeast Asian states to deal with their domestic problems and the outcome of these efforts also affected regionalism. The communist victory in North Vietnam ended any possibility of its participation in a regional forum involving the non-communist Southeast Asian states. In Myanmar, a campaign against communist rebellions and separatism undermined democracy and led to the advent of a military regime under General Ne Win in 1962 that professed no interest in regionalism and pursued an isolationist policy. In Malaysia, Thailand, the Philippines and Indonesia after Sukarno, on the other hand, domestic problems created a shared predicament. All these states had pursued free-market policies and relied on rapid economic growth to combat communism. They perceived a common internal threat and saw regional cooperation as an important way to combat it.

In this respect, it should be recognized that the pro-Western regimes facing the threat of communism shared a common perception about its sources. They saw it as essentially domestic. Even as these insurgencies derived support from China and Russia, international support was not their root cause. Communist movements in Southeast Asia established themselves internally by exploiting the nationalist campaign against colonial and external powers, as in the case of Indonesia and Malaysia.[54] In terms of their origins and appeal, the insurgencies corresponded to what Michael Leifer identifies as being the common feature of such insurrections in post-colonial societies: "organized armed opposition to successor elites to colonialism by alternative elites who offer a radically different vision of modernity and social order", and whose appeal is "cast doctrinally in terms of the values of distributive justice and are designed to attract groups alienated by poverty, by gross disparities of private wealth and by the intolerance of a dominant culture".[55] To the extent that the socioeconomic patterns in all Southeast Asian countries in the post-colonial period were marked by these features, communist movements in the region were a product, first and foremost, of internal contradictions. It was this realization that was to prove crucial to the emergence of ASEAN and its inward-looking focus as a group of like-minded regimes. This focus was made further evident when these governments collaborated against the threat of communism. In fact, one of the main catalysts of political cooperation among the non-communist Southeast Asian countries leading to the formation of ASEAN was the development of joint counter-insurgency measures along their common borders.

Another important development affecting political cooperation in Southeast Asia was the decline of democratic experiments and the rise of authoritarianism in the pro-Western states of Southeast Asia. Indeed, the link between authoritarianism and regionalism has been a neglected aspect of study in Southeast Asia's international relations. The decline of constitutional government and the growing authoritarian turn of governments in the region initially dampened prospects for regionalism, but over the longer term it created the political basis for a common subregional political and ideological framework.

As Chan Heng Chee observes, many Southeast Asian countries "emerged from the colonial era experimenting with Western liberal democracy, but each abandoned the original model for variations of authoritarian forms which accommodate degrees of democracy".[56] A common thread running through the shift towards authoritarianism was its justification by the ruling regimes in terms of communist threat, ethnic unrest and a belief that economic development required a certain amount of authoritarian control. And it is this thread that provided an important basis for regional cooperation in the 1960s and 1970s, especially through the ASEAN framework.

Myanmar provides the clearest case where the retreat of democracy dampened the prospects for regional cooperation in Southeast Asia. Myanmar had been swept into independence by revolutionary nationalism. Its nationalist leadership under Aung San was an early advocate of regionalism, although, as noted earlier, this was not necessarily Southeast Asian in scope. But whatever interest Myanmar had in regionalism ended with the collapse of its democratic experiment in March 1962. The Ne Win regime suspended the constitution, suppressed the opposition and set up the Revolutionary Council, which assumed sweeping legislative, executive and judicial powers under his leadership. The junta set up its own political party, called the Burma Socialist Programme Party, and made itself the only legal political party in 1964. In April 1962, the Revolutionary Council announced a programme called "The Burmese Way to Socialism", which aimed at achieving economic self-sufficiency by combining Theravada Buddhism with Marxism-Leninism. It adopted non-alignment as its foreign policy posture and maintained good relations with both India and China at a time when they were at war, but gradually reduced its contacts with the outside world. This posture of isolationism was Ne Win's way of insulating Myanmar from external intervention in whatever form. Although it remained a member of the UN, the World Bank, the International Monetary Fund (IMF) and the ADB, Myanmar scaled down its involvement in these organizations, refused to send students abroad and discouraged tourism. Moreover, it no longer professed an interest in regional cooperation and effectively excluded itself from proposals to form a regional organization in Southeast Asia.

While in Myanmar domestic troubles led to foreign policy isolationism, in the case of Indonesia domestic strife led to expansionism and interstate tensions. Sukarno's flirtation with democracy cooled after the first national elections held in 1955. Thereafter, Javanese attempts to centralize the country sparked serious separatist campaigns, leading to the setting up of independent governments by local army commanders in Sumatra and Sulawesi in late 1956. Sukarno also had to deal with the communist movement at home. The Indonesian Communist Party (PKI) was rebuilding its strength after the disastrous 1948 revolt, drawing support from China and Russia. The combination of ethnic separatism and communist pressure led Sukarno to impose martial law in March 1957, followed by the abolition of the parliamentary constitution in 1959 and the declaration of what he called "Guided Democracy", which placed considerable power in his own hands. These domestic troubles contributed to Sukarno's tendency to divert attention from domestic problems through regional adventures that threatened the security of neighbours.[57] These included his policy of *Konfrontasi*. Sukarno regarded the Malaysian Federation created in 1963 with the merger of Malaya, North Borneo (Sabah), Sarawak and Singapore as an artificial creation of colonialism. The British had seen the federation as the best way to ensure the viability of the small and vulnerable states. But Sukarno took an ideological stand against the Malaysian Federation, arguing that because of its continuing defence and economic links with Britain, including the Anglo-Malayan Defence Agreement (AMDA) of 1957 that in 1963 was extended to the whole of Malaysia covering Malaya, North Borneo, Sarawak and Singapore, Malaysia was not genuinely independent. He contrasted Indonesia's armed struggle with Malaysia's constitutional path. Soon after the formation of the Malaysian Federation, Sukarno launched a "Crush Malaysia" campaign, which continued for three years. Indonesia's campaign combined raids on the Sarawak-Kalimantan border, with incursions into the Malay Peninsula and Singapore. He even took Indonesia out of the UN in 1965 to protest the admission of Malaysia into the UN.

Soeharto's "New Order" regime initially promised to be less authoritarian than Sukarno's "Guided Democracy", but hopes for this soon faded.

Explaining its actions in terms of the need for national "resilience", as manifested through internal stability and economic development, the regime imposed authoritarian rule and put down hopes for the more participatory political climate raised by the 1965 coup. But while Sukarno's foreign policy directly undermined regionalism, the New Order saw regionalism as an important tool for its domestic goals.

A similar turn to authoritarianism in Malaysia and the Philippines, while not crucial to the initial development of regionalist concepts among the pro-Western regimes in Southeast Asia, did help to sustain it later. In Malaysia, the democratic experiment also ran into problems as a result of domestic troubles, including communist rebellions and ethnic unrest. Communal riots following the May 1969 elections were blamed on economic injustice and the failure of free-market economics to reduce racial inequalities. The government of Tunku Abdul Rahman responded with the suspension of parliament (restored in January 1971), but sought to enlarge and strengthen the corporatist form of governance by creating an even bigger alliance among political groups under the National Front. It also created a national ideology, called *Rukunegara*, and banned public debate on sensitive issues such as race relations and the status of the Malay monarchies. While ethnic unrest led to the decline of the Malaysian democratic experiment, in the Philippines concerns about regime survival in the face of communist rebellion contributed to the retreat of democracy. In September 1972, Ferdinand Marcos, approaching the end of his second and last term in office, suspended the constitution and declared martial law, citing communist insurgency as the reason. Marcos' "New Society" programme emphasized the need for stability and promised land reform and economic justice, but extracted the price of "constitutional authoritarianism" as the necessary political framework. The army was strengthened and given a place in mainstream Filipino politics for the first time, and political dissidence was suppressed.

Thus, the governments of Malaysia, Singapore, the Philippines and Indonesia came to focus on political stability and continuity of leadership, while downgrading the Western model of participatory liberal democracy. The case of Thailand was not substantially different. Thailand had experienced alternations between democratic experiments and military rule. Democracy seemed to have prevailed in 1946 when Seni Pramoj, who became prime minister after the defeat of the Japanese, lost the 1946 general elections. But the ensuing government of Pridi Phanomyong was overthrown in 1947 by Field Marshal Phibul Songkram.

Democracy returned briefly in 1957 when political parties were legalized and general elections were held as a result of domestic and Western pressure. But Field Marshal Sarit Thanarat, who had been forced out of power as a result of the election, returned the country to military rule in October 1958. The government suppressed the left-wing opposition and promoted economic development, education and social reform to dispel the underlying sources of social discontent. In the late 1960s, the military government of Thanom Kittikachorn and Praphas Charusathien faced a serious escalation of the rebellion led by the Communist Party of Thailand, both in the northern and southern parts of the country. The government responded with harsh measures. Although these would lead to massive protests and the brief restoration of civilian rule between 1973 and 1976 — first under Seni Pramoj and then his brother Kukrit — an authoritarian and bureaucratic polity continued to shape Thai regional foreign policy for much of the 1950s and 1960s.

Facing similar predicaments of communism, ethnic separatism and challenges to regime survival, the governments of Malaysia, Singapore, Thailand, the Philippines and Indonesia responded with a common turn to authoritarianism, emphasizing domestic stability and economic development. This became a source of solidarity among these regimes. As Jorgensen-Dahl points out:

> the various countries [in ASEAN] ... have the same internal enemy ... the common internal enemy is seen to feed and depend for its success on a cluster of social conditions that are essentially the same in the various countries. From this point of view regional cooperation and organization is seen as an instrument which will allow the countries involved to more effectively strike at the roots of these conditions, and therefore at the very base of the most crucial support of their common internal enemy.[58]

Among these governments, regionalism was seen as a more effective way of dealing with internal threats than external support. In some cases, the turn to regionalism spurred by domestic changes was quite dramatic. In the Philippines, after imposing martial law, Marcos moved to make his country more independent of the United States, stressing regionalism in the foreign policy framework. Domestic politics also began to facilitate a shift in Thailand away from the United States and towards regionalism. During the fight against the communists in the late 1960s, the fear of a U.S. withdrawal and doubts about its credibility, as well as security concerns raised by the escalation of the Vietnam War, caused Thailand to rethink its stance. Indonesia's foreign policy shift was the most dramatic and influential. Sukarno's anti-colonialism was replaced by Soeharto's anti-communism. The Soeharto regime shifted its foreign policy, not only by cutting off diplomatic ties with Beijing and Moscow (placing the blame for the attempted 1965 coup on Beijing's support for the Indonesian communists), but more importantly by becoming an active promoter of regionalism, leading to the formation of ASEAN.

Great-Power Rivalry and Regional Autonomy

At the onset of the post-colonial era, the attitude of the great powers and Cold War geopolitics served to undermine the prospects for Southeast Asian regionalism. The availability of external (Western) security guarantees against both domestic and external threats rendered the need of some Southeast Asian states for regional cooperation less urgent in dealing with security challenges. Thailand and the Philippines, while ostensibly interested in regional defence cooperation, could actually be relaxed about it since their security needs were met, at least partially, by the United States-Philippines Mutual Defense Treaty of 1951 and the beginning of the U.S. military assistance to Thailand in 1950. Moreover there was little agreement among the Western powers on the need for regional security cooperation in Southeast Asia. The French and the British had hoped for some form of collaboration, especially in defending against popular insurgencies in Malaya and Vietnam backed by China. However, the United States was not prepared to support any such proposals, having been stretched by the Korean War. This was to change in the 1950s, but the United States would face considerable obstacles in developing a regional defence system in Southeast Asia.

At the end of World War II, neither the United States nor the Soviet Union considered Southeast Asia to be an area of major strategic significance. Their involvement in the region was minimal. Stalin considered Southeast Asia to be peripheral to his interest in spreading communism; the Soviet Union had not envisaged the possibility of major geopolitical or ideological gain either in Indonesia or Indochina. This lack of interest was further confirmed by its failure to support the Indonesian Communist Party's Madiun revolt in 1948.

During the immediate post-war period, the United States and Britain had key influence over the framework of regional associations in Southeast Asia. At the Potsdam Conference of July 1945, the victorious Allied Powers decided to divide the responsibility for administering Japan's colonial possessions in Southeast Asia among the Americans, Chinese and British. Accordingly, the United States would be responsible for the Philippines; the Chinese would have responsibility for North Vietnam; and the Southeast Asia Command (SEAC), led by Britain, would have responsibility for the remainder of colonial Southeast Asia. This made Britain the only external power to have the opportunity to develop a semi-regional approach to Southeast Asia. By 1948, Britain had become convinced that Southeast Asia would become a major arena of U.S.-Soviet rivalry. The British also came up with one of the first formulations of the "domino theory". The British Commissioner-General in Southeast Asia predicted in 1949 that the fall of China would precipitate communist takeovers in Indochina, followed by Siam (Thailand), Myanmar and Malaya. Although President Eisenhower expressed belief in the domino theory in April 1954, the United States rejected a British proposal to create some sort of Marshall Plan for Southeast Asia. To a certain extent, Britain's interest in developing the Colombo Plan[59] within the framework of the Commonwealth was partly an effort to compensate for its inability to influence the Americans in this regard. The Plan was created at a meeting of the Commonwealth Foreign Ministers in Colombo in January 1950. It was meant to be a framework for the provision of economic and technical aid. Britain had hoped that the scope of the Plan be extended to cover security issues, although this failed to materialize.

The U.S. policy towards Southeast Asia in the immediate aftermath of the war was more hesitant about the necessity for a regional organization. In general, Southeast Asia was not a priority area in U.S. global strategic policy, thanks to the continued streak of hemispheric isolationism and the burdens imposed by the need to police other theatres of the Cold War. U.S. policy did recognize an opportunity for American business to invest in the Southeast Asian colonies created by post-war rehabilitation. There was support for this from the colonial powers; this in turn served to moderate the U.S. interest in seeing a hasty end to the age of empire in Southeast Asia. Thus, while as a champion of national liberation President Roosevelt proposed in 1942–43 an international trusteeship system for the former Southeast Asian colonies that would prepare them for independence, the stability afforded by the restoration of colonial rule was seen by the United States as a more useful tool against communist advance than the instability associated with weak nation-states. Thus, the real U.S. interest in thinking about Southeast Asia as a regional unit and about regional cooperation had less to do with anti-colonialism than anti-communism. Even then, Washington was cautious about being too closely involved in a regional organization. As a Policy Planning Staff Paper on U.S. policy towards Southeast Asia in March 1949 noted:

> We should avoid at the outset urging an area organization, our effort should initially be directed toward collaboration on joint or parallel action and then, only as a pragmatic and desirable basis for intimate association appears, should we encourage the areas to move step by step toward formal organization. If Asian leaders prematurely precipitate an area organization, we should not give the impression of attempting to thwart such a move but should go along with them while exerting a cautiously moderating influence ... In order to minimize suggestions of American imperialist intervention, we should encourage the Indians, Filipinos and other Asian states to take the public lead in political matters. Our role should be the offering of discreet support and guidance ...[60]

The U.S. reluctance to support the establishment of an anti-communist security alliance in the Pacific was reflected in its response to one such proposal, made by President Elpidio Quirino of the Philippines, calling for a Pacific equivalent of the North Atlantic Treaty Organization (NATO). This proposal drew support from President Syngman Rhee of South Korea and General Chiang Kai-Shek of nationalist China. A meeting between Chiang and Quirino in Baguio in July 1949 led them to call for an anti-communist front, with the involvement of South Korea, India, Australia, New Zealand, Thailand and Indonesia. While Australia, New Zealand and Thailand were willing to consider this idea, the Truman administration was not interested.

But the U.S. attitude shifted in the early 1950s in response to the communist challenge. As the survival of non-communist regimes (whether as vestiges of old colonial rule or newly installed nationalist regimes) was recognized as a major U.S. interest in Southeast Asia, the United States began assisting the French against the Vietminh as well as supporting the nationalist regimes that showed a determination to challenge communists — a policy that explained U.S. support for Indonesian independence, which became stronger following Sukarno's stand against the Indonesian communists in Madiun. The "loss" of China further strengthened the U.S. decision to extend its containment policy to Southeast Asia. On 18 July 1949, the U.S. Secretary of State, Dean Acheson, expressed American interest in preventing "further communist domination on the continent of Asia or in South-East Asia".[61] This development came in the midst of major developments in the Cold War in Europe, including the formation of the NATO in 1949 and signs of intensified armed struggle by communist movements in Myanmar, Indonesia, Malaya, the Philippines and Vietnam. Regional alliance-building became an important part of the U.S. containment strategy to prevent the emergence of pro-Soviet regimes in Asia, an objective rendered more urgent by the outbreak of the Korean War and the Vietminh offensive against French forces in September 1950. These developments gave rise to Washington's own "domino theory", which assumed that communist victory in any single country would have a contagious effect, leading to communist victories in the other countries of the region. Other strategic interests and objectives also contributed to the U.S. interest in regional security cooperation. These included ensuring access to strategically located overseas bases and a desire to counter pan-Asian movements, such as the Asian Relations Conference of 1947, the New Delhi Conference of 1949 and the Bandung Conference of 1955, which were seen as being unfriendly and anti-Western.

Washington's attitude towards Asian (including Southeast Asian) regional cooperation in the immediate post-war period was thus marked by contradictory impulses. Being aware of the growing Asian nationalism, U.S. planners and policy-makers had refrained from taking any initiative in the formation of regional associations in Asia. Any such U.S. initiative, it was thought, might give rise to suspicions of "imperialist intervention". On the other hand, the United States was eager to provide assistance to a regional association born out of Asian initiative that would be pro-Western in orientation and anti-communist by nature. In the absence of a desirable Asian initiative, and faced with the growing influence of communist forces in Indochina, Washington took the initiative and was instrumental in the establishment of the Southeast Asia Treaty Organization (SEATO).

While the United States began looking for a regional security structure to contain communism, the Eisenhower administration emphasized the development of bilateral alliances with the Philippines and Thailand. But the defeat of the French in 1954 at the hands of Vietminh forces led by General Vo Nguyen Giap at Dien Bien Phu led to a U.S. effort to internationalize the war, and spurred new interest in a regional defence alliance. U.S. support for the French in Indochina had been increased, due to China's entry into the Korean War in November 1950 and its backing of the Vietminh. While the Geneva Accords on Indochina in 1954 produced a ceasefire agreement between the French and North Vietnamese governments,[62] it did not assuage U.S. concerns over communist expansion. In fact, the Geneva Accords sowed the seeds of the ideological and strategic polarization of Southeast Asia, which was to affect the prospects for regional cooperation. As A.J. Stockwell writes:

> In international relations it presented the pursuit of war by other means. Predicated upon a Manichean division of the world into two hostile blocs, it reinforced belief in the existence of Western and communist monoliths. Instead of providing for the agreement of the Great Powers, it set the scene for another phase in their future confrontation. None of the participants (including the co-chairmen, Britain and the USSR) had either the will or the means to stand firm on the implementation of the Geneva settlement and to convert the ceasefire into a political agreement. The United States came to hate everything Geneva stood for; China soon claimed it had been duped as regards the position of Cambodia and Laos; and the opposing Vietnamese felt betrayed by their respective sponsors. Some weeks later the creation of the Southeast Asia Treaty Organization (SEATO) at the Manila Conference (September 1954) introduced a new phase in the conduct of containment in the region by replacing the outworn structures of French colonialism and military imperialism with a system of collective security. Geneva may have prevented the internationalization of the Vietnam War in the summer of 1954, but it provided for the formal entanglement of Indochina in the international relations of Cold War.[63]

The legal framework for SEATO, the Southeast Asia Collective Defense Treaty (or the Manila Pact) was signed on 8 September 1954 at a meeting in Manila attended by Britain, the United States, France, Australia, New Zealand, Pakistan, Thailand and the Philippines. The meeting also adopted a Pacific Charter, which, among other things, endorsed SEATO's role in protecting the security and stability of the members from aggression and subversion. The establishment of SEATO did contribute to a greater awareness of Southeast Asia as a region in the international arena. However, the concept of "region" embodied by SEATO was loose and flexible. According to Article VIII of the Manila Pact:

> As used in this Treaty, the "Treaty Area" is the general area of South-East Asia, including also the entire territories of the Asian Parties, and the general area of the South-West Pacific not including the Pacific area north of 21 degrees 30 minutes north latitude. The Parties may, by unanimous agreement, amend this Article to include within the Treaty Area the territory of any State acceding to this Treaty in accordance with Article VII or otherwise to change the Treaty Area.[64]

As a regional security framework, SEATO was plagued by several problems. Key differences emerged between its two leading players, the United States and Britain. Britain had wanted to delay the consideration of a pact until the Geneva Conference was over, hoping that it would produce a settlement and bring about lasting peace. John Foster Dulles, the U.S. Secretary of State who masterminded the U.S. Cold War alliances, saw it differently. He did not believe the conference would succeed (this proved to be a self-fulfilling prophecy). Even before the start of the conference, in March 1954, Dulles had called for a collective defence treaty against communist aggression. Britain argued that such a treaty would jeopardize the conference's prospects and instead suggested a non-aggression pact that would include India and other Asian countries. In the end the organization only came about through a compromise, whereby Britain gave up its demand for a non-aggression pact and the United States gave up the idea of a unified field command. These compromises undermined SEATO at birth.

The establishment of SEATO was greeted with considerable antagonism by China and Vietnam. Beijing accused the United States of destroying the Geneva agreement, despite U.S.-British claims that SEATO was meant to reinforce the Geneva principles. But SEATO's main problem had to do with the gap in expectations between the Asian members on the one hand and those of the Western sponsors, especially the United States, on the other. The credibility of the alliance suffered, as the Asian parties to SEATO were disappointed by the lower level of assurances and security guarantees offered by the United States. Adding to this were the divergent security objectives of the Western powers and the Asian parties. For the latter, internal challenges to regime survival were the main threat to security, rather than overt communist aggression or subversion, as had been advanced by the United States as the major rationale for creating a regional security structure. Moreover, SEATO, like other Cold War alliances, failed to provide any mechanism for conflict resolution within the region. Given that intraregional conflicts constituted a serious challenge to the security of Southeast Asia, a regional security system that did not contain a mechanism to deal with such conflicts was questionable in terms of relevance and utility.

For the region's officially non-aligned countries, especially Indonesia and Malaysia, SEATO represented a flawed approach to regional security. For them, while military pacts might be useful against a threat of outright aggression — an unlikely scenario as far as many non-communist

Southeast Asian states were concerned — they could not address revolutionary social challenges. Indonesia's Foreign Minister, Adam Malik, drew attention to this danger when he warned that "military alliances or foreign military presence does not enhance a nation's capacity to cope with the problem of insurgency. The price for such commitments is too high, whereas the negative ramifications for the nation are too great."[65] Mohammed Ghazali bin Shafie, a former Malaysian Foreign Minister, later wrote, "External support for internal insurgencies, or for governments combating insurgencies, have the effect of raising the level of violence and complicating both conflict management and the peaceful resolution of conflicts through political means. Internal stability cannot after all be imposed from the outside."[66] Seeking the help of external powers in situations of domestic instability could undermine the legitimacy of the threatened regime; after all, the most important and painful lesson of the Vietnam War was that relying on external backing in domestic upheavals could "easily serve to insulate it [the threatened regime] from political and economic realities and render it insensitive to the social forces with which in the long run it must come to terms if it is to survive on its own".[67]

A major development affecting SEATO's fortunes was the superpower détente of the early 1970s, which severely undermined the credibility of the U.S. commitment to anti-Soviet regional coalitions in the Third World. Détente also raised the unsavoury prospect of a superpower condominium that might compromise or ignore the security interests of the Third World states in general. Faced with these prospects, some members of the Cold War alliances chose to change track and distance themselves from the superpower sphere of influence, thereby rapidly rendering these alliances obsolete. The failure of such alliances in turn led to renewed interest in regional organizations that promised "regional solutions to regional problems".

The United States came to acknowledge the limitation of SEATO. President Nixon wrote in October 1967, "SEATO was useful and appropriate to its time, but it was Western in origin."[68] This suggests that even the United States had become convinced that regional cooperation in Southeast Asia could not thrive without an indigenous basis. The decision to dissolve SEATO by mid-1977 was announced in September 1975. By this time, ASEAN had come into a life of its own. Some attempt was made by SEATO's protagonists to see ASEAN as a more civilian successor to SEATO. In May 1977, the then Secretary-

General of SEATO, Sunthorn Hungladarom, said, "I don't think it is possible to revive SEATO. We have to let some organization like ASEAN assume some of SEATO's functions."[69] But ASEAN would be very sensitive to any such comparison. The United States did turn its attention to supporting ASEAN. This was consistent with the Johnson administration's 1965 policy declaring its intention to support regional cooperation in Southeast Asia. But the U.S. backing of ASEAN would be mainly indirect, and ASEAN would be very careful about not being seen as a tool of U.S. policy.

In the late 1960s, a major shift in the international environment affected the international relations of Southeast Asia. The chief trend was the easing of Cold War tensions and a shift from the rigid bipolarity of the early Cold War period towards a more fluid situation, resulting from the Sino-Soviet rift and the rise of the European Community. U.S.-Soviet relations had steadily evolved towards greater understanding after the Cuban missile crisis in 1962, when the danger of nuclear war was brought home to their leaders.

In Southeast Asia, these developments helped to increase the appeal of regionalism among the pro-Western regimes. They lessened the credibility and usefulness of relying on Western security guarantees, even for the Philippines and Thailand, which had developed close defence links with the United States. The Philippines' dependence on the United States had increased significantly as a result of the U.S. help in suppressing the Huk insurgency, at its height in the 1950s. The Philippines then became a major link in the U.S. containment strategy, providing troops to fight in the Korean War from August 1950. In August 1951, the United States and the Philippines signed a Mutual Defense Treaty. Thailand too had become a close U.S. ally, signing military, economic, and technical cooperation and assistance agreements in 1950. Like the Philippines, the Thai Government under Phibul sent troops to Korea. Facing a communist insurgency dominated by an ethnic Chinese element, Thailand had adopted some anti-Chinese measures.

Against this backdrop, two developments had a major impact on the attitudes of the pro-Western regimes of Southeast Asia, especially Thailand, the Philippines, Malaysia and Singapore, towards Western security guarantees. The first was the announcement by the Harold Wilson government in 1966 of Britain's "east of Suez" policy, which in effect meant the withdrawal of British military forces "east of Suez" (initially by the mid-1970s but brought forward to 1971). The other development was the Nixon administration's new "doctrine" on regional security, called the "Nixon doctrine", which ruled out U.S. involvement in a future land war in Southeast Asia and called upon America's Asian allies to assume a greater share of the burden for their own defence. Despite the different historical roles played by the British and the Americans in Southeast Asia's international relations, these developments had the same effect: they signalled to the pro-Western countries of the region the need for greater self-reliance, through both national effort and regional cooperation.

The British withdrawal was particularly significant for Singapore and Malaysia. Long reliant on Britain and other Commonwealth partners (Australia and New Zealand) for protection against both internal as well as external threats, they received the announcement at a time when the development of their indigenous defence capabilities was still at a rudimentary stage. The British decision to withdraw prompted the replacement of the Anglo-Malaysian Defence Agreement (AMDA) with a regional security system called the Five Power Defence Arrangement (FPDA), involving Britain, Australia, New Zealand, Singapore and Malaysia. Mindful of their financial limitations and political constraints, the British produced a greatly watered down commitment: a consultative arrangement backed by a small air defence (centred on Australian combat aircraft) and ground force component (contributed by New Zealand).[70] Against this backdrop, for both Singapore and Kuala Lumpur, regional cooperation that was aimed at minimizing the potential for intraregional conflict seemed to be a natural course to follow, complementing the rapid buildup of their military forces in order to achieve the greater self-reliance dictated by the weakening Western strategic umbrella.[71]

The British withdrawal contributed to the urgency of efforts towards regional cooperation on the part of Singapore, which saw it as an essential means through which local countries could address the non-military, especially political and economic, requirements of security. The Foreign Minister of Singapore, S. Rajaratnam, observed:

> The British decision to withdraw from the region in the seventies brings ... to an end nearly two centuries of dominant European influence in the region. The seventies will also see the withdrawal of direct American influence in Southeast Asian affairs. For the first time in centuries, Southeast Asia will be on its own. It must fill what some people call the power vacuum itself or resign itself to the dismal prospect of the vacuum being filled from the outside ... we can and should fill it ourselves, not

necessarily militarily, but by strengthening our social, economic, and political foundations through cooperation and collective effort.[72]

The Nixon Doctrine was a by-product of the Nixon administration's efforts to simultaneously reduce tensions with the Soviet Union while seeking a new opening with China. This meant an easing of the side effects of the U.S.-Soviet and Sino-U.S. geopolitical rivalries over Southeast Asia. While this contributed to a more relaxed atmosphere in Southeast Asia, the U.S. policy also had the effect of magnifying the evolving Sino-Soviet conflict, especially with the use of the "China card" in the Nixon-Kissinger geopolitical framework. This meant that, insofar as Southeast Asia was concerned, the Sino-Soviet rivalry would remain an important aspect of the region's international relations. Thus, the pro-Western regimes of Southeast Asia could no longer count on their external security guarantees, while not being totally free from the influence of great-power rivalry. It is in response to both these situations that the pro-Western governments in Southeast Asia looked to regional solidarity.

The U.S. failure in Indochina had become apparent by the late 1960s, and the Nixon Doctrine, by calling on the United States' regional allies to assume greater responsibilities for their own security, was a warning signal of the eventual U.S. disengagement from mainland Southeast Asia. One major impact of the shifting U.S. posture was to further stimulate Thailand's efforts to steer a more independent course in foreign policy, a move also in keeping with Bangkok's traditional policy of avoiding "too much dependence on any single power or patron".[73] The impact on the Philippines was similar, spurring Manila's desire to shed its image as a strategic client of the United States and to assert its "Asian" identity.[74] For these two states, the geopolitical reverses suffered by the United States due to its engagement in Vietnam and the Nixon Doctrine made imperative a drive towards self-reliance in the framework of greater regional cooperation. For Singapore and Malaysia, the U.S. withdrawal was a further blow to the credibility of the Western security guarantees that had already been severely undermined by the announcement of British withdrawal from the region.

These developments in great-power relations interacted with developments at the regional level. Here, contrasting trends emerged, in Indochina on the one hand and the rest of Southeast Asia (excluding Myanmar) on the other. As Indochina's international relations were shaped by war and revolution and continuing great-power intervention, the non-communist Southeast Asian countries, alarmed by the developments in Indochina and exposed to the common dangers of rebellions and interventionism, closed ranks and launched an experiment in regionalism with a view to reducing great-power influence and to ensure their political survival.

While the Cold War aggravated a great deal of intraregional conflict in Southeast Asia, it also helped to bring the region into the international limelight. Prior to the advent of the Cold War in Southeast Asia, the region had consisted of separate countries that had been linked far more closely to their colonial masters than to each other. By identifying the region as a "trouble-spot", and asserting regionwide solutions to their problems there, the superpowers changed all that. The Cold War also provided a strong impetus for regionalism by creating a common fear of superpower rivalry among the countries of the region.

For much of this early Cold War period, Southeast Asia presented the image of a highly unstable segment of the international system, an image captured by Milton Osborne's famous phrase, "region of revolt".[75] The region's proneness to strife became a distinctive feature, prompting the comments by Bernard Gordon, that one of the factors "which makes Southeast Asia a 'region' is the widespread incidence of conflict, along with some attempts at cooperation" and that "instability is the one feature of Southeast Asia that gives the region much of its contemporary importance".[76] The prevalent Cold War geopolitical view of Southeast Asia in the West, particularly in the United States, was that it was a region of likely dominos.

Conclusion

The international relations of Southeast Asia in the 1950s and 1960s were deeply influenced by a complex interaction between three fundamental forces: nationalism, the nature of the decolonization process and the advent of the Cold War. The main outcome of this was the achievement of only limited national and regional autonomy by the Southeast Asian states. Nationalism had spurred a search for self-reliance and autonomy. However, in reality, the weakness of the nation-state, and intraregional divisions caused by both the pressures of the Cold War and contending nationalisms, served to create a regional pattern of international relations in Southeast Asia that was largely dominated by outside powers and influences. Superpower rivalry gradually replaced colonialism as the chief determinant of international affairs in the region. The newly independent states of Southeast Asia were too weak and disorganized to override these external constraints and resist great-power intervention. Attempts to develop "regional solutions to regional problems" faltered, due to existing suspicions and rivalries among the Southeast Asian states as well as their continued dependence on external security guarantees.

The fact that the political, economic and strategic conditions in Southeast Asia remained substantially unfavourable to regional cooperation during the first two decades of the post-war period was confirmed by an important study of regional economic interdependence in Southeast Asia. Although the study was concerned mainly with economic linkages, it helped to identify the obstacles to regionalism in general. These included:

1. The tendency among Southeast Asian leaders to advance proposals for regional cooperation for domestic and foreign political effect (examples include Sukarno's "Newly Emerging Forces" idea);
2. The persistence of intraregional antagonisms such as *Konfrontasi*, the Vietnam-Thailand, Cambodia-Vietnam and Malaysia-Philippines rivalries, which created great sensitivity towards the development of political and military institutions of regional cooperation;
3. The impact of the Cold War in polarizing national foreign policy postures, with countries such as India (still regarded at the time as a likely member of a Southeast Asian regional co-operation framework), Laos, Cambodia and Myanmar choosing a non-aligned posture between East and West, and Malaysia, Singapore, Thailand and the Philippines adopting a pro-Western posture (Indonesia, according to this study, was shifting from a neutral to a pro-Western stance); and
4. Differences in basic economic policy among regional countries, with Myanmar, Indonesia and India adopting an "inward-looking" trade and investment policy, and Malaysia, Thailand and the Philippines relying on a relatively "outward-looking" approach through private enterprise and free trade.[77]

Another pessimistic assessment of the regional situation was provided by Kenneth T. Young, a former U.S. ambassador to Thailand. Writing in 1966, he argued:

It is doubtful that political regionalism or area-wide defense will emerge to play a part in encouraging regional equilibrium or regional institutions for political collaboration or collective defense. Centrifugal and divisive tendencies are too strong. Leaders will be more interested in relations with outside countries than among themselves, and more inclined to participate in Pan-Asian or international conferences and organizations than in exclusively Southeast Asian formations. They know that real power and needed resources, which the Southeast Asian countries do not possess, will continue to come from outside the region. Even the common fear of Communist China and the threat of Chinese minorities will not develop any sense of solidarity or serve to coordinate the divergent policies of neutrality and alignment. One political dilemma in Southeast Asia is that these new governments are trying desperately to become viable nation-states in an area where the individual state may, despite internal nationalism and good leadership, be turning obsolescent for the security and development of the area, and where at the same time a sense of regional community and purpose is lacking to complement and reinforce the nation-state.[78]

Young was correct in identifying the lack of resources, the divisive tendencies in Southeast Asia and the negative impact of nationalism on regionalism. But with the benefit of hindsight, it is clear that he did not foresee the motivation for cooperation among a subregional group of like-minded regimes fearful of Chinese-backed communist expansion. By the mid-1960s, there were already indications of a shift in domestic and external conditions that would culminate in the development of regionalist concepts among the non-communist states of Southeast Asia. Some of these changes were linked to great-power policies. The declining willingness and ability of the Western powers, Britain and the United States, to maintain their security umbrella in the region, further encouraged the quest for regional cooperation and identity. The non-communist states of Southeast Asia had now to look to themselves for developing a collective political resistance to communism. Thus, Singapore's Foreign Minister, S. Rajaratnam, would explain the emergence of ASEAN as a "response on the part of non-communist Southeast Asia to the Western abandonment of its role as a shield against communism".[79]

These external developments interacted with the domestic situations of pro-Western Southeast Asian states, which were marked by a number of similarities. These included the commonly faced threats of communist rebellions and ethnic separatism. These challenges also produced a common shift towards authoritarianism, as well as an emphasis on regime legitimation via rapid economic growth through market capitalism, thereby creating a commonality of predicament and policy outlook among these states. Ultimately, this proved to be the key driving factor behind the formation of ASEAN in 1967.

The first two decades of the post-World War II period saw a major shift in approaches to regional order in Southeast Asia. The 1950s were marked by a direct or indirect push by the Western powers to involve their Southeast Asian allies in developing regional alliances that could act as bulwarks against communism. In these years, then, Southeast Asian efforts in developing regional groupings were minimal and largely rhetorical. But from the late 1950s, there emerged the first serious initiatives among Southeast Asian leaders to develop regional associations with an essentially Southeast Asian scope and character. The 1960s saw a growing recognition among the Southeast Asian elite of the dangers and futility of being involved in the kind of regionalism advocated by the West, and their consequent desire to develop a more "self-reliant" form of regionalism, geared to managing intraregional security relationships and shielding the region from the harmful effects of great-power rivalry. While the initial efforts in this regard were short-lived, they had an important cumulative effect, moving the countries of the region towards a more viable form of regionalism in 1967.

NOTES

[1] Constance Mary Turnbull, "Regionalism and Nationalism", in *The Cambridge History of Southeast Asia*, vol. 2: *The Nineteenth and Twentieth Centuries*, edited by Nicholas Tarling (Cambridge: Cambridge University Press, 1992), p. 589.

[2] See Anthony Reid, "A Saucer Model of Southeast Asian Identity", *Southeast Asian Journal of Social Science* 27, no. 1 (1999): 7–23.

[3] Christopher E. Goscha, *Thailand and the Southeast Asian Networks of the Vietnamese Revolution, 1885–1954* (Richmond, Surrey: Curzon Press, 1999), p. 244.

[4] Cited in Chintamani Mahapatra, *American Role in the Origin and Growth of ASEAN* (New Delhi: ABC Publishing House, 1990), p. 15.

[5] Cited in William Henderson, "The Development of Regionalism in Southeast Asia", *International Organization* 9, no. 4 (1955): 462–76.

[6] Cited in Goscha, *Thailand and the Southeast Asian Networks of the Vietnamese Revolution*, p. 255.

[7] Josef Silverstein, "The Political Legacy of Aung San", Data paper no. 86 (Ithaca, NY: Department of Asian Studies, Southeast Asian Program, Cornell University, 1972), p. 101.

8   Ibid., pp. 101–2.
9   Aung San, *Burma's Challenge* (South Okklapa, Myanmar: U Aung Gyi, 1974), p. 192.
10   Aung San, *Burma's Challenge*, p. 193.
11   "Blue Print for Burma", originally printed in *The Guardian*, March 1947, pp. 33–35; reprinted in Silverstein, "The Political Legacy of Aung San", p. 21.
12   Ibid.
13   Ibid., p. 22.
14   Ibid., p. 21.
15   Ibid.
16   Silverstein, "The Political Legacy of Aung San", p. 101.
17   Aung San, "Problems for Burma's Freedom" [General Aung San's speeches] (Rangoon: Sarpay Bait Man Press, 1971), pp. 38–39.
18   Ibid., p. 36.
19   Ibid.
20   Ibid.
21   Ibid.
22   Ibid.
23   Ibid.
24   Silverstein, "The Political Legacy of Aung San", p. 101.
25   Ibid.
26   Ibid.
27   Ibid., p. 102.
28   Aung San, "Defence of Burma, January 30, 1945", DSHRI Classification: GR60/P III c/1945 Jan DR 49/P III c/1945 Jan (Defence Services Historical Research Institute, Rangoon, Burma); reprinted in Silverstein, "The Political Legacy of Aung San", pp. 23–24.
29   Ibid.
30   "Welcome India", address of welcome delivered at the reception given in honour of Mr Sarat Bose, a member of the Working Committee of the Indian National Congress, at the City Hall of Rangoon on 24 July 1946. In *Bogyoke Aung San Maint-Khun-Myar (1945–1947)* [General Aung San's speeches] (Rangoon: Sarpay Bait Man Press, 1971), p. 86.
31   Aung San, "Problems for Burma's Freedom", pp. 36–37.
32   Cited in Amry Vandenbosch and Richard Butwell, *The Changing Face of Southeast Asia* (Lexington: University of Kentucky Press, 1966), p. 341.
33   Ibid.
34   Goscha, *Thailand and the Southeast Asian Networks of the Vietnamese Revolution*, p. 257.
35   Ibid., pp. 258–59.
36   Ibid., p. 341.

[37] Cited in Goscha, *Thailand and the Southeast Asian Networks of the Vietnamese Revolution*, p. 348.

[38] Wang Gungwu, "Nation Formation and Regionalism in Southeast Asia", in *South Asia Pacific Crisis: National Development and World Community*, edited by M. Grant (New York: Dodd, Mead and Company, 1964), p. 134.

[39] Ibid., pp. 125–35.

[40] Bernard K. Gordon, *The Dimensions of Conflict in Southeast Asia* (Englewood Cliffs, NJ: Prentice Hall, 1966), p. 145.

[41] Ibid., p. 164.

[42] Norman Owen, "Economic and Social Change", in Tarling, *The Cambridge History of Southeast Asia*, vol. 2, p. 493.

[43] Ibid., pp. 473–74.

[44] Hla Myint, *Southeast Asia's Economy: Development Policies in the 1970s* (New York: Praeger, 1972). This was, of course, not the first book on the subject. Books written by Western scholars with a Southeast Asian focus include F.H. Golay, R. Anspach, M.R. Pfanner and B.A. Eliezer, *Underdevelopment and Economic Nationalism in Southeast Asia* (Ithaca, NY: Cornell University Press, 1969); T. Morgan and N. Spoelstra, eds., *Economic Interdependence in Southeast Asia* (Madison: University of Wisconsin Press, 1969).

[45] Cited in Myint, *Southeast Asia's Economy*, p. 13.

[46] Ibid., p. 25.

[47] Ibid., p. 23.

[48] Ibid., p. 13.

[49] Ibid., p. 27.

[50] Ibid., pp. 26–27.

[51] Ibid., p. 71.

[52] Ibid., pp. 71–72.

[53] Ibid., p. 159.

[54] Joo-Jock Lim and Shanmugaratnam Vani, "Introduction", in *Armed Communist Movements in Southeast Asia*, edited by Joo-Jock Lim and S. Vani (Aldershot, Hants: Gower, 1984), p. xiii.

[55] Michael Leifer, *Conflict and Regional Order in Southeast Asia*, Adelphi Paper no. 162 (London: International Institute for Strategic Studies, 1980), p. 4.

[56] Chan Heng Chee, "Political Stability in Southeast Asia", paper presented to the seminar on "Trends and Perspectives in ASEAN", Institute of Southeast Asian Studies, Singapore, 1–3 February 1982, p. 11.

[57] Turnbull, "Regionalism and Nationalism", p. 610.

[58] Arnfinn Jorgensen-Dahl, *Regional Organization and Order in Southeast Asia* (London: Macmillan, 1982), p. 102.

[59] The Colombo Plan, which began to function from 1 July 1951, was not strictly a regional organization. Under this plan, seventeen Asian countries were to

receive technical assistance and capital aid from the United States, Britain, Canada, Australia, New Zealand and Japan. The assistance arrangements were based on bilateral understandings between aid givers and recipients. The United States considered expanding the Colombo Plan into a multilateral grouping and privately sounded out a proposal to this effect with some members at the Ministerial Conference of the Colombo Plan in Ottawa. Although the Colombo Plan was useful in facilitating American cooperation with Asian countries without inviting the usual criticism of imperialist intervention, the plan to strengthen the Plan failed to materialize, due to U.S. reluctance to agree to the creation of a permanent secretariat.

60   Mahapatra, *American Role in the Origin and Growth of ASEAN*, p. 48.

61   Cited in Anthony John Stockwell, "Southeast Asia in War and Peace: The End of European Colonial Empires", in Tarling, *The Cambridge History of Southeast Asia*, vol. 2, p. 361.

62   The Geneva settlement established an International Supervisory Commission to oversee the end of hostilities, divided the country at the seventeenth parallel, ensured French withdrawal and recognized the independence, security and integrity of Laos and Cambodia. The eventual reunification of Vietnam was envisaged, pending a political settlement and the holding of elections to be held in July 1956.

63   Stockwell, "Southeast Asia in War and Peace", p. 373.

64   *History of SEATO* (Bangkok: Public Information Office, SEATO Headquarters, n.d.), pp. 42–43.

65   Adam Malik, "Djakarta Conference and Asia's Political Future", *Pacific Community* 2, no. 1 (1970), p. 74.

66   Mohammed Ghazali bin Shafie, "ASEAN's Response to Security Issues in Southeast Asia", in *Regionalism in Southeast Asia* (Jakarta: Centre for Strategic and International Studies, 1975), p. 23.

67   George McT. Kahin, "The Role of the United States in Southeast Asia", in *New Directions in the International Relations of Southeast Asia*, edited by T.S. Lau (Singapore: Singapore University Press, 1973), p. 77.

68   Cited in Evans Young, "Development Cooperation in ASEAN: Balancing Free Trade and Regional Planning", Ph.D. dissertation, University of Michigan, Ann Arbor, 1981, p. 89.

69   Ibid.

70   Chin Kin Wah, "The Five Power Defence Arrangement and AMDA: Some Observations on the Nature of an Evolving Partnership", Occasional Paper no. 23 (Singapore: Institute of Southeast Asian Studies, 1974).

71   Kannan Kutty Nair, "Defence and Security in Southeast Asia: The Urgency of Self-Reliance", *Asian Defence Journal*, no. 1 (1975): 9–17.

72   Statement at the Second ASEAN Ministerial Meeting, Jakarta, 6 August 1968, cited in T. Phanit, "Regional Integration Attempts in Southeast Asia: Problems

and Progress", Ph.D. dissertation, Pennsylvania State University, 1980, pp. 32–33.

[73] Barbara Pace et al., *Regional Cooperation in Southeast Asia: The First Two Years of ASEAN — 1967–1969* (McLean, VA: Research Analysis Corporation, 1970), p. 18.

[74] Phanit, *Regional Integration Attempts in Southeast Asia*, pp. 35–36.

[75] Milton Osborne, *Region of Revolt: Focus on Southeast Asia* (Rushcutters Bay, NSW: Pergamon Australia, 1970).

[76] Gordon, *The Dimensions of Conflict in Southeast Asia*, pp. 1 and 3.

[77] "Introduction", in *Economic Interdependence in Southeast Asia*, edited by Theodore Morgan and Nyle Spoelstra (Madison: University of Wisconsin Press, 1969), pp. 10–11.

[78] Kenneth T. Young, *The Southeast Asia Crisis* (New York: The Association of the Bar of the City of New York, 1966), p. 64.

[79] Cited in Evans Young, "Development Cooperation in ASEAN", p. 87.

5

The Evolution of Regional Organization

In Southeast Asia's international relations, the first two decades after World War II were characterized and shaped by nationalism, decolonization, great-power intervention and failed attempts at regional (mainly pan-Asian) cooperation. It is fair to say that attempts at regional cooperation played a marginal role in shaping international order and were overwhelmed by domestic politics on the one hand and externally determined Cold War geopolitics on the other. But the situation during the next two decades would be different. While the domestic strife characteristic of post-colonial states persisted and great-power rivalry continued to plague the region, Southeast Asia's international relations during the 1970s and 1980s would be marked chiefly by a dynamic involving the competing forces of regional conflict and cooperation. An important factor shaping this dynamic was the establishment of the Association of Southeast Asian Nations (ASEAN) in 1967.

During this period, regionalism would have a paradoxical effect on Southeast Asia's unity and identity. On the one hand, it brought together to an unprecedented degree the non-communist Southeast Asian states under a political and security framework. This subregional framework was spurred by a collective quest for security and development in the face of common external and internal challenges. The outcome was the first viable regional organization in the history of Southeast Asia: ASEAN. On the other hand, regionalism reflected, and contributed to, the ideological polarization of Southeast Asia. The latter, in turn, generated an intense and wide-ranging pattern of regional conflict that engulfed the region for much of the 1970s and 1980s.

ASA and Maphilindo

At the beginning of the 1960s, the prospects for a viable regional organization in Southeast Asia looked bleak. Referring to Southeast Asia as the "Balkans of Asia", the American scholar Albert Ravenholt observed that "increasingly, these eight newly-independent nations [Singapore was yet to be separated from Malaysia] and Thailand are drifting into the grip of petty nationalisms and jealousies, complete with border disputes and rivalries among their leaders".[1] Moreover, the continued dependence of regional countries on extraregional powers for protection against internal as well as external threats also served to undermine early attempts at regional organization. The strong security links of Thailand and the Philippines with the United States, and that of Malaysia and Singapore with Britain, made the idea of regional cooperation less urgent.[2] The membership of the Philippines and Thailand in the Southeast Asia Treaty Organization (SEATO) also created a schism in strategic perspectives between these two states and Indonesia, which had been a strong advocate of non-alignment and which, even with the advent of a pro-Western regime, opposed any security role for outside powers in the region.

Against this backdrop, the establishment of the Association of Southeast Asia (ASA) in 1961, with the membership of Malaya, Thailand and the Philippines, was an unlikely development. The idea of ASA was initially proposed by Tunku Abdul Rahman soon after Malaya became independent in 1957. Rahman envisaged a regional grouping to fight communist subversion by targeting what he deduced to be its major cause: poverty. At a meeting with Philippine President Garcia in January 1959, the two had agreed on a Southeast Asian Friendship and Economic Treaty as the core of a regional association. The objectives of the proposed group, as revealed in portions of the Tunku's message to Sukarno, dated 28 October 1959, were:

to encourage closer relations among the countries of Southeast Asia by discussion, conferences, or consultation, and to achieve agreement freely. It is hoped by this method that countries will be able to understand each other more deeply. It is also the objective of this association to study ways and means of helping one another — particularly in economic, social, and cultural and scientific fields.... You will understand that because of historical circumstances, the economic growth of most of the countries in Southeast Asia in this century has been influenced by relations with countries outside the region. Because of this, the feeling of "one region" has been stunted, ... and because of these historical circumstances, we have looked for help and examples from the outside and seldom look to ourselves ...[3]

The Tunku's idea received support from the then Thai Foreign Minister Thanat Khoman, who wanted a broad, inclusive grouping with the exception of North Vietnam. The Thais also prepared a "Preliminary Working Paper on Cooperation in Southeast Asia",[4] which emphasized the need for an organization with minimal administrative machinery. Although the Tunku attempted to convince other regional leaders of his idea, Indonesia remained suspicious of the organization, viewing it as a front for SEATO. Though the idea of a broader grouping failed, ASA was set up with the three members in 1961.

ASA's goals were modest. In the economic arena, it agreed to consider streamlining customs procedures and administration in each member country, to exchange information on imports and exports of manufactured goods in each country, and to consider the possibility of creating and developing wider intraregional markets for the export commodities of ASA countries. Another stated objective, classified under social and cultural cooperation, was the "promotion of Southeast Asian studies".[5]

The Tunku described ASA as "an alliance of three friendly countries formed to build a happy region in South-East Asia".[6] The purpose of ASA was to "show the world that peoples of Asia can think and plan for themselves".[7] Of all the ASA members, it was the Tunku who focused most on the issue of regional identity:

In the past — and this is one of the faults of our history — the countries of South-East Asia have been very individualist, very prone to go different ways and very disinclined to co-operate with each other. In fact, those with more rather tended to look down on others with less, there was no desire to try and help one another.[8]

Replying to critics of ASA, including some of the neighbouring states in Southeast Asia, the Tunku stated:

They [the critics] do not believe, as we do, that ASA is a practical idea of benefit to all. They say it is all up in the air, just so much talk and no substance. This is the sort of attitude some neighbours appear to adopt. This is a regional defect, a failure to realise the importance of regional co-operation. There is no reason at all why this state of affairs should continue. Whatever others may think, we three nations are determined to work closely together for the common good of all.[9]

Malaysia's approach to ASA provides a clear illustration of a mutually reinforcing relationship between nationalism and regionalism. Under the Tunku's stewardship, ASA reflected Malaysia's quest to use regionalism as a means of advancing its nationalist agenda. The idea of such a regional association had been conceived even when the Tunku was leading Malaya's transition to independence in the late 1950s. At this time, joining a regional association with countries that had already emerged as nation-states was a means of securing legitimacy for the Malaysian nation. It was also useful in mitigating opposition to the Malaysian concept and thwarting territorial claims on the Malaysian states from neighbours such as Indonesia and the Philippines.

The Philippines seemed more interested in the practical aspects of regional cooperation. Its Vice-President and Secretary of Foreign Affairs, Emmanuel Pelaez, saw the rationale for ASA as lying in the fact that "we are entering an era of international regional cooperation which, as the experiences of other countries have already shown, opens the door to faster and greater economic progress." ASA, he contended, would help its members to achieve "better work opportunities and greater income", while at the same time "meeting the increasing challenge of economic blocs from other parts of the world". For this reason, he called for ASA to "fully explore and exploit the possibilities and potentialities of greater intra-regional trade".[10]

Despite being an association of Southeast Asia, ASA's proponents saw themselves as part of a larger Asian cultural, political and economic context. For the Thai Foreign Minister and key architect of ASA, Thanat Khoman, ASA was rooted in "Asian culture and traditions". Describing ASA as an example of "Asian mutual co-operation", he argued: "For Asian solidarity must be and will be forged by Asian hands and the fact that our three countries: the Federation of Malaya, the Philippines, and Thailand, have joined hands in accomplishing this far-reaching task cannot be a mere coincidence."[11] While ASA considered the possibility of establishing a "Southeast Asian Voting Group" in the IMF and World

Bank, the "Asian" rather than "Southeast Asian" context of ASA was further reflected in its proposal for an "Organization for Asian Economic Cooperation". Moreover, ASA remained open to the membership of countries that would later be excluded from ASEAN. As one study of the grouping put it, "ASA has demonstrated that it is not inward-looking in nature by its declared willingness to include other Asian countries" including India, Ceylon and Pakistan.[12]

Khoman described the process of ASA as "practical cooperation" rather than political cooperation. But the political nature of ASA was evident in his call for regional self-reliance. In his view, ASA reflected a faith "in our capability to shape and direct for ourselves the future destiny of our nations".[13] Moreover, ASA was clearly anti-communist in orientation, despite being a non-political group. The Malaysian Foreign Minister in 1963 stated that the members of ASA were determined to "make a success of this organization" because ASA's commitment to improve the "lives of our peoples" was "the best possible way of preventing the communists from trying to destroy the lives and souls of our nations".[14]

Certainly, Sukarno had no doubts about ASA's political nature. The fact that its members were all pro-Western, with Thailand and the Philippines having defence treaties with the United States and Malaysia with Britain, was sufficient to provoke his opposition, even though ASA did not have an explicit security focus. Indonesia criticized ASA as a "Western-inspired", anti-communist bloc.[15] ASA soon joined as an object of Indonesian ire the proposed Malaysian Federation, which also sparked opposition from the Philippines. The latter laid claim to the formerly British-controlled territory of North Borneo (Sabah) in June 1962, challenging its decision to join the Malaysian Federation. This and Indonesia's armed campaign to "crush" the newly independent Malaysian state spelled doom for ASA. Despite its swift demise, ASA's creation was significant in that it was a local initiative geared to local Southeast Asian concerns. Given that earlier efforts at the Asian Relations Conferences in New Delhi and Bandung had failed to set up a permanent organization, ASA's existence, though brief, set an important precedent. Additionally, the organization did produce some diplomatic results, including Thanat Khoman's mediation between the Philippines and Malaysia. Ironically, as Bernard Gordon notes, the Sabah claim that had stood in the way of ASA had been a catalyst in Manila's interest in closer association with Indonesia, in the search for a regional grouping. This, in turn, helped the Philippines shift towards an Asian and Southeast Asian identity, thereby offsetting its image as an appendage of the United States.[16]

Manila's attitude was evident in President Diosdado Macapagal's proposal for a new group, Maphilindo, a loose confederation of the three independent states of Malay stock (Malaysia, Philippines and Indonesia). The idea of Maphilindo had been born amidst a growing crisis in the region resulting from several factors: Sukarno's nationalism, his opposition to the Malaysian Federation and the resulting policy of *Konfrontasi*, and the Philippines' claim to North Borneo. According to the "Macapagal Plan", the organization aimed to "restore and strengthen the historic unity and common heritage among the Malay peoples, and draw them to closer political, economic, and cultural relations".[17]

Maphilindo may be regarded as one of the first attempts at finding "regional solutions to regional problems", since the impetus for its creation came as a result of British refusal to discuss with Manila its claim to Sabah. That led to the hosting in Manila on 31 July 1963 of a "Summit Conference" among Sukarno, Macapagal and Tunku Abdul Rahman, where the three leaders tried to find a formula for settling the controversy arising from the impending formation of Malaysia. The formula agreed upon was Malaya's promise to seek British agreement for a UN team to determine whether the recently held elections in Sarawak and North Borneo had enabled their peoples to express a choice on joining the federation of Malaysia. The agreement ultimately failed because the Tunku, pressed by the British timetable for withdrawing sovereignty, announced that the Federation of Malaysia would become a reality on 16 September 1964, two days after the UN had said it would release the findings of its survey (which confirmed that the people of Sarawak and North Borneo had agreed to join the Malaysian Federation of their free will). This announcement was seen by Indonesia and the Philippines as unduly hasty and a breach of the agreement, and it led both countries to announce their rejection of the Malaysian Federation.

Despite its failure, Maphilindo underscored the potential uses of culture in advancing the political and strategic objectives of Southeast Asian nations. In pushing for Maphilindo, one of President Macapagal's aims was also to prevent Indonesia from falling into the communist bloc, by ensuring its integration into the "greater Malayan family".[18] Thus, a limited and culture-specific regional framework was seen as important for Philippine security objectives. Moreover, Maphilindo was important for the Philippines' own regional identification. It signalled Manila's realization that the Philippines could not live alone in the region. The U.S. defence umbrella was an important but insufficient basis for security. Regional identification was necessary.

Maphilindo was dismissed by one study as "hardly more than a slogan and sentiment".[19] But even as that, it was a forerunner of some of the key principles of ASEAN. Its three member countries pledged not to let foreign military bases on their soil be used to "subvert the national independence" of any member. This was not an outright call for the removal of foreign bases, but implied a political intent to restrict the use of British bases in Singapore and U.S. bases in the Philippines, although the Philippines may also have been seeking to preclude the establishment of Soviet bases in Indonesia. The member countries also undertook not to use "collective defense to serve the interests of any among the big powers".[20] Second, Maphilindo brought about a declaratory commitment to the principle of *musyawarah*, or consultation, as the basis for settling differences among its members. This principle would be integral to ASEAN's approach to regional cooperation.

The Establishment of ASEAN: Motivating Factors

ASEAN was created in Bangkok on 8 August 1967, with Indonesia, Malaysia, the Philippines, Singapore and Thailand as its founding members. ASEAN members have subsequently claimed that its founders had actually envisaged a regional grouping of ten countries (Brunei, Cambodia, Indonesia, Laos, Malaysia, Myanmar, the Philippines, Singapore, Thailand and Vietnam). Historical evidence suggests that assertions to this effect are misleading. The vision of Southeast Asia's regional space held by ASEAN's founders was much more uncertain than the ASEAN-10 concept suggests. ASEAN's founding statement, the Bangkok Declaration of 1967, left membership in the organization open to "all States in the South-East Asian region subscribing to the ... aims, principles, and purposes of ASEAN". But it did not provide a definite sense of where to draw the boundaries of the region itself.[21] Reinforcing this uncertainty is the fact that while signing the Bangkok Declaration, the foreign ministers of the five original members decided to "open the doors" of ASEAN to Myanmar, Cambodia, Laos, Ceylon (Sri Lanka) and both North and South Vietnam.[22] Ceylon did not take up the offer (ironically, its subsequent application to join ASEAN was rejected on the ground that it did not belong to Southeast

Asia) and, as it happened, Myanmar and Cambodia refused to join ASEAN.

The invitation to join ASEAN clashed with Sihanouk's policy of neutrality. Having broken ties with the United States and warmed up to the Chinese, Sihanouk was not about to join a grouping that he saw as patently pro-Western and anti-Chinese. Moreover, his choice on this matter was limited by the fear of upsetting Vietnam, which had already indicated its hostility towards the ASEAN concept. A visit by Adam Malik to discuss the proposed regional organization failed to persuade him, as in the case of Myanmar, which Malik also visited. The official reason for Myanmar's rejection of ASEAN was the presence of the U.S. military bases in the Philippines.[23] Like Cambodia, the Burmese Government too viewed the proposed regional organization as an anti-Chinese front. Participation in ASEAN detracted from Myanmar's non-aligned and isolationist stance in international affairs, as articulated by strongman Ne Win in his highly idiosyncratic approach to foreign policy.[24]

The declared objectives of the association were not only to "accelerate the economic growth, social progress and cultural development in the region", but also to "promote regional peace and stability". ASEAN disavowed a security focus, but Thanat Khoman coined the term "collective political defense" to describe one of its goals.[25] The relative importance of "peace and stability" objectives in the formation of ASEAN was later stressed by Adam Malik, a founder of ASEAN:

> Although from the outset ASEAN was conceived as an organization for economic, social and cultural cooperation, and although considerations in these fields were no doubt central, it was the fact that there was a convergence in the political outlook of the five prospective member-nations, both with regard to national priority objectives as on the question of how best to secure these objectives in the emergent strategic configuration of East Asia, which provided the main stimulus to join together in ASEAN … Whether consciously or unconsciously, considerations of national and regional security also figured largely in the minds of the founders of the ASEAN.[26]

ASEAN's formation reflected several changes in the regional climate. A major impetus came from regime change in Indonesia. The downfall of President Sukarno and the advent of a new regime with vastly different priorities in domestic and foreign policy spheres created a similar political outlook among the five governments, "which had been involved in confrontation, whether as adversaries or as conciliators".[27]

The New Order regime of Soeharto in Indonesia became an enthusiastic proponent of ASEAN. Its motives were threefold. First, Jakarta saw a regional group like ASEAN as convincing proof of its final abandonment of *Konfrontasi*, which had never been very popular within the military, which wielded real power in the new regime. Second, Indonesia's new regime also saw regionalism as a vital adjunct to its national development plan, the essential part of its efforts to ensure domestic stability and establish the legitimacy of the New Order. Third, Jakarta saw ASEAN as having the potential "to serve as a forum for the expression of Indonesia's leadership in Southeast Asia", with the express approval and participation of its neighbours.[28]

This had special relevance for Singapore. While Singapore's separation from the Malaysian Federation in 1965 had left an air of considerable bitterness in bilateral relations between the two countries, its ties with Indonesia were even more problematic.[29] Feeling acutely vulnerable for its smallness, the island republic was profoundly suspicious of Indonesia's intentions towards its smaller neighbours. Even after the latter abandoned *Konfrontasi*, Singapore's relations with both Malaysia and Indonesia would be described as being marked by "an acute sense of vulnerability ... as the government of a conspicuously Chinese Republic, which was alarmed by the effusive expression of Malay blood-brotherhood which had attended the end of confrontation".[30]

Against this backdrop, developing a positive regional role for Indonesia "was a key purpose behind its neighbours' interest in ASEAN". As one Indonesian analyst puts it:

> Indonesia's membership in ASEAN would reduce the possibility of threat to their security posed by their giant neighbour ... Indonesia would appear to be placed in what amounts to a "hostage" position, albeit in a "golden cage." ... [I]t is within ASEAN that Indonesia might be provided with an opportunity to realize its ambitions, if any, to occupy a position of primacy or *primus inter pares* without recourse to a policy of confrontation ...[31]

Apart from the need to mollify the regional power, each member had its own needs for viewing ASEAN in a positive light. Singapore, in particular, could use its participation in ASEAN "to gain acceptance as being part of Southeast Asia and playing a bigger role by being able to influence other like-minded countries on issues of mutual interest".[32] Along with Indonesia and Singapore, Thailand, Malaysia and the Philippines recognized ASEAN's potential as a forum for the peaceful settlement of intraregional disputes by helping to "foster and strengthen mutual trust and understanding amongst" its members.[33] To this end, the value of ASEAN also lay in the creation of a set of norms for governing relations among the member countries. The basic norms were spelled out by the Bangkok Declaration itself, which urged members to observe also "the rule of the law" in their relationships with one another.

Another major factor contributing to ASEAN's formation was the changing pattern of great-power rivalry. Towards the end of the 1960s, the Sino-Soviet rift and competition for influence in Southeast Asia was assuming prominence over traditional Cold War patterns. The prospect of China emerging as the dominant force in the region — and, as Lee Kuan Yew was to put it later, the related prospect of Southeast Asia becoming "to her what the Caribbean is to America or Eastern Europe to the USSR"[34] — was one aspect of ASEAN members' collective apprehensions. Sino-Soviet competition — featuring both the Soviet quest for regional influence through the establishment of links in Indochina and the advancement of proposals regarding an "Asian Collective Security Arrangement" and Chinese warnings concerning Soviet "hegemonism" — made the ASEAN countries realize the need for a united response to the new form of great-power rivalry.[35] At the same time, the relaxation of tensions between the United States and the Soviet Union on the one hand and the United States and China on the other aroused a different kind of concern. ASEAN members were fearful that such great-power compromises would leave their security interests ignored or undermined. Malaysia's Prime Minister, Hussein Onn, was to put it succinctly on the eve of the Bali summit, when he noted that the big powers "can create tension in any area ... especially, when they try to settle their differences and impose their ideologies forcefully in other countries ... there is a Malay saying that when two elephants fight, the mouse deer wedged in between will suffer".[36]

It should be noted that the regionalism of Southeast Asia at this time reflected developments in regionalism in other parts of the world. The latter was marked by a shift from continental or macro-regional to micro-regional or subregional groupings. The credibility of three larger regional organizations, the Organization of American States (OAS), the Arab League and the Organization of African Unity (OAU), had eroded in the 1970s.[37] This was due to several factors, including a lack of resources and inability to deal with internal conflicts, which accounted for a large percentage of the conflicts in the developing world.[38] Nor were these organizations able to limit superpower meddling and intervention in regional affairs. Their decline gave impetus to more compact subregional frameworks for conflict mediation and management that enjoyed the benefits of greater homogeneity.[39] In the economic sphere, subregionalism was also becoming prominent during the 1960s and 1970s. Several subregional groups had emerged, seeking to emulate the European Economic Community (EEC) (later the European Union), such as the Central American Common Market and the East African Community.

But the creation of ASEAN was not simply a reflection of these global trends. It was largely the product of local circumstances. The immediate motivating factors behind ASEAN had to do, firstly, with a common desire for collective diplomatic clout against external powers. ASEAN was expected to enhance the bargaining power of its small and weak members in their dealings with the great powers. ASEAN might not enable its member states to prevent the great powers from interfering in the affairs of the region, but it could, as Prime Minister Lee Kuan Yew of Singapore pointed out, help them to "have their interests taken into consideration when the great powers make their compromises".[40] Adam Malik, the Indonesian Foreign Minister, made the same point:

> Southeast Asia is one region in which the presence and interests of most major powers converge, politically as well as physically. The frequency and intensity of policy interactions among them, as well as their dominant influence on the countries in the region, cannot but have a direct bearing on political realities. In the face of this, the smaller nations of the region have no hope of ever making any impact on this pattern of dominant influence of the big powers, unless they act collectively and until they develop the capacity to forge among themselves an area of internal cohesion, stability and common purpose.

> Thus regional cooperation within ASEAN also came to represent the conscious effort by its member countries to try to re-assert their position and contribute their own concepts and goals within the on-going process of stabilization of a new power equilibrium in the region.[41]

The establishment of ASEAN also reflected shared threat perceptions among its members. To be sure, there was limited agreement on external threats.[42] China's potential to pose a long-term security threat to Southeast Asia was viewed with considerably more seriousness by Indonesia and Malaysia than by other ASEAN partners. Thailand and Singapore, for their part, were less optimistic about Vietnam's post-war intentions towards its ASEAN neighbours than Indonesia. But the ASEAN leaders agreed more on the nature of their internal enemy and were strongly united by a "common interest in preventing radical internal political change".[43] This was partly the basis of their response to the communist victories in Indochina, which were feared for their demonstrative effect on the incipient "national liberation movements" within their own territories. Thus, the similarities of their domestic political orientation and a common fear of communist-led national liberation movements in Vietnam, Laos and Cambodia provided important glue for ASEAN.[44] In this context, an early feature of relations among the ASEAN states was joint security measures undertaken on a bilateral basis but reinforced by ASEAN's collective political and ideological concerns against communism.[45]

Bilateral cooperation to combat insurgent activity along their common border areas had already developed between Malaysia and Indonesia and between Malaysia and Thailand, even before the formation of ASEAN. The arrangement between Thailand and Malaysia had been initiated in 1959; a joint border committee was established in 1965 to oversee this effort. A similar agreement to control border movement had been signed between Indonesia and the Philippines in January 1964. And after the end of hostilities between Indonesia and Malaysia, the two countries signed an agreement in March 1967 that covered cooperation between their air, naval and land forces for the purpose of curbing communist insurgency, piracy and smuggling along their common border. The establishment of ASEAN would not only reflect the members' shared concern over domestic insurgencies, but also provide a further boost to bilateral security measures among them.

While superpower aid was in general a major factor in the ideological polarization of Southeast Asia, in the case of the pro-Western ASEAN members it also contributed to their economic growth and hence regime security, which in turn had become a fundamental basis of ASEAN's approach to regional order.[46] In this context, the Vietnam War helped the economies of the ASEAN members in the 1960s and 1970s. The case of Thailand and Singapore is particularly illustrative. The United States had begun to funnel aid into Thailand from the mid-1950s onwards and, as the Vietnam War gathered momentum in the 1960s, that aid increased. By 1975 the United States had spent nearly $3.5 billion in military and economic aid to Thailand.[47] The economic infrastructure was greatly improved, especially the highway system and key ports and airports, and the Thai bureaucracy, which had a long tradition of being at the centre of power in the country, was expanded and strengthened.[48]

The war helped Singapore, which had separated from Malaysia to become an independent state in 1965. It became the regional petroleum-refining centre, providing petroleum products for the U.S. military campaign in Indochina. Its traditional entrepôt trade rapidly increased as U.S. spending generated greater regional prosperity. Singapore also became a destination for the U.S. servicemen on leave in the region. The income generated for the Singapore economy by these developments helped the government to put in place its economic and social infrastructure programmes and to pursue an export-oriented development strategy.[49] Thus, while the U.S. withdrawal from Indochina encouraged regional cooperation among those who had relied on its security umbrella, U.S. wartime aid and spending helped to foster domestic economic conditions conducive to the kind of ideologically moderate and free-market-oriented regionalism that ASEAN represented. In addition, the United States, as Owen puts it, "subsidized right-wing movements throughout the region", supporting coups in Indonesia (1965) and Thailand (1976) and the imposition of martial law in the Philippines.[50] In the meantime, Chinese and Soviet aid was confined mainly to Indochina (although some failed overtures were made towards Myanmar and Indonesia, the two countries gave about US$90 million annually to North Vietnam during 1955–65 and US$400 million a year during the 1965–75 period).[51] This, while bringing the Indochinese countries closer together, sustained the ideological polarization of Southeast Asia that ASEAN itself reflected.

Finally, growing economic policy convergence also contributed to the emergence of ASEAN. The evolution of the post-war economies of ASEAN member countries had gone through three phases.[52] The first was the rehabilitation and reconstruction of primary-producing export economies created during the colonial era. This was followed by the advent of import-substitution industrialization (ISI), motivated and accompanied in many cases by economic nationalism. The third stage, export-oriented industrialization (EOI), became the dominant feature of the international political economy of Southeast Asia from the late 1970s onwards, although Singapore had been a pioneer of this strategy since the mid-1960s.

As noted in Chapter 2, by the late 1960s, Southeast Asian countries were experiencing differing economic growth rates. Singapore, Malaysia and Thailand showed the best economic performance. Indonesia from 1966 attracted growing foreign investment and began to improve education and living conditions. But the Philippines experienced economic stagnation, so much so that President Marcos imposed martial law in 1972 to regain public confidence. The economic conditions of the Indochinese countries were severely affected by war, while the socialist methods of Myanmar (the "Burmese Way to Socialism") plunged the country into prolonged and deep stagnation under the Ne Win regime.

While the differing economic predicaments and policies of Southeast Asian countries were to some degree reflected within the ASEAN grouping, it was, as Owen points out, "not the differences of policy within this bloc that are striking, but the broad similarities".[53] While in the 1950s nationalism might have aggravated economic competition, by the 1960s and 1970s a certain amount of homogenization was taking place among the capitalist countries of the region. These economies had begun from a similar position of "uneven development, limited national integration and plural societies".[54] More importantly, they had reacted to this predicament in similar ways. All had emphasized rapid urban industrial development and maintained a relatively high degree of openness to the world economy. Consequently, through institutions such as the World Bank and the IMF, these economies were also highly receptive to ideas about economic liberalization and export-led development. Moreover, the lack of adequate indigenous capital that characterized the capitalist economies of the region led them to seek and forge close alliances between the state, foreign corporations and domestic capitalists. This created a common pattern of economic development.

In the 1960s, the ISI strategies pursued by the Philippines, Thailand and Malaysia were producing less encouraging results. Indonesia, where these strategies were still in the early stages of implementation, was an exception. But structural changes in the global economy would offer new incentives to the ASEAN countries to shift towards export-led development strategies.[55]

As the ASEAN members began to pursue similar development strategies, there emerged a certain ideological commonality among them that provided an important political foundation for ASEAN. With the war in Indochina having prompted its members to focus on economic growth within the free-market model, Ghazali Shafie of Malaysia would proclaim that:

> The concept of free enterprise as they apply [sic] in the ASEAN region is the philosophical basis of ASEAN. The appreciation of this is vital in the understanding of ASEAN and its sense of direction. The countries of the ASEAN region had come together to protect the system of free

enterprise as a counterpoise against communism on the one hand and monopolistic capitalism on the other ... When the leaders of Malaysia, Indonesia, Philippines, Singapore and Thailand got together in Bangkok in 1967 to officiate at the establishment of the Association of Southeast Asian Nations, they were in fact making a commitment to jointly strengthen and promote the system of free enterprise in their countries in the belief that together they could harness the strength of the system to bring about the kind of national and regional resilience that would serve as a bulwark against communism.[56]

The leaders of ASEAN countries recognized that the root causes of communism lay in domestic economic and social conditions. The most serious of these conditions were poverty and social inequality, then endemic features of all ASEAN societies.[57] As such, the long-term answer to the communist threat lay not in its military suppression but in the achievement of rapid economic development, which could diffuse the fundamental sources of sociopolitical discontent. As one study described it, economic growth would not only eradicate poverty but also lead to greater equity. The use of advanced technology to sustain the progress of urban industrial development would lead to the accumulation of wealth. This could then have a "trickle-down" effect, producing automatic adjustments to the distribution of wealth in society as a whole. Thus:

> Development strategies generally chosen and implemented by non-Communist Southeast Asian governments are aimed at bringing about rapid economic growth with focus on urban-based industrial promotion and utilization of advanced technology in an environment of free enterprise. The underlying assumption is that sooner or later there will be 'trickle-down' effects and any maladjustments in terms of distribution will automatically be corrected. In that eventuality equity in terms of equal shares will not be achieved, but everyone's demands and requirements will be 'satisfied' and there will be further incentive to work for another round of growth and trickle-down effects.[58]

General acceptance of these ideas, coupled with persistent concern over the common internal enemy, fostered a common understanding of how to promote regional economic security. While rejecting a military role for ASEAN, its members hoped that political cooperation would create an atmosphere of stability, which in turn would facilitate economic growth. As Carlos Romulo, the Foreign Minister of the Philippines, put it:

> The main enemy we have is subversion, and the only way to counteract subversion is to improve the lot of the masses, to give them social justice,

to have economic development. That is why the main thrust of ASEAN is economic development.[59]

In stressing the importance of economic regionalism, President Marcos went as far as to speak of "estimates" made by ASEAN leaders, according to which the ASEAN countries could, by working jointly for "anywhere between five to seven years", achieve the necessary economic conditions to eliminate the threat of subversion, whereas it "could take two decades" to achieve this goal if the members were to work for such development individually.[60] At this stage, no one thought ASEAN would follow the model of West European economic integration. However, its founders believed that the Association could make a contribution to national economic development by ensuring domestic tranquillity in member states through its non-interference doctrine. Moreover, ASEAN's prospective economic security role was seen to lie not in creating regional wealth and equity through economic integration but in fostering a climate free from interstate tensions so that its members could devote their resources to national economic development. As Lee Kuan Yew put it, "each ASEAN country has to ensure sufficient economic growth and social justice that will make insurgency unattractive and unlikely to succeed."[61] In addition, by limiting the interference of members in each other's affairs, and thereby contributing to an atmosphere of stability, ASEAN could affect the flow of foreign investment into the region, which in turn was viewed as the key to fostering rapid economic growth.

Dimensions of ASEAN Regionalism

The new regional organization in Southeast Asia almost suffered a hasty demise because of a sudden escalation of the Sabah dispute. Just as it had in the case of ASA and Maphilindo, the Philippines' claim to Sabah threatened the early years of ASEAN's development. Between April 1968 and December 1969, relations between Malaysia and the Philippines worsened considerably over the issue, although Sabah was now firmly within the Malaysian Federation. Though the dispute dated back to 1961, the bilateral crisis was renewed because of reports in the Manila press in March 1968 that a secret army was being trained on the island of Corregidor in preparation for an impending invasion of Sabah. While the government of the Philippines denied its involvement in any such plan, its reaction to the so-called "Corregidor affair" showed a renewed pursuit of its claim on Sabah. The affair not only plunged Manila's relationship with Kuala Lumpur into crisis but also threatened the very survival of ASEAN, barely six months after its creation in August 1967.

At first, other ASEAN members carefully avoided publicly voicing any views on the dispute that might be construed by the disputants as an indication of partiality. Their neutrality deprived Manila of the kind of international diplomatic support it needed to pursue its claim effectively. It might also have discouraged further action by President Marcos in escalating the dispute.

Although Thailand and Indonesia offered their good offices in urging the two sides to reach a negotiated settlement, both shied away from directly mediating in the dispute. Initially, the other ASEAN members tried to keep the Sabah issue separate from ASEAN, hoping that this would limit the dispute's damaging effects on the fledgling organization. But as bilateral talks in June 1967 between Malaysia and the Philippines failed, followed by the severance of their diplomatic relations and Malaysia's refusal to take part in any further ASEAN meetings where the Philippines might raise the Sabah issue, the link between ASEAN and the Sabah dispute could no longer be avoided.

In a bid to contain the crisis, ASEAN foreign ministers met in Jakarta in August and in Bangkok in December 1968 to persuade the two sides to minimize their public airing of the dispute and accept a "cooling off period". Statements by Thailand and Indonesia urged restraint on both sides for the sake of ASEAN. Until their suspension, various ASEAN ad hoc and standing committees provided crucial channels of communication between the two sides when no others existed. In March 1969, Manila agreed not to raise the Sabah issue at future ASEAN meetings, thereby indicating a new flexibility and meeting a key Malaysian demand. It was an ASEAN committee meeting in Indonesia in May 1969 that brought the two countries together for the first time in eight months (excluding the ad hoc December 1968 foreign ministers' meeting). The softening of Manila's stand was partly due to the ASEAN factor, since the prior suspension of all ASEAN meetings had deprived Manila of a major channel through which to pursue its claim and threatened its relations with the other ASEAN members — Indonesia, Thailand and Singapore.

At an ASEAN Foreign Ministers' Meeting in December 1969, Malaysia and the Philippines agreed to resume diplomatic relations, thereby effectively putting the issue on the back burner. The episode gave ASEAN a new sense of confidence and purpose. The avoidance of any further escalation of the Sabah dispute was all the more significant because it took place at a time when the degree of economic interdependence within the region was not significant enough to act as an incentive against interstate tensions. In the words of the joint communiqué of the December ASEAN Foreign Ministers' Meeting, the resumption of diplomatic ties was possible "because of the great value Malaysia and the Philippines placed on ASEAN".

To be sure, ASEAN did not and could not *resolve* the Sabah dispute, which continued to elude a decisive settlement. Nor did ASEAN play the role of conflict mediator or manager in a formal and legalistic sense. But ASEAN members, through direct and indirect measures of restraint, pressure, diplomacy, communication and trade-offs, did succeed in preventing any further escalation of the crisis that might have led to armed hostilities and destroyed the organization.[62]

After surviving the intramural dispute over Sabah, ASEAN faced the challenge of responding to the changing pattern of great-power rivalry in the region. The first major initiative considered by the association was a Malaysian proposal for the neutralization of Southeast Asia. This proposal reflected Malaysia's disenchantment with external security guarantees, aggravated by the British withdrawal. The implementation of neutralization required reciprocal obligations on regional countries as well as those external powers that were to guarantee the neutral status of the region. The former were required to abstain from military alliances with the great powers and prevent the establishment of foreign military bases on their soil, while the latter were asked to "refrain from forging alliances with the neutralised states, stationing armed forces on their territory, and using their presence to subvert or interfere in any other way with other countries".[63]

But the neutralization proposal ran counter to Indonesia's foreign policy beliefs. Because neutralization was to be secured through guarantees from the major powers, Jakarta saw it as giving the latter an undue say in the maintenance of regional order. Indonesia's reservations led to the neutralization proposal being revised. The new framework, known as the Zone of Peace, Freedom and Neutrality (ZOPFAN) in Southeast Asia and adopted by the foreign ministers of ASEAN countries in Kuala Lumpur in November 1971, gave greater emphasis to Indonesia's preferred approach, in which the regional countries themselves would have principal responsibility for ensuring regional security. No guarantees from outside powers were to be sought. The ZOPFAN concept also emphasized the need for regional countries to "respect one another's sovereignty and territorial integrity, and not participate in activities likely to directly or indirectly threaten the security of another".[64]

ZOPFAN also encouraged ASEAN members to stay away from alliances with foreign powers, refrain from inviting or giving consent to intervention by external powers in the domestic affairs of the regional states, abstain from involvement in any conflict of powers outside the zone, and ensure the eventual removal of foreign military bases in the territory of zonal states.[65]

But the implementation of the ZOPFAN concept was plagued by intramural disagreements. The view of Thailand, Singapore and the Philippines regarding the need for a U.S. presence in the region was at variance with the professed principles and objectives of ZOPFAN, which were strongly espoused by Indonesia and Malaysia. Singapore warned that the ZOPFAN concept made the continuation of the U.S. presence all the more necessary, since there was no certainty that all the other great powers would abide by the restraints placed upon their geopolitical behaviour by ZOPFAN. As Lee Kuan Yew put it, "in the event of one or more great powers not respecting, it may be useful that there would be some [U.S.] naval and air base facilities so that some balance can be maintained".[66]

Apart from the difficulties encountered in securing the implementation of ZOPFAN, ASEAN also faced problems in moving towards greater security and defence cooperation. The U.S. withdrawal from Indochina and the communist takeover of South Vietnam, Cambodia and Laos provided the impetus for the historic first ASEAN summit in Bali in February 1976, which in turn gave ASEAN's latent security objectives their most serious public expression. On the eve of the Bali summit, the threat of insurgency and subversion had pushed the ASEAN members towards regular exchanges of intelligence, both on a bilateral and multilateral basis. In the course of preparations for the first ASEAN summit, there were indications that sections within the Indonesian leadership were willing to propose multilateral defence cooperation within ASEAN. An Indonesian study paper circulated prior to the summit was believed to have suggested the formation of a "joint council" for defence cooperation and holding joint military exercises among the ASEAN states.[67] However, deliberations over security issues at the pre-summit meeting of ASEAN foreign ministers in Pattaya indicated, as Carlos Romulo put it, "a general view ... that security considerations should not be institutionalised on an ASEAN basis". At the Pattaya meeting, "complete agreement was reached on the desirability of continued" bilateral cooperation, "some of which ante-date the association".[68]

The Bali summit confirmed ASEAN's rejection of a military pact. The Prime Minister of Malaysia, Hussein Onn, stated just after the Bali summit:

> It is obvious that the ASEAN members do not wish to change the character of ASEAN from a socio-economic organisation into a security alliance as this would only create misunderstanding in the region and undermine the positive achievements of ASEAN in promoting peace and stability through co-operation in the socio-economic and related fields.[69]

In the Declaration of ASEAN Concord signed at the Bali summit, the ASEAN leaders expressed their approval of the "continuation of cooperation on a non-ASEAN basis between the member states in security matters in accordance with their mutual needs and interests", a clear reference to the border and intelligence cooperation arrangements that had already developed among ASEAN states on a bilateral basis. While ASEAN states did not fully agree on the role of great powers in their security environment, and while progress towards ZOPFAN was decidedly slow, they were united in asserting the need for self-reliance in countering their domestic security problems. Moreover, through collective diplomatic efforts, they hoped to reduce, if not eliminate, their dependence on external security guarantees.

At Bali, ASEAN stressed the need to manage great-power competition and intervention through the ZOPFAN framework, which would render the external security links of individual members somewhat non-provocative (to adversaries such as Vietnam and China). The Treaty of Amity and Cooperation signed at the Bali summit outlined the norms that were to form the basis of ASEAN's code of interstate behaviour. These norms included: (1) "Mutual respect for the independence, sovereignty, territorial integrity of all nations"; (2) "The right of every state to lead its national existence free from external interference, subversion and coercion"; (3) "Non-interference in the internal affairs of one another"; (4) "Settlement of differences and disputes by peaceful means"; and (5) "Renunciation of the threat of use of force".[70]

In the aftermath of the Bali summit, ASEAN policy-makers continued to reject the idea of multilateral security and defence cooperation. At the annual ASEAN foreign ministers' conference in Singapore in July 1977, the representatives from Malaysia and Indonesia issued a joint statement proclaiming that the main threat to the region was the possibility of increased subversive activities that could be handled on a national and bilateral basis.[71] The Thai Foreign Minister declared that military alliances were "obsolete" and stressed that ASEAN had "nothing to do with military cooperation".[72] This position was reaffirmed at the Kuala Lumpur summit held later that year, where the leaders were believed to have consulted closely on the threat posed by subversive activities, but rejected any change to ASEAN's position on, and preference for, security bilateralism.[73] Bilateral cooperation against border insurgencies that had developed between Malaysia and Indonesia and between Malaysia and Thailand was considered to be an acceptable model for security cooperation and sufficient to deal with the threat at hand.

These arrangements had increased in scope after the formation of ASEAN. In 1969, Malaysia and Thailand announced an agreement permitting "hot pursuit" of insurgents by the security forces of both sides into each other's territory. While joint operations were initially carried out by police, from 1970 onwards regular troops were deployed alongside the police. Similar joint operations against communist insurgents along the Kalimantan border were conducted in 1971 by Indonesia and Malaysia.

ASEAN's rejection of multilateral defence cooperation was largely motivated by a desire to prevent comparisons with SEATO. This was especially important in view of Vietnam's increasingly shrill accusations at the time that "ASEAN will become another SEATO and Japan and the U.S. may use ASEAN as an organisation to expand their influence in Southeast Asia …"[74] Indonesia, which prided itself as the only genuinely non-aligned country in ASEAN, opposed any ASEAN military pact that smacked of dependence on Western security guarantees. As Adam Malik put it, "Pacts are of no value and don't really add strength to a region."[75] Carlos Romulo, the Foreign Minister of the Philippines, agreed with this view: "We did not phase out SEATO in order to set up another one."[76] A military role for ASEAN was deemed both unnecessary and inappropriate, as the ASEAN states were concerned primarily with security issues within their own borders that could be best dealt with through non-military means.

ASEAN was more open to multilateral economic cooperation. But two Asia-wide multilateral economic institutions were already in existence. These were the Economic and Social Commission for Asia and the Pacific (ESCAP) and the Asian Development Bank (set up in 1966).[77] They provided concepts and resources for the development efforts of ASEAN members within the framework of global financial institutions. Prospects for economic cooperation within the ASEAN framework had to be seen in the context of a number of similarities and differences among the members. First, in terms of the level of development, ASEAN members remained a diverse lot. According to a 1975 World Bank report, the Philippines and Thailand were classified as "very poor" (with a per capita GNP of less than $520), while Indonesia was among the "poorest" nations (with a per capita GNP of less than $265). Singapore and Malaysia were well above these categories, with per capita GNPs of $2,450 and $760 respectively. But in terms of growth rates, the ASEAN economies could all be classified as middle-income, less developed economies. During the 1960–70 period, the real growth rate in Indonesia averaged 3.9 per cent, in Malaysia 5.8 per cent, the Philippines 5.1 per cent, Singapore 9.4 per cent and Thailand 8 per cent. The average annual growth rate for all five countries was estimated at 5.6 per cent. The growth rates for the 1970–77 period were more impressive: Indonesia 7.7 per cent, Malaysia 7.5 per cent, the Philippines 6.2 per cent, Singapore 8.9 per cent and Thailand 6.6 per cent, for a total ASEAN average of 7.1 per cent.[78]

As noted in the previous chapter, ASEAN members differed in terms of their openness to foreign investment. During the 1971–77 period, Singapore and Malaysia were the most accessible to FDI. In the Philippines, the low level of FDI reflected the strength of economic nationalism. In Thailand, political uncertainty and instability, as well as the communist victories in Indochina, accounted for a declining level of FDI. For example, during 1976, the ratio of FDI to total capital in Indonesia was 0.17 per cent (this may not reflect the trend for the 1971–77 period, because the figure was 0.32 in 1971 and 0.74 in 1975); in Malaysia it was 0.69 per cent; the Philippines 0.11 per cent; Singapore 0.77 per cent; and Thailand 0.15 per cent (down from 0.41 in 1971).[79]

With the exception of Singapore, primary commodities accounted for the larger share of the exports of ASEAN members, reflecting the colonial pattern of development despite policies to change the export structure. But, for all ASEAN economies, foreign trade formed a major part of national economic activities. The ratio of foreign trade to GDP in Malaysia was over 90 per cent during each of the three years 1974, 1975 and 1976. The figure for Indonesia ranged from 31 per cent in 1971 to 50 per cent in 1974. Indonesia's ratio hit 50 per cent in 1974 and was never less than 31 per cent (1971). For the Philippines, the ratio was

38 per cent in 1971 and 42 per cent in 1976, with a peak of 48 per cent in 1974. For Thailand, the ratio was 38 per cent in 1971 and 45 per cent in 1976, with a peak of 48 per cent in 1974.[80]

By the early and mid-1970s, ASEAN members had emerged as middle-level developing economies with rapid growth rates. All were highly export-dependent and their fortunes were therefore closely linked to the international economic situation. At the same time, their economies were competitive rather than complementary, thereby rendering the common dependence on foreign trade a divisive factor as each country turned away from the region to external trading partners and sought separate bilateral trade and economic ties. This meant low levels of intra-ASEAN trade. Indeed, total intra-ASEAN trade in 1975 was estimated at 15 per cent of the total trade of its five members.[81]

Against this backdrop, ASEAN's initial efforts at economic cooperation involved a modest programme of trade liberalization. This was centred on the scheme called the ASEAN Preferential Trading Arrangements (PTA), with a basic agreement signed in 1977. The PTA provided for a number of measures to liberalize and increase intra-ASEAN trade, including long-term quantity contracts, liberalization of non-tariff measures on a preferential basis, exchange of tariff preferences, preferential terms for financing of imports, and preference for ASEAN products in procurement by government bodies. Yet the impact of the PTA remained limited, even though intra-ASEAN trade as a proportion of total ASEAN trade rose from 13.5 per cent in 1973 to a peak of 20 per cent in 1983 (it fell to 16 per cent in 1985). Much of the total intra-ASEAN trade volume would be accounted for by bilateral trade between Singapore and Malaysia and between Malaysia and Indonesia. In addition, about 65 per cent of intra-ASEAN trade was fuel trade (mineral fuels, lubricants and related materials).[82] Thus, the increase in intra-ASEAN trade in the early 1980s was due largely to the increase in fuel prices rather than to increased trade in industrial products.

ASEAN's avoidance of EU-style regional economic integration had much to do with the national development strategies of its members. Heavily dependent on access to international capital and markets, the ASEAN states were wary of the harmful effects of inward-looking regional integration approaches. The perceived dangers of such integration were highlighted in a 1980s report on ASEAN economic cooperation:

> ASEAN countries owe their economic prosperity to trade and investment links with the outside world. Measures in the name of regional integration

that discriminate against more efficient producers can undermine this. ASEAN must continue to maintain its outward-looking orientation and remain competitive in world markets.[83]

To this end, ASEAN's economic cooperation was geared towards expanding and maintaining access to international markets and capital. Its role in collective external bargaining took precedence over the goal of intraregional trade liberalization. Beginning in the early 1970s, the collective external bargaining role of ASEAN included negotiating favourable commodity prices.[84] A major example was bargaining with Japan over natural rubber. Japan had been accused of producing and dumping synthetic rubber in the international market, thereby undercutting ASEAN producers of natural rubber. ASEAN's efforts were successful in winning major concessions from Japan. Another aim of collective bargaining was to secure greater market access for ASEAN products. The highlight of this effort was ASEAN's success in expanding the coverage of its exports in the EC's generalized system of preferences. Finally, ASEAN sought to develop a united position at multilateral trade negotiations, starting with the coordination of positions at the Tokyo Round of the GATT talks. This was followed by similar coordination at the Uruguay Round, which as will be seen in the Chapter 5, played an important part in ASEAN's growing attention to economic regionalism.[85]

Conclusion

Some Southeast Asian scholars have discerned important similarities between nation-building and region-building in Southeast Asia. "The search for national solidarity and unity", writes the Filipino Alejandro Melchor, "… is replicated, albeit on a broader scale and less urgent, but equally persistent, in the relations among nations of Southeast Asia".[86] Later, Russell Fifield, an American observer investigating Southeast Asia's claim to be a region, pointed out that the development and acceptance of the regional concept of Southeast Asia was akin to the development of nationalism, especially in the way Benedict Anderson had studied the process. Anderson had argued that the idea of nationalism was, among other things, "learned" by the indigenous elite while receiving their education in the West.[87] Fifield found that, like concepts such as nationalism, Marxism and social humanism, the idea of regionalism was "brought to Southeast Asia by the indigenous upper class", who often received their education in the capitals of the colonial powers.[88]

In this context, one may note the essentially elite-driven nature of ASEAN regionalism. Moreover, like nationalism, ASEAN regionalism came to represent an imagined community underpinned by its own organizing myths and principles. From the very outset, its leaders recognized the importance of regional identity-building. While the first ASEAN declaration (the Bangkok Declaration of 1967) had assured its members that the grouping would "preserve their national identities", S. Rajaratnam, then Foreign Minister of Singapore and a founding figure of ASEAN, argued that this objective should be reconciled with the development of a "regional existence". In his view, the success of ASEAN depended on "a new way of thinking about our problems". Since ASEAN member states had been used to viewing (intramural) problems from the perspective of their national interests or existence, the shift to a "regional existence means painful adjustments to those practices and thinking in our respective countries".[89]

The leaders of ASEAN also saw their organization as a framework for providing "regional solutions to regional problems". This hope was articulated by Adam Malik, then Foreign Minister of Indonesia and another founding figure of ASEAN, in 1975. As Malik put it:

> Regional problems, i.e. those having a direct bearing upon the region concerned, should be accepted as being of primary concern to that region itself. Mutual consultations and cooperation among the countries of the region in facing these problems may ... lead to the point where the views of the region are accorded the primacy they deserve in the search for solution.[90]

This quest for regional autonomy was initially shaped by a concern, prevalent in the Cold War milieu, that regional conflicts not managed at the regional level would invite intervention by outside powers, which in turn would aggravate existing intraregional tensions and polarization. To this end, ASEAN regionalism championed the principles of mutual non-interference, non-intervention and non-use of force. Through ZOPFAN, ASEAN emphasized its concern over the danger of great-power rivalry and the need for greater security self-reliance as the basis of a common regional identity.

Yet, the identity-building process undertaken by ASEAN was rudely and severely jolted by developments in Southeast Asia's international relations towards the end of the 1970s. Vietnam's invasion of Cambodia marked an end to prospects for a single Southeast Asian regional entity based on an inclusive form of regionalism. The ensuing ASEAN-Indochina rivalry, featuring ASEAN's campaign to drive Vietnam out of Cambodia, led to further polarization of Southeast Asia — a division that would persist through the 1980s.

NOTES

[1] Albert Ravenholt, *Maphilindo: Dream or Achievable Reality,* American University Field Staff Reports, Southeast Asia Series 7, no. 1 (1964), p. 2.

[2] Arnfinn Jorgensen-Dahl, *Regional Organization and Order in Southeast Asia* (London: Macmillan, 1982), p. 229.

[3] Bernard K. Gordon, *The Dimensions of Conflict in Southeast Asia* (Englewood Cliffs, NJ: Prentice Hall, 1966), p. 170.

[4] Ibid., p. 167.

[5] Association of Southeast Asia, *Report of the Special Session of Foreign Ministers of ASA* (Kuala Lumpur/Cameron Highlands, Federation of Malaya, April 1962), p. 13.

[6] Ibid., Annex A, p. 21.

[7] Ibid., p. 22.

[8] Ibid., p. 24.

[9] Ibid.

[10] Speech before the Special Session of Foreign Ministers of ASA, Annex B, ibid., pp. 27–28.

[11] Ibid., p. 33.

[12] Hiroshi Kitamura and A.N. Bhagat, "Aspects of Regional Harmonization of National Development Plans", in *Economic Interdependence in Southeast Asia,* edited by Theodore Morgan and Nyle Spoelstra (Madison: University of Wisconsin Press, 1969), p. 53.

[13] Ibid., pp. 32–33.

[14] Cited in Evans Young, "Development Cooperation in ASEAN: Balancing Free Trade and Regional Planning", Ph.D. dissertation, University of Michigan, Ann Arbor, 1981, p. 90.

[15] Ibid., p. 91.

[16] Gordon, *Dimensions of Conflict in Southeast Asia,* p. 21.

[17] Ibid., p. 189.

[18] Ravenholt, *Maphilindo,* pp. 8–9.

[19] "Introduction", in Morgan and Spoelstra, *Economic Interdependence in Southeast Asia,* p. 10.

[20] Ibid.

[21] ASEAN, *The ASEAN Declaration* (Bangkok: Association of Southeast Asian Nations, 1967), p. 2.

[22] Ranjit Gill, *ASEAN: Coming of Age* (Singapore: Sterling Corporate Services, 1987), p. 15.

[23] Daw Than Han, "Common Vision: Burma's Regional Outlook", Occasional Paper (Washington, D.C.: Institute for the Study of Diplomacy, Georgetown University, 1988).

[24] I am grateful to Tin Maung Maung Than for offering helpful views on Myanmar's reasons for not joining ASEAN in 1967.

[25] Constance Mary Turnbull, "Regionalism and Nationalism", in *The Cambridge History of Southeast Asia*, vol. 2, *The Nineteenth and Twentieth Centuries*, edited by Nicholas Tarling (Cambridge: Cambridge University Press, 1992), p. 616.

[26] Adam Malik, "Regional Cooperation in International Politics", in *Regionalism in Southeast Asia* (Jakarta: Centre for Strategic and International Studies, 1975), pp. 161–62.

[27] Michael Leifer, *Indonesia's Foreign Policy* (London: George Allen and Unwin, 1983), p. 120.

[28] Franklin Weinstein, "Indonesia Abandons Confrontation", Interim Report Series, Modern Indonesia Project, Southeast Asia Program, Department of Asian Studies, Cornell University, 1969, pp. 87–88.

[29] Lau Teiek Soon, "The Role of Singapore in Southeast Asia", *World Review* 19, no. 3 (1980), p. 35.

[30] Leifer, *Indonesia's Foreign Policy*, p. 123.

[31] J. Soedjati Djiwandono, "The Political and Security Aspects of ASEAN: Its Principal Achievements", *Indonesian Quarterly* 11, no. 3 (1983), p. 20.

[32] Seah Chee Meow, "Singapore's Position in ASEAN Cooperation", Occasional Paper no. 38, Department of Political Science, National University of Singapore, p. 18.

[33] Statement by President Soeharto at the opening of the Seventh ASEAN Ministerial Meeting in Jakarta.

[34] Lee Kuan Yew, quoted in *Straits Times*, 11 May 1975.

[35] Thakur Phanit, "Regional Integration Attempts in Southeast Asia: A Study of ASEAN's Problems and Progress", Ph.D. dissertation, Pennsylvania State University, 1980, pp. 218–22.

[36] *Straits Times*, 7 February 1976.

[37] Ernst B. Haas, "Regime Decay: Conflict Management and International Organizations", *International Organization* 37 (1983): 189–256; and *Why We Still Need the United Nations: The Collective Management of International Conflict* (Berkeley: University of California, Institute of International Relations, 1986); M.W. Zacher, *International Conflicts and Collective Security, 1946–1977* (New York: Praeger, 1979).

176									The Making of Southeast Asia

38	Linda B. Miller, "Regional Organization and the Regulation of Internal Conflict", *World Politics* 19, no. 4 (1967): 582–600.

39	See Arnfinn Jorgensen-Dahl, *Regional Organization and Order in Southeast Asia* (London: Macmillan, 1982); M.Z. Ispahani, "Alone Together: Regional Security Arrangements in Southern Africa and the Arabian Gulf", *International Security* 8, no. 4 (1984): 152–75; E. Peterson, *The Gulf Cooperation Council: Search for Unity in a Dynamic Region* (Boulder, CO: Westview Press, 1988).

40	*Sunday Times* (Singapore), 18 March 1978.

41	Malik, "Regional Cooperation in International Politics", pp. 162–63.

42	For a comprehensive study of external threat perceptions of the ASEAN countries, see Robert O. Tilman, *Southeast Asia and the Enemy Beyond: ASEAN Perceptions of External Threats* (Boulder, CO: Westview Press, 1987).

43	Michael Leifer, "The Paradox of ASEAN: A Security Organisation Without the Structure of an Alliance", *The Round Table* 68, no. 271 (1978), p. 268.

44	M. Zarkovic, "The Revival of ASEAN", *Review of International Affairs*, 5 October 1977, pp. 29–31.

45	For discussion of these arrangements, see Ronald D. Palmer, *Building ASEAN: 20 Years of Southeast Asian Cooperation*, The Washington Papers no. 127 (New York: Praeger/Center for Strategic and International Studies, 1987), pp. 116–27; Howard M. Federspiel and K.E. Rafferty, *Prospects for Regional Military Cooperation in Southeast Asia* (McLean, VA: Research Analysis Corporation, 1969), pp. 67–69; S. Simon, "The ASEAN States: Obstacles to Security Cooperation", *Orbis* 22, no. 2 (1978): 415–34; "A New Era of Cooperation", *Asian Defence Journal*, March–April 1977, pp. 14–20; "Operation Cooperation: The Malaysian-Thai Joint Border Operations", *Asian Defence Journal*, October 1977, pp. 18–21.

46	This section draws heavily from Amitav Acharya and Richard Stubbs, "The Perils of Prosperity? Security and Economic Growth in the ASEAN Region", in *Security Issues in the Post-Cold War World*, edited by Jane Davis (London: Edward Elgar, 1995), pp. 99–112.

47	John L.S. Girling, *Thailand: Society and Politics* (Ithaca, NY: Cornell University Press, 1981), pp. 235–36. See also Economist Intelligence Unit, *The Economic Effects of the Vietnam War in East and Southeast Asia*, QER Special no. 3 (London: Economist Intelligence Unit, November 1968).

48	See Donald E. Nuechterlein, "Thailand: Another Vietnam?" *Asian Survey* 7, no. 2 (1967): 126–30; J.A. Caldwell, *American Economic Aid to Thailand* (Lexington, MA: D.C. Heath, 1974); and Robert J. Muscat, *Thailand and the United States: Development, Security, and Foreign Aid* (New York: Columbia University Press, 1990).

49	Richard Stubbs, "Geopolitics and the Political Economy of Southeast Asia", *International Journal* 44, no. 3 (1989): 517–40.

50 Norman Owen, "Economic and Social Change", in Tarling, *The Cambridge History of Southeast Asia*, vol. 2, p. 479.

51 Ibid., p. 481.

52 Ibid., p. 474.

53 Ibid.

54 Chris Dixon, *South East Asia in the World-Economy: A Regional Geography* (London: Cambridge University Press, 1991), p. 150.

55 Richard Robison, Richard Higgott, and Kevin Hewison, "Crisis in Economic Strategy in the 1980s: The Factors at Work", in *South East Asia in the 1980s: The Politics of Economic Crisis*, edited by Richard Robison, Richard Higgott and Kevin Hewison (Sydney: Allen and Unwin, 1987), pp. 1–15.

56 M. Ghazali bin Shafie, "Confrontation Leads to ASEAN", *Asian Defence Journal*, February 1982, p. 31.

57 Malaysian prime minister Hussein Onn, cited in *New Straits Times*, 5 August 1977. For a discussion of the similarities and differences in the perceptions of ASEAN leaders of the time in relation to internal threats, see Estrella David Solidum, *Towards a Southeast Asian Community* (Quezon City: University of the Philippines Press, 1974), pp. 103–10.

58 Sukhumbhand Paribatra and Chai-Anan Samudavanija, "Internal Dimensions of Regional Security in Southeast Asia", in *Regional Security in the Third World*, edited by Mohammed Ayoob (London: Croom Helm, 1986), p. 67.

59 *Straits Times*, 3 August 1977.

60 *Straits Times*, 9 July 1977.

61 *Straits Times*, 24 April 1975.

62 The discussion of ASEAN's role in the Sabah dispute draws heavily from Arnfinn Jorgensen-Dahl, *Regional Organization and Order in Southeast Asia*; T.S. Lau, "Conflict-Resolution in ASEAN: The Sabah Issue", Department of Political Science, University of Singapore, n.d.; T.S. Lau, ed., *New Directions in the International Relations of Southeast Asia* (Singapore: Singapore University Press, 1973).

63 Noordin Sopiee, "The Neutralisation of Southeast Asia", in *Asia and the Western Pacific: Towards a New International Order*, edited by Hedley Bull (Melbourne and Sydney: Thomas Nelson, 1975), p. 144.

64 M. Ghazali bin Shafie, "The Neutralisation of Southeast Asia", *Pacific Community* 3, no. 1 (1971), p. 115.

65 Heiner Hanggi, "ASEAN and the ZOPFAN Concept", Pacific Strategic Paper no. 4 (Singapore: Institute of Southeast Asian Studies, 1991), p. 25.

66 *Straits Times*, 6 February 1976.

67 Frank Frost, "The Origins and Evolution of ASEAN", *World Review* 19, no. 3 (1980), p. 10; Tim Huxley, "The ASEAN States' Defence Policies, 1975–81: Military Response to Indochina?", Working Paper no. 88 (Canberra: Australian National University, Strategic and Defence Studies Centre, 1986), p. 52. See

also *Straits Times*, 10 February 1976. An indication of Indonesia's interest in greater ASEAN military cooperation was the composition of the Indonesian delegation to the pre-summit meeting of ASEAN foreign ministers in Pattaya. It included at least four senior military and intelligence officers. Also important was the timing of a strong statement by the Indonesian foreign minister, Adam Malik, on the Chinese threat to the region. Just prior to the Pattaya meeting, Malik criticized the complacency that he sensed in the attitude of his ASEAN partners, especially Thailand, towards China. His statement was seen as an attempt to put defence and security at the top of the Bali summit agenda. See *Straits Times*, 22 December 1975; 7 February 1976; 10 February 1976; and 12 February 1976.

[68] *Straits Times*, 12 February 1976.

[69] *New Straits Times*, 1 April 1976.

[70] Tarnthong Thongswasdi, "ASEAN After the Vietnam War: Stability and Development through Regional Cooperation", Ph.D dissertation, Claremont Graduate School, 1979, p. 123.

[71] *Straits Times*, 6 July 1977.

[72] Ibid.

[73] *Manila Journal*, 21–27 August 1977.

[74] Cited in *Straits Times*, 12 February 1976.

[75] *Straits Times*, 22 August 1974.

[76] *Straits Times*, 22 December 1975.

[77] J. Walton, "Economics", in *An Introduction to Southeast Asian Studies*, edited by Mohammed Halib and Tim Huxley (London: I.B. Tauris, 1996), p. 192.

[78] Marjorie Leemhuis Suyriyamongkol, "The Politics of Economic Cooperation in the Association of Southeast Asian Nations", Ph.D dissertation, University of Illinois at Urbana-Champaign, 1982, p. 55.

[79] Ibid., p. 78.

[80] Ibid., p. 64.

[81] Ibid., p. 68.

[82] M. Hadi Soesastro, "Prospects for Pacific-Asian Regional Trade Structures", in *Regional Dynamics: Security, Political and Economic Issues in the Asia-Pacific Region*, edited by Robert Scalapino et al. (Jakarta: Centre for Strategic and International Studies, 1990), p. 391.

[83] "Summary Record: New Directions for ASEAN Economic Cooperation", in Proceedings of the Second ASEAN Roundtable, Kuala Lumpur, Institute of Strategic and International Studies, 20–21 July 1987, p. 8.

[84] Apart from trade liberalization and collective bargaining, ASEAN's economic regionalism during the 1970s included measures to promote industrial development and energy and food security. ASEAN industrial development cooperation had three main aspects. The first was ASEAN Industrial Projects, launched in 1978. These included an ammonia-urea project in Indonesia, an

urea project in Malaysia, a rock salt soda ash project in Thailand, a copper fabrication plant in the Philippines, and a Hepatitis B vaccine project in Singapore. The second was the ASEAN Industrial Complementation Scheme, the basic agreement of which was signed in June 1981. The Scheme was aimed at promoting industrial development in the region by permitting the private sector to agree in advance to industrial specialization, thereby eliminating "unnecessary competition among ASEAN countries". It provided for vertical and horizontal specialization. But the number of industrial projects suitable for component production was limited and getting ASEAN members to agree on a scheme proved to be difficult. Hence the rationale for the third element in ASEAN industrial cooperation, called the ASEAN Industrial Joint Venture (AIJV) Scheme. Launched in 1980, this scheme aimed at encouraging private sector participation in intra-ASEAN industrial cooperation. AIJV schemes required participation by only two private sector partners.

In addition, ASEAN economic cooperation included food and energy security programmes. In 1977, ASEAN members agreed to an ASEAN emergency petroleum-sharing scheme, comprising the national oil corporations of the member countries. An ASEAN Food Security Reserve System was set up in 1979 to provide mutual support in the time of emergencies as well as an early warning system for such emergencies. An ASEAN Emergency Rice Reserve of 50,000 tonnes was one offshoot of this.

See Chng Meng Kng, "ASEAN Economic Cooperation: The Current Status", *Southeast Asian Affairs 1985* (Singapore: Institute of Southeast Asian Studies, 1985), pp. 31–53; Marjorie Leemhuis Suyriyamongkol, *Politics of ASEAN Economic Co-operation* (Singapore: Oxford University Press, 1988). For a review of the main literature on ASEAN economic cooperation, see H.C. Rieger, "Regional Economic Cooperation in the Asia-Pacific Region", *Asia-Pacific Economic Literature* 3, no. 2 (1989): 5–33.

[85] For an overview of ASEAN's role in GATT, see M. Hadi Soesastro, "ASEAN's Participation in the GATT", *Indonesian Quarterly* 15, no. 1 (1987): 107–27.

[86] A. Melchor Jr., "Security Issues in Southeast Asia", in *Regionalism in Southeast Asia* (Jakarta: Centre for Strategic and International Studies, 1975), p. 46.

[87] Benedict Anderson, *Imagined Communities: Reflections on the Origin and Spread of Nationalism* (London: Verso, 1983).

[88] Russell Fifield, "'Southeast Asia' and 'ASEAN' as Regional Concepts", in *Southeast Asian Studies: Options for the Future*, edited by Ronald A. Morse (Lanham, MD: University Press of America, 1984), p. 128.

[89] Cited in C.P.F. Luhulima, *ASEAN's Security Framework*, CAPA Reports no. 22 (San Francisco: Center for Asia Pacific Affairs, The Asia Foundation, 1995), p. 1.

[90] Malik, "Regional Cooperation in International Politics", p. 160.

6

Southeast Asia Divided:
Polarization and Reconciliation

The period from 1979 to 1991 may be regarded as a distinctive phase in modern Southeast Asian history. It began with the most serious challenge to peace and stability in the region since the end of the Vietnam War — the Vietnamese invasion of Cambodia in December 1978. The ensuing crisis saw the polarization of Southeast Asia into two antagonistic political groups, one represented by ASEAN, the other by the three Indochinese states led by Vietnam. As the rivalry between the two groups intensified, ASEAN's concept of regionalism was opposed by that of Vietnam, which held Indochina to be a single strategic unit. The regional conflict in Southeast Asia reflected changes in the international security environment, especially the collapse of the superpower détente and the advent of the "second Cold War". Renewed superpower tensions fuelled the stalemate in the Cambodian conflict and were manifested in heightened U.S.-Soviet strategic rivalry, part of which was played out in the form of naval competition in the Pacific. Sino-Soviet and Sino-Vietnamese ties too plunged to new lows during the period, with China putting military pressure on Vietnam on their common border and providing military support to the

Cambodian rebels so as to impose a heavy cost on Hanoi's occupation of Cambodia.

But the crisis in regional relations was also in many respects a blessing in disguise, not only for ASEAN, but also arguably for the whole region of Southeast Asia. For it provided the ASEAN grouping with a new sense of unity and purpose, brought international recognition and support for its diplomatic and political role in finding a solution to the Third Indochina War, and strengthened the recognition among ASEAN regimes that economic development was the best guarantee of their political legitimacy and national stability. While the accelerated pace of economic liberalization and globalization in the non-communist part of Southeast Asia was due to a variety of factors, such as the southward movement of Japanese capital in the wake of the 1985 Plaza Accord and the spread of post-Fordist transnational production, it was also a response by ASEAN governments to the sense of insecurity and vulnerability in the wake of the ideological polarization of the region. In the end, what began as a period of crisis and conflict turned out to be a period of remarkable transformation in Southeast Asia's economic and strategic landscape, one that paved the way for a more united and resilient region by the early 1990s.

Vietnam and ASEAN

The U.S. withdrawal from Indochina and the communist takeover in Vietnam, Laos and Cambodia entrenched the polarization of Southeast Asia into two ideologically hostile blocs. The communist takeovers were unexpectedly swift. The Khmer Rouge was first, seizing Phnom Penh in mid-April 1975. Less than two weeks passed before Saigon fell as the result of a final attack by Hanoi. In Vientiane, the Pathet Lao took over in November 1975 as the existing coalition government collapsed and the king abdicated. From this point onwards, this intraregional divide became the principal determinant of international relations in Southeast Asia, outweighing even the traditionally decisive impact of the Cold War.

The communist takeovers in Indochina were received by the ASEAN states with a mixture of both anxiety and hope. The impact of these takeovers on regional stability had to be seen against the backdrop of the effects of the Sino-Soviet split. The Sino-U.S. rapprochement of 1972 changed the political context of Sino-Vietnamese relations. Hanoi felt betrayed by Beijing and suspected a Sino-U.S. deal at the expense of

Vietnam's interests. Despite the fact that China had provided massive support to Vietnam's war effort, it showed no interest in helping its reunification effort. Part of the reason may have been its traditional fear of a strong, united Vietnam. Cooperation among communists in the two countries dated back to the Comintern days of the early 1920s. China had helped Ho Chi Minh launch the communist organization and, until Ho's death in 1969, remained a close ally. But international developments — such as the Sino-Soviet split, changes in Sino-U.S. relations and domestic developments in Vietnam, especially reunification — changed all that.

Fears of communist domination in the region undermined hopes that had been raised by the détente at the global level. The formation and early life of ASEAN was greeted with considerable suspicion by Vietnam, despite the fact that ASEAN had carefully avoided intramural military cooperation, precisely for fear of provoking Hanoi. That the communist states in the region viewed ASEAN as a pro-Western and anti-communist front is not hard to understand. Not only were ASEAN members engaged in the suppression of communist insurgencies backed by China and the Soviet Union and maintaining security links with the Western countries, they also received substantial economic aid from the West. Vietnam saw ASEAN as a Western tool replacing SEATO but serving essentially the same function of imposing Western capitalist political and economic domination. ASEAN feared the emergence of a unified Indochinese federation under Vietnamese hegemony. To be sure, Vietnam, Cambodia and Laos proclaimed a "militant solidarity", but no political integration ensued.

There was little evidence that post-reunification Vietnam saw its destiny as lying within the Southeast Asian community of nations. Hanoi seemed to make greater efforts to project its image as a non-aligned nation within the developing world. But Hanoi during the 1976–77 period also began a diplomatic effort to underscore its independence from socialist powers. This meant distancing itself from China and identifying itself as a Southeast Asian nation. Indeed, Southeast Asia did figure in Vietnam's own perception of its place in the world; the Party leader Le Duan on 15 May 1975 proclaimed the nation's intention to turn itself "into a civilised, prosperous and powerful country, an inviolable bastion of national independence, democracy and socialism in Indochina and South East Asia".[1] During 1976–77, Hanoi began adopting a softer stance towards ASEAN, despite continuing to criticize it for its anti-communist underpinnings and the development of bilateral defence ties among its members.

As Vietnam seemed to concentrate on reunification and reconstruction, in September 1975 Premier Pham Van Dong offered an olive branch to ASEAN, declaring a commitment to peaceful reconstruction and acknowledging that this would require building good relations with other countries in Southeast Asia. He affirmed his nation's commitment to non-interference and mutual respect. After the reunified state of the Socialist Republic of Vietnam was established in July 1976, Hanoi expected normal ties and aid from the United States under the 1973 Paris Agreement. While undertaking collectivization, changing from the capitalist to the socialist mode in the south and promoting socialist ideology and culture at home, Vietnam was seeking external aid to support its economic and political programme. It joined the World Bank, IMF and ADB, and developed trade relations with India, Sweden, Singapore, Japan and Australia. During this period it seemed as though Hanoi was more interested in rebuilding its economy than in fostering the spread of communism.

But despite its conciliatory tone towards ASEAN, Hanoi's own vision of regional order clashed with that of ASEAN. Specifically, Hanoi's relations with Laos and Cambodia, both of which fell under communist rule, rekindled fears in ASEAN of Hanoi's old plan for an Indochinese federation. The Vietnamese Communist Party had begun life as the Communist Party of Indochina, with the goal of achieving power not just in Vietnam but also in the entire Indochina area. Ho Chi Minh, in his role as Comintern representative before World War II, was tasked with revolution not just in Indochina but also in the entire Southeast Asian region, and Hanoi had supported, albeit in a minor way, communist insurgencies in Malaysia, Myanmar and Thailand.[2] Although this goal had been abandoned as an immediate objective after the end of World War II (to be revived again in 1951 and abandoned reluctantly after 1954), it now seemed to be on Hanoi's foreign policy agenda.

The conception of Indochina as a region was based not just on common colonial legacy, but also ideology and geopolitics. There were several ways in which this regional concept could be achieved. An extreme form would be formal integration, which seemed remote. A different form would be a gradual move towards a loose federation in which Laos and Cambodia would retain their own ethnic governments under Vietnamese dominance. The regime in Laos was more receptive to this idea than that in Cambodia, though some sections of its leadership seemed favourably disposed for ideological and practical reasons. A realization of this idea would have meant a form of regionalism different from that represented by ASEAN. In it, Vietnam would have been the dominant power, without having to accept any norms of self-restraint towards its lesser partners; by contrast, ASEAN was based on the understanding that the leading member, Indonesia, would not seek regional hegemony and exercise restraint towards its smaller neighbours.

But Hanoi's vision of Indochina faltered amidst diverging political conditions in Laos and Cambodia. The ruling communist regime in Laos, despite its collectivization programme and re-education camps, sought to develop a more moderate version of communist rule than Vietnam by tolerating Buddhism and accepting foreign aid. While Laos' foreign policy was staunchly pro-Vietnamese, it did not want to be seen as a Vietnamese puppet. Cambodia was a different case. Under the brutal Khmer Rouge, it experienced far more domestic turmoil than Vietnam and Laos. The regime ordered the mass evacuation of the capital to the countryside and sought to bring about the rapid transformation of society and economy by forcible restructuring towards communal living. This process was accompanied by mass killings of intellectuals, peasants and former leaders; the abolishment of private property; the banning of the Buddhist church; and abolition of the use of money. Norodom Sihanouk was put under house arrest and later exiled to Beijing; a new constitution established Democratic Kampuchea in January 1976. The Party then turned upon itself to weed out disloyal elements. In total, more than a million Cambodians died. While the domestic violence continued, the Khmer Rouge pursued a much more nationalist and thus anti-Vietnamese posture. As its conflict with Vietnam escalated, it moved closer to Beijing, seeking economic and military support, thereby ensuring that Vietnam's vision of an alternative regional order centred on Indochina could be realized only by the military overthrow of the Khmer Rouge regime.

In the meantime, Hanoi's policy towards ASEAN remained ambiguous. On the one hand, it sought improvement in bilateral ties. But its support for ASEAN was more qualified. The Vietnamese Foreign Minister, Nguyen Duy Trinh, during a tour of all ASEAN member states (except Singapore) between 20 December 1977 and 12 January 1978, called for Southeast Asia to achieve "peace, independence, and neutrality", echoing ASEAN's official doctrine of "peace, freedom, and neutrality". But his deputy, Vo Dong Giang, suggested during a visit to Kuala Lumpur that

ASEAN ought to be wound up as it was "American-backed" and replaced with a new regional body that Hanoi would join.[3] Later, in June 1978, Hanoi proposed the creation of a Zone of Peace, Independence, and Neutrality, but faced with suspicion from ASEAN was willing to revert to the original term "freedom" instead of "independence". This failed to assuage the fears of some ASEAN members, such as Singapore, who suspected Soviet prodding behind Vietnam's shift.

Hanoi's hesitant wooing of ASEAN reflected its concern over the developing relationship between Cambodia and China, as Hanoi's own ties with the Khmer Rouge deteriorated. It is also noteworthy that the Khmer Rouge regime rejected regionalism. While stating that it was opposed neither to ASEAN nor to its ZOPFAN proposal, the Khmer Rouge proclaimed its intention to "avoid leaning towards or associating with any bloc or join any regional grouping".[4] By 1978, the earlier hopes created by Vietnam's peace offensive towards ASEAN had died down.

The communist victory in Vietnam was not seen by its ASEAN neighbours as a direct military threat. In fact, few ASEAN policy-makers believed that either China or Vietnam could pose a direct military threat to non-communist Southeast Asia. The threat of Chinese aggression in particular appeared remote, with the advent of the Sino-Soviet rift and the Sino-U.S. rapprochement. Vietnam after 1975 was a different story, but even in this case there were few apprehensions that Vietnamese hostility to ASEAN could take the form of a military attack. In the immediate aftermath of the fall of Saigon, and until its military intervention in Cambodia, such a possibility was hardly likely. This was not just because a war-weary Vietnam needed to pay urgent attention to the formidable task of reconstruction. To pose a military threat, Hanoi would have required strong external assistance from either China or the Soviet Union or both, and each of these powers was then seeking better ties with the United States. At a meeting of ASEAN foreign ministers in Singapore in July 1977, the then Foreign Minister of Thailand, Dr. Upadit Pachariyangkun, described the prospect of any ASEAN member being threatened by external aggression as "obsolete". Rather, "we are more preoccupied with the possibility of increased subversive activities which get aid from outside ... I am sure that there will be no external aggression, not even from North Vietnam."[5] Even in the aftermath of Vietnam's invasion of Kampuchea (the official name of Cambodia under the Khmer Rouge), the possibility of a direct Vietnamese attack on any ASEAN member was not credible for a number of reasons. Not only was Vietnam preoccupied with the pacification of Kampuchea as well as with the maintenance of its military and political presence in Laos, it also lacked any significant power projection capability. Moreover, insofar as the prospect of an attack on Thailand was concerned, Vietnam did not host a faction of exiled Thais who could be used to justify a direct military attack (as was the case with Kampuchea).[6]

Nor did the communist victories in Indochina signal an intensified Vietnamese campaign to export its communist revolution, as predicted by the "domino theory". This theory was met with considerable scepticism in ASEAN. As a Malaysian newspaper editorialized: "The domino theory is a cold-war relic. If the non-communist [Southeast Asian] states are toppled, they will almost certainly be toppled from within."[7] While the possibility of Vietnamese-backed communist subversion was noted by ASEAN leaders (who also expressed concern that weapons left by the United States in Vietnam could find their way to insurgents in their countries), they regarded the communist threat in the ASEAN context as more likely to be internally inspired. ASEAN leaders were all too aware that the communist insurgencies and subversion they were facing or might have to face in the future were rooted, first and foremost, in the internal contradictions of their societies. The origin of these insurgencies pre-dated the fall of Saigon. As noted in Chapter 2, they had established themselves internally by exploiting the nationalist campaigns against colonial and external powers.

Thus, President Marcos of the Philippines predicted that the danger from within would continue to be the main security problem for the ASEAN states.[8] He also warned that if external powers, including the superpowers, were to destabilize the ASEAN states, the only way they would succeed was by taking advantage of the internal vulnerabilities of the latter:

> [The threat of great power rivalry] ... is not an open threat of aggression. It is exploitation of internal weaknesses, and exploitation of internal contradictions — lack of economic development and / or the lack of an even spread of the benefits of economic development, leading to guerilla insurgency.[9]

Nowhere was the emphasis on internal stability in ASEAN's collective security perceptions better illustrated than in Indonesia's concepts of "national resilience" and "regional resilience", phrases that were to become something of a rallying slogan for all the ASEAN regimes. According to the Indonesian view, domestic stability in the individual ASEAN states was an indispensable prerequisite for regional security and regional collaboration. The concept of national resilience emphasized the non-military, internal dimensions of security; it was "an inward-looking concept, based on the proposition that national security lies not in military alliances or under the military umbrella of any great power, but in self-reliance deriving from domestic factors such as economic and social development, political stability and a sense of nationalism."[10] On the face of it, the emphasis on national security and nationalism would seem to go against the spirit of regionalism. But the Indonesian view was exactly the opposite; as a prominent Indonesian scholar on regional security put it: "If each member nation can accomplish an overall national development and overcome internal threats, regional resilience will automatically result much in the same way as a chain derives its overall strength from the strength of its constituent parts."[11] The underlying assumption was that, with their houses in order, ASEAN countries would find it easier to settle their disputes and devise collective plans to promote long-term stability and security in the region.

The foregoing analysis suggests that communist victories in Indochina in 1975 did not by themselves plunge Southeast Asia into intraregional turmoil and competition. Preoccupied with internal problems, both Vietnam and ASEAN entertained hopes of accommodating each other's security interests and concerns. The ASEAN members seemed prepared to live with Vietnam if Hanoi would express a commitment to regional peace and stability and accept the principle of non-interference. Indonesia and Malaysia seemed most willing to cooperate with Hanoi in developing a framework of political accommodation that might lead to the admission of the Indochinese states into ASEAN. But any hope for such an outcome was dashed by Vietnam's invasion of Cambodia in December 1978.

ASEAN and the Cambodian Conflict

Vietnam's move into Cambodia was the culmination of deteriorating relations between the two communist governments. Soon after seizing power in Phnom Penh, the Pol Pot regime not only launched a brutal domestic programme of building a rural utopia, involving the wholesale expulsion of the capital's residents to the countryside, it also carried out increasingly violent incursions into Vietnamese territory. In retaliation,

Vietnam's leadership extended support to a breakaway faction of the Khmer Rouge led by Heng Samrin and Hun Sen. Invading Vietnamese forces toppled the Pol Pot regime and installed Heng Samrin as the leader of Cambodia, thereby plunging Southeast Asia into a new crisis with profound international implications.

Vietnam tried unsuccessfully to convince the international community that what was going on in Cambodia was essentially a domestic power struggle between rival Cambodian factions, in which the genocidal Pol Pot regime had been justly overthrown by a Cambodian "salvation" front. It also hinted that its actions in support of the Heng Samrin regime were a defensive move to counter the threat of Chinese expansionism, given Beijing's strong backing for Pol Pot. Hanoi refused to accept that it was a direct party to the Cambodian conflict. The question of the withdrawal of its troops could be decided only by the Heng Samrin regime, as the sole legitimate government of Cambodia. The domestic situation in Cambodia, that is, the replacement the Pol Pot regime by Heng Samrin, was "irreversible".[12] While Vietnam was willing to discuss the security concerns of ASEAN arising from the crisis in Cambodia — proposing, among other things, the creation of a demilitarized zone on the Thai-Cambodian border to be supervised by a joint commission, and expressing willingness to sign non-aggression treaties with Thailand and other ASEAN countries — it rejected ASEAN's idea of an international conference on Cambodia, which would include all the belligerent sides. Instead, Hanoi tried to persuade Thailand to accept a limited withdrawal of its forces to be decided by Hanoi and Phnom Penh.

The Vietnamese invasion swept away any incipient idea on the part of ASEAN of developing accommodation with Hanoi. ASEAN claimed that Hanoi's move had decisively rebuffed its overtures for peaceful coexistence with communist Indochina, a condition that might have created a place for the latter within the regional grouping. Furthermore, Hanoi's move showed contempt for the cardinal principles of non-interference and non-use of force in interstate relations. Hardline elements in ASEAN argued that the invasion of Cambodia showed Hanoi's aspirations towards regional hegemony, beginning with the strategic domination of Indochina and extending into other parts of Southeast Asia through the use of subversion and intimidation. ASEAN was presented with another security challenge from Vietnam when Hanoi nationalized private trade in March 1978, severely affecting its ethnic Chinese community. This led to an exodus of ethnic Chinese, the so-called "boat people", into the ASEAN states, creating a new source of tension between ASEAN and Vietnam.

The Vietnamese invasion dashed hopes that the U.S. disengagement from Indochina would usher in an era of relative peace and stability in the Southeast Asian region. It also marked the beginning of a period of heightened great-power rivalry, with the Sino-Vietnamese confrontation aggravating the existing Sino-Soviet rivalry. Ironically, Vietnam, which had been dismissive of ASEAN's desire to limit the role of external powers in Southeast Asian security, was the main victim of renewed great-power interventionism, as it faced considerable military pressure from China. Military tensions between China and Vietnam had already escalated through their territorial dispute over the South China Sea islands, especially after Chinese forces seized the Paracels in January 1974 and began extending China's claims to the Spratly Islands, also claimed by Vietnam. But these tensions were nothing compared to the aftermath of Vietnam's invasion of Cambodia. In February 1979, China launched an attack into the northern border zone of Vietnam, ostensibly to "teach Hanoi a lesson", but the attack proved costly for Beijing. While it failed to force Vietnam's hand and produced no change in the political situation in Cambodia, it also had the effect of forcing Vietnam deeper into the Soviet orbit.

The Soviet Union had given considerable military aid to Hanoi during the last stages of the Vietnam War. Moscow, sensing Washington's China card, courted Hanoi as a counter. Its interests coincided with Vietnam's own enmity with China. The strategic relationship between the two countries had already grown closer following the December 1975 visit by Vietnam's leader Le Duan to Moscow; a bilateral economic agreement in 1976; Vietnam's incorporation into the Council for Mutual Economic Assistance (COMECON) in June 1978; and, in November that year, a twenty-five-year Treaty of Friendship and Cooperation. The fact that Vietnam had invaded Cambodia a month after signing the treaty confirmed for Beijing that Soviet hegemonism was in collusion with Vietnam. Beijing blamed the Vietnamese invasion on the massive Soviet backing for Hanoi. The presence of Vietnamese forces in Cambodia was listed by China as one of the principal obstacles to normalizing ties with Moscow in future "normalization" talks between the Soviet Union and China. China would reiterate its demand that Moscow discipline Hanoi over Cambodia as a precondition for improved relations. But little progress was achieved. As a result, Beijing continued to pursue a "counter-hegemony" platform, aimed at resisting Soviet geopolitical moves in the region. As part of this policy, Beijing continued to improve its ties with the United States, maintained strong support for ASEAN's hardline stance against Vietnam, and cultivated influence with ASEAN by extending a commitment to discontinue its support for communist insurgencies in Southeast Asia.

Apart from renewing the spectre of great-power rivalry, the Third Indochina War also raised the possibility of a wider intraregional military confrontation. The Vietnamese military presence in Cambodia and the spillover of its military raids into Thai territory led Thailand to perceive a direct military threat from the instability in Indochina. Presenting itself as a "frontline state", Thailand turned to China and the United States for military assistance. It acquired Chinese arms for the Thai military and reaffirmed the Thai-U.S. security alliance. In addition, Thailand secured assurances of military support from several ASEAN partners, such as Singapore and Malaysia, although this fell short of a formal ASEAN military alliance. Intra-ASEAN political differences and suspicions aside, ASEAN remained reluctant to develop military ties for fear of aggravating Hanoi's hostility. This in turn served to highlight ASEAN's continued dependence on external security guarantees, despite the professed goal of self-reliance in the wake of the British and U.S. withdrawals from the region.

ASEAN's immediate priority in responding to the Vietnamese invasion was to deny Vietnam a *fait accompli* in Cambodia. This meant denying recognition and legitimacy to the Heng Samrin government while mobilizing support for Pol Pot's Democratic Kampuchea (which had been overthrown by Hanoi) and ensuring Hanoi's international isolation both diplomatically and economically.[13] ASEAN focused its diplomatic energies at the UN, mobilizing the international censure of Hanoi. But ASEAN's diplomacy suffered from internal divisions, with Indonesia and Malaysia showing a greater willingness (as evidenced by the so-called Kuantan principle jointly enunciated by their leaders in March 1980) to recognize Vietnam's security interests in Indochina, if Hanoi were to reduce its strategic links with and dependence on the Soviet Union.[14] The position of Malaysia and Indonesia reflected a growing concern that the Cambodian conflict, if left unresolved, would become a grave threat to the security of all regional states. For both Jakarta and Kuala Lumpur, it was China that posed the real long-term threat to Southeast Asia; Vietnam could be a bulwark against Chinese expansionism. If ASEAN went along with China's "bleed Vietnam" policy, this would lead not only to a more entrenched Soviet-Vietnam strategic alliance, including the acquisition by the former of military bases in Cam Ranh Bay, but it would also contribute to a dangerous degree of Chinese influence in the region.[15] This view conflicted with the position of Singapore and Thailand, which saw Vietnam as the main threat to regional peace and security.

It was not only the differences within ASEAN or between ASEAN and Vietnam that undermined early attempts to find a diplomatic solution to the Third Indochina War. Sharp differences between ASEAN and China surfaced at the International Conference on Kampuchea (ICK), held under the auspices of the UN in 1981. Boycotted by Hanoi and the Soviet Union, the ICK saw a clash between China and ASEAN over how to handle the Khmer Rouge. ASEAN pushed for a formula that would ensure the total withdrawal of Vietnamese forces from Cambodia, disarm all Cambodian factions and give all factions representation in an interim government. This would prevent the return of the Khmer Rouge to power. But China, backed by the United States, rejected the ASEAN proposal on the ground that it would give the Vietnamese aggressor and the resistance factions equal status. The resulting failure of the ICK was a major blow to the Cambodian peace process, creating a diplomatic stalemate that had already taken root through the refusal of the Indochinese states to accept ASEAN's position on the conflict.

The stalemate in the Cambodian conflict was also fuelled by geopolitical rivalry among the great powers. Since the Soviet invasion of Afghanistan in December 1979, U.S.-Soviet relations had reached a new low, making dialogue difficult on resolving regional conflicts. While, in contrast to its massive support for the Afghan resistance, Washington provided no overt military assistance to the Cambodian resistance, it did encourage support from China and ASEAN for the resistance factions. The United States remained largely inactive in the Cambodian peace process, lending support to ASEAN's diplomatic efforts while at the same time siding with China's "bleed Vietnam" policy, to the discomfort of Indonesia and Malaysia.

Because China and ASEAN provided military assistance to the Cambodian resistance factions, the stalemate in the Cambodian peace process was both matched and conditioned by the stalemate on the battlefield.[16] Hanoi's failure to pacify Cambodia was amply evident by the mid-1980s. Frustrated by its inability to decimate the forces of the regime it had toppled, estimated to be some 60,000 in 1980, Hanoi succeeded only in forcing the retreat of the resistance to the Thai-Cambodian border, from where they were able to reorganize and fight back. They did this with the help of massive Chinese aid, Thai willingness to grant sanctuaries, and political and material support from the ASEAN states. The Khmer Rouge was joined by two non-communist resistance armies: the Khmer People's National Liberation Front (KPNLF) and Armee Nationale Sihanoukist (ANS). Their emergence forced Hanoi to switch to a regular pattern of cross-border, dry-season offensives into Thailand, which produced in January 1984 direct engagements between Thai and Vietnamese forces. The Vietnamese dry-season offensive during 1984–85 wiped out almost every resistance camp inside Cambodia and sent about 200,000 civilians fleeing to refugee camps in Thailand. But while damaging the resistance, Vietnam failed to destroy it. The inefficiency of the forces of the Heng Samrin regime and the creation of a resistance coalition called the Coalition Government of Democratic Kampuchea (CGDK) served to reinforce the stalemate on the battlefront. At the same time, the resistance was not capable of inflicting a military defeat on Vietnam or of toppling the Vietnamese-installed regime in Phnom Penh, thanks to internal divisions within the factions (especially the KPNLF, which had received a large chunk of the aid from ASEAN). Nonetheless, the resistance was able to thwart Hanoi's desire to consolidate the rule of the Heng Samrin regime. The stalemate was reflected in the fact that the dry season of 1987 passed without military engagements.

The polarization of Southeast Asia that accompanied the Third Indochina War was not confined to the political and strategic spheres. It was also reflected in the economic arena. The economic development policies among the region's capitalist countries, all of which belonged to ASEAN, presented a marked contrast to those in the socialist segment. With communist Indochina now excluded from trading with both the United States and ASEAN, Vietnam, despite its own poverty, played the role of regional hegemon. It developed special ties with Laos after 1975 and Cambodia after 1979, and even made interest-free loans to Laos in 1975. However, its greater size and better educational and economic facilities were not enough to underwrite such a role. Vietnam became increasingly dependent upon the USSR to supply it with several crucial import items such as oil, iron, steel, chemical fertilizers and cotton.[17]

In contrast, revolution and war in Indochina served to improve the positioning of the ASEAN economies *vis-à-vis* the world economy.

Prompted by the Vietnamese invasion of Cambodia, and subsequent fears in the region of Vietnamese expansionism, and spurred on by the United States, Japan increased its aid to the ASEAN members. For example, during the height of the Cambodian conflict from 1982 to 1986, the four largest ASEAN states — Indonesia, Malaysia, the Philippines and Thailand — together received nearly $1 billion in development assistance from the Japanese.[18] For the government of Japan, this was the best way of ensuring that a region that was increasingly vital to Japanese companies seeking lower-cost sites for producing manufacturing goods for export to the United States and Europe, and that sat astride key sea lanes linking Japan to Europe and the Middle East, was kept relatively stable. Hence, once again, security issues paved the way for the injection of capital into the ASEAN region, which in turn promoted economic growth.

In contrast to Indochina and Myanmar, the ASEAN states were committed to economic liberalization and structural change, facilitated by a conscious integration into the new international division of labour. Moreover, the Third Indochina War created a more favourable external climate for the economic development of ASEAN states. Although mostly an urban phenomenon, the progressive integration in the early 1970s of Malaysia and Thailand into the world economy enhanced their economic development prospects. In Indonesia and the Philippines, however, economic development was still stalled, though under both the Soeharto and Marcos governments internationalization programmes were instituted and economic collapse was avoided.[19] Overall, the impressive economic growth rates of the ASEAN members — at times reaching well over nine per cent per year in Thailand, Singapore and Malaysia — could be attributed in good part to the impact that security issues had on the region's economies. The Korean War, the Vietnam War and the Vietnamese occupation of Cambodia all produced much-needed external funds that helped to create greater prosperity in ASEAN countries. In addition, the communist threat helped ASEAN regimes to justify strong domestic institutions, to which their citizens were generally willing to cede considerable authority for the sake of security and stability.[20]

At the international level, the Third Indochina War became a flash-point of the "New Cold War" between the United States and the Soviet Union. That had resulted from the breakdown of the détente following the Soviet invasion of Afghanistan and what the United States perceived to be Soviet geopolitical gains throughout the Third World, including

Southeast Asia where the Soviet-Vietnamese alliance had seemed to Washington to indicate a general expansion of Soviet geopolitical interest in the region. These fears, shared by some of Washington's allies in Southeast Asia (especially Singapore) were aggravated by the buildup of the Soviet naval fleet in the Pacific. The Soviet move, which involved the acquisition of bases in Cam Ranh Bay, was seen by the pro-Western countries of the region as dramatically enhancing its power projection capabilities in Southeast Asia, posing a threat to the security of the sea lanes.[21]

The advent of the Reagan administration in 1981 saw a major intensification of U.S. measures against Soviet gains in the Third World by imposing a heavy political, economic and military burden on Moscow. Instead of providing a focus for mutual dialogue, regional conflicts such as Cambodia were cited by the administration as a major factor in the deterioration of East-West relations and as justification for a massive U.S. military modernization programme. The administration's attitude towards the Cambodian conflict was shaped by its overall policy framework towards regional conflicts, called the "Reagan Doctrine". Cambodia, which the administration held to be a direct result of Moscow's military and economic backing for Vietnam, was included among the targets of the Reagan Doctrine, which aimed to achieve a "roll-back" of Soviet geopolitical advances by supporting directly or indirectly (as in the case of Cambodia) guerilla groups resisting Soviet-backed regimes.

Despite Washington's fear of a Soviet geopolitical offensive, Moscow's influence in Southeast Asia remained quite limited. Moscow had earlier courted the region with a plan for a Collective Security System for Asia, first proposed by General Secretary Leonid Brezhnev in 1969. However, this proposal had received a cold response from the ASEAN states, largely due to their perception that Moscow's real objective was to isolate the United States, China and the Western European powers from the region. Even later Soviet proposals, such as those made by Mikhail Gorbachev in the late 1980s concerning regional security, were not very enthusiastically received by ASEAN members because of the larger issue of the Soviet refusal to push Vietnam into withdrawing from Cambodia. As long as their suspicion of Soviet motives in Indochina remained, the ASEAN states did not embrace too warmly any Soviet initiatives for regional cooperation.

While the Third Indochina War aggravated the security dilemma in Southeast Asia and further undermined ASEAN's professed security framework (especially ZOPFAN), it also had a dramatic impact in giving a more substantive meaning to ASEAN political and security cooperation. Moreover, the search for a political solution to the Cambodian conflict helped propel ASEAN from being a relatively unknown grouping to the centre stage of international diplomacy.

Towards Regional Reconciliation

By the mid-1980s, the military and diplomatic situation in the Cambodian conflict showed little sign of victory for either of the contending parties. On the one hand, Hanoi's goal of making the rule of Heng Samrin's PRK "irreversible", and thereby extending its influence over Indochina, had not been fulfilled. On the other hand, the efforts by the anti-Vietnamese coalition, consisting of the CGDK, China and ASEAN with backing from Western countries, to put pressure on Vietnam both politically (through condemnation and isolation) and militarily (through backing for the military efforts of the CGDK) had not succeeded in securing a Vietnamese roll-back. In fact, the "bleed Vietnam" strategy may have been counter-productive. As the *Strategic Survey* published by the London-based International Institute for Strategic Studies (IISS) pointed out:

> The strategy of diplomatic isolation and support for the Khmer resistance's guerilla campaign of attrition, which ASEAN, China, and the West pursued, far from forcing concessions from her [Vietnam], only reinforced her intransigence and her insistence that the situation in Kampuchea was both "irreversible" and an "internal" matter.[22]

After some time, the rival Khmer factions and their principal external backers, China and Vietnam, came increasingly to the realization that their objectives could not be achieved by military means within acceptable costs. Moreover, at least for three major players in the conflict, namely Vietnam, the Soviet Union and ASEAN, the costs of the stalemate seemed to be higher than the cost of a political settlement. For Vietnam, whose intervention had been the key issue, the cost of the conflict in human, political and economic terms was high. In July 1988, the vice-commander of Vietnamese troops in Cambodia estimated that about 55,000 Vietnamese troops and civilians had perished. The conflict not only deprived Vietnam of access to international capital and aid urgently needed for economic development, it also increased Vietnamese dependence on the Soviet Union. Vietnam also remained politically isolated, as reflected in the increasing majorities supporting the annual, ASEAN-sponsored resolution in the UN General Assembly condemning its invasion of Cambodia.

For the Soviet Union, the Cambodian stalemate imposed major costs in political as well as economic terms. The massive amount of economic and military aid to Hanoi, estimated at between four and six billion U.S. dollars a year,[23] without which the latter's campaign in Cambodia could not have been sustained, was an increasingly unacceptable burden on an ailing Soviet economy. Politically, Soviet support for Hanoi's Cambodian venture had obstructed the normalization of its ties with China and the prospect of superpower rapprochement. Moscow's role in bringing about a settlement to the Cambodian conflict was sure to help its standing within the Asia-Pacific region, especially in the eyes of those ASEAN countries with which it was actively seeking closer economic ties. On the other hand, the possible "losses" for the Soviet Union from a Cambodian settlement — a Vietnam that was less dependent on Moscow and reduced Soviet access to military installations at Cam Ranh Bay — would not be critical. Towards the end of the 1980s, Moscow had begun to withdraw its forces from Vietnam as part of Gorbachev's overall force-reduction programme. As diplomacy replaced a strong regional military presence as the chief instrument of policy towards the Asia-Pacific, the fear of losing these bases did not deter Moscow from pressuring Hanoi to adopt a more flexible stand on the Cambodian problem.

Gorbachev's famous speech at Vladivostok on 28 July 1986[24] heralded a new era in Soviet strategic thinking on the Asia-Pacific region and indicated an eagerness to win recognition as a peaceful player in the region. Although the Soviet leader offered no concessions on the Cambodian conflict, he signalled the Soviet desire to disengage from Afghanistan and make concessions on its border dispute with China, the other "obstacles" to Sino-Soviet rapprochement. With Vladivostok marking the beginning of a thaw in Sino-Soviet rivalry, the stakes and interests of external powers in the Cambodian conflict were dramatically altered. The Soviet desire to extricate itself from regional hotspots reduced its support for Vietnam's continuing occupation of Cambodia and forced Hanoi's decision to withdraw its troops. The Sino-Soviet rapprochement also lessened Beijing's interest in using its support for the Cambodian resistance factions to bleed the Soviet Union.

For ASEAN, a stalemate in the Cambodian conflict had been a mixed blessing at best. The Cambodian problem clearly helped ASEAN's unity and its international reputation initially. But as the stalemate continued, ASEAN began counting the costs. The stalemate had severely tested ASEAN's unity, and brought to the surface the differing intramural perceptions of China and Vietnam. It also sustained Chinese influence over the security concerns of the grouping, a factor especially unwelcome to Indonesia and Malaysia.

The changing international political climate and the role of a group of mediators were major factors in generating hopes for a breakthrough in Paris. The evolving Reagan-Gorbachev détente created hope for mutual restraint and understanding on regional disputes in the Third World, including Cambodia. The activism and success of the UN in mediating regional disputes had further contributed to a positive international climate for an agreement on the Cambodian problem. Several so-called "middle powers", such as Australia, France, Japan, Canada and India, showed a similar interest, and their willingness to contribute to the reconstruction of the war-devastated country was an additional factor that created hopes for a settlement.

As the conflict entered the second half of the 1980s, the major parties realized that the stalemate on the battlefield could not be broken without a dramatic increase in military operations and its attendant risks; they became more willing to search for compromises in the diplomatic arena. The possibility of such a negotiated settlement, as seen earlier, had been marred by the lack of agreement on an appropriate negotiating forum. While ASEAN had tried to "internationalize" the conflict, Hanoi preferred a "regional" dialogue. With the evident failure of the ICK, however, another international gathering to discuss the conflict seemed unrealistic. In addition, although ASEAN's effort to keep the issue alive at the UN by sponsoring an annual resolution condemning the Vietnamese invasion was successful in isolating Hanoi, it had made little difference to the task of conflict resolution. Thus, it was soon advocated that the peace process take place through more limited, "regional" forums, with Indonesia (ASEAN's officially designated interlocutor with Hanoi on the Cambodia issue) playing a key role.

The regional peace process took the form of two Jakarta Informal Meetings (JIM I in July 1988 and JIM II in February 1989). These meetings marked a high point in ASEAN diplomacy, particularly for Indonesia. While not producing a decisive outcome, the JIM process helped to narrow the differences between the Cambodian factions and the external powers on the crucial issue of power-sharing in post-conflict Cambodia.

The final stages of the Cambodian conflict were dominated by the two sittings of the Paris Peace Conference. Here, the five permanent members of the UN Security Council (P5) and Australia took centre stage, to some extent at ASEAN's expense. While the first sitting of the conference in 1989 did not resolve the issue of power-sharing among the Cambodian factions and had to be postponed, the second sitting in 1991 resulted in a diplomatic settlement that led to the signing of the Final Act of the Paris Conference on 23 October 1991.[25]

The Paris Agreement was not without its limitations. While it marked an end to the so-called "external aspects" of the conflict — that is, the competitive intervention of China and Soviet-backed Vietnam — its provisions for power-sharing among the Khmer factions was left uncertain and in the hands of a United Nations authority.[26] But insofar as ASEAN was concerned, the accord was a cause for celebration for two reasons. First, the peace settlement conformed to terms set by ASEAN from the very outset, including the end of the Vietnamese occupation and the replacement of the regime installed by its invasion. Vietnam had to abandon its desire to impose its security framework on Indochina. Second, the accord was seen by the international community as a vindication of ASEAN's diplomatic efforts, notwithstanding the fact that ASEAN's role in the final stages of the process had been overshadowed by that of the permanent members of the UN Security Council.

ASEAN also gained new momentum in realizing its vision of regional order in Southeast Asia. The positive turn in the Cambodian peace process was accompanied by movement towards bridging the ideological divide of Southeast Asia. The transformation of ASEAN-Vietnam relations had begun as a slow and tortuous process.[27] It was driven by a thaw in Thai-Vietnamese rivalry, which in turn was helped by domestic changes in both countries. Domestic reform in Vietnam aimed at transforming its socialist economy into a market economy. The Vietnamese Communist Party's adoption in 1986 of the policy of "renovation", or *doi moi,* signalled Hanoi's realization that its occupation of Cambodia entailed severe economic costs that it could no longer afford. Managing the economic crisis at home to ensure regime survival became a more important concern for Hanoi than maintaining its occupation of Cambodia, ostensibly to counter external threats to national security.[28] "Renovation" was adopted by the Sixth National Congress of the Vietnamese Communist Party and strengthened by a Conference of the Politburo in May 1989 and the Seventh National Congress of the Party in June 1991.

Initially, the ASEAN states had ignored the implications of Vietnamese reform for ASEAN-Indochina relations, choosing instead to focus on Hanoi's continued occupation of Cambodia. But the advent of a new Thai Government under Prime Minister Chatichai Choonhavan in August 1988 produced a major shift in Thailand's hitherto hardline policy towards Hanoi. Chatichai recognized the opportunities offered by Vietnam's efforts to create a "market mechanism economy", and declared that Thai policy would now aim at "turning the Indochinese battlefields to marketplaces". Initially, the Thai economic and political initiatives that flowed from Chatichai's new policy served to undermine ASEAN's Indonesia-led consensual diplomacy on Cambodia.[29] In particular, Bangkok's move to invite Prime Minister Hun Sen in January 1989 caused discomfort and apprehension in other ASEAN capitals, especially Singapore and Jakarta.[30] Yet the shift in Thai policy, followed by steady progress in the Cambodian peace process, led to a common ASEAN interest in bringing Vietnam into its fold. By 1988, Vietnamese inclusion within ASEAN had already been foreseen by Malaysia and Indonesia. As Malaysian Prime Minister Mahathir had put it, "if Vietnam subscribes to the ideas of ASEAN, the system of government it practices should not be something that stands in the way of becoming a member of ASEAN."[31]

Continued emphasis on economic reform increased Hanoi's stakes in improved relations with ASEAN. ASEAN membership, it calculated, would create the necessary external political environment for economic growth, help it to normalize ties with the West, attract foreign technology and investment, and reduce dependence on the Soviet Union.[32] ASEAN had the potential to be Vietnam's "bridge" to the West.[33] For ASEAN, Vietnam's transition to a capitalist economy provided significant economic opportunities at a time when traditional Western markets were turning protectionist. Thus, Chatichai's policy of turning the Indochinese "battlefields to marketplaces" was vindicated, as ASEAN governments moved to develop significant trade and investment linkages with Vietnam.

On 5 April 1989, Hanoi surprised the international community by announcing that it would pull its troops out of Cambodia by September 1989, irrespective of the result of the forthcoming peace talks. While ASEAN members, including Thailand, waited for proof of Hanoi's good intentions,[34] there was no question that the Vietnamese move would remove two of ASEAN's most serious concerns: (1) Vietnam as a security threat to Thailand, and (2) Vietnam's domination of Indochina as a single strategic unit. Thus, it was not surprising that the announcement of the Vietnamese withdrawal produced speculation about Vietnam partnering with ASEAN through functional cooperation as well as acquiring formal membership status.[35] But ASEAN became a victim of its own success in keeping international interest in the conflict alive, because in the final stages of the peace process its own diplomacy was overwhelmed by that of the great powers. Thus, by seeking closer relations with Indochina, ASEAN tried to regain some initiative on issues of regional order in the post-Cambodia context.

Another factor conducive to improved ASEAN-Vietnam relations was the changing relationship among the principal great powers involved in Southeast Asian security. The normalization of Sino-Soviet relations meant that Vietnam could no longer count on Soviet backing against China, with which it had a major territorial dispute. The Vietnamese sense of insecurity was further compounded by the Soviet military retreat from Asia and the cessation of Soviet aid to Vietnam. Furthermore, the prospective withdrawal of the United States from the Philippines and the general cutbacks to the superpower military presence in the Asia-Pacific contributed to a greater sense of vulnerability on the part of both ASEAN and Vietnam, especially *vis-à-vis* China, which seemed the likely candidate to step into the vacuum created by the end of the Cold War. Such insecurity initially led Hanoi to seek accommodation with Beijing, but Beijing soon made it clear that any improved relations would be on its own terms, and hence not entirely satisfactory to Hanoi. Better relations with ASEAN could, from Hanoi's perspective, offset some of the vulnerabilities arising from the changing great-power relationship in the Asia-Pacific. ASEAN could be a valuable political ally, if not a strategic and economic partner of enough consequence to offset the loss of the Soviet Union as a donor and security guarantor.

The ASEAN-Vietnam rapprochement was visible in both economic and political arenas. Between 1987 (when Vietnam's economy began to be liberalized) and 1990, the total volume of official trade (exports and imports) between ASEAN and Vietnam increased almost sixfold, from $58.2 million to $337.2 million.[36] Vietnam became an increasingly attractive target for investments by the ASEAN states, as the latter came to recognize the economic potential of Vietnam, with its rich natural and human resource base.[37] ASEAN-Vietnam political accommodation also received a boost in November 1990, when Indonesian President Soeharto became the highest-ranking ASEAN leader to visit Hanoi since the Vietnamese invasion of Cambodia. Despite warnings from Singapore against "undue haste" in helping Vietnam,[38] opposition within ASEAN to reconciliation with Vietnam became progressively muted. As a sign of the changing times, between October 1991 and March 1992, Vo Van Kiet, Chairman of the Council of Ministers of Vietnam, visited all six ASEAN countries. While in Singapore in October 1991, Vo listened to Singapore's Prime Minister, Goh Chok Tong, speak of his hope for "a more relaxed strategic environment in Southeast Asia as Vietnam's economy and policies became more compatible with the ASEAN countries".[39] Not long afterwards, in January 1992, Thai Prime Minister Anand Panyarachun arrived in Hanoi for the first visit by a Thai head of government since the establishment of diplomatic relations between Thailand and Vietnam in 1975. And in April 1992, Mahathir Mohamad became the first ever Malaysian Prime Minister to visit Hanoi.

An important development in the political arena was the seeming convergence of Vietnam's security philosophy with ASEAN's. Hanoi not only abandoned its past policy of seeking close ties with one great power (the Soviet Union) to oppose another (first the United States, then China) and its neighbouring states (ASEAN). Its new security policy sought "appropriately balanced relationships with great powers outside the region, with a view to resolving disputes for influence between them over the region".[40] This conformed to ASEAN's philosophy of regional autonomy and marked the end of Hanoi's opposition to regional cooperation within the ASEAN framework.

East Asian Regionalization and Southeast Asian Regionalism

While ASEAN was working hard to achieve greater regional autonomy in the political and security sphere, in the economic arena its members were actively pursuing policies of greater integration into the global capitalist system as well as the East Asian regional economy. The outward-looking economic focus of ASEAN members could be explained by several factors. During the 1970s and 1980s, the ASEAN countries were reaping the benefits of export-led industrialization strategies, with average annual growth rates during the 1965–70 and 1980–90 periods reaching 7.0 and 5.5 per cent for Indonesia, 7.4 and 5.2 per cent for Malaysia, 5.7 and 0.9 per cent for the Philippines, 10.0 and 6.4 per cent for Singapore, and 7.3 and 7.6 per cent for Thailand.[41] From 1965 to 1986, when the Third

World almost doubled its share of world FDI, the ASEAN states were a major recipient of this trend in international investment.[42] Although Singapore and Malaysia were the major beneficiaries, the ASEAN states as a whole increased their share of Third World FDI from 10.2 per cent in 1973 to 16.9 per cent in 1986.[43]

Even more importantly, the ASEAN countries became major targets of the southward movement of Japanese capital. This followed an agreement among the finance ministers of the Group of Seven (G-7) industrialized nations in 1985 that made their central banks responsible for raising the value of the yen against the dollar. The agreement, called the Plaza Accord, resulted in a rapid appreciation of the yen. Japanese corporations, already facing high costs at home, were now endowed with vastly increased capital assets. They began relocating to lower-cost countries, initially to South Korea and Taiwan, but later, as the currencies of these countries also appreciated, to Southeast Asia. For Japanese investors, Southeast Asia had the advantages of geographical proximity, reasonably good infrastructure, a cheap but relatively skilled workforce, relative political stability, strong bureaucracy and policies of economic liberalization, including the relatively "open" stance of Southeast Asian governments towards trade, foreign investment and the operations of multinational corporations.[44] Added to these were Southeast Asia's resource endowments and the market potential of a population over 300 million.[45] During the 1985–89 period, Japan's FDI grew at an average annual rate of 62 per cent.[46] The main beneficiaries of the massive flow of Japanese investment were four Southeast Asian countries: Malaysia, Singapore, Indonesia and Thailand. Between 1987 and 1991, Japanese FDI in ASEAN amounted to $16.7 billion. Japan's FDI in Thailand rose from $250 million in 1987 to $1.3 billion in 1989, while in Singapore the figure rose from $302 million in 1986 to $1.9 billion in 1989.[47] Another $15 billion of Japanese FDI flowed to Southeast Asia between 1990 and 1993, compared to $10 billion from the United States.[48] Taiwan (often for political reasons) and South Korea also directed major portions of their investment towards Southeast Asia. These investment flows and the ensuing trade linkages among these countries contributed to the growing regionalization of production among the East Asian economies.[49]

This pattern of regionalization covered both inter- and intra-industry or intra-firm trade. In the early 1990s, the regionalization of East Asian economies was often described in terms of a three-tier production structure. In this structure, Japan exported the most technologically advanced products; the NICs (Singapore, Hong Kong, South Korea and Taiwan) exported skilled labour-intensive products; and the ASEAN-4 (Malaysia, Indonesia, Thailand and the Philippines) and China exported labour-intensive products. But this missed the extent of intra-firm trade, that is, trade taking place between multinational corporations operating in East Asia. According to one estimate, the rise in the index of intra-industry trade during the 1979–88 period was 91 per cent for the Philippines, 90 per cent for Indonesia, 85 per cent for Thailand and 64 per cent for Malaysia.[50]

The question now emerges whether the regionalization of East Asian economies helped shape a new regionalism and regional identity.[51] The trade and investment linkages among Japan, China, Taiwan and South Korea on the one hand and the ASEAN economies on the other implied a trend towards greater *East* Asian, rather than *Southeast* Asian integration. It is interesting to note that the percentage of intra-ASEAN trade actually declined during the 1980s. But the regionalization of East Asian economies contributed to pressures for trade liberalization among the ASEAN countries in several ways. One of the main consequences of the inflow of Japanese investment was the emergence of a series of production networks of parts and component producers linked to assembly plants, especially in the auto and electrical sectors. As a result, Japan wanted to be able to move components from country to country without facing intra-ASEAN trade barriers. As such, Tokyo began urging the ASEAN states to move towards greater trade liberalization, often using its official development assistance (ODA) and other means to this end. Moreover, Northeast Asian investments in Southeast Asia had a major impact in altering the composition of intra-ASEAN trade, creating a new rationale for ASEAN economic cooperation. While in 1980 the percentage of manufactured goods accounted for 28.2 per cent of total intra-ASEAN trade, in 1990, the figure was 61.3 per cent. Much of the increase was due to the activities of multinational corporations in spreading their production bases to several countries in ASEAN. The ASEAN governments realized that an ASEAN trade arrangement would present the ASEAN region as a single investment area to outside investors and thereby make it much more attractive by offering incentives that no country could individually offer.[52]

While the regionalization of East Asian economies did create new incentives for greater ASEAN regionalism, it also posed questions as to

TABLE 6.1
Share of Intra-ASEAN Exports in ASEAN Total Exports*

Intra-ASEAN Exports as Percentage of ASEAN Total Exports (%)

Year	1967	1970	1975	1980	1985	1990	1994
Percentage	20.9	21.4	17.2	17.9	19.2	19.3	20.8

* The statistics are based on Ravenhill's calculations using IMF Direction of Trade data accessed through the International Economic Data Bank, Australian National University. *Source:* John Ravenhill, "Economic Cooperation in Southeast Asia: Changing Incentives", *Asian Survey* 35, no. 9 (1995): 851.

whether Southeast Asia was following the "Japanese model" or an "East Asian model" of economic development. The idea of such models had emerged when political economists challenged neo-classical assumptions about the invisible hand of the marketplace that underplayed the role of government while stressing the role of "vigorous, competitive and entrepreneurial private business".[53] Chalmers Johnson, for example, outlined a "four-fold structural model of East Asian high-growth systems". The model consisted of the following elements:

> Stable rule by a political-bureaucratic elite not acceding to political demands that would undermine economic growth; cooperation between public and private sectors under the overall guidance of a pilot planning agency; heavy and continuing investment in education for everyone, combined with policies to ensure the equitable distribution of the wealth created by high-speed growth; and a government that understands the need to use and respect methods of economic intervention based on the price mechanism.[54]

While the question of whether the Southeast Asian economies fit into this pattern would become a matter of intense debate, Singapore and Malaysia consciously evoked Japan as a role model for their own development. Mahathir's "Look East" policy followed Singapore's "Learn from Japan" campaign in late 1970s. At the same time, Southeast Asia's position as an integral part of the East Asian regional political economy was popularized by the somewhat loose and rhetorical notion of "flying geese". The analogy was linked to the Japanese "flying wild geese pattern", in which the leader of the inverse "V" formation of geese is periodically replaced by a newcomer. In this sense, some Southeast Asian countries, especially Thailand, Malaysia and Indonesia, would represent the next "geese" by picking up the light manufacturing industries (e.g., textiles, food-processing and simpler electronics) that had been shed by the original NICs (South Korea, Taiwan, Hong Kong and Singapore). Thus, all of Southeast Asia would progressively be integrated into the process of technological diffusion emanating from Japan.

On the other hand, the validity of models assuming similarities between Southeast and Northeast Asian development could be questioned on the basis of major differences in economic situation and development policy.[55] While some aspects of the Japanese model of industrialization were to be found in other East and Southeast Asian countries — emphasis on universal primary education, high savings rates, and institutional and anti-monopoly reforms by the government to promote competition within the private sector — other factors remained peculiar to Japan. These included Japan's restrictions on private foreign investment (not found in Southeast Asia) and its guarantee of lifetime employment. Moreover, the economies of the Southeast Asian countries, including Indonesia, Malaysia, Thailand and the Philippines (called the near-NICs), shared a number of characteristics that differed from those of the original NICs. These included a shortage of qualified technical, professional and managerial manpower, owing partly to rigid social structures, religious influences and greater rural poverty. In addition, the Southeast Asian near-NICs showed greater wage differentials across different categories of the workforce and a greater incidence of individualism among the workers. While their domestic savings were high, they were less stable than the original NICs because of fluctuations in the price of commodities, on which their economies were much more dependent. In the Southeast Asian near-NICs, pervasive government intervention had the effect of reducing innovation and risk-taking in the private sector. Against this backdrop, one could speak of not one but several growth and industrialization models in East Asia. R. Hirono identified three: the Japanese, the newly industrializing and the near-industrializing country models, while insisting that the performance of more advanced countries could not be copied by the less advanced countries.[56]

The fact that the near-NICs of Southeast Asia could not be regarded simply as the latest "geese" could also be seen from the fact that the growth of their manufacturing sectors was not built on successful import-substituting industrialization. Instead, in many cases, exporting industries were "grafted" onto economies featuring small manufacturing sectors with a high incidence of rent-seeking behaviour. In addition, the Southeast Asian economies had a much higher degree of technological dependence than Korea and Taiwan, and much greater dependence on transnational corporations and their subsidiaries for manufactured exports. Southeast Asia had experienced a technology-less industrialization.[57] Overall, the second-generation NICs differed considerably from the first in terms of their initial conditions of development and their political institutions. This helped to establish claims that Southeast Asia's economic growth was linked to its subregional circumstances, despite economic globalization and integration with the Northeast Asian economies.

The "ASEAN Way"

While the extent to which the political economy of ASEAN was distinct from that of Northeast Asia was a matter of debate, there was little question as to the distinctive nature of the diplomatic style and pattern of elite socialization prevailing within ASEAN. In a variety of ways, ASEAN was able to reinforce its claim to be a cohesive regional grouping that had developed a special and successful approach to peace, stability and development. Part of this was articulated in contrast to the ideological and economic currents sweeping the communist societies of Indochina. Before the eyes of the international community, ASEAN was able to contrast Vietnamese "expansionism" with ASEAN's "good neighbourliness" and desire for regional political stability (implying a territorial and political status quo in Southeast Asia); Vietnam's alliance with the Soviet Union with ASEAN's professed goal of a Zone of Peace, Freedom and Neutrality (ZOPFAN) in Southeast Asia; Vietnam's intense nationalism and ideological fervour with ASEAN's pragmatism and developmentalism; and Vietnam's military suppression of the Cambodian rebels with ASEAN's efforts for a political settlement of the conflict. Moreover, the ASEAN members pointed to the superiority of their model of economic development and political management *vis-à-vis* the Indochinese model. By stressing its "free-market", "anti-communist" and "pro-Western" image, ASEAN gained for itself international goodwill as well as political and economic support from the West.

A more controversial claim made by ASEAN members concerned the so-called "ASEAN Way".[58] Presented by ASEAN leaders as a distinctive approach to interstate relations and regional cooperation, the ASEAN Way supposedly consisted of the avoidance of formal mechanisms and legalistic procedures for decision-making, and the reliance on *musyawarah* (consultation) and *mufakat* (consensus) to achieve collective goals.[59]

Moreover, the ASEAN Way implied emphasis on quiet diplomacy and rejection of adversarial posturing in negotiations. A former Indonesian Foreign Minister described *musyawarah* as a setting in which negotiations take place "not as between opponents but as between friends and brothers".[60]

An important example of the ASEAN Way could be found in the provisions concerning dispute settlement contained in ASEAN's Treaty of Amity and Cooperation. This Treaty (Chapter IV, Articles 13 to 17) provided for an official dispute settlement mechanism called High Council, consisting of ministerial-level representatives from each member state. The role of the Council was to encourage direct negotiations between the parties of a dispute and to take appropriate measures such as good offices, mediation, inquiry or conciliation to facilitate a settlement. But the ASEAN members never chose to convene a meeting of the High Council, despite numerous intramural disputes. While some would see this as a sign of weakness,[61] ASEAN leaders found in it a vindication of the ASEAN Way. Thus, Noordin Sopiee, a Malaysian scholar, pointed to "the intangible but real 'spirit' of ASEAN, which has been effective in sublimating and diffusing conflicts as in actually resolving them".[62] The implication was that, unlike other multilateral bodies, including European regional organizations, ASEAN's approach rested on an assumed capacity to manage disputes without resorting to formal, multilateral measures.

The ASEAN Way of informality was also reflected in its decision to keep its bureaucratic apparatus relatively small, although there was a proliferation of official ASEAN meetings (exceeding 300 a year in the 1990s). While legalistic procedures would be evident in some subsequent ASEAN initiatives (such as the Southeast Asia Nuclear Weapon Free Zone Treaty of 1995), the ASEAN brand of "soft regionalism", relying primarily on consultations and consensus, has remained the norm for much of the organization's history. The Asian economic crisis in the late 1990s has led some ASEAN leaders to adopt a more institutionalized approach to cooperation, but any initiatives in this regard are unlikely to turn ASEAN into a European Union-style bureaucracy.

Conclusion

For Southeast Asia, the end of the regional Cold War came with the Vietnamese withdrawal from Cambodia, which culminated in the May 1993 Cambodian elections. It became obvious that Vietnam was no longer a significant security concern for the ASEAN states. In December 1989, an agreement was signed by the Malaysian Government, the Thai Government and the Communist Party of Malaysia (CPM), which ended a more than forty-year-long guerilla struggle to overthrow the Malayan / Malaysian Government. This preceded the collapse of the Communist Party of Thailand, and was followed by the decline of the Communist New People's Army in the Philippines. Thus ended the threat of communist subversion in the region, which itself had contributed to the intraregional polarization of Southeast Asia. These developments secured for Southeast Asia a greater and more positive international recognition than was the case during the 1970s, a decade dominated by the Vietnam War and myriad internal revolts. While the 1980s had begun with Southeast Asia projecting the image of a region divided, the rhetorical quest for "One Southeast Asia" became the organizing slogan for the region in the 1990s.

NOTES

[1]   Cited in The Parliament of the Commonwealth of Australia, Joint Committee on Foreign Affairs and Defence, *Power in Indochina Since 1975* (Canberra: Australian Government Publishing Service, 1981), p. 64.
[2]   Allan W. Cameron, *Indochina: Prospects After "the End"* (Washington, D.C.: American Enterprise Institute for Public Policy Research, 1976), p. 25.
[3]   Kannan Kutty Nair, "ASEAN-Indochina Relations Since 1975: The Politics of Accommodation", Canberra Papers on Strategy and Defence no. 30 (Canberra: Australian National University, Strategic and Defence Studies Centre, 1984), pp. 94–95.
[4]   Ibid., p. 94.
[5]   *Straits Times*, 6 July 1977.
[6]   See Sheldon Simon, *ASEAN States and Regional Security* (Stanford, CA: Hoover Institution Press, 1982), p. 53; Tim Huxley, "Indochina as a Security Concern of the ASEAN States 1975–81", Ph.D. dissertation, Australian National University, 1986, pp. 130–88.
[7]   *New Straits Times*, 14 May 1975.
[8]   *Straits Times*, 18 February 1976.
[9]   *Straits Times*, 26 November 1975.
[10] David Irvine, "Making Haste Less Slowly: ASEAN from 1975", in *Understanding ASEAN*, edited by Alison Broinowski (London: Macmillan, 1982), p. 40.
[11] Jusuf Wanandi, "Security Issues in the ASEAN Region", in *ASEAN Security and Economic Development*, edited by Karl D. Jackson and M. Hadi Soesastro,

Research Papers and Policy Studies no. 11 (Berkeley: Institute of East Asian Studies, University of California, 1984), p. 305.

[12] Hari Singh, "Understanding Conflict Resolution in Cambodia: A Neorealist Perspective", *Asian Journal of Political Science* 7, no. 1 (1999): 41–59.

[13] Chan Heng Chee, "The Interests and Role of ASEAN in the Indochina Conflict", paper presented to the international conference on "Indochina and Problems of Security and Stability in Southeast Asia", held at Chulalongkorn University, Bangkok, 19–21 June 1980, p. 12.

[14] Justus Maria van der Kroef, "ASEAN, Hanoi, and the Kampuchean Conflict: Between Kuantan and a Third Alternative", *Asian Survey* 21, no. 5 (1981): 516–21.

[15] Ibid., pp. 517–18.

[16] Elizabeth Becker, "Stalemate in Cambodia", *Current History* 86, no. 519 (1987), p. 158.

[17] David J. Steinberg, ed., *In Search of Southeast Asia: A Modern History*, rev. ed. (Honolulu: University of Hawaii Press, 1987), p. 449.

[18] Japanese Economic Institute, JEI Reports, various dates.

[19] Lucian W. Pye, *Southeast Asia's Political Systems*, 2nd ed. (Englewood Cliffs, NJ: Prentice Hall, 1974), p. 92.

[20] Richard Stubbs, "The Political Economy of the Asia-Pacific Region", in *Political Economy and the Changing Global Order*, edited by Richard Stubbs and G.R.D. Underhill (London: Macmillan, 1994), pp. 370–71.

[21] Amitav Acharya, "The United States Versus the U.S.S.R. in the Pacific: Trends in the Military Balance", *Contemporary Southeast Asia* 9, no. 4 (1988): 282–99.

[22] International Institute for Strategic Studies, *Strategic Survey 1982–1983* (London: International Institute for Strategic Studies, 1983), p. 95.

[23] Gerard Hervouet, "The Return of Vietnam to the International System", Occasional Paper no. 6 (Ottawa: Canadian Institute for International Peace and Security, 1988), p. 42.

[24] For details and implications of Gorbachev's Vladivostok speech, see Amitav Acharya, "The Asia-Pacific Region: Cockpit for Superpower Rivalry", *The World Today* 43, nos. 8–9 (1987): 155–59.

[25] The Final Act of the Paris Conference, signed on 23 October 1991, consists of three documents: (1) "An Agreement on a Comprehensive Political Settlement of the Cambodia Conflict"; (2) "An Agreement Concerning the Sovereignty, Independence, Territorial Integrity and Inviolability, Neutrality and National Unity of Cambodia"; and (3) "Declaration on the Rehabilitation and Reconstruction of Cambodia". The first document contained annexes on "the mandate for UNTAC, military matters, elections, repatriation of Cambodian refugees and displaced persons, and the principles for a new Cambodian constitution".

[26] See Michael Leifer, "Power-sharing and Peacemaking in Cambodia", *SAIS Review* 12, no. 1 (1992): 139–53.

[27] Hari Singh, "Vietnam and ASEAN: The Politics of Accommodation", *Australian Journal of International Affairs* 51, no. 2 (1997): 215–29.

[28] Carlyle A. Thayer, "The Challenges Facing Vietnamese Communism", *Southeast Asian Affairs 1992* (Singapore: Institute of Southeast Asian Studies, 1992), p. 352.

[29] For an excellent discussion of the implications of the Chatichai initiative, see D. Weatherbee, "ASEAN the Big Loser in Thai Race for Profit in Indochina", *Straits Times*, 5 May 1989.

[30] S. Rajaratnam, "Riding the Vietnamese Tiger", *Contemporary Southeast Asia* 10, no. 4 (1989): 343–61.

[31] *Bangkok Post*, 16 December 1988.

[32] *International Herald Tribune*, 21 March 1989. The Vietnamese desire to join ASEAN was clearly conveyed to visiting Philippine Foreign Secretary Raul Manglapus by Party Chairman Nguyen Van Linh and Foreign Minister Nguyen Co Thach in November 1988. *Straits Times*, 18 April 1989.

[33] Cited in Frank Frost, "Vietnam and Asean: From Enmity to Cooperation", *Trends*, 29 December 1991, p. 26.

[34] P. Sricharatchanya, "Wait and See", *Far Eastern Economic Review*, 11 May 1989, p. 21.

[35] See Muthiah Alagappa, "Bringing Indochina into Asean", *Far Eastern Economic Review*, 29 June 1989, pp. 21–22.

[36] International Monetary Fund, *Direction of Trade Statistics Yearbook*, as reported in M. Than, "ASEAN, Indochina and Myanmar: Towards Economic Cooperation", *ASEAN Economic Bulletin* 8, no. 2 (1991), p. 183.

[37] Institute of Southeast Asian Studies, *Regional Outlook 1991* (Singapore: Institute of Southeast Asian Studies, 1992), p. 58.

[38] "Sense of Place, Sense of Time", *Straits Times*, 23 November 1990.

[39] Goh Chok Tong, "Towards a Positive Relationship with Vietnam", *Speeches*, vol. 15, no. 5 (September–October 1991), p. 9.

[40] Vietnamese Assistant Foreign Minister H.C. Tran, cited in Thu My, "Renovation in Vietnam and its Effects on Peace, Friendship and Cooperation in Southeast Asia", in *Unity in Diversity: Cooperation Between Vietnam and Other Southeast Asian Countries*, edited by D.Q. Nguyen (Hanoi: Social Science Publishing House, 1992), pp. 141–42.

[41] John Bresnan, *From Dominos to Dynamos* (New York: Council on Foreign Relations Press, 1994), p. 19.

[42] Chris Dixon, *South East Asia in the World-Economy: A Regional Geography* (London: Cambridge University Press, 1991), pp. 12–13.

[43] Ibid., p. 12.

44   Richard Stubbs, "Signing on to Liberalization: AFTA and the Politics of Regional Economic Cooperation", *The Pacific Review* 13, no. 2 (2000): 297–318.

45   Dixon, *South East Asia in the World-Economy*, p. 4.

46   Paul Bowles, "ASEAN, AFTA and the New Regionalism", *Pacific Affairs* 70, no. 2 (1997): 219–33.

47   Stubbs, "Signing on to Liberalization".

48   Margaret Mason, "Foreign Direct Investment in East Asia: Trends and Critical Issues", CFR Asia Project Working Paper (New York: Council on Foreign Relations Press, 1994), p. 6.

49   Richard Stubbs, "Regionalization and Globalization", in Stubbs and Underhill, *Political Economy and the Changing Global Order*, p. 232.

50   Bowles, "ASEAN, AFTA and the New Regionalism", p. 223.

51   Stubbs, "Regionalization and Globalization", p. 232.

52   Bowles, "ASEAN, AFTA and the New Regionalism", p. 223.

53   S. Awanohara, "'Look East' — The Japan Model", *Asia-Pacific Economic Literature* 1, no. 1 (1987): 75–89.

54   Chalmers Johnson, "Political Institutions and Economic Performance: The Government-Business Relationship in Japan, South Korea, and Taiwan", in *The Political Economy of New Asian Industrialism,* edited by Frederic C. Deyo (Ithaca, NY: Cornell University Press, 1987), p. 145.

55   For further discussion, see Walter Hatch and Kozo Yamamura, *Asia in Japan's Embrace: Building a Regional Production Alliance* (New York: Cambridge University Press, 1996).

56   Ryokichi Hirono, "Japan: Model for East Asia Industrialization?", in *Achieving Industrialization in East Asia,* edited by Helen Hughes (Cambridge: Cambridge University Press, 1988), p. 259.

57.   Mitchell Bernard and John Ravenhill, "Beyond Product Cycles and Flying Geese: Regionalization, Hierarchy, and Industrialization of East Asia", *World Politics* 47, no. 2 (1995): 171–209.

58   For a more detailed discussion of the "ASEAN Way" and its role in building regional cooperation, see Amitav Acharya, "Ideas, Identity, and Institution-Building: From the 'ASEAN Way' to the 'Asia-Pacific Way'?" *Pacific Review* 10, no. 3 (1997): 319–46.

59   J.N. Mak has identified some of the key features of the ASEAN process: (1) it is unstructured, with no clear format for decision-making or implementation; (2) it often lacks a formal agenda, issues are negotiated on an ad hoc basis "as and when they arise"; (3) it is an exercise in consensus-building; (4) decisions are made on the basis of unanimity; (5) decision-making can take a long time because of the need for consensus, there is no fixed timetable, negotiations may go on as long as it takes to reach a position acceptable to all parties; (6) it is closed, behind-the-scenes and lacking transparency. J.N. Mak, "The ASEAN Process ('Way') of Multilateral Cooperation and

Cooperative Security: The Road to a Regional Arms Register?", paper presented to the MIMA-SIPRI Workshop on "An ASEAN Arms Register: Developing Transparency", Kuala Lumpur, 2–3 October 1995, p. 6.

[60] Cited in Arnfinn Jorgensen-Dahl, *Regional Organization and Order in Southeast Asia* (London: Macmillan, 1982), p. 166.

[61] Michael Leifer, "Debating Asian Security: Michael Leifer Responds to Geoffrey Wiseman", *Pacific Review* 5, no. 2 (1992), p. 169.

[62] Noordin Sopiee, "ASEAN and Regional Security", in *Regional Security in the Third World*, edited by Mohammed Ayoob (London: Croom Helm Ltd., 1986), p. 228.

Section B

1. Malaysian Merdeka (Independence)
From left to right: the Duke of Gloucester, the Yang Di-Pertuan Agong (the king of Malaya), an aide-de-camp and Tunku Abdul Rahman (1903–90), the first prime minister of Malaya, attend the Malayan Proclamation of Independence ceremony at Merdeka Stadium, Kuala Lumpur, 31 August 1957. The Tunku played a key role in the creation of Association of Southeast Asia (ASA) in 1960, the first formal regional organization of Southeast Asian countries, comprising Malaysia, the Philippines and Thailand. Although ASA did not last, it was a direct precursor to ASEAN.

Source: Photo by Central Press/Getty Images.

2. Ho Chi Minh: The Revolutionary Leader of Vietnam (1940 photo)

In 1945, Ho was keen to mobilize pan-Asian sentiments (even proposing a "Federation of Free Peoples of Southern Asia") to further Vietnamese independence. But once he took to armed struggle to fight the French and then the United States, he focused on the strategic unity of Indochina as a single revolutionary battlefield that was viewed in the West as a formula for Vietnamese expansionism. Vietnam's position thus became distinct from that of the "moderate" nationalists in Malaya, Thailand, the Philippines and Indonesia (under Soeharto). ASEAN was founded in 1967 but was denounced by Hanoi (until the late 1980s) as a front for Western imperialism.

Source: Photo by Keystone/Getty Images.

3. Insurgency, Malaya

British troops of the Special Air Service (SAS) in the Malayan jungle in search of communist rebels, 1953. A shared concern for regime survival against common internal threats such as the Communist Party of Malaya insurgents was a catalyst of ASEAN's formation.

Source: Photo by Popperfoto/Getty Images.

4. Insurgency: Southern Philippines

Muslim rebels from the Moro Islamic Liberation Front (MILF) gather on 27 January 2010 in the Southern Philippine town of Mamasapano in Maguindanao as peace talks are resumed in Malaysia. The Philippine government and the MILF had resumed peace talks to try to reach an agreement to end the decades-long conflict which has left over 120,000 people dead and as many displaced from their homes. The rebellion was rebranded as a terrorist movement after 9/11, posing a test for ASEAN counter-terrorism cooperation.

Source: Photo by Jeoffrey Maitem/Getty Images.

5. Sukarno to Soeharto

President Sukarno (R) of Indonesia walks with the Major General Soeharto (L) in Indonesia, 11 March 1966. Sukarno was asked by the Indonesia Army to give Soeharto supreme authority to restore order after the 30 September 1965 murders of six generals, which the Army blamed on the Indonesia Communist Party (PKI). In March 1976, the Indonesian Parliament (The People's General Assembly) stripped President Sukarno of all powers and appointed Soeharto as the Acting President. Sukarno was placed under house arrest until his death in June 1970. Compared to his predecessor, Soeharto proved to be a stronger advocate of Southeast Asian regional cooperation, including ASEAN.

Source: Photo by Beryl Bernay/Getty Images.

6. Thanat Khoman
Foreign Minister Thanat Khoman of Thailand, 1 January 1966. Khoman played a key role reconciling Indonesia and Malaysia after Sukarno's Konfrontasi policy, a reconciliation that paved the way for ASEAN's creation in 1967.

Source: Photo by Bill Ray/Time Life Pictures/Getty Images.

7. Adam Malik
Indonesian Foreign Minister, Adam Malik, returning to Djakarta after the Bangkok Conference on 1 January 1966. The Bangkok Conference ended the Indonesia-Malaysia conflict (Konfrontasi), and presaged ASEAN's conflict mitigation role.

Source: Photo by Co Rentmeester/Time Life Pictures/Getty Images.

8. Signing of the ASEAN Declaration, Bangkok, 8 August 1967
From left: Narciso Ramos, Secretary of Foreign Affairs of the Philippines, Adam Malik, Minister for Foreign Affairs of Indonesia, Thanat Khoman, Minister for Foreign Affairs of Thailand, Tun Abdul Razak, Deputy Prime Minister of Malaysia, and S. Rajaratnam, Minister for Foreign Affairs of Singapore. The Declaration founded ASEAN.

Source: Courtesy of the ASEAN Secretariat.

9. ASEAN Heads of Government at the First ASEAN Summit, Bali, Indonesia, 23–24 February 1976
From left to right: Prime Minister Hussein Onn of Malaysia, Prime Minister Lee Kuan Yew of Singapore, President Soeharto of Indonesia, President Ferdinand Marcos of the Philippines, and Prime Minister Kukrit Promoj of Thailand.

Source: Courtesy of the ASEAN Secretariat.

10. Vietnamese Invasion of Cambodia

Khmers Rouge prisoners after the fall of Phnom Penh to Vietnamese forces, Cambodia, 1 January 1979. Vietnam's full-scale invasion of Cambodia on 25 December 1978 toppled the murderous Khmer Rouge regime and started the Third Indochina War, which tested ASEAN's role in regional conflict management.

Source: Photo by Jean-Claude Labbe/Gamma-Rapho via Getty Images.

11. Brunei Joins ASEAN

Soon after gaining its independence from Britain in January 1984, Brunei Darussalam was admitted into ASEAN as its sixth member.

Source: Courtesy of the ASEAN Secretariat.

12. The Paris Peace Agreement on Cambodia, Paris, 23 October 1991
Cambodian faction leaders including Hun Sen (second from left), Prince Norodom Sihanouk (fourth from left) and Khieu Samphan (extreme right), applaud after signing the peace treaty which ended the Cambodia conflict.

Source: Photo by Eric Feferberg/AFP/Getty Images.

13. Economic Development, Rubber
A young Tamil girl pulling sheets of crepe off a roll in a rubber factory in Malaya, circa 1955.

Source: Photo by Horace Bristol/Three Lions/Getty Images.

14. Economic Scene: Batik
Women make batik by hand in Surakarta, Java Island, Indonesia, 1955.

Source: Photo by J. Baylor Roberts/National Geographic/Getty Images.

15. Japan and Southeast Asian Industrialization
A worker prepares colour television sets on a production line at Japanese giant Sony Corp.'s Malaysian factory in Kajang, 2 October 2000. Investments by Japanese corporations created a transnational production structure that promoted the economic development and regional integration of Southeast Asia.

Source: Photo by Jimin Lai/AFP/Getty Images.

16. Singapore, 1955
Raffles Quay, Singapore Harbour, circa 1955.

Source: Photo by Three Lions/Hulton Archive/Getty Images.

17. Singapore, 2012
Raffles Quay, Central Business District, Singapore, January 2012.

Source: Photo taken by the author.

18. Malaysia, Industrialization
Malaysia, Shah Alam, Proton car factory. Rapid economic growth in Southeast Asian countries involved a shift from resource-based economic development to manufacturing.

Source: Photo by Gary Cralle/Getty Images.

19. Skyline of Kuala Lumpur, Malaysia.
Source: Photo by Getty Images.

7

Constructing "One Southeast Asia"

The end of the Cold War brought fundamental changes to the international relations and regional identity of Southeast Asia. The image of a region divided, fuelled by the ASEAN-Vietnam conflict, was coming to an end, in parallel with breakthroughs in the Cambodian peace process in the late 1980s. ASEAN's vigorous diplomacy on Cambodia had not only earned it positive international recognition, but also contributed to the impression of Southeast Asia as a region able to provide indigenous solutions to its own problems. Regional cohesion and unity had been bolstered by the easing of intramural disputes within ASEAN. The ASEAN model or "ASEAN Way" was presented by leaders and commentators both inside and outside the region as an example of how a region can manage its problems and develop a positive identity in international relations. Both in terms of intraregional interactions and extraregional perceptions, Southeast Asia had become the symbol of a dynamic and largely peaceful region.

Yet, looking at the period from Southeast Asia's emergence from the Cold War until the period of the Asian financial crisis in 1997, it becomes clear the elements of integration and cohesion went hand in hand with the forces of conflict and fragmentation. Much of the latter stemmed from the need to adapt to external developments, such as the changing global economic and security order, including globalization and strategic multipolarity. There also emerged fresh challenges to intraregional relations, including territorial and political disputes, which had been dormant or sidelined during the Cold War years. ASEAN, which had been widely praised for its contribution to stability and prosperity, was presented with a host of new problems, including those stemming from the expansion of its membership to realize the aspirations of its founders towards a united Southeast Asia. Buoyed by its Cambodian success, ASEAN also felt confident enough to assume a major role in developing cooperative security frameworks for the larger Asia-Pacific region, partly in response to a perceived strategic void caused by superpower retrenchment and anxieties linked to the rise of China. Finally, Southeast Asia's integration into the wider regional (East Asian) economy, which accelerated in the late 1980s and early 1990s, created its own host of problems. As the Asian economic crisis in the later part of the 1990s demonstrated, Southeast Asian states had to exist and interact within a larger context of globalization that would redefine their quest for regional identity and autonomy.

Towards "One Southeast Asia"

Perhaps the most significant project undertaken by Southeast Asian countries following the end of the Cold War was the fulfilment of the "One Southeast Asia" concept. This was a conscious region-building exercise seeking to redefine the Southeast Asian political space. It was the logical extension of the political settlement of the Cambodian conflict following the Paris Agreement of 1991. As the Thai Prime Minister, Anand Panyarachun, contended, ASEAN was working "towards a new regional order that embraces all nations of South-east Asia in peace, progress and prosperity".[1] Foreign Minister Ali Alatas of Indonesia offered an even loftier vision:

> one quintessential dividend of peace in Cambodia to strive for would be the dawning of a new era in Southeast Asian history — an era in which for the first time Southeast Asia would be truly peaceful and truly free to deal with its problems in terms of its own aspirations rather than in terms of major-power rivalry and contention; an era marking the beginning of a new Southeast Asia, capable of addressing itself to the

outside world with commensurate authenticity and able to arrange its internal relationships on the basis of genuine independence, equality and peaceful cooperation.[2]

At the first post-Cold War summit held in Singapore in 1992, ASEAN leaders declared that they would "forge a closer relationship based on friendship and cooperation with the Indo-Chinese countries, following the settlement on Cambodia". As a first step, the Singapore Summit Declaration opened the door to all countries of Southeast Asia to sign the Treaty of Amity and Cooperation. Vietnam and Laos were to be the first signatories, followed by Cambodia, once its internal political structure was settled through elections held under the UN.[3] By accepting the Indochinese states into the Treaty, ASEAN would commit them to a regional code of conduct, including norms such as the pacific settlement of disputes and non-interference in the internal affairs of each other.

ASEAN pursued the vision of "One Southeast Asia" as a matter of faith. The realization of this vision, argued Thai scholar Sukhumbhand Paribatra, would "enhance the region's security and well-being", and represent "the fulfillment of a dream to create a region-wide organization, which had begun some three decades before …"[4] Several non-governmental initiatives made the same point, including documents such as *Shared Destiny: Southeast Asia in the 21st Century*, issued in 1993, and *Southeast Asia Beyond the Year 2000: A Statement of Vision*, issued by prominent academics and think tanks in 1994. These documents attested to the fact that, as Carolina Hernandez wrote, "one Southeast Asia … is a goal increasingly captivating the imagination and support of the region's political and other opinion leaders from academe, the media, the private sector, and other professionals".[5]

Vietnam became ASEAN's seventh member in July 1995. Laos and Myanmar (Burma) were admitted in 1997, while Cambodia's entry was delayed by ASEAN until April 1999 because of domestic difficulties that followed the breakdown of the Hun Sen-Ranariddh coalition in 1997. The most significant new member was clearly Vietnam, whose entry was not only of profound symbolic value (in terms of ending the polarization of Southeast Asia) but was also expected to strengthen ASEAN's collective political clout in dealing with the great powers. But the expansion of ASEAN would not be without costs and difficulties.

One key uncertainty was, and remains, whether the new members would be able to fit into the "ASEAN Way" of diplomacy and decision-making, based on the principles of consultation and consensus, which the original members of ASEAN had developed over a long period during the Cold War. This was an important challenge due to the additional bilateral disputes and problems, such as the Thai-Vietnamese, Vietnamese-Cambodian and Thai-Burmese disputes over territory and resources, that now became matters of concern for the organization. That the new members would place the same degree of importance upon ASEAN's norms concerning the non-use of force and pacific settlement of disputes could not be taken for granted.

Moreover, the entry of the new members complicated ASEAN's relations with external powers. Vietnam's inclusion brought ASEAN's "diplomatic border" right up to the frontier with China.[6] Capitalizing on existing Malaysian and Indonesian suspicions of the growing Chinese naval power, Vietnam publicized the "common fear of Chinese policy in the South China Sea" that it shared with certain ASEAN members and sought ASEAN's support in its protest against Chinese oil exploration activities in its claimed territorial waters.[7] The anti-China stance that Vietnam provoked carried the potential to divide the organization.

Myanmar's induction into the regional organization at its July 1997 Annual Ministerial Meeting posed a more serious test for ASEAN. It created considerable tension with Western powers, especially the EU, while drawing condemnation from Southeast Asian non-governmental organizations as well. ASEAN refused to bow to international pressure to keep Myanmar out, on the grounds that doing so would violate its principle of non-interference. Yet granting membership to Myanmar, while essential to the realization of the ASEAN-10 concept, reinforced the negative image of ASEAN as a champion of authoritarianism.

The postponement of Cambodia's membership by ASEAN foreign ministers at a meeting on 10 July 1997 was also a test of ASEAN's non-interference doctrine. Since the decision to postpone was prompted by internal political developments in Cambodia, that is, Cambodian leader Hun Sen's ouster of his Co-Prime Minister Prince Norodom Ranariddh, it seemed like a departure from ASEAN's non-interference doctrine. Yet, as a signatory to the Paris Agreement on Cambodia of 1991, ASEAN did have a legal basis — indeed, an obligation — to respond to domestic developments that threatened to unravel the peace process. But the episode underscored the complexities and pitfalls of bringing the "One Southeast Asia" concept to fruition, especially the burden it imposed on ASEAN in dealing with its weaker and politically less stable new member states.

The expansion of ASEAN also reshaped regional economic interdependence and integration. It increased the volume of both intraregional and total trade in ASEAN. The participation of the new members in the ASEAN Free Trade Area (AFTA) was expected to increase ASEAN's collective competitiveness and expand the appeal of ASEAN's internal market to foreign investors, and to prevent the diversion of investment to other areas such as China and India. For existing members, the liberalization programmes pursued by the new members provided important new markets in the face of increasing protectionism in the West. These programmes also offered access to cheaper sources of raw materials and production locations. The new members stood to benefit economically, in ending their economic isolation, expanding the potential for subregional cooperation, increasing investment in manufacturing and infrastructure, and sustaining the momentum of attempts at economic reform. On the negative side, the expansion widened economic disparities within ASEAN, creating the basis for polarization and friction between richer old members and the poorer new ones.

Overall, ASEAN's expansion was celebrated as a political victory for those seeking the unity and integrity of Southeast Asia as a region. In the words of Ali Alatas, the Indonesian Foreign Minister at the time, expansion would "increase our ability to deal with these problems now that we are together, not divided nations of seven plus three".[8] But a less sanguine view of ASEAN's expansion was offered by a Thai newspaper, the *Bangkok Post*: "There is also the distinct possibility that the happy 10 will become something of a dysfunctional family unless the more progressive members grasp the formidable challenges that the three newcomers ... present."[9] An expanded ASEAN made it more difficult for the group to achieve consensus on key issues, which in turn constrained its ability to provide leadership and direction to the new members. The expansion threatened to dilute ASEAN's unity and consultative decision-making style and thereby to reduce the credibility of the organization in the eyes of the international community. Furthermore, the presumed economic benefits of ASEAN membership for the newly anointed were hard to come by, especially after the economic crisis that hit the region in 1997, impoverishing many of the original members such as Thailand, Indonesia and Malaysia.

Apart from the burdens imposed by membership expansion, Southeast Asian regionalism faced a host of new challenges in the 1990s. One set of challenges had to do with the danger of intraregional conflict. As noted in Chapter 4, some of the sources of regional tension in the Cold War period, such as the spillover effect of communist insurgencies in Thailand and Malaysia, had declined by the early 1990s. The decline of communist insurgency had also occurred in the Philippines and Indonesia. On the one hand, this contributed to the ASEAN states' confidence in normalizing ties with Vietnam, thereby reviving the prospects for regional unity and vindicating the ASEAN states' approach to economic development and regional order. On the other hand, the collapse of communist insurgency removed a major basis for ASEAN solidarity, since the common fear of this danger had served as a catalyst for ASEAN's formation and continued survival in the 1960s and 1970s. Moreover, the transborder spillover effect of ethnic separatist movements, including those in the southern Philippines, Aceh and southern Thailand, remained a source of interstate tension. For example, the exodus of refugees from Aceh to Malaysia soured Indonesia-Malaysia relations in the 1990s, while Manila's worry that the Moro separatists in Mindanao were receiving support from the Malaysian state of Sabah led Philippine politicians to take a hardline stand on formal renunciation of the Philippine claim to Sabah.

Intra-ASEAN relations were marked by a number of bilateral disputes, such as between Malaysia and Singapore over Pedra Branca Island (later settled in Singapore's favour by International Court of Justice (ICJ), between Malaysia and Indonesia over Sipadan and Ligitan islands in the Sulawesi Sea (also subsequently settled in Malaysia's favour by the ICJ), between Thailand and Malaysia over border-crossing rights, and between Malaysia and Brunei over the Limbang territory. Disputes in the maritime sphere were another source of regional discord. Thanks largely to the Law of the Sea Convention, such disputes had proliferated during the 1980s. In 1989, of the fifteen maritime boundaries in the South China Sea (excluding the Gulf of Thailand), twelve were in dispute, two had been agreed (one partially) and one resolved through a joint exploitation agreement. Six of these boundary disputes were between ASEAN member countries, with Malaysia having disputes with every other ASEAN country.[10] A different category of intraregional conflict that acquired a new importance in the post-Cold War era was the Spratly Islands dispute, involving China, Vietnam, Taiwan, Malaysia, Brunei and the Philippines.[11] This dispute was seen as having the potential to become the next regional "flashpoint of conflict" in Southeast Asia, after Cambodia.[12] Overall, as the Governor of Indonesia's Defense Institute warned, Southeast Asia had the potential to become the theatre of "prolonged, low-intensity conflicts without directly involving strong nations" that would replace larger conflicts fuelled by superpower rivalry during the Cold War.[13]

A related challenge to regional order were the military modernization programmes undertaken by Southeast Asian states.[14] Despite the improved security climate brought about by the end of the Cold War and the peace agreement on Cambodia, Southeast Asia witnessed a large-scale arms buildup. Defence expenditures increased significantly in all the ASEAN states,[15] which also modernized their armed forces by purchasing sophisticated weapons systems (especially combat aircraft, naval platforms and missiles), in order to enhance their capacity for interstate conventional warfare.[16] The regional military buildup could not simply be regarded as a full-blown "arms race" driven by inter-active rivalry. A number of other factors contributed to it. The end of the Cold War had left the major defence manufacturers of the world with large quantities of weapons that had to be exported to save jobs. Their consequent scramble for new markets presented the increasingly prosperous ASEAN states with an opportunity to indulge in post-Cold War bargain-hunting. Other considerations behind the military buildup included the perceived need for greater self-reliance in the wake of superpower retrenchment from the region, anxieties about rivalry among extraregional actors such as China, Japan and India, domestic inter-service rivalries, the prestige value of sophisticated weapons, and the technological spin-offs of advanced weapon acquisitions. Yet, whatever the cause, the increase in defence spending and arms purchases raised questions about the future of regional unity and order, especially at a time when ASEAN was making strong assertions about its contribution to peaceful relations in the region.

Apart from these somewhat conventional challenges, Southeast Asia was also faced with relatively new sets of issues with significant implications for regional cohesion. Foremost among them were human rights, democracy and the environment. The early 1990s saw human rights and democracy gaining a new salience as a result of the changing international environment, especially with the greater emphasis on human rights and democracy on the policy agendas of Western governments. The anti-communist thrust of Western policy, which had tolerated blatant human rights abuses by pro-Western Asian governments in the past, had ended. Lee Kuan Yew lamented that, with the end of the Cold War, U.S.

policies towards China, Japan and the countries of East Asia were no longer "guided by strategic and economic considerations as they used to be". Instead, "issues of human rights and democracy have become an obsession with the US media, Congress and the administration".[17] In general, Southeast Asian governments faced increasing pressure from the West over their human rights records. Violent military suppression of political protesters in Thailand in 1992 and East Timor separatists in 1991 attracted a great deal of negative international publicity. Other Southeast Asian countries, especially Malaysia and Singapore, were criticized by international human rights watchdogs for their internal security detention laws and lack of democratic freedoms. Faced with the loss of jobs to foreign (especially East Asian) competition, trade unions and human rights groups in the United States increasingly demanded linking trade privileges for countries such as Malaysia with their allowance of workers' rights.

Initially, it appeared that Southeast Asian governments, especially the ASEAN members, would be capable of presenting a collective front before the West on human rights and democracy. There were two broad areas of relative agreement in their perspectives. The first focused on cultural relativism, which argued that human rights should "vary because of differences in socio-economic and cultural backgrounds".[18] In 1993, prior to the Vienna World Conference on Human Rights, ASEAN had worked with other like-minded Asian countries (including China) to draft a declaration that stated that human rights "must be considered in the context of a dynamic and evolving process of international norm-setting, bearing in mind the significance of national and regional particularities and various historical, cultural and religious backgrounds".[19] To strengthen the case for relativism, Southeast Asian elites also presented a communitarian view of governance. Ali Alatas, speaking at the Vienna UN World Conference on Human Rights, argued that Indonesia and the developing world had to maintain a balance between an "individualistic approach" to human rights and the interests of the society as a whole. Singapore invoked the Confucian principle of "community over self".[20]

The second point of commonality among Southeast Asian states was the view that political freedom should not be stressed over economic and social rights. The ASEAN foreign ministers, meeting in Singapore in July 1993, issued a statement contending that:

> human rights are interrelated and indivisible comprising civil, political, economic, social and cultural rights. These rights are of equal importance.

They should be addressed in a balanced and integrated manner and protected and promoted with due regard for specific cultural, social, economic and political circumstances ... the promotion and protection of human rights should not be politicised.[21]

ASEAN's stance of cultural relativism came under criticism from both Western and local sources. Critics saw it as a justification for authoritarian political control. Moreover, the definition of what constituted cultural standards for defining human rights was not uniform between or within regional societies. Singapore's invoking of Confucian values could not be shared by Islamic Malaysia or Catholic Philippines or Buddhist Thailand. Nor did values converge within individual ASEAN states. In multi-ethnic ASEAN states, any attempt by the ruling elite to articulate a "national" position on human rights would be contested by other groups — especially religious and ethnic minorities. Thus, it was spurious to talk about a Southeast Asian position on human rights when individual countries could not overcome inter-ethnic competition within their own territories.[22]

Moreover, despite the talk about "Asian values", championed by Singapore's Lee Kuan Yew and Malaysia's Mahathir Mohammed, and the "ASEAN Way", even the elites in ASEAN did not necessarily share the same views on human rights and democracy. As Carolina Hernandez has argued, differences among the ASEAN states on human rights questions arose because their governments:

follow different paths (1) in the way they interpret human rights and democracy, (2) in their assumption of international legal obligations as indicated by their acceptance of international human rights norms embodied in various international human rights documents, (3) in the manner in which they have organized their domestic constitutional, legal and judicial systems as they relate to human rights concerns, and (4) in the degree of political openness of their societies ...[23]

As with human rights, authoritarian Southeast Asian leaders — Indonesia's Soeharto, Malaysia's Mahathir and Singapore's Lee Kuan Yew — were alarmed by what they saw as Western efforts to promote democracy in the region. Dismissing the suitability of Western-style democracy for the region, they argued that external pressures, including economic sanctions, would not be effective in bringing about democratic change. They also warned that the West's democratic zeal risked undermining the foundations of regional order based on the inviolability of state sovereignty. It went against one of the most vaunted

ASEAN norms: the doctrine of non-interference in the internal affairs of members. With the possible exception of its unprecedented collective support for the democratic Aquino regime, ASEAN, instead of promoting democratic norms, had regarded the internal political structure of its member countries as irrelevant to its regional framework.

In the case of Myanmar, ASEAN was instrumental in resisting Western calls for sanctions against the military regime and pushing for a policy of "constructive engagement".[24] Similarly, Vietnam was allowed to join ASEAN despite its communist political structure. These confirmed the nature of Southeast Asian regionalism as an elite-driven process in which human rights and democracy did not figure. Despite its claim to be based on broad historical, cultural and societal ties, the drive for regionalism to a large extent reflected the need of the post-colonial elite to ensure regime survival. The definition of what constituted the region, and who was to be included and excluded, was determined by the political and security interests of states, with non-state actors playing a rather marginal role.

But this situation began to change somewhat during the late 1990s, when non-governmental organizations (NGOs) increasingly made their presence felt over a host of issues, including development, environment and human rights, thereby developing a parallel track of regionalism. In the 1990s, Southeast Asian governments faced increasing demands for respect for human rights from these NGOs (especially in Thailand, Malaysia, Indonesia and the Philippines).[25] Despite scant resources and government suppression, these groups were encouraged by the favourable international climate for their cause. Their perspectives contrasted sharply with those of the Southeast Asian elites and provided an alternative channel for the development of human rights norms. The NGO community became especially active in the Philippines and Thailand, and in Indonesia after the fall of Soeharto.

While the development of human rights NGOs in Southeast Asia owed partly to financial support from Western donor countries, these groups did have strong domestic roots.[26] Some of the larger human rights NGOs in the region developed in response to political crackdowns by their own governments without being prompted by the West. This was the case in the emergence of NGOs in the Philippines after the declaration of martial law in 1972, in the establishment of the Legal Aid Institute (later called The Indonesian Legal Aid Foundation) in Indonesia in 1971, and in the emergence of Thai human rights groups after the coup of 1973.

Apart from action within the domestic sphere, there were some examples of concerted international action by Southeast Asian human rights NGOs. An example of this was the Bangkok NGO Declaration of March 1993, which was a clear rejection of the stand adopted by regional governments. The meeting revealed strong coordination among Southeast Asian NGOs (especially Thai, Malaysian, Filipino and Indonesian) as well as between South and Southeast Asian NGOs. Subsequently, Southeast Asian human rights activists tried unsuccessfully to submit their recommendations to the ASEAN foreign ministers during the inaugural ARF meeting in July 1994. Consequently, they accused the ASEAN foreign ministers of adopting "double standards by only showing concern for problems outside the region such as Bosnia and Rwanda while not demonstrating similar concern for problems that exist within the region, especially in Burma and East Timor". Exiled East Timorese leader Jose Ramos-Horta stated, "while ASEAN can be proud of its contribution to the resolution of the Cambodian conflict, it cannot be proud of its role on East Timor or on Burma." Regional NGOs also pointed out that, while the ASEAN foreign ministers were rejecting Western policies linking trade with workers' rights, labour standards and environmental issues as a new type of protectionism, "the ASEAN governments should primarily be held responsible for continued violations of workers' rights, the undermining of labour standards and degradation of the environment in their respective countries."[27]

The wider transboundary focus of human rights NGOs became more pronounced in the case of Thai groups that had "gone regional" and organized joint meetings with Indonesian human rights NGOs. This development prompted one observer to note that "official solidarity [among the ASEAN members] is mirrored by a greater sense of regionalism among non-governmental activists".[28]

While the development of human rights NGOs in Southeast Asia remains limited, the emergence of an NGO perspective on human rights already has important implications for the regional identity and international politics of Southeast Asia. Among other things, it ensures that the demand for human rights extends to and becomes more vocal in every Southeast Asian country. It refutes the government view that human rights is an externally imposed cause from the liberal West. It creates a more receptive audience for Western human rights policies. And finally, the pressure from NGOs forces Southeast Asian governments to respond and exercise greater sensitivity towards human rights, as shown by Indonesia's creation of a national human rights commission in June 1993. The campaign of NGOs to oppose ASEAN's policy of "constructive engagement" towards the military regime in Myanmar and to seek self-determination in East Timor marked the beginning of a "bottom-up" vision of regionalism, and a more inclusive approach to defining Southeast Asia's regional identity and role in the international system. (Further discussion of the role of civil society in Southeast Asian regionalism and identity can be found in Chapter 8.)

Southeast Asia and the Asia-Pacific Idea

One post-Cold War development with important implications for Southeast Asian regional identity was the emergence of Asia-Pacific multilateral institutions in the security and economic spheres. While the "One Southeast Asia" concept was motivated by a desire to enhance regional cohesion within Southeast Asia, participation in these wider regional groupings was conditioned by the need to preserve a Southeast Asian regional identity in the face of apparently overpowering extraregional security and political challenges.

The emergence of the Asia-Pacific idea was gradual, and responded to growing economic interdependence in the region. In the late 1980s and early 1990s, ASEAN took steps to develop a free trade area. This was in marked contrast to the lackadaisical attitude it had taken towards regional economic cooperation in the 1960s and 1970s. That attitude, as Stubbs points out, had to do with a concern for sovereignty as well as domestic economic conditions in the member states. Until the late 1980s, the most populous ASEAN countries — Indonesia, the Philippines, Thailand and Malaysia — had remained heavily reliant on raw material exports and import-substitution strategies. Indonesia's oil boom of the 1970s discouraged export promotion strategies. In Malaysia, the advent of the New Economic Policy (NEP) (aimed at giving indigenous Malays a greater share of the national wealth) resulted in massive government intervention, especially in creating import-substituting heavy industries. These conditions lessened the urgency of intraregional trade liberalization, more commonly associated with economies geared towards export promotion. Moreover, the level of intra-ASEAN trade had remained fairly low due to colonial linkages and the impact of the Vietnam War. As the 1990s approached, ASEAN members' trade with the United States, Western Europe and Japan was considerably higher than with each other.[29]

A number of developments led to a shift in the attitude of ASEAN states towards trade liberalization. The first had to do with changes in the international political economy in the 1980s, especially the global economic downturn early in the decade; rising protectionism in the United States; the international debt crisis and the consequent reduction in the flow of Northern capital to the South; and the economic recession in the ASEAN countries in the early 1980s. These developments made the ASEAN countries more aware of their economic vulnerabilities and contributed to moves towards regional cooperation. A second factor was the growing influence in the ASEAN member states of business pressure groups with an interest in regional trade liberalization. A third factor was political in nature. It stemmed from ASEAN's own desire to retain its relevance in the face of the proposals for and formation of newer and wider regional institutions such as the Asia-Pacific Economic Cooperation (APEC).[30]

At the Singapore Summit in 1992, ASEAN decided to create an ASEAN Free Trade Area (AFTA). Under AFTA, members were given until the year 2003 (new members were given an extension) to bring down their tariffs to between 0 and 5 per cent (AFTA's original deadline for reducing tariffs to that level was a fifteen-year period beginning in January 1993, but it was brought forward for the original ASEAN-Six to 2003). AFTA's evolution, its scope and the extent of its institutionalization conformed to the "ASEAN Way".[31] This meant a preference for informality, non-adversarial bargaining, consensus-building and non-legalistic procedures for decision-making rather than formal institutions and legal commitments.[32] ASEAN members agreed that AFTA be moved forward at a pace with which all governments felt comfortable.[33]

Apart from AFTA, ASEAN undertook a number of new initiatives to promote regional economic cooperation in the 1990s. These included cooperation in securing greater foreign investment through the creation of an ASEAN Investment Area, an ASEAN Investment Plan and an ASEAN Investment Code. Another initiative, aimed at generating greater trade in services, would be achieved by liberalizing market access and national treatment in key service sectors such as tourism, maritime transport, air transport, telecommunications, construction, business and financial services. Cooperation in intellectual property matters would be encouraged through the creation of an ASEAN Patent System and an ASEAN Trademark System.

Despite AFTA and these other initiatives, state-centric trade liberalization measures remained too modest to create a noticeably high degree
of regional interdependence in Southeast Asia. The level of intra-ASEAN
trade as proportion of total ASEAN trade remained around 16–17 per
cent in the 1980s.[34] From 1991 to 1995, trade among the ASEAN Six
grew at an annual rate of 21.6 per cent, totalling $137 billion, or 23 per
cent of their total trade. In comparison, the world trade of the ASEAN
Six grew at a slower annual rate of 15 per cent over the same period.
(But if transshipment through Singapore is discounted, the level of intra-
ASEAN trade falls to about 12 per cent.)[35] Moreover, AFTA remained
plagued by fears among ASEAN members about the unequal distribution
of gains. This was aggravated by the differing levels of development
between the ASEAN Six and the new ASEAN members, even though
the latter were allowed extensions beyond the 2003 deadline to bring
their tariffs down to the required level.

The low level of intraregional trade was not the only challenge facing
ASEAN in developing Southeast Asia as an economic region. A second
challenge came from the global economic situation in the late 1980s
and early 1990s. For the ASEAN states, one of the most troubling
developments was rising protectionism in the West. This pre-dated the
crisis in the Uruguay Round of GATT talks in the late 1980s, but the
latter contributed to a sense of urgency. In March 1991, Singapore's Goh
Chok Tong specifically argued that it was in ASEAN's interests to see
free trade and GATT work, but if this was not the case "and others
[were] forming trading arrangements, then there would be no choice
but for us to look after our own interests by following what others
do".[36] A related development was the prospect of a declining flow of
investment from Western countries to Southeast Asia, as the Eastern
European market opened up. A former Finance Minister of Malaysia,
Daim Zainuddin, warned that "the expected diversion of private foreign
capital to Eastern Europe would ... necessitate that ASEAN lay greater
stress on the intra-regional flow of capital, to lessen the dependence
on external sources to maintain the momentum of growth".[37] Though
overstated, the chances of a crunch in the availability of investment
capital aggravated ASEAN's concerns regarding the competition it could
face in attracting Western capital.

These perceived global economic trends shaped ASEAN's interest
in, and attitude towards, the development of wider regional economic
frameworks, especially APEC. APEC grew out of various academic and

semi-official initiatives, especially the Pacific Economic Cooperation Conference (PECC), set up in 1980 to explore and advance free trade and economic cooperation in the Asia-Pacific region. APEC was conceived as a more formal intergovernmental vehicle for cooperation that could allow the region as a whole to coordinate an approach to GATT and increase the liberalization of trade in the area.[38] Growing support for Asia-Pacific economic regionalism was partly in anticipation of European integration and the free trade agreement between Canada and the United States. The first meeting of APEC, attended by ministers from twelve Pacific states (Australia, Canada, Japan, South Korea, New Zealand, the United States and the six countries in ASEAN) was held on 5–7 November 1989 in Canberra, Australia. ASEAN governments were initially lukewarm to APEC, fearing that it would be dominated by non-Southeast Asian countries such as Japan, Australia and the United States. ASEAN wished to be the model for APEC and was keen to ensure that the new grouping should not on any account reduce the activities or status of ASEAN. ASEAN wished to remain as the core of multilateral processes in the region; other regional institutions should assess the ASEAN experience and proceed from there. Subsequently, ASEAN came to accept APEC, recognizing ASEAN and APEC as "concentric circles".[39] But its endorsement of the wider regional economic body came with a number of conditions: (1) APEC should not deal with political and security issues; (2) APEC should not lead to the formation of a trade bloc; (3) APEC's institutional arrangements should not reduce the importance and role of existing Asia-Pacific institutions for cooperation; and (4) ASEAN's machinery should be the centre of the APEC process.[40]

ASEAN saw APEC as a useful forum for managing trade conflicts within the region, as well as a platform to advance ASEAN's interest in global multilateral trade negotiations.[41] Another contribution of APEC was seen to lie in countering some of the uncertainties in the regional investment climate caused by developments in Eastern Europe. At a time when Eastern Europe was attracting more attention from Western countries, APEC would provide an extra incentive for Japan and other major regional economies to invest in Southeast Asia.[42]

Despite their acceptance of APEC, some ASEAN members felt that a regional economic group involving the developed and developing economies of the Asia-Pacific was not the most desirable way to address the economic problems of the 1990s. Malaysia in particular resented the fact that APEC was an Australian initiative, that it was dominated by

Western members at the expense of ASEAN and that it did not reflect the level of de facto economic integration achieved within the East Asia region, which by some measures exceeded trans-Pacific integration. These factors led Malaysia's Prime Minister, Mahathir Mohamad, to call for the establishment of an exclusive East Asian Economic Grouping (EAEG), later changed to the East Asian Economic Caucus (EAEC), in December 1990, soon after the collapse of the Uruguay Round talks over agricultural subsidies. Malaysia described the proposal as a move to "counter the emergence of protectionism and regionalism in world trade".[43] The most striking aspect of the EAEC was the exclusion from its membership of the key members of APEC, including the United States and Australia. The EAEC was to comprise the ASEAN countries, Taiwan, Hong Kong, South Korea and Japan, with the latter clearly being assigned the pivotal role.[44]

On the face of it, the EAEC concept was firmly rooted in the economic realities of the region.[45] Not only was trade among East Asian countries expected to exceed trans-Pacific trade in the 1990s in terms of investment, but the 1980s had seen a massive increase in Japanese private investment in the region.[46] South Korean and Taiwanese investment in Southeast Asia had added to the massive influx of Japanese capital, creating a strong sense of East Asian economic interdependence.

However, if Malaysia's intention was to test the reaction of ASEAN partners to the idea of a trade bloc that would "counter the emergence of protectionism and regionalism in world trade" through similar methods, then it clearly made little headway. Its ASEAN partners, not convinced that a genuine trade bloc would be possible within the GATT framework or acceptable to the major trading partners of ASEAN, expressed reservation. Strong opposition from the United States was clearly stated by Richard Solomon, Assistant Secretary of State for East Asia and Pacific, who argued that the EAEC would be a "very unwise direction to proceed".[47] In the face of U.S. opposition and Japanese reluctance, the EAEC concept remained stagnant despite a compromise formula adopted by ASEAN, which called for the EAEC to function as a caucus within APEC. But the subsequently convened summits under the Asia-Europe Meeting (ASEM) framework would see all the projected members of the EAEC participate with members of the EU, prompting Malaysia to claim that the EAEC idea had in effect become a reality. Another significant development, given a strong push in November 1999, was the proposal for an East Asian Forum comprising ASEAN members and Japan, China and South Korea.

But the ASEAN countries continue to adhere to an economic approach that rejects inward-looking trade structures and seeks the maintenance of an open and multilateral international trade regime.

Asia-Pacific multilateral institutions like the APEC and EAEC were not the only entities raising questions about the concept of Southeast Asia as a distinct economic region. Another challenge came from trends in transnational production, in the form of what has been known variously as "growth triangles", "natural economic territories", or "subregional economic zones" (here the term "growth triangle" will be used as a generic concept). At least four such areas emerged in the first part of the 1990s: the Singapore-Johor-Riau (SIJORI) triangle; the Indonesia-Malaysia-Thailand Growth Triangle (IMT-GT); the East ASEAN Growth Area (EAGA) involving Sabah, Sarawak and Labuan in Malaysia, North Sulawesi, East Kalimantan and West Kalimantan in Indonesia, the Mindanao region of the Philippines, and Brunei; and finally, the Growth Quadrangle of mainland Southeast Asia, consisting of China's Yunnan province, Laos, Thailand and Myanmar.

By their very nature, the growth triangles challenged the traditional, state-centric regional concept of Southeast Asia that consisted of the officially defined state boundaries of the ten member countries of ASEAN. But these triangles have contributed to the enhanced intraregional security accruing from greater economic integration and confidence-building.[48] They have also reestablished some of the intra-Southeast Asian economic linkages lost during the colonial period. Moreover, their emergence reflected an attenuation of economic nationalism, which had in the past thwarted the development of a regional identity and regional cooperation. Many of the states involved in the growth triangles had been bitter enemies in the not-too-distant past. The emergence of a growth triangle linking Borneo and Mindanao, for example, was striking, given the long-standing dispute between Malaysia and the Philippines over Sabah. The case of the IMT-GT was also significant, given the periodic strains in the Thai-Malaysian relationship over Malaysian support for Thai Muslim separatists and the problems in Malaysia-Indonesia ties over the exodus of Acehnese refugees to Malaysia. Thus, the shared commitment of these states to a growth triangle suggested at the very least that the traditional element of the region's high politics was no longer a sufficient barrier to serious attempts at economic regionalism. On the other hand, these entities remained underdeveloped and their management was plagued by intramural differences. They could not overcome the political suspicions and differences in economic approach among Southeast Asian countries.

The organization of security relations within the Asia-Pacific framework region was shaped by trends in the international system that accompanied the end of the Cold War.[49] The post-Cold War milieu, some Southeast Asian analysts feared, would see an unleashing of conflicts that had been effectively frozen or "suppressed" during the colonial era and the subsequent period of superpower rivalry.[50] A major determinant of the early post-Cold War international environment had to do with the reduction of superpower forces in the Asia-Pacific region. The withdrawal of the Soviet presence in Cam Ranh Bay in Vietnam was followed by the removal of the U.S. bases in the Philippines. At its peak in the mid-1980s, the Soviet presence in Cam Ranh Bay had aroused strong concerns in ASEAN about the threat it could pose to the security of sea lanes and the impetus it might give to Vietnamese designs on Southeast Asia. But by January 1990, the Soviets had reportedly withdrawn most of their forces at Cam Ranh Bay.[51] The Soviet withdrawal caused concern that it would reduce the stakes of the United States in its Philippines bases and precipitate a reduction in the U.S. military presence in the Pacific, which ASEAN considered vital to regional stability. And for at least some ASEAN states, particularly Malaysia, the Soviet withdrawal from Vietnam removed a useful counterweight to China's regional ambitions.

Adding to the concern were uncertainties about the U.S. military presence in the Pacific in general, and in the Philippines bases in particular. Despite repeated U.S. statements that any cutbacks in its military presence would not be substantial, the initial U.S. plan to reduce its military presence in Japan, South Korea and the Philippines by 15 per cent became a source of concern to ASEAN.[52] All ASEAN member states acknowledged the role of the United States as a stabilizing force in the region. Even Indonesia and Malaysia, the staunchest supporters of ASEAN's ZOPFAN concept, conceded the need for a U.S. presence in the region.[53]

Although there was no regional consensus as to the nature of the threat posed by developments in great-power relations, it was clear that the rise of China evoked the most immediate concern in Southeast Asia in the post-Cold War era. Sino-ASEAN relations had improved dramatically during the Cambodian conflict. Not only was ASEAN able to secure a Chinese pledge to cease its support for communist insurgencies in the region, but China was also seen as a potential guarantor of ASEAN's security against the Vietnamese threat. Thailand became a de facto ally of Beijing, developing a substantial arms-transfer relationship. The end of the Cold War and the Cambodian conflict coincided with the growing military and economic power of China. The end of the Sino-Soviet conflict and Soviet force withdrawals from their common border enabled Beijing to devote more resources and attention to contingencies in the South China Sea.[54] While watching these developments with concern, the ASEAN countries also continued to maintain a very ambivalent attitude towards Japan, although, as Lee Kuan Yew said, in ASEAN, "fear of Japan's re-militarisation [was] more emotional than rational".[55] Any prospect of a unilateral Japanese security posture was viewed with grave suspicion. Japan's role in UN peacekeeping operations through the use of non-combatant soldiers could be tolerated.[56] But in the late 1980s increased U.S. pressure on Tokyo to enhance its maritime defence capabilities caused discomfort in Southeast Asia, where some also feared that a major U.S. military withdrawal from the region would prompt Japanese remilitarization.[57] And concerns persisted in ASEAN capitals about further U.S. force reductions in the region, despite assurances by U.S. officials to the contrary. In addition, ASEAN governments feared that the retreat of the United States, by prompting Japan to become a more self-reliant military power, could provoke China to increase its own military capability, thereby creating a new security dilemma in Asia.

The shift from superpower to regional power rivalry formed the core of security concerns in Southeast Asia. By seeking to balance each other, regional powers might engage in a competition that would create a multipolar regional order much less stable than the Cold War system. Regional order could also be challenged by rivalry between the United States and two of the leading regional powers, China and Japan. The prospect that the U.S.-Japan trade dispute might escalate and thereby threaten the fate of the U.S.-Japan security relationship constituted the worst-case scenario. The state of the Sino-U.S. relationship was another key factor in Southeast Asian security. The growing friction between the United States and China over human rights and Washington's threat of economic sanctions against China was seen by Lee Kuan Yew as having "serious long-term consequences for Asia-Pacific peace and stability".[58]

It is against the backdrop of these concerns and uncertainties that ASEAN began to develop new frameworks and responses in the political and security spheres. While the project to complete "One Southeast Asia" proceeded, ASEAN governments also felt that Southeast Asia-specific solutions would not suffice, given the seriousness of the challenges facing them on the security front. They would also need to address these challenges at the wider Asia-Pacific level. This would be a major departure from ASEAN's traditional security approach, which had during the Cold War focused essentially on the subregional environment of Southeast Asia. Then the ASEAN framework had professed the need for regional autonomy, with a strong distrust of externally inspired solutions to regional problems. Now, ASEAN's approach to regional security came to embrace a wider concept of "region" than in the previous era. Southeast Asia could no longer hope to insulate itself from the impact of security trends in the wider Asia-Pacific region that had been set in motion by new patterns of interaction among the United States, China, Japan and Russia.

This realization also necessitated a rethinking of the ZOPFAN concept. ZOPFAN had already proved to be an impracticable concept because some ASEAN members, especially Singapore and Thailand, saw it as detrimental to regional stability, given the need for the region to retain the "balancing wheel" role of the United States to ensure its security and economic progress.[59] Now, in the post-Cold War context, the relevance of ZOPFAN was even further undermined. Although ASEAN members maintained a declaratory commitment to ZOPFAN, even its staunchest supporters conceded that the ideal required reassessment and adjustment in view of the changing regional strategic environment.[60] Frameworks of security that were more inclusive of regional and extraregional powers had to be given due consideration.

Such rethinking was further pushed along by proposals for "common security" and "cooperative security" advanced by other Asia-Pacific nations.[61] These proposals, initiated by Russia, Australia and Canada, called for the creation of a regional security institution to facilitate confidence-building and conflict resolution within the region. Security multilateralism was viewed by these proponents as a more desirable alternative to deterrence-based security, underpinned by United States military alliances. The very fact that the region's former adversaries, such as the ASEAN states and Vietnam, Russia and Japan, and China and Russia, had been searching for common ground in which to bury the Cold War hatchet further encouraged ideas concerning multilateral approaches to security issues.

ASEAN's initial response to these proposals was marked with some apprehension and scepticism. ASEAN leaders argued that the Asia-Pacific theatre was too complex and diverse to allow for European-style multilateral security cooperation. Moreover, the fact that almost all the proposals for regional security cooperation came from "outside" powers, and that some of these were based on European models of security cooperation, aroused suspicions in ASEAN, which had hitherto believed that regional order must be based on indigenous conceptions of security without any kind of influence or interference by countries outside the region.

But ASEAN could not ignore the growing calls for multilateralism. Lest the outside powers seize the initiative, ASEAN had to come up with an "indigenous" framework that would enable it to play a central role in developing any multilateral framework for regional security. In this sense, ASEAN was given an opportunity to project its subregional experience in security cooperation onto a larger regional arena and thereby enhance its relevance and role as a regional institution in the post-Cold War era. Against this backdrop, on 28 January 1992, at the end of the fourth summit meeting held in Singapore, ASEAN leaders agreed to "promote external dialogues on enhancing security as well as intra-ASEAN dialogues on ASEAN security cooperation".[62] They expressed support for informal and consultative mechanisms within the existing ASEAN framework, especially through the annual meeting between ASEAN foreign ministers and their dialogue partners (called the ASEAN Post-Ministerial Conferences — ASEAN-PMC). This move, which ensured that ASEAN would remain at the centre of the evolving security apparatus in the Asia-Pacific, culminated in the formation of the ASEAN Regional Forum (ARF) in 1994.

The ARF began life with eighteen members: Brunei, Indonesia, Laos, Malaysia, the Philippines, Singapore, Thailand, Vietnam, Australia, Canada, China, the European Union, Japan, South Korea, New Zealand, Papua New Guinea, Russia and the United States (Cambodia joined a year later, while India and Myanmar were accepted as members in 1996). The ARF was not only the first truly "multilateral" security forum covering the wider Asia-Pacific region, it was also the only "regional" security framework in the world in which all the great powers (including the United States, Russia, Japan, China and India, as well as Britain, France and Germany as part of the European Union delegation) were represented.

The founding statement of the ARF defined its goal as the creation of a "more predictable and constructive pattern of relations for the Asia Pacific region".[63] The key principle underlying the ARF was the notion of "cooperative security", defined by Gareth Evans, then Foreign Minister of Australia, as an effort to build "security with others rather than against them".[64] Through the ARF, ASEAN sought to influence and manage regional order in five ways. The first was to offset the strategic uncertainties of the post-Cold War period. A multilateral security forum could help to avoid misperceptions and generate new ideas about, and approaches to, regional order. The second was to "engage" China in a system of regional order to dilute the threat to regional stability posed by its unprecedented economic growth and military buildup. This strategy was seen as being preferable to the alternative of "containment", which ASEAN members saw as an impractical and dangerous strategic option. Thirdly, the ARF could be a useful device to ensure the continued engagement of the United States in the region's security affairs. This in turn would preclude the emergence of an independent Japanese security role, a development that ASEAN viewed as highly destabilizing. The fourth goal that ASEAN sought to pursue through the ARF was to ensure that intraregional conflicts, such as the territorial disputes in the South China Sea, could be managed peacefully through multilateral norms and principles. To this end, the ARF sought to develop measures of confidence-building and preventive diplomacy to constrain the use of force in interstate relations. Finally, the ARF provided ASEAN, a coalition of small powers, with a measure of influence over great-power geopolitics in the region. Acting collectively through a multilateral forum, ASEAN members could shape the development of a set of ideas and principles that might persuade the region's major powers to use diplomacy and "rules of acceptable conduct", rather than arms races and alliances, as the principal means of preserving regional equilibrium.

Since its inception, the ARF has been characterized by two broad features: incrementalism and soft institutionalism. Incrementalism, implying a step-by-step approach to security collaboration, is evident from a document entitled "The ASEAN Regional Forum: A Concept Paper", developed by ASEAN in 1995. The paper envisaged three stages of security cooperation: confidence-building, preventive diplomacy and conflict resolution.[65] The initial measures of confidence-building selected by the ARF include the annual and voluntary exchange of information on defence postures, increased dialogues on security issues on bilateral, subregional and regional bases, the forging of senior-level contacts and exchanges among military institutions and the participation of the ARF members in the UN Conventional Arms Register. Though limited, the ARF's confidence-building initiatives are an important step towards greater regional security cooperation. The outlook for preventive diplomacy, however, is more constrained due to concerns by some members (especially China) that it would violate the principle of non-interference in the internal affairs of states. By the end of 2009, more than a decade and a half after its founding, the ARF had yet to move beyond confidence-building to a preventive diplomacy role.

ASEAN's involvement in the ARF has been marked by a number of problems. Under its guidance, the ARF adopted an evolutionary and non-legalistic approach to security cooperation. Critics of the ARF argue that it would remain essentially a "talk shop", rather than an instrument of collective action in regional conflicts. ASEAN's style in the leadership of the ARF does not sit well with some of the Western members, who would like the ARF to develop quickly and adopt concrete measures.[66] They doubt whether the so-called "ASEAN Way" of consultation and consensus-building will be effective in the Asia-Pacific context. Finally, by getting too closely involved in a wider regional cooperation framework, ASEAN may have risked the dilution of its own quest for Southeast Asian autonomy and identity. Its leadership role in the ARF challenges the conception of Southeast Asia as a distinct security region.

Conclusion

The preceding discussion dealt with the challenges to Southeast Asia emerging from the "deepening" and "widening" of the regional space managed by ASEAN. Challenges to the regional concept of Southeast Asia stemmed from its intraregional and external environment. Intraregionally, progress towards "One Southeast Asia" had paradoxical implications. While realizing a foundational dream of ASEAN (at least according to official lore), it also extended ASEAN's political, economic and diplomatic diversity. The lack of familiarity of the new members with the "ASEAN process" may have undermined somewhat the sense of regional identity that had been painstakingly constructed over the past three decades. Externally, the challenge came from Southeast Asia's closer interdependence and integration with the wider Asia-Pacific region. Of particular significance here was ASEAN's involvement in the Asia-

Pacific multilateral institutions APEC and ARF, although an even more significant challenge, the ASEAN Plus Three (the basis for an East Asian Community, to be discussed in the next chapter) was also conceived during the early 1990s.

But there was a further and more serious challenge to Southeast Asia in the late 1990s. The forces of economic globalization, as manifested through the economic crisis plaguing the region from mid-1997 on, also exposed the precarious dependence of Southeast Asian countries on external forces, and called into question their professed aspirations towards regional autonomy. Together, as will be discussed in the following chapter, these developments created pressures on Southeast Asia's regional unity and identity.

NOTES

[1]	Thai prime minister Anand Panyarachun, cited in the *Straits Times*, 25 June 1991.
[2]	Statement by H.E. Ali Alatas, Minister for Foreign Affairs and Co-Chair of the Paris Peace Conference on Cambodia, 23 October 1991, p. 4.
[3]	*Straits Times*, 17 February 1992, p. 11.
[4]	Sukhumbhand Paribatra, "ASEAN Ten and Its Role in the Asia Pacific", paper prepared for the conference, "Asia in the XXI Century", organized by the Institute for International Relations, Hanoi, 28–29 April 1997, p. 5.
[5]	Carolina Hernandez, "One Southeast Asia in the 21st Century: Opportunities and Challenges", paper presented to the 1995 Convention of the Canadian Council for Southeast Asian Studies on "The Dynamism of Southeast Asia", University of Laval, Quebec City, 27–29 October 1995, p. 4.
[6]	"Vietnam Joins ASEAN", *Strategic Comments*, no. 5, 8 June 1995, p. 2.
[7]	Martin Gainsborough, "Vietnam II: A Turbulent Normalisation with China", *The World Today* 48, no. 11 (1992), p. 207.
[8]	K. Chaipipat, "ASEAN Agrees to Burma's Entry", *The Nation*, 1 June 1997.
[9]	"Coping with a Larger Family", editorial, *Bangkok Post*, internet edition <www. bangkokpost.com> (accessed 13 June 1997).
[10]	Commodore A. Ramli Nor, "ASEAN Maritime Cooperation", paper presented to the Defence Asia '89 Conference on "Towards Greater ASEAN Military and Security Cooperation: Issues and Prospects", Singapore, 22–25 March 1989, pp. 2–6.
[11]	Marko Milivojevic, "The Spratly and Paracel Islands Conflict", *Survival* 31, no. 1 (1989): 70–78.
[12]	"Spratly Islands: Jakarta's Next Target for Peace", *Sunday Times*, 6 January 1991, p. 10.

[13] *Straits Times,* 24 August 1992, p. 12.

[14] See Tim Huxley, "South-East Asia's Arms Race: Some Notes on Recent Developments", *Arms Control* 11, no. 1 (1990): 69–76; M. Vatikiotis, "Measure for Measure: Malaysia, Singapore Poised to Acquire New Arms", *Far Eastern Economic Review,* 30 April 1992, p. 18.

[15] See S. Kondo, "The Evolving Security Environment: Political", paper presented to the workshop on "Arms Control and Confidence-Building in the Asia-Pacific Region", organized by the Canadian Institute for International Peace and Security, Ottawa, 22–23 May 1992, pp. 4–5; A. Mack, "Asia's New Military Build-up", *Pacific Research* 4, no. 1 (1991), p. 12.

[16] The procurement of fighter aircraft became a key regionwide trend in the mid- and late 1980s, when three countries, Indonesia, Thailand and Singapore, acquired the F-16 from the United States, as well as advanced airborne early warning capabilities. Other states have entered the fray since, with Indonesia, Malaysia and Brunei acquiring Hawk advanced jet trainer/strike aircraft from Britain, Russian-built MiG-29 Fulcrum fighters and U.S.-built FA-18 fighters. Singapore's air force, already the region's most advanced, further increased its combat aircraft strength by acquiring additional F-16 fighter aircrafts from the United States. Thailand also purchased additional F-16A/B fighters as well as E-2C Hawkeye Airborne Early Warning and Control aircraft from the United States. See Amitav Acharya, "An Arms Race in Post-Cold War Southeast Asia? Prospects for Control", Pacific Strategic Paper no. 8 (Singapore: Institute of Southeast Asian Studies, 1994).

[17] Michael Richardson, "For the Planners, a Time to Decide", *International Herald Tribune,* 18 November 1993, p. 5.

[18] Gordon Fairclough, "Standing Firm", *Far Eastern Economic Review,* 15 April 1993, p. 22.

[19] "Vienna Showdown", *Far Eastern Economic Review,* 17 June 1993, p. 17.

[20] Kishore Mahbubani, "New Areas of ASEAN Reaction: Environment, Human Rights and Democracy", *Asean-ISIS Monitor* 5 (1992), p. 15, and at <www.aseansec.org>.

[21] Joint communiqué of the Twenty-Sixth ASEAN Ministerial Meeting, Singapore, 23–24 July 1993, p. 7.

[22] Yash Ghai, *Human Rights and Governance: The Asia Debate* (San Francisco: The Asia Foundation, Center for Asian Pacific Affairs, 1994), p. 10.

[23] Carolina Hernandez, "ASEAN Perspectives on Human Rights and Democracy in International Relations: Problems and Prospects", Working Paper 1995–1, Centre for International Studies, University of Toronto, p. 13.

[24] See Amitav Acharya, "Human Rights and Regional Order: ASEAN and Human Rights Management in post-Cold War Southeast Asia", in *Human Rights and International Relations in the Asia-Pacific,* edited by James T. H. Tang (London: Pinter, 1995), pp. 167–82; Amitav Acharya, *Human Rights in Southeast Asia: Dilemmas of Foreign Policy* (Toronto: Joint Centre for Asia Pacific Studies, 1995).

[25] On the role of human rights NGOs in Asia, see S. Jones, "The Organic Growth", *Far Eastern Economic Review*, 17 June 1993, p. 23.

[26] Sidney Jones, "The Impact of Asian Economic Growth on Human Rights", Asia Project Working Paper (New York: Council on Foreign Relations, 1995).

[27] "Thailand: Rights Activists Get Cold Reception", *Bangkok Post*, 26 July 1994, p. 10.

[28] Michael Vatikiotis, "Going Regional", *Far Eastern Economic Review*, 20 October 1994, p. 16.

[29] Richard Stubbs, "Signing on to Liberalization: AFTA and the Politics of Regional Economic Cooperation", *The Pacific Review* 13, no. 2 (2000): 297–318.

[30] Paul Bowles, "ASEAN, AFTA and the New Regionalism", *Pacific Affairs* 70, no. 2 (1997), p. 221.

[31] Stubbs, "Signing on to Liberalization".

[32] Ibid.

[33] Ibid.

[34] M. Hadi Soesastro, "Prospects for Pacific-Asian Regional Trade Structures", in *Regional Dynamics: Security, Political and Economic Issues in the Asia-Pacific Region*, edited by R. Scalapino et al. (Jakarta: Centre for Strategic and International Studies, 1990), p. 391.

[35] For an excellent study of the economic implications of an expanded ASEAN that is the main source for the discussion in this paragraph, see *The New ASEANs: Vietnam, Burma, Cambodia and Laos* (Canberra: Department of Foreign Affairs and Trade, 1997).

[36] He was of course referring to worries about the apparent formation of trade blocs in Europe and North America and making the point that ASEAN might be forced to consider similar measures in response. See *Straits Times*, 5 March 1991.

[37] *Straits Times* (weekly overseas edition), 31 March 1990.

[38] For instance, see James Cotton, "APEC: Australia Hosts Another Pacific Acronym", *The Pacific Review* 3, no. 2 (1990): 171–73.

[39] *Far Eastern Economic Review*, 16 November 1989, p. 11.

[40] Noordin Sopiee, "Pan-Pacific Talks: ASEAN is the Key", *International Herald Tribune*, 4–5 November 1989, p. 4.

[41] Text of speech by Lee Hsien Loong, Minister for Trade and Industries, Singapore, to the Indonesia Forum, Jakarta, 11 July 1990, p. 9.

[42] Ibid.

[43] *Far Eastern Economic Review*, 31 January 1991, p. 32.

[44] Later, in the wake of concerns regarding the exclusion of important regional actors such as Australia, Malaysia was to insist that there was no "exclusion list" for EAEG and that Australia's participation would be possible at a subsequent stage.

45 See Paul Evans, "The Changing Context of Security Relations in Eastern Asia", paper prepared for the workshop on "Korea and the Changing Asia-Pacific Region", 8–9 February 1990.

46 *International Herald Tribune*, 8–9 December 1990.

47 *Straits Times*, 22 December 1990.

48 Amitav Acharya, "Transnational Production and Security: Southeast Asia's Growth Triangles", *Contemporary Southeast Asia* 17, no. 2 (1995): 173–85.

49 Hari Singh, "Prospects for Regional Stability in Southeast Asia in the Post-Cold War Era", *Millennium* 22, no. 2 (1993): 279–300.

50 Leszek Buszynski, "Declining Superpowers: The Impact on ASEAN", *Pacific Review* 3, no. 3 (1990), p. 258.

51 Michael Richardson, "Soviets Cutting Vietnam Force", *International Herald Tribune*, 16 January 1990, p. 1.

52 "Asia Shudders in the Grip of New Fears after the Cold War", *Straits Times*, 29 December 1990, p. 23.

53 "Asean Talks about Security at Last, But How Far Will it Go?", *Straits Times*, 1 February 1992, p. 24.

54 Cheung Tai Ming, "China's Regional Military Posture", *International Defense Review*, June 1991, pp. 618–22.

55 Lee Kuan Yew, "Japan's Key Role in the Industrialization of East Asia", *Straits Times*, 14 February 1992, p. 22.

56 Michael Richardson, "Asians Urge Japan to be Peacekeeper", *International Herald Tribune*, 8 March 1991, p. 1.

57 Sheldon W. Simon, "United States Security Policy and ASEAN", *Current History* 89, no. 545 (1990), p. 98.

58 Lee Kuan Yew, *Straits Times* (weekly overseas edition), 14 November 1992, p. 24.

59 Muthiah Alagappa, "Regional Arrangements and International Security in Southeast Asia: Going Beyond ZOPFAN", *Contemporary Southeast Asia*, vol. 12, no. 4 (1991): 269–305.

60 "Asean Must Stick to Zopfan Plan, Says Alatas", *Straits Times*, 31 December 1990, p. 11.

61 For a discussion of the evolution of ideas and initiatives concerning a multilateral security system in the Asia-Pacific region, see Amitav Acharya, *A New Regional Order in Southeast Asia: ASEAN in the Post-Cold War Era*, Adelphi Paper no. 279 (London: International Institute for Strategic Studies, 1993).

62 *Singapore Declaration of 1992*, ASEAN Heads of Government Meeting, Singapore, 27–28 January 1992, p. 2.

63 "The ASEAN Regional Forum: A Concept Paper", document circulated at the Second Annual Meeting of the ASEAN Regional Forum, Brunei, 1 August 1995.

64 *Straits Times*, 4 August 1994, p. 2.

65 "The ASEAN Regional Forum: A Concept Paper", Annex A and B, pp. 8–11.

66 "New Framework for Security", *Straits Times*, 26 July 1994, p. 15.

8

Globalization and the Crisis of Regional Identity

A key question about regions is their permanence and transience. Regional identity can be altered or undermined by a variety of forces, external and internal to the region. In modern times, the forces that are especially likely to affect regional identity are globalization, the rise of new power centres within or in proximity to a region, altered political interactions with countries outside the region, and regional social forces that compete with state-sponsored national and regional identities. In this chapter, I discuss four key challenges to Southeast Asia that have arisen since the turn of the last century: (1) the perils of globalization, including the "Asian financial crisis" of 1997 and the "global financial crisis" of 2008, and new transnational dangers, such as pandemics, environmental degradation, natural disasters and terrorism; (2) the emergence of a civil society regionalism; (3) the rise of China and India; and (4) the emergence of the idea of an East Asian Community (EAC). These challenges have raised serious questions about whether the regional idea of Southeast Asia can endure into the future.

The Perils of Globalization

Southeast Asia's exposure to the forces of globalization, such as financial downturns, terrorism, pandemics and environmental degradation, was amply evident throughout the post-Cold War period. The Asian financial crisis (or the Asian economic crisis, as it is also called) began in mid-1997, underscoring the pitfalls of economic development strategies that were based on an emphasis on foreign investment and export-oriented industrialization without adequate regulatory mechanisms.[1] Commenting on the seriousness of the crisis for Southeast Asia, Rodolfo Severino, then Secretary-General of ASEAN, commented: "Since ASEAN's founding thirty-one years ago, no disaster has hit the countries of Southeast Asia with such widespread impact as the financial crisis."[2] While the crisis was not "Southeast Asian" in scope (apart from South Korea, it acquired the attributes of a global crisis affecting countries as far apart as Russia and Brazil), the "contagion" effect of the crisis was most seriously felt in Southeast Asia. Moreover, the crisis was peculiarly Southeast Asian in the way it threatened to unravel and reshape intraregional politics, and created the impetus for a broader East Asian Community.

The Asian economic crisis confronted the regional concept and the regionalism of Southeast Asia with a number of challenges, undermining intra-Southeast Asian relations, aggravating latent bilateral tensions and damaging ASEAN's credibility as an instrument of regional cooperation. The crisis severely affected four Southeast Asian countries: Thailand, Indonesia, Malaysia and the Philippines. The Indonesian currency lost 80 per cent of its value, while the currencies of Thailand, Malaysia and Philippines suffered smaller but significant losses of value (40, 40 and 30 per cent against the dollar respectively) during the first weeks of January 1998.[3] The currencies of Singapore, the regional trade hub, and Brunei (tied to the Singapore dollar) also lost value. Other Southeast Asian countries, Vietnam, Laos and Myanmar and Cambodia, lost a good deal of the foreign investment that came from their neighbours. During 1997–98, over US$30 billion fled Indonesia, Malaysia, the Philippines and Thailand. Unemployment almost doubled in Malaysia and nearly tripled in Indonesia and Thailand.[4] Overall growth rates in Southeast Asia plunged to minus 7.5 per cent in 1998,[5] prompting the World Bank to call the crisis "the biggest setback for poverty reduction in East Asia for several decades".[6]

Despite the diversity among the economies of Southeast Asian countries, it was possible to locate some common factors behind the crisis, including dependence on foreign investment, property and stock market bubbles, large external deficits and a lack of financial oversight.[7] It was possible to speak of a *regional "contagion"* effect.[8] Speaking of the *regional* dimensions of the crisis, a senior ASEAN official observed:

> ASEAN countries are more closely linked to one another than previously perceived. Investors have clearly considered ASEAN as an integrated region ... Hence, each ASEAN country should not only consider the impact of the crisis on their own economy but on that of the region as a whole. This implies the crucial need for regional strategies and regional action.[9]

In terms of its political and security impact, the crisis toppled the Soeharto regime and generated intraregional strains — especially evident in relations between Singapore, Indonesia and Malaysia. The rise of Islamic political forces in Indonesia following the downfall of Soeharto rekindled anxieties in Singapore about its large and unstable neighbour. The forced repatriation of illegal workers by Malaysia and Thailand challenged domestic stability (as evident in rioting by Indonesian workers) in Malaysia. Moreover, in precipitating the downfall of Soeharto, a founding figure and key anchor of Southeast Asian regionalism, the crisis also cast a shadow over the future of ASEAN.

Singapore-Malaysia relations were poisoned by Malaysia's perception that Singapore was not interested in helping it out of the economic downturn by offering unconditional financial assistance. While some contentious bilateral issues in Singapore-Malaysia relations pre-dated the economic downturn, the latter certainly contributed to their escalation, especially because securing financial assistance from Singapore might have reduced Malaysia's need to seek outside help. Similar charges were levelled against Singapore by Soeharto's immediate successor, President B.J. Habibie, who openly criticized Singapore for not being "a friend in need".[10] This was notwithstanding the US$5 billion in aid that Singapore agreed to provide Indonesia in conjunction with the IMF rescue package to Indonesia. (The real reason for Habibie's anger was Lee Kuan Yew's earlier criticism of Soeharto's choice of Habibie as Vice-President, which Lee implied would be poorly received by the market and hinder Indonesia's recovery.)

The crisis exacerbated intra-Southeast Asian differences in attitudes to human rights and democracy, with Thailand and the Philippines openly championing the virtues of democracy over authoritarianism in ensuring economic progress. The crisis put the proponents of cultural relativism and "Asian values" on the defensive.[11] By showing the relative ability of democratic political systems in Thailand and the Philippines in managing the crisis, in contrast to the collapse of authoritarian Indonesia, the crisis provided a powerful argument to pro-democracy forces in the region.

The political and security implications of the Asian economic crisis led, at least temporarily, to a rethinking of globalization and interdependence as tools of development and security, although perspectives on this issue varied among Southeast Asian governments, especially Malaysia and Singapore. Malaysia's Mahathir Mohamad was the most vocal critic of globalization, pointing to its negative impact on sovereignty and security. In June 1998, Mahathir argued, "Globalisation, liberalisation and deregulation are ideas which originate in the rich countries ostensibly to enrich the world. But so far the advantages seem to accrue only to the rich."[12] In contrast, Singapore's leaders continued to affirm the positive impact of globalization on economic well-being and security. Its Foreign Minister, S. Jayakumar, reminded that "it was the forces of globalization that gave the developing countries in our region direct access to the financial resources, technology and markets of the developed world ... it was also globalization that allowed many developing countries, including those in East Asia, to enjoy decades of sustained economic growth, rapid industrialization and massive improvement in their standards of living, health and education."[13] A retreat from globalization, warned Singapore's then deputy Prime Minister, Lee Hsien Loong, would undermine not just the prospects for further development, but also security: "countries will be *less secure, and more prone to conflicts*"[14] (emphasis added). In the end, instead of retreating from globalization, the market economies of Southeast Asia sought to build some resilience against its negative aspects so that they could better handle the next crisis. The measures taken included building larger foreign exchange reserves, better macroeconomic and regulatory management (especially of the financial sector), and joining hands with other East Asian states to develop currency swap agreements.

Despite escalating bilateral tensions, both Singapore and Malaysia rejected the possibility of military conflict.[15] Lee Kuan Yew likened the Singapore-Malaysia verbal spat to a "war dance, plumed feathers and so on", which would release latent tensions in their relationship, but not lead to a war because the two countries had "a long history of such ups and downs".[16]

A further challenge to regionalism was the weakness of ASEAN in responding to the crisis. The crisis diminished ASEAN's international standing. Within ASEAN, hopes that the crisis would engender greater unity and a sense of solidarity among the member states, prompting them to deepen existing level of cooperation and develop common responses to the crisis, proved too optimistic.[17] Apart from exposing the region's dependence on foreign capital and its vulnerability to global market and political forces, the crisis showed the limits of ASEAN's collective clout.[18]

One challenge to ASEAN unity concerned its time-honoured principle of non-interference in the domestic affairs of states and the "ASEAN Way" of quiet and consensual diplomacy. *The Economist* argued that, despite its achievements in settling old animosities in the early years of the organization, "the 'ASEAN way' no longer works".[19] Indeed, ASEAN's norm of non-interference was blamed as the reason why none of its ASEAN partners had made any effort to warn Bangkok of the evident mismanagement of its national economy leading to the crisis collapse of its currency. Nor could anyone in ASEAN put a clamp on Malaysia's Mahathir, despite the damage that his frequent outbursts against Western capitalism and financial speculators did to the regional markets.[20] The new Thai Foreign Minister, Surin Pitsuwan, openly called for ASEAN to review its non-interference doctrine so that it could develop a capacity for "preventing or resolving domestic issues with regional implications".[21] But Surin's initiative, dubbed "flexible engagement", received support from just one other ASEAN member, the Philippines. ASEAN foreign ministers, at their annual meeting in Manila in July 1998, decided to stick to the old principle of non-interference.[22] Subsequently, Mahathir's sacking of Anwar Ibrahim, his Deputy Prime Minister and the proponent of the idea of "constructive intervention" as a framework for helping ASEAN's newer members such as Myanmar and Cambodia, further weakened the forces advocating more openness in ASEAN.[23]

The crisis generated demands for ASEAN to be more receptive to formal and institutionalized mechanisms for cooperation. As Tommy Koh pointed out, the region had pursued cooperation by "building trust, by a process of consultation, mutual accommodation and consensus", while displaying a "general reluctance to build institutions and to rely on laws and rules". But the crisis showed the need to supplement the "ASEAN Way" with institutions.[24] Similarly, the Foreign Secretary of the Philippines raised the possibility of a EU-style ASEAN. ASEAN needed to move "towards institutionalising closer coordination of national economic policies and performance and fostering rule-based transparency in governance".[25]

Southeast Asian countries remained divided on the issue of non-interference. Myanmar, Vietnam and Laos were clearly opposed to any departure from this doctrine, while Thailand under Chuan Leekpai and the Philippines were most active in pushing for a shift. ASEAN's addiction to non-interference explained its muted response to the violence in East Timor in 1999. But more importantly, post-Soeharto Indonesia added its voice to those calling for relaxing the doctrine of non-interference, reflecting its democratizing domestic politics. Within ASEAN generally, there would gradually emerge a greater willingness to re-examine the issue of non-interference in the light of emerging transnational challenges to the region.[26] Moreover, ASEAN's decision in 2000 to institute a "Troika" system — consisting of three ASEAN representatives, including the current, previous and forthcoming chairs of the ASEAN Standing Committee, who could undertake preventive diplomacy and provide rapid diplomatic response to unfolding crisis situations — indicated a shift from the previously rigid non-interference doctrine. This shift was further underscored by ASEAN's development of financial cooperation, including conduct of "peer reviews" on national economies.

Southeast Asia would face another financial crisis a decade later. The crisis of 2008 was not an "Asian crisis" but a global one, with its origins clearly lying in the housing and banking (subprime mortgages) sectors in the United States. But with some 20 per cent of Southeast Asia's exports going to the United States, the region could not escape being hit. Evidence for this could be found in the 32 per cent fall in the market capitalization (average stock market value) of Malaysia, Indonesia, Thailand and Singapore in the first three quarters of 2008. While the 1997 crisis had underscored intraregional (both East and Southeast Asian) interdependence and shared vulnerabilities, the crisis of 2008 was indicative of Southeast Asia's collective reliance on the West.[27] But the region, along with other Asian economies, also earned plaudits for having learned the lessons of the 1997 crisis, particularly in instituting stronger and more prudent supervisory, regulatory and risk management practices in the financial sector. Hence, there was a general optimism that the region would escape the worst spillover effects of the U.S. subprime mortgage crisis and enjoy renewed growth, a forecast that proved to be reasonably accurate.[28]

The 2008–09 crisis underscored a few new realities about Southeast Asia's fate as a region. First, the region was not "autonomous" from global market and financial forces. Some argued, at least during the initial stages of the crisis, that Southeast Asia needed to rethink its fundamental economic strategy of relying on FDI to generate economic growth and prosperity. But this was not a challenge that could be met easily or swiftly. A more powerful aspect of the new reality was the role of China as the anchor of Southeast Asia's economic prospects.[29] The resilience of China and India, economies with which Southeast Asia is increasingly linked, to the financial downturn meant the 2008 global recession would not affect Southeast Asia to the extent initially feared. But does this mean its neighbours to the west and north will replace the West as the principal challenge to Southeast Asian identity? I will turn to this question later.

Intra-Southeast Asian relations fared much better in the aftermath of the 2008 crisis. The Badawi government in Malaysia (replaced by Najib Tun Razak in 2009) had already helped to stabilize Malaysia-Singapore relations by pursuing a more moderate approach towards Singapore than the Mahathir government. But the real reason for avoiding a major setback to intra-Southeast Asian relations had to do with Indonesia's growing political and economic stability. Indonesia survived the 2008 crisis in much better shape than it had the 1997 crisis. While the latter had engendered a revolution, the 2008–09 period was marked by consolidation. But Jakarta's growing self-confidence created leadership ambitions that went well beyond Southeast Asia, a development that may strike at the roots of Southeast Asia's coherence. And while ASEAN's older members managed their relationships better in 2008 than in 1997, the same was not true of the relationship between an older and a newer member, Thailand and Cambodia, as will be discussed later in this chapter.

While at its origin the regional identity of Southeast Asia was shaped by concerns about the fledging nation-states and national identities, the forces challenging Southeast Asia since the mid-1990s onwards were primarily transnational in nature. Aside from the financial crises of 1997 and 2008, these included terrorism, pandemics, natural disasters and environmental hazards.

Although the terrorist attacks of 11 September 2001 on the World Trade Center and Pentagon in the United States were events far removed from Southeast Asia, they nonetheless had a major impact on the region. The vulnerabilities of the region to this new menace were demonstrated by the bombings in Bali in October 2002. To some observors, Southeast Asia offered an attractive home to international terrorism, thanks to its multiethnic societies; the tenuous hold of central authorities in the Philippines, Indonesia, Thailand and Myanmar over their peripheral areas; ongoing separatist movements that lent themselves to infiltration by foreign elements; governments that were weakened by the financial crisis; and the newly created democratic space in Indonesia, where public support was low for security regulations to ensure the preventive suppression of terrorism. With the defeat of Al Qaeda in Afghanistan as a result of the U.S. attack on the Taliban regime in December 2001, some Al Qaeda elements shifted their attention to Southeast Asia. A few Southeast Asians who had trained with the Taliban in Afghanistan returned home, where they would respond to the Al Qaeda leadership's periodic call for (both low- and high-impact) terrorist strikes against targets including entertainment spots frequented by Western tourists. This development helped one radical group already established in Southeast Asia, known as Jemaah Islamiyah (JI). Working sometimes but not always in concert with the Al Qaeda network, the JI became more noticeably active in terrorism. The discovery of a terrorist plot in Singapore in December 2001, targeted at the U.S. military personnel stationed there, highlighted the threat posed by terrorism to the region. The suspected perpetrators of the planned attacks were believed to have been members of JI, whose objectives included the creation of a pan-Southeast Asian Islamic state comprising the Muslim-majority areas of the southern Philippines, Indonesia, Malaysia, Singapore and southern Thailand and even extending to northern Australia.[30]

To be sure, this aspiration for a Pan-Islamic regional unity never had the potential to overwhelm the Southeast Asia of nation-states. The JI, like most terrorist groups around the world, consisted of elements with markedly divergent objectives and territorial bases. They developed transnational linkages as a matter of tactics, because external aid was necessary to compensate for the limited resources of individual groups. This, rather than a strategic ambition of redefining national and regional boundaries, was what really drove extremist groups. Even the Taliban, often seen as an extreme form of a Pan-Islamic movement, was more concerned with establishing its authority within the internationalized frontiers of Afghanistan than with sponsoring a regional or global caliphate.[31]

The challenge posed by transnational terrorism in general and the JI in particular spurred Southeast Asian governments into a certain amount of concerted action. The agenda of regional cooperation in Southeast Asia after September 11 reflected the growing recognition of this challenge. But caught in a moment of weakness caused by intramural bickering, the burdens of membership expansion and the lingering effects of the Asian economic crisis, ASEAN members could offer only a mixed response to the terrorist challenge. Terrorism emerged as a common challenge that could galvanize regional cooperation. It led to some new areas of cooperation, including information exchanges and measures to deal with money laundering and illegal migration. But governments in the region also realized that the fight against terrorism had to be carried out primarily through national means, through instruments such as intelligence services, polices forces, military, immigration and customs services, etc. Regional cooperation could complement national action, but some areas of cooperation such as intelligence-sharing would have to be undertaken on a bilateral basis only. Moreover, across the region, differences in the seriousness of terrorist threats, limitations on the resources available, and divergent political imperatives made it difficult to devise common responses. Hence, Indonesia would initially refuse to crack down on elements identified by its neighbours as leaders of Al Qaeda-linked terrorist organizations. The Bali bombings of 12 October 2002 would prompt Jakarta to toughen its stance on terrorism, including the passage of internal security measures, but the government remained sensitive to domestic opposition to such measures.

To be sure, ASEAN and its related organizations did help to reinforce the commitment of member countries to fight terrorism and build capacity in various areas. Some of the multilateral measures against terrorism included a trilateral pact (later expanded to include Thailand) between the Philippines, Indonesia and Malaysia, providing for information exchanges and other forms of cooperation. Regional anti-terror cooperation was also undertaken in the form of a U.S.-ASEAN agreement providing for intelligence-sharing and training. Bilateral agreements proved more useful than multilateral means, with the U.S.-Philippines joint training and operations in the southern Philippines and the U.S.-Malaysia accord against terrorism constituting important examples. Domestic political considerations prevented some national governments from extending full support to the "war on terror" launched by the United States, with Malaysia and Indonesia showing open opposition to the U.S. invasion of Iraq in 2003, in contrast to Singapore, Philippines and Thailand, who joined "the coalition of the willing" put together by the United States for the invasion. The latter two countries would win U.S. recognition as "major Non-NATO Allies" for their support.

Terrorism was cited by some regional governments (Singapore in particular) and terrorism analysts as the most serious threat to Southeast Asia in the post-Cold War period. But in reality, terrorism has cost fewer lives in Southeast Asia than other transnational calamities that have befallen the region. Indeed, in terms of fear and anxiety, if not of actual lives lost, the Severe Acute Respiratory Syndrome (SARS) crisis of early 2003 was clearly a more serious challenge. SARS affected 8,096 individuals in 29 countries, with 774 total deaths.[32] Vietnam was the second country to face an outbreak of SARS after China, and would report 63 cases and 5 deaths between 26 February 2003 (when the outbreak began) and 8 April, when it was declared SARS-free by the World Health Organization (WHO).[33] Singapore's toll was 33 deaths out of 238 cases.[34] Although Singapore and Vietnam were the only two Southeast Asian countries to be seriously affected by SARS (according to some reports, there were SARS-related deaths in Philippines and Thailand — two in each country)[35] the fear of potential regionwide contagion from the pandemic was substantial and visible. As the then ASEAN Secretary-General, Ong Keng Yong, put it, "The philosopher Bertrand Russell once said, 'Neither a man nor a crowd nor a nation can be trusted to act humanely or to think sanely under the influence of a great fear.' This is indeed the case when we met the challenge of SARS. Fear is taking charge of businesses and people world-wide and that is why our economies are suffering."[36]

Perhaps a more significant aspect of the SARS episode was that the borders of Southeast Asia remained open through the crisis despite strict surveillance and quarantine procedures. No ASEAN citizen was denied entry to another ASEAN country on suspicion of SARS, but instead was given access to medical assistance. In view of the widespread climate of panic, keeping national borders within ASEAN open was no small matter. SARS was also a turning point in China-ASEAN relations. China was widely blamed for its secrecy about the outbreak of the disease and for not notifying the WHO of the outbreak until February

2003, when the disease had already spread to nearby Hong Kong and Vietnam and thence to other countries via international travellers. But China also had to be part of the solution to the crisis. A crucial step in responding to SARS was an East Asian Ministers of Health Special Meeting held on 26 April 2003 in Kuala Lumpur. An emergency meeting of the leaders of China and the ASEAN states (plus Hong Kong), held on 29 April 2003, saw Chinese premier Wen Jiabao (who attended the meeting along with the chief executive of Hong Kong, Tung Chee-Hwa) signing onto a Joint Declaration on SARS. Southeast Asia was declared a SARS-free region, free of local transmission, with the last case in the region being isolated on 11 May 2003.

If SARS topped the list of transnational threats to Southeast Asia in terms of fear, the earthquake off the coast of Sumatra and the tsunami that followed on 26 December 2004 was by far the biggest killer. The quake, measuring 9.15 on the Richter scale, went beyond Southeast Asia. Indonesia was the hardest hit — the epicentre of the earthquake was located off the coast of Sumatra, where coastal regions were destroyed. An estimated 226,041 people died in Indonesia, Sri Lanka, India and Thailand. In Indonesia alone, over 165,000 people were killed and 36,804 others remained missing.

Interestingly, if tragically, the tsunami swept through an area — the Coromandel coast of India, Sri Lanka, Sumatra and the west coast of Malaysia — that had been intimately linked in ancient times through commerce, migration and the flow of ideas and religions.[38] The scale of the devastation wrought, and the vast and coordinated relief operations sparked by the disaster, underscored the importance of the "Indian Ocean" rim as a regional concept. It challenged existing regional distinctions between "South Asia" and "Southeast Asia", developed after the Bandung Conference, which, as noted in Chapter 4, had brought together the leaders of India, Ceylon, Pakistan, Myanmar and Indonesia as the Conference of South East Asian Prime Ministers. As ASEAN developed greater cohesion and its own sense of regional identity, and as India's regional leadership in Asian regionalism became a casualty of its border war with China and rivalry with Pakistan over Kashmir, "South Asia" had progressively become a notion distinct from that of "Southeast Asia". In challenging such regional exclusivities, the tsunami followed several longer term developments. India's relative isolation from Southeast Asia had effectively ended, as its "Look East Policy", backed by economic reforms, created new opportunities for linkages with ASEAN. The rise of China as an economic and security giant created in Southeast Asia a renewed interest in New Delhi as a possible counterweight to Chinese dominance. And terrorism emerged as a common threat binding the western part of the Indian Ocean with the Indian subcontinent, Southeast Asia and even Australia. Both India and Pakistan are now members of the ASEAN Regional Forum, the first time that the two countries have belonged to the same regional security organization (an important contrast, given New Delhi's stringent opposition to the Southeast Asian Treaty Organization, to which Pakistan enthusiastically belonged).

While the tsunami produced an outpouring of aid and relief from the international community at large, Southeast Asian countries played a significant role in drawing international attention to the disaster and organizing the diplomatic framework for concerted international action. A leaders' meeting in Jakarta on 6 January 2005 helped coordinate all international relief efforts and discuss ways to establish a regional early warning system. ASEAN's proposed resolution on "Strengthening Emergency Relief, Rehabilitation, Reconstruction and Prevention on Aftermath of the Indian Ocean Tsunami Disaster" was adopted by consensus by the UN General Assembly on 19 January 2005. Although the contribution of Southeast Asian countries to the overall relief effort was relatively insignificant compared to outside powers,[39] Southeast Asian countries did make a contribution. Singapore provided a total of S$150 million (US$94 million) in aid,[40] and was one of the first countries to send an assistance mission to Aceh, a 900-strong contingent deploying aircraft, landing ships and helicopters. Singaporean units opened up Aceh's air and naval facilities to all countries helping in the massive relief and reconstruction effort. Malaysia deployed a 250-man police contingent to Aceh and offered engineering expertise in areas designated by Indonesia for rehabilitation. The Sultan of Brunei inspected the affected areas in Indonesia and also donated US$150,000 by mid-January. Thailand, where the tsunami had killed 5,000 people, many of them foreign tourists, had politely declined a Japanese offer for financial assistance worth US$20 million and instead recommended that it be sent to those countries deemed more needy. Cash-strapped countries like Laos and the Philippines provided token assistance in the form of cash donations or the deployment of medical missions. Laos raised US$55,000 for countries hit by the tsunami while the Philippines sent medical missions that had the added task of locating Filipino victims.[41]

Another natural calamity tested ASEAN even more severely. This was Cyclone Nargis, which hit Myanmar in 2008. Whereas the principal victim of the 2004 earthquake and tsunami, Indonesia, had had no qualms about accepting international aid, the military junta in Myanmar was quite fearful of opening its borders to foreign humanitarians. In terms of ASEAN's doctrine of non-interference, Nargis posed an acute dilemma, because Myanmar's ASEAN allies did not want to be seen as not doing anything to help a member state in distress. In the end, ASEAN devised a plan to act as the conduit of international humanitarian assistance to Myanmar. The regime in Myanmar was prepared to accept such a role from its neighbours, on whom it could count for not interfering in its domestic politics. While reviews of the humanitarian assistance mission have been mixed, it marked a turning point in Southeast Asia. The regional element was highlighted, even though the material assistance came mainly from non-Southeast Asian donors.

Rainforests and Regional Identity

It is hard to think of Southeast Asia without its rainforests.[42] Home to "the oldest, most consistent rainforests on Earth", Southeast Asia enjoys a "biological richness and diversity unequalled by that of the Amazon or African rainforests".[43] But Southeast Asia's forest cover has been declining at a rapid rate. According to a 2004 study, Southeast Asia had "the highest relative rate of deforestation of any major tropical region, and could lose three quarters of its original forests by 2100 and up to 42% of its biodiversity".[44] The deforestation has been a long-term phenomenon. It began as a result of the expansion of agriculture in the early nineteenth century and accelerated with the planting of export crops like rubber, oil palm and coconut. Commercial logging of timber further contributed to deforestation after 1950. According to the environmental group Rainforest Relief, "By 1986, Peninsular Malaysia was the largest source of sawtimber from tropical logs and Sabah (a Malaysian state on the island of Borneo) was the world's leading log exporter."[45] Along with agricultural expansion, cash crops and logging, development projects also had a major impact on Southeast Asia's rainforest cover. For example, millions of square kilometres of forest area were opened up due to the construction of the North-South Expressway in Malaysia. Dam projects, and the resulting need for resettlement programmes, led to the large-scale loss of forest cover in Thailand during the 1980s. During the

1994–2004 period, Southeast Asia was experiencing an average annual loss of forest cover of 1.4 per cent, a rate "which was higher than the deforestation rates of other speciose tropical regions, such as Central America and the Caribbean (1.2%), and South America (0.5%). By 2004, only 'less than half' (41.3–44.2%) of the original forests of Southeast Asia remained."[46]

According to the United Nations Food and Agriculture Organization (FAO), the rate of deforestation in Southeast Asia accelerated during the 1980s, doubling between 1976–80 and 1986–90.[47] Another estimate found a drop of approximately 17 per cent in the region's forest cover between the late 1960s and the late 1980s. The countries where deforestation had been most rapid between 1970 and 1990 were Vietnam (68.8 per cent, or over 124,820 sq. km), the Philippines (56.0 per cent, or over 83,980 sq. km), and Thailand (41.7 per cent, or over 106,900 sq. km). However, Indonesia (17.1 percent, or over 243,769 sq. km) had lost the most rainforest in gross terms. Thailand and the Philippines, threatened with the near-extinction of their existing reserves, banned logging in 1989.[48] With more than 10 per cent of the world's rainforests, and 40 per cent of Asia's, Indonesia increasingly became the main source of tropical timber in the region. Each year, according to the international environmental organization Earth Action, the nation had been destroying a forested area larger than Lebanon, reflecting its role as one of the world's largest exporters of wood products.[49]

Nothing has highlighted the plight of Southeast Asian rainforests more dramatically than the Indonesian forest fires. The massive fires of 1997 reflected the scale of deforestation in Southeast Asia. Fires on the islands of Sumatra and Kalimantan had been a severe problem for many years,[50] leading to the loss of vast tracts of virgin rainforest, which according to one estimate could take up to 500 years to recover. A particularly dramatic account of the 1997 haze was found in the pages of the *New York Times*:

> Tigers and elephants are fleeing the burning jungles. Birds are falling from the murky skies. School children are fainting at their desks. Ships are colliding at sea. As a filthy haze from vast Indonesian forest fires continues to darken the sky across seven Southeast Asian nations, illness, ecological destruction and economic hardship are growing.After four months, the man-made fires, set on the heavily forested islands of Borneo and Sumatra to clear land for crops, are spreading rather than shrinking.[51]

Independent reports confirmed the losses of between 750,000 and 1.7 million hectares of forest due to the 1997 fires.[52] An estimate in 1997 suggested that the health of over 40,000 people across the region had been affected by the haze.[53] The Economy and Environment Program for Southeast Asia (EEPSEA) put the economic cost of 1997's haze at $1.4 billion. Private estimates put the total cost of the forest fires and the ensuing haze to the Southeast Asian region at $5–6 billion.[54] A subsequent report by the International Development Research Centre of Canada called the 1997 haze "certainly one of the century's worst environmental disasters", which had affected the lives and health of some of 70 million people. That study put the cost of the haze at US$4.5 billion, an amount that would exceed the combined cost of the Exxon Valdez oil spill and India's Bhopal chemical spill.[55] Moreover, deforestation has contributed to climate change. One study found that the burning of rainforests and peatlands in Indonesia, Malaysia and Papua New Guinea released an average of 128 million tonnes of carbon (470 million tonnes of carbon dioxide) per year between 2000 and 2006.[56]

The 1997 haze from Indonesia drew the ire of Singapore and Malaysia, prompting an apology from then President Soeharto. It also ensured that environmental issues would come onto the agenda of regional intergovernmental cooperation. Regional efforts to help Indonesia cope with the haze problem included the institutionalization of a new ministerial meeting on the haze in November 1997, the implementation of a regional haze action plan and the establishment of a new haze task force coordination unit at the ASEAN Secretariat. But the result of cooperation has not been encouraging, suggesting inadequate political will and collective capacity for regional disaster management. In 2006, another major incidence of regional haze from Indonesia occurred, blanketing Singapore and large areas of Indonesia and Malaysia. There were anti-Indonesia demonstrations in Malaysia, and Singapore's Prime Minister wrote to the Indonesian President to express his "disappointment".[57] This prompted an apology from President Susilo Bambang Yudhoyono, who also promised to ratify the ASEAN Agreement on Transboundary Haze Pollution, which Jakarta had signed in 2002 but was yet to ratify.[58] Yet, responding to neighbourly criticism, the Indonesian Forestry Minister would say, "Our forests produce oxygen which makes the air cool for them (regional neighbours), but they have never been grateful."[59]

Identity and Community

The transnational dangers facing Southeast Asia during the first decade of the new millennium offer two lessons. On the one hand, because of their severity and scope, responses relying exclusively on the resources of Southeast Asian states — singly or collectively — would be futile. Southeast Asia has to work with outside countries and institutions, including UN bodies like the WHO, drawing upon their resources and adapting them to local circumstances, in fighting these dangers. At the same time, intraregional solidarity is of critical importance in generating international attention and response to these perils. Currency speculators, terrorists, viruses and earthquakes have scant regard for national boundaries. Hence the realization that collective responses to these dangers should be seen not as an abrogation of sovereignty, but rather the pooling of it. As such, the shared transnational dangers that have confronted Southeast Asia do have a silver lining. To quote Surin Pitsuwan, the former Thai Foreign Minister who became the Secretary-General of ASEAN in 2008, "One good thing about the repeated crises we are having is that a sense of community is growing very fast in the region."[60] These crises challenged old attitudes towards sovereignty and non-interference associated with the "nation-state" in Southeast Asia, and contributed to the impetus towards regional "community-building".

As Southeast Asia went through the financial and other crises, there was a widespread perception, both outside and inside the region, that ASEAN's institutional mechanisms had not kept up with the new challenges it has faced and would therefore need to be redesigned. ASEAN responded to these criticisms with a community-building agenda that was an extension of its 1997 ASEAN Vision 2020 concept. Meeting in Kuala Lumpur on 15 December 1997, the leaders of ASEAN had congratulated themselves for having "created a community of Southeast Asian nations at peace with one another and at peace with the world", and for having the "strength and inspiration ... to help one another foster a strong sense of community". The challenge now was to "chart a vision for ASEAN on the basis of today's realities and prospects in the decades leading to the Year 2020". This was to be the vision of a "concert of Southeast Asian nations, outward looking, living in peace, stability and prosperity, bonded together in partnership in dynamic development and in a community of caring societies". This would include the establishment of a region "where each nation is at peace with itself and where the causes for conflict have been eliminated" and "where territorial and other disputes are resolved by peaceful means". The future, as they saw it, would consist of "vibrant and open ASEAN societies consistent with their respective national identities, where all people enjoy equitable access to opportunities for total human development regardless of gender, race, religion, language, or social and cultural background."[61]

Six years later, meeting in Bali on 7 October 2003, ASEAN leaders outlined a plan for community-building that would consist of "three pillars": an ASEAN Security Community (ASC — later renamed as the ASEAN Political-Security community, or APSC), an ASEAN Economic Community (AEC) and an ASEAN Socio-Cultural Community (ASCC). The three pillars are supposed to be "closely intertwined and mutually reinforcing", and the resulting ASEAN Community "open, dynamic and resilient".[62]

The APSC is designed to bring ASEAN's political and security cooperation to "a higher plane". It exhorts member states to "regard their security as fundamentally linked to one another and bound by geographic location, common vision and objectives". Yet it also reaffirms the "sovereign right of the member countries to pursue their individual foreign policies and defense arrangements". While the APSC identified some new areas of cooperation, especially concerning common approaches to maritime security and "strengthening national and regional capacities to counter terrorism, drug trafficking, trafficking in persons and other transnational crimes", it did so without significant departure from traditional ASEAN norms, including "principles of non-interference, consensus-based decision-making, national and regional resilience, respect for national sovereignty, the renunciation of the threat or the use of force, and peaceful settlement of differences and disputes".[63] The APSC was a truncated version of an original, much more ambitious Indonesian proposal, which had urged ASEAN to develop a variety of new institutions to promote security and defence cooperation, including the meetings of police and defence ministers, an ASEAN Centre for Combating Terrorism and an ASEAN Centre for Peace Keeping Training.[64] But objections from fellow ASEAN members, worried about the challenge to non-interference and wary of Jakarta's lack of prior consultation in developing the proposal, forced a significant dilution of the measures originally envisaged.

While the APSC underscored continued tensions between the reality of national sovereignty and the aspirations towards regional integration, the non-interference norm, despite being upheld in theory, did come under increasing pressure in dealing with the political issues of the day, especially Myanmar. ASEAN relented to international pressure and growing dissatisfaction among some of its members over the lack of progress in Myanmar's so-called "road map" to democracy. The outcome was sufficient to persuade Myanmar to relinquish its rotational right to the chairmanship of ASEAN in 2006. And ASEAN meetings in 2005 and thereafter did discuss the issue of political reform and the progress of constitution-drafting in Myanmar with the junta's representatives. In other words, the issue of Myanmar could no longer be swept under the carpet in the traditional ASEAN way.

The second element of the community-building project, the AEC, is aimed at establishing an "ASEAN economic region".[65] Its goal is to ensure a free flow of goods, services and capital, and the reduction of poverty and socio-economic disparities. Southeast Asia is to become a single market and production base; the diversity among national economies could be turned into an opportunity for business complementation. Greater ease of movement of business and skilled labour throughout the region is another important and related goal. Moreover, the AEC seeks to provide a legally binding mechanism for settling economic disputes and to reduce the gap between the new members of ASEAN and its more developed members.

The third pillar of ASEAN's community-building project, the ASCC, is aimed at "building a community of caring societies". Its scope is fairly expansive, ranging from addressing poverty, promoting equity and human development to developing human resources and providing greater social protection. Perhaps conscious of ASEAN's state-centric nature, it pays special attention to improving people-to-people contacts, including "interaction among ASEAN scholars, writers, artists and media practitioners to help preserve and promote ASEAN's diverse cultural heritage" with a view to "fostering regional identity" and "cultivating people's awareness of ASEAN".[66] Moreover, the goal of developing a sociocultural community also includes the protection and management of the region's environmental and natural resources, and engaging the civil society in "providing inputs for policy choices".[67] The last objective touches on one of the most critical gaps in Southeast Asian regionalism, and the challenges facing its realization will be discussed in some detail in the next section.

Another major step taken by ASEAN was the adoption of the ASEAN Charter in December 2007 (ratified a year later). The Charter consolidates all of ASEAN's agreements and institutions, and confers on ASEAN "a legal personality", giving it the authority "to act as an organisation in its relations with the world, rather than as a mere collective of 10 countries".[68] As such, it accentuates ASEAN as an anchor for regional identity. The Charter also provides for an ASEAN human rights mechanism, leading to the creation of the ASEAN Intergovernmental Commission on Human Rights (AICHR) in October 2009. Yet, initial hopes created by the Charter for expanding and deepening ASEAN's engagement with the regional civil society, and thereby creating a regional identity from below and not just from top down, are far from being realized.

Regional Identity and Civil Society

Is Southeast Asia a people's region? While regional construction may well start with elites, its authenticity depends on the civil society getting involved. To be viable, regions must be imagined as much, if not more, by its peoples as by its governments. As much of the preceding discussion in the book shows, constructing Southeast Asia's regional identity has been primarily elite-driven. Regional interactions have been largely intergovernmental. But this is no reason to ignore the other side of the coin: regionalism involving non-state actors, or non-official regionalism.

Taking stock of non-official regionalism in Southeast Asia is important for several reasons. First, such regional interactions present an alternative conception of regional order and often pose a challenge to official regionalism, especially when the latter remains circumscribed and takes an oppressive form. Second, some forms of non-official regionalism complement the official regionalism of Southeast Asia, thereby broadening its scope and base. Third, non-official regionalism reflects the level of popular participation in regionalist projects, which is crucial to the legitimacy of official regionalism and its ability to foster a regional identity. Fourth and most important, the growing interaction between the two traditionally distinct and often conflicting types of regionalism state and non-official, has led to the emergence of what might be called "participatory regionalism" in Southeast Asia. This has important implications for regional cooperation, identity-building and order.

Non-state regionalism in Southeast Asia falls into two broad categories. The first may be called semi-official regionalism: it consists of those networks and processes that complement the work of official regionalism in distinct issue areas. The second may be called non-official regionalism: it consists of social movements, groups and processes that challenge state dominance and present an alternative conception of regional identity and order.

Semi-official regionalism in Southeast Asia is of two main types. The first is the so-called Second Track (or Track-II) processes. Although the idea of Track-II is by no means unique to Southeast Asia, it has been quite significant to the evolution of ASEAN's security role in the 1980s and 1990s. Track-II processes are meetings (both bilateral as well as multilateral) sponsored by non-governmental organizations (usually think tanks) that bear explicitly and directly on policy-relevant issues. Such mechanisms have two main characteristics. First, the think tanks[69] involved are, in most cases, closely linked to their respective national governments and rely on government funding for their academic and policy-relevant activities. As Stuart Harris puts it, Track-II diplomacy is dependent "upon the consent, endorsement and commitment, often including financial commitment, of governments".[70] Second, these meetings feature participation by government officials (although usually in a private capacity) alongside academics and other non-official actors. Although the participating officials seldom venture beyond the positions of their respective governments, the principle of "private capacity" enables governments to test new ideas without making binding commitments and, if necessary, backtrack on positions.[71]

The most prominent group of Track-II regionalism in Southeast Asia is the ASEAN Institutes for Strategic and International Studies (ASEAN-ISIS). ASEAN-ISIS is a pro-state, state-supported, knowledge-based network of think tanks, whose main function has been to provide ASEAN and its member governments with policy inputs. It has a track record of providing the impetus for the establishment of the ASEAN Regional Forum and the idea for the ASEAN Free Trade Area. ASEAN-ISIS has also established a wide network of research institutions with like-minded counterparts in Northeast Asia, North America and Europe and was instrumental in the creation of the Council for Security Cooperation in the Asia Pacific (CSCAP), whose role in fostering discussion of regional political and security issues in the Asia-Pacific has been recognized by the ASEAN Regional Forum and by ASEAN governments. ASEAN-ISIS is the official sponsor of the annual Asia-Pacific Roundtable on Confidence Building and Conflict Reduction, held annually in Malaysia. Its other key Track-II conference programmes include "The ASEAN Young Leaders Programme", which identifies and brings together younger-generation elite from various sectors, and the ASEAN-ISIS Colloquium on Human Rights, which seeks to promote mutual understanding about human rights and related issues, and to improve human rights performance in the region. It had backed the establishment of a human rights mechanism for Southeast Asia.

A second form of semi-official regionalism involves educational, cultural and the so-called "people-to-people" contacts. Examples of this type of regionalism include the ASEAN Tourism Association,[72] (ASEANTA), an umbrella organization that comprises the public and private travel sectors of the ASEAN countries, including as charter members the various national tourist promotion agencies, hotel and travel associations, and national airlines. Another institution created to forge sociocultural contacts is the ASEAN Foundation,[73] whose functions include promoting ASEAN awareness at the ordinary citizen level, student exchange programmes, and scholarships. Other goals of the Foundation include human resources development and cooperation for promoting intra-ASEAN assistance. The ASEAN University Network represents yet another semi-official network, the goal of which is to promote exchanges in cultural, social, economic and political areas, through the incorporation of ASEAN studies in university course curricula, teaching materials and the creation of an online course on ASEAN studies. The Southeast Asia Ministers of Education Organization (SEAMEO) acts as an umbrella organization that coordinates many scholarships on offer by the various universities within the region, in addition to offering a well-regarded English language training programme.

Despite the proliferation of such networks and institutions, semi-official regionalism in Southeast Asia remains underdeveloped and marginal to regionalism of the official variety. The policy autonomy of the Track-II processes in Southeast Asia could be overstated. The space separating the "official line" and the positions taken by many, if not all, the think tanks is not that wide. Moreover, a key principle of Track-II, the participation of government officials "in their private capacity", has been rarely upheld in practice. Seldom have these officials been able to rise above national interests and concerns. The contribution of semi-official regionalism to the development of a regional identity has been modest, if not entirely insignificant, for four reasons. First, the education sector of Southeast Asian states remains heavily state-dominated, which gives little space for private universities to develop networking on their own. Language barriers remain another major obstacle; few ASEAN countries offer facilities for learning the indigenous languages of their neighbouring countries. Third, ASEAN countries have devoted few resources to developing sociocultural link-ages or training programmes that would foster a common identity or common sense of belonging to the region, notwithstanding the official rhetoric. Finally, the weakness of civil society organizations in individual ASEAN countries, largely due to official restrictions on their activities and lack of resources, creates barriers to the development of a non-official regional identity.

While semi-official regionalism is sovereignty-conforming, non-official regionalism can be sovereignty-challenging. Non-official regionalism in Southeast Asia is undertaken mainly by NGOs with a regional and transnational membership and focus.[74] It could also be the result of networking and concerted action among national civil society groups in specific issue areas, such as environmental protection and human rights promotion. Table 8.1. provides a partial listing of some of the more prominent NGOs in Southeast Asia operating regionally, although not necessarily on a "Southeast Asian" basis.

Among the more prominent regional NGO networks is the Asia-Pacific Coalition for East Timor (APCET),[75] a network of local, national, regional and international organizations that were involved in solidarity initiatives on East Timor when it was under Indonesian rule. This group was founded in 1994 and played a major role in mobilizing international opinion for the liberation of East Timor. Another prominent Southeast Asian NGO is the Alternative ASEAN Network on Burma (ALTSEAN-Burma),[76] a network of activists, NGOs, academics and politicians who support human rights, democracy and peace in Myanmar. ALTSEAN-Burma initiated a regional campaign plan to pressure member states of ASEAN and the ASEAN Regional Forum to seek positive reforms in Myanmar and to advocate Myanmar's democratization at the local, national, regional

TABLE 8.1

Selected Southeast Asian NGOs and International NGOs Active in Southeast Asia

Name	Head Office	Issue Areas
Focus on the Global South	Bangkok	Campaign against neoliberal globalization
Asian Forum for Human Rights and Development (Forum-Asia)	Thailand	Promotion of democracy, human rights and a regional response
ALTSEAN-Burma (Alternative ASEAN Network on Burma)	Bangkok	Support for the movement for human rights and democracy in Myanmar
APCET (Asia Pacific Conference in East Timor)	Sittings varied	Human rights and self-determination in East Timor
Third World Network	Penang, Malaysia	Campaign against neoliberal globalization; human, social and economic rights
Towards Ecological Recovery and Regional Alliance (TERRA)	Thailand	Environmental protection issues in Myanmar, Laos, Cambodia, Thailand and Vietnam
Committee for Asian Women	Bangkok	Women's issues, especially labour
La Via Campesina (Southeast Asia and East Asia)	Indonesia	Farmers' rights, agrarian reform, biodiversity and genetic resources, food sovereignty and trade, migration and rural workers' human rights
Coalition Against Trafficking in Women in Asia-Pacific (CATW-Asia-Pacific)	Philippines	Women's rights (anti-prostitution and trafficking)
Child Workers in Asia (CWA)	Thailand	Children's rights (especially child labour issues)

TABLE 8.1 *(Cont'd)*

Name	Head Office	Issue Areas
Global Alliance Against Trafficking in Women	Thailand	Women's rights (especially trafficking issue)
Asian Indigenous Peoples' Pact (AIPP)	Thailand	
Asia Pacific Forum on Women, Law and Development (APWLD)	Thailand	Women's rights; impact of climate change on women
Asian Coalition for Housing Rights (ACHR)	Thailand	Urban poverty and development
People's Empowerment Foundation	Thailand	ASEAN civil society, Thai democracy, Burmese refugee and migrant worker communities, exchanges with Sri Lanka and southern Philippines
ASEAN People's Assembly (APA)		Promoting greater awareness of ASEAN community; mutual understanding and tolerance amidst diversity; bridging of gaps between societies of ASEAN
Solidarity for Asian People's Advocacy (SAPA)	Bangkok	Accountability within ASEAN on human rights Coalition of more than 70 NGOs
ASEAN Peoples' Forum		People-to-people platform for civil society inputs on issues within ASEAN states

Source: Personal interviews with NGO officials in Bangkok; *A Directory of Asia and the Pacific Organizations Related to Human Rights Education Work*, 2nd ed. (Bangkok: Asian Regional Resource Center for Human Rights Education, 1999); <http://www.altsean.org/Aboutus.htm>; <http://www.prachatai.com/english/node/1461> (accessed 18 December 2009); <http://www.aippnet.org/>; <http://www.achr.net/strategies_2000.htm>; <http://www.apc.org/en/events/all/asiapacific/asean-peoples-forum>.

and international levels through information dissemination, workshops and other means.

Forum-Asia, one of the largest and most prominent NGOs in Southeast Asia, seeks to "facilitate collaboration among human rights organizations in the region so as to develop a regional response on issues of common concern in the region".[77] Forum-Asia's activities include monitoring and reporting on human rights violations, conducting human rights educational activities, and organizing fact-finding missions and trial observations.[78] Forum-Asia has also called for alternative approaches to national security that stress the security of people over that of states and regimes.[79] The Manila People's Forum on APEC, created as a parallel grouping to challenge the Manila APEC Summit in 1996, described itself as a "dynamic consultative process aimed at ... formulating a people's response to APEC and coming up with a regional strategy of equitable and sustainable development".[80] The Bangkok-based Focus on the Global South and the Malaysia-based Third World Network have been at the forefront of campaigns to create greater awareness of the dangers of globalization and have organized protests against the exploitation of labour and the environment by multinationals. The environment has also become another key issue for mobilizing social movements, especially in the wake of massive forest fires in Indonesia in 1997, which led to widespread ecological and economic damage.

A key force behind the increased prominence of non-official regionalism in Southeast Asia is the trend towards democratization in the region. Democratization has created greater tolerance for civil society groups in several countries, such as Philippines, Thailand and Indonesia. It has also engendered greater attention and sensitivity in these governments to civil rights issues, thereby giving human rights NGOs more space. Political openness in these countries has empowered NGOs with respect to a regional and transnational agenda. As an example, Indonesian activists and parliamentarians in 2000 showed increasing support for Myanmar opposition leader Aung San Suu Kyi, and opposition to ASEAN's tolerance of military rule there. Greater western support for Asian NGOs, induced by post-Cold War policy initiatives towards human rights promotion and sustainable development, has also helped the regional NGO movement. This is now supplemented by the call for "human security", espoused both by Western countries and Japan.[81] At the root of the human security concept is the recognition of threats to the safety and dignity of the individual. The attendant shift from state or regime security provides a conceptual justification for the closer involvement of civil society and social movements in regional cooperation, which had traditionally been the exclusive preserve of governments. Moreover, thanks to democratization, issues that authoritarian regimes might have considered too sensitive (such as human rights promotion) were brought onto the regional agenda. Newly empowered civil society movements could now apply pressure on their own governments to find regional approaches to transnational issues such as the environment, refugees and migration. Moreover, regional and international cooperation among the NGOs is a way of overcoming the constraints imposed by limited domestic resources and support, especially in cases where the home governments remain intolerant of NGO activism.[82]

Initially, Southeast Asian NGOs had developed their own separate identities, networks and approaches, adopting mainly confrontational tactics that condemned ASEAN's pursuit of economic globalization and its neglect of, and tolerance for, human rights abuses and anti-democratic practices in the region.[83] A recent trend in Southeast Asia shows some degree of convergence between official, semi-official and non-official regionalisms. Traditionally separate and even conflicting, they have now begun to find a certain common ground. The outcome of this is a phenomenon that may be described as "participatory regionalism", because of the willingness of governments to listen to the region's civil society groups.[84] Participatory regionalism has been stimulated by new transnational dangers to the region, as discussed earlier. Dealing with challenges such as environmental degradation and refugee flows has led to a greater appreciation by governments of the role of NGOs, especially those that may possess specialist local knowledge of these issues and experience in dealing with them.

One example of this mutual accommodation is the ASEAN People's Assembly (APA), which held its first meeting in November 2000 in Indonesia, bringing together government officials, Track-II groups (mainly government-supported think tanks) and NGOs. [85] Another example is Solidarity for Asian People's Advocacy (SAPA), inaugurated in Bangkok in 2006 with the participation of over fifty NGOs. SAPA is not strictly Southeast Asian in scope, but it has a working group on ASEAN and participated in the consultations over the ASEAN Charter, organized by the Eminent Persons' Group (EPG) on the ASEAN Charter. SAPA has organized the ASEAN Civil Society Conference (ACSC), and taken a strong interest in the ASEAN Intergovernmental Commission on Human

Rights (AICHR), established in 2009. For example, it claims credit for ensuring that the official terms of reference for the mechanism would deal not just with human rights "promotion", but also "protection".[86]

The ASEAN People's Forum (APF) was established in 2009 with a view to "strengthen civil society across the ASEAN region, through direct People-to-People engagement". The forum would operate on "a two-way process, in which domestic issues are escalated to higher regional forums and the local impacts of regional issues are highlighted for community level groups". Moreover, the forum "encourages regional civil society to engage on critical ASEAN issues both among itself and with ASEAN institutions".[87] The APF held its first session in February 2009, in tandem with the ASEAN Civil Society Conference (already on its fourth session), with a mandate to ensure the regional "civil society's continuous engagement with the ASEAN bodies". The coming together of the two bodies fuelled hopes for a greater role for civil society in Southeast Asian regionalism. The forum held some thirty workshops, whose recommendations were debated before being forwarded to the ASEAN leaders. Included in this event was a two-hour dialogue with the ASEAN Secretary-General and the Thai Minister of Foreign Affairs. This was followed by a half-hour informal meeting between representatives of the forum and the ASEAN leaders in Cha-am, Thailand. The themes of the workshops conducted by the forum reflect its broad agenda, including "(1) peace and human security dimension of ASEAN regionalism; (2) social and cultural dimensions of regionalism — focus on environmental and sustainable development, special interest groups, media, women's rights, and youth; (3) the socio-economic dimension of regionalism — focus on globalization, labor, trade and global financial crises; and (4) avenues of action and participation for ASEAN civil society — a People's ASEAN: civil society, social movements, active citizenship, and democracy".[88] Yet hopes generated by the relative success of the first APF were dashed when the second APF, held on 18–20 October 2009 in Cha-am, Thailand, failed to attract ASEAN officials, prompting the organizers to be "deeply disappointed", calling it "a step backward on ASEAN's commitment to promote a people-oriented ASEAN".[89]

There remain important obstacles to the further development of participatory regionalism in Southeast Asia. ASEAN itself continues to show resistance to post-sovereign regional norms. It shows no deep commitment to democracy and human rights, as adopted by European or Latin American regional institutions. Thailand's support for human rights and democracy in its regional foreign policy agenda declined under the Thaksin Shinawatra government. The AICHR has been criticised for lacking powers to "protect" human rights through sanctions and enforcement. Moreover, the democratization process in Southeast Asia remains incomplete and uneven, with several states, such as Myanmar despite the signs of a shift there in 2011 and Vietnam, remaining firmly under authoritarian rule. Democratic consolidation in Indonesia, although defying expectations, still faces a number of serious challenges and constraints. Moreover, some of the measures undertaken by regional governments to counter the threat of terrorism have undermined civil liberties in the region. Indonesia enacted new security laws, and the harsh internal security laws in Singapore and Malaysia came to enjoy the backing of Western countries, including the United States. Muslim civil society groups came under government scrutiny for their alleged links with terrorist networks. ASEAN governments developed new forms of internal security cooperation to counter transborder terrorism. This led to a reassertion of Southeast Asia's official regionalism at the expense of civil society networks.[90]

There is still a long road to travel before regionalism in Southeast Asia takes on the character of a peoples' regionalism. An official ASEAN website for culture and information (<http://www.asean-infoculture. org/>) claims that "ASEAN cultural cooperation is aimed at the vigorous development of an awareness of regional identity, the preservation of the region's cultural heritage, and the exertion of efforts to create a strong ASEAN community." But developing true regional identity would require greater interaction at the popular level, so that ordinary people in ASEAN states would identify with the regional entity. ASEAN has not done enough thus far to draw the citizenry and civil society into the ambit of regional interactions. Today, there are a variety of associations affiliated with the ASEAN Secretariat whose work is relevant to the creation of a regional sociocultural community: the ASEAN Music Industry Association (AMIA), the ASEAN University Sports Council (AUSC), the ASEAN Federation of Furniture Manufacturers Association (AFFMA), and the ASEAN Chambers of Commerce and Industry (ACCI), to name a few. There is also the ASEAN Arts Festival, ASEAN Bird Singing Contest, and ASEAN Rickshaw Run. But the reach of these activities into the hearts and minds of ordinary people remains limited and they have not created a robust sense of community from below.

Democratization in Indonesia has important implications for Southeast Asian identity. An important goal of Indonesia behind its ASEAN Security Community idea was the promotion of human rights and democracy through ASEAN. Indeed, in 2002–03, Indonesia tried to secure a commitment from other ASEAN members to accept democracy and human rights as fundamental principles of ASEAN. Underlying Jakarta's effort was a belief that a newly democratic Indonesia should project its own values and persuade its neighbours to change. But this effort did not go very far in the face of opposition from within the grouping, especially from those states that did not have a democratic political system. This, and the dilution of other proposals from Indonesia to reform and strengthen ASEAN (such as the creation of a peacekeeping force), has certainly caused disillusionment in Jakarta about ASEAN and prompted it to rethink its role in Southeast Asia. Enjoying closer ties with Australia and with a seat in the G-20 grouping, Jakarta has indicated a larger role for itself in world politics; while not abandoning ASEAN, it is less willing to make ASEAN the cornerstone of its foreign policy. Jakarta's move to cast its net beyond Southeast Asia raises questions about the future of the regional concept, at a time when the region's identity is under increasing pressure from the two traditional giants in its neighbourhood, China and India.

A dramatic shift in the prospects for human rights and democracy in Southeast Asia occurred in 2011, when Myanmar's regime, following flawed parliamentary elections in 2010 under a new constitution that was internationally condemned as undemocratic, started showing signs of liberalization. Released from house arrest in November 2010, Aung San Suu Kyi was allowed to hold talks for the first time with the new President Thein Sein in August 2011. She signalled confidence in the President's commitment to political reform and expressed hope for a democratic Myanmar, hopes that were furthered by the releasing of several hundred political prisoners in January 2012. Some ASEAN leaders took credit for encouraging gradual and peaceful reform in Myanmar, although it was not entirely convincing given its history of constructive engagement with and tolerance for military rule there, despite growing signs of impatience with the Myanmar government in the last few years.

China, India and Southeast Asian Identity

In September 2005, Singapore's then Foreign Minister, George Yeo, made a remarkable speech before the Global Leadership Forum in Kuala Lumpur.

A good deal of the speech was about the fate of Southeast Asia as a region in the era of the rise of China and India:

> In every area, we have to think and act strategically so that South-east Asia becomes a major intermediary between China and India. This is our historical position and this should also be our future ... Some historians explain that, whatever our diversity, we are still a collection of states which lie along the trade routes between East Asia and South Asia, alternately receiving the cultural influence of both and, more recently, from the West. ... In our historical memory, we have had to respond to the waxing and waning of powers nearby and farther away. Every time the East-West trade flourished, we prospered with it. The growth of the East-West trade in this century will dwarf anything that has ever been seen before and will open up a whole new horizon for us.[91]

Yeo's basic point was that "the growth of China and India will sweep us along in this century". Otherwise, this might mean the end of Southeast Asia: "Either we become stronger as a region or we will fragment."[92] While the financial crisis, the terrorist bombings in Bali, the SARS pandemic and the tsunami were dramatic challenges for Southeast Asia, a more evolutionary challenge to the region's affairs and the regional idea of Southeast Asia has been the simultaneous rise of China and India.

Some Southeast Asians and Western observers do worry about the region becoming a vassal of China. They foresee the emergence of a Chinese sphere of influence in Southeast Asia, or a Chinese Monroe Doctrine.[93] Southeast Asians are also concerned about economic marginalization. The single most important concern has been investment diversion to China. ASEAN and China each received US$14 billion in FDI. From 1995 to 2000, ASEAN received US$23.3 billion in FDI while China received US$40.9 billion — 56 per cent more than ASEAN. From 2001 to 2003, ASEAN's FDI decreased by 21 per cent to US$18.1 billion, while China's increased dramatically to US$51 billion.[94] Optimistic assessments of China's economic rise argue that it will offer opportunities for a new regional division of labour that would benefit Southeast Asian countries as much as China. China could become a "regional integrator".[95] Driven by China's cheap and surplus labour, large market, geographical proximity and overseas Chinese capital in Southeast Asia, investment from ASEAN states to China stood at US$38.22 billion in November 2005.[96] Hence the optimistic argument that "rather than considering China as a threat, ASEAN could ride on China as an engine of growth".[97]

The level of two-way trade between China and ASEAN increased from US$8 billion in 1991 to over US$40 billion in 2001 and US$231 billion in 2008.[98] The China-ASEAN free trade area (called ACFTA by ASEAN and CAFTA by the Chinese), formally proposed by China in 2001 and coming into effect on 1 January 2010, is billed as the third-largest FTA in the world (after EU and NAFTA) in terms of trade volume (US$4.5 trillion) and the largest in the world in terms of the combined population of the partners (1.9 billion). The agreement eliminates tariffs on 90 per cent of products, by 2010 for China and six ASEAN members (Indonesia, Malaysia, Singapore, Brunei, Thailand and Vietnam), and for the remaining four members by 2015. The deal has generated concerns about the increasing dominance of Chinese companies and products in ASEAN, although these concerns may be overstated, given the diversified nature of ASEAN's trade (Japan, EU and the US remain significant trading partners with ASEAN), and terms that allow each country to exclude "dozens of sensitive areas from ports to cars to popcorn".[99]

As economic modernization in China progresses, competition with ASEAN economies could intensify and result in crowding-out effects on the ASEAN economies' exports in the markets of developed countries.[100] But this is still a far cry from ASEAN becoming a backyard for Chinese raw material imports and manufactured exports, as a sphere of influence framework would imply. China might gain additional clout over ASEAN, including an ability to offer incentives and punishments. China may be able to develop a strong economic influence in the less developed ASEAN members: Laos, Myanmar and Cambodia. Selective Chinese trade concessions and economic aid could persuade these countries to support Chinese foreign policy and strategic objectives. And if China pursues a strategy of bilateral trade deals with ASEAN members, this could have a divisive impact on ASEAN.[101] But this does not mean Southeast Asian countries such as Malaysia, Indonesia, Thailand, Philippines, Vietnam and Singapore would sacrifice their national and regional interests and identities to be part of a Chinese sphere of influence.

Concerns about the South China Sea conflict (contested by China, Taiwan, the Philippines, Malaysia, Vietnam and Brunei), a point of tension and anxiety in Southeast Asia concerning Chinese expansionism, have grown considerably. In 1992, ASEAN issued a Declaration on the South China Sea, urging all claimants to seek a peaceful settlement of the dispute. Following a period of Chinese resistance, ASEAN managed to secure Beijing's agreement to deal with it multilaterally on this issue in 1995. Subsequent efforts to seek a common ground — marred by periodic accusations from ASEAN members (especially the Philippines) of Chinese military buildup in the area and its "creeping" takeover of a number of islands (the most serious being the "Mischief Reef episode" in 1995) — focused on the development of a code of conduct. These efforts led to the Declaration on a Code of Conduct in the South China Sea at the ASEAN summit in Cambodia in 2002, calling on the parties "to exercise self-restraint in the conduct of activities that would complicate or escalate disputes and affect peace and stability including, among others, refraining from action of inhabiting on the presently uninhabited islands, reefs, shoals, cays, and other features and to handle their differences in a constructive manner".[102]

The Declaration was not a legally binding document, however; nor did it include a specific commitment to freeze the erection of new structures in the disputed area, a commitment that was sought by the Philippines but refused by China. A demand by Vietnam, that the proposed code should apply to the Paracel Islands (claimed by Hanoi but now occupied by China), was resisted by China, although the problem was overcome through the acceptance of a Philippine initiative that suggested dropping any reference to the geographical boundaries of the Declaration, thereby allowing Hanoi to claim that the code applied to the entire South China Sea. But it did represent China's willingness to deal with ASEAN multilaterally on a subject that it had previously insisted on resolving exclusively on a bilateral basis. The Declaration also signalled that China saw a military confrontation over the Spratlys as being detrimental to its interests. China had stepped up its involvement in regional institutions, paying much more attention to ASEAN and the ARF and playing a key role in the development of the ASEAN Plus Three (APT).

This is not to say that China adopted a mainly conciliatory approach to the South China Sea issue. There has been a harder and more assertive Chinese posture in the South China Sea subsequent to the Declaration on the Code of Conduct. At the same time, China's building of dams in the upper reaches of the Mekong River has created concerns in Southeast Asia about its ability to control the flow of water to other riparian states such as Laos, Cambodia and Vietnam.[103] Myanmar is another place where China's political clout raised a great deal of concern in Southeast Asia. Reports about China's links with Myanmar cover a wide variety of activities, including the sale of military equipment and the stationing of Chinese military personnel for training and the operating of sophisticated electronic communication and surveillance equipment.[104] While some of these reports may have been "based on unsubstantiated rumours or idle speculation",[105] they nonetheless shaped ASEAN's opposition to Western sanctions against the repressive military junta in Myanmar and the decision to admit it as a full member in 1997.

In considering the long-term implications of the rise of China for Southeast Asia, some scholars have maintained that the future regional order might resemble the old tributary system, or at least as David Kang puts it, a "hierarchical" interstate order with China at its core. This might engender greater regional stability, since, as he argues, "East Asian regional relations have historically been hierarchic, more peaceful, and more stable than those in the West."[106] But such an institutionalized hierarchy is implausible under the sovereign-state system, which China both accepts and defends. Historically, the Chinese world order featured a single great power — China. Today, Southeast Asian countries have several major powers to contend with, and to play against one another. Although Sino-ASEAN relations seem unequal at present, hence conducive to a hierarchical pattern reminiscent of the past, ASEAN is not without bargaining clout in its dealings, especially collective dealings, with China. To sustain its economic growth, China needs Southeast Asian resources and markets, as well as a stable regional environment, which ASEAN can help provide. China also requires Southeast Asia's acquiescence and cooperation to realize its leadership ambitions in Asia and the world. Its relationship with ASEAN is a test case of Beijing's credibility as an engaged and constructive world power. While Beijing remains wary of ASEAN's pressure on the South China Sea dispute and the pro-U.S. defence orientation of many ASEAN members, there are also reasons for Beijing to view Southeast Asia as a relatively "safe" and "benign" area within which to cultivate positive and mutually beneficial relationships. Beijing is also mindful that an adverse relationship with Southeast Asia could move many of the states there towards a closer alignment with China's competitors, such as Japan and the United States. This presents an opportunity for Southeast Asian states, provided they can stay united and purposeful, to extract strategic restraint from China and develop cooperative security strategies.

India's role in Southeast Asia differs from China's in three respects. First, to a much greater extent than China, India was an active champion of Southeast Asian regionalism in the 1940s and 1950s. Second, the growth of India's economy is not comparable to that of China. This means India would pose less of an economic challenge to Southeast Asia, but it could also imply that Southeast Asia has less to gain from India. The volume of trade between India and Southeast Asia pales in comparison with that between China and Southeast Asia. In 2008–9, the total trade between ASEAN and China was about four times that between ASEAN and India.[107] Third, while India's military, especially its naval reach, in Southeast Asia is significant, at least potentially, it (including its potential blue-water navy) is viewed as more benign than China's military. As a Chinese scholar put it, "India enjoys a much better situation in Southeast Asia [than China]. India's potential as a big power and China's possible threat have prompted many ASEAN nations to rethink their relations with India."[108] In his view, India and China "are competitors for ASEAN's favor: from visible trade and investment for their domestic modernization to invisible cooperation and support for their increasing international influence".[109]

There is a growing sense in Southeast Asia that India could act as a counterbalance to China in the region. Several Southeast Asian states, including Singapore and Malaysia, have developed closer contacts with the Indian navy. But the view of India as a counterbalance is not shared by all. In the words of a Southeast Asian diplomat, "If [Asean countries] wanted to offset China's influence by bringing in India, they would have done it a long time ago … It's a seductive story [to pit India against China], but it's not true. China is too influential to have its power offset by India."[110]

In reality, a combination of geography and geopolitics, economics and culture, forms the basis of India's engagement in Southeast Asia. "Look East", India's slogan for its East Asia policy, was driven principally by economic factors, including India's desire to develop trade and investment links with East Asia; in this plan, Southeast Asia, especially Singapore, acts as a springboard. Singapore has argued that ASEAN should not throw all its economic eggs into the China basket. Geography also matters. "On clear days, you can see the islands of Indonesia and Thailand" from India, joked P.K. Kapur, the Indian ambassador to Cambodia.[111] Kapur also explained how the rich cultural ties between India and Myanmar, Singapore, Malaysia, Indonesia, Thailand and Cambodia have helped shape India's policy towards the region. These sentiments echoed those expressed by the Indian Prime Minister, Atal Behari Vajapayee, in 2001, when he gave a speech in Singapore. As Vajpayee put it, referring to Myanmar, "The admission of new countries brought ASEAN literally to India's doors. From a maritime neighbour, ASEAN became our close neighbour with a land border of nearly 1,600 kilometers."[112] With regard to cultural ties, he argued that "the most basic historical factor, which unites us is a civilisational bond formed from the strands of spiritualism, culture and commerce. The cross-fertilization of our human experiences was not through conquest or domination, but through a meeting of minds. Evidence of this confluence between India and Southeast Asia abounds in the art, architecture, language and culture of every ASEAN country."[113] But while Indian scholars and policy-makers hope these past cultural connections might increase the "comfort level" between India and Southeast Asian countries, in reality, there is little evidence that this is the case. There is not as much appreciation of India's historical role in Southeast Asia as some Indians would like to see. But from both the Indian and Southeast Asian perspectives, the growth of Chinese power and the size and dynamism of the Indian economy cannot be discounted as factors shaping their mutual relationship without posing the risk of Indian domination or entanglement in the region.

On balance then, the simultaneous rise of China and India on Southeast Asia's doorstep does not threaten to eclipse Southeast Asia's regional identity, as feared by some observers. China possesses unmistakably superior economic resources, and it is a giant continental power. However, India's geographical and cultural proximity, together with its economic potential (though this is sometimes exaggerated, not the least by Indians themselves), are countervailing factors. This is not a classic balance-of-power situation, because there is little evidence that the Southeast Asians are playing one against the other (although this might have been attempted by the military regime of Myanmar before the 2010 elections). Nor is there any evidence that India or China are seeking Southeast Asian proxies to compete with each other. But Southeast Asia's strategy of engaging both of its big neighbours along with other more distant powers has served the region well, and will continue to do so if pursued consistently and with a measure of unity and cohesion. The key element of this strategy is ASEAN's pursuit of the idea of East Asian Community.

An East Asian Community?

While the rise of China and India challenges the Southeast Asian concept geopolitically and economically, following the crisis of 1997 a new factor in Southeast Asia's regional identity was the rapid development of East Asian regionalism. The initial development of East Asian regionalism was through the ASEAN Plus Three (APT) framework, which evolved into the East Asian Summit (EAS), as a stepping stone to an aspirational East Asian Community.

Comprising the ten ASEAN members and China, Japan and South Korea, the APT had its roots in the Asian economic crisis, especially in what the ASEAN members perceived as the West's lukewarm and somewhat insincere assistance to crisis-hit regional economies. The APT was in a sense a revival of Malaysian Prime Minister Mahathir Mohamad's proposal for an East Asian Economic Caucus (EAEC), which was discussed in the previous chapter. As noted, the EAEC had remained moribund, as Japan, its putative leader, refused to endorse it out of deference to the United States, which had strongly opposed the EAEC. But the advent of the Asia-Europe Meeting (ASEM) in 1996 saw the EAEC concept get a new lease of life, as the Asian component of the ASEM comprised of essentially the same countries that Mahathir had wanted in the EAEC (with the exclusion of Western members of APEC such as Australia, the United States, Canada and New Zealand).

The APT framework gave ASEAN a fresh start, after the credibility of the grouping had suffered for its perceived failure to offer an effective response to the economic crisis. The APT also offered a framework for regional financial cooperation, after the proposal in 1997 by Japan for an Asian Monetary Fund had been shot down by the United States. Indeed, the major project undertaken by the APT has been the Chiang Mai Initiative (CMI). The CMI was established by APT members in May 2000. Its main instrument is a system of bilateral currency swap agreements among the APT members. By the end of 2003, sixteen such swap agreements, amounting to $36.5 billion, had been agreed upon.[114] Critics noted that the bilateral nature of the CMI swaps would limit its flexibility and effectiveness in a future crisis. Moreover, the total value of currency swap agreements was relatively small, given that fact that the foreign exchange reserves held by the APT countries amounted to $1.5 trillion. In view of the fact that Thailand alone had requested $17.2 billion from the IMF during the 1997 crisis, the amount was hardly sufficient to deal with a future crisis. The total value of currency swaps under the CMI had risen to US$75 billion by May 2006.[115] In March 2010, a multilateral component called CMI Multilateralization (CMIM) came into effect, with an initial size of US$120 billion.

Nonetheless, advocates of the APT were fairly optimistic about its potential. Philippine President Joseph Estrada hoped that the APT concept might in due course lead to an "Asian common market", "one East Asian currency" and "one East Asian community".[116] Mahathir himself went so far as to claim that an East Asian monetary system might have made a big difference to the region's ability to cope with the economic crisis of 1997: "Had such an EAMF [East Asian Monetary Fund] existed, I believe that the East Asian currency crisis of 1997 and 1998 would not have occurred, would not have endured and would not have gone to such ridiculous depths."[117]

The security role and benefits of the APT remained unclear. As Ali Alatas, the former Foreign Minister of Indonesia, pointed out, it was unlikely to develop a significant security role for itself.[118] At the same time, the APT raised concerns that China might displace ASEAN from regional leadership at a time when a weakened ASEAN was increasingly dependent on China's markets. The possibility of Chinese leadership was one key difference between the APT and Mahathir's EAEC, which had assumed Japanese leadership. This may have been one reason for Japan to call for the inclusion of Australia and New Zealand in the East Asian cooperation process, while others, such as Singapore, backed the entry of India.

For Southeast Asia, the emergence of APT foreshadowed a broader and potentially competing source of regionalism. The APT was described as reflecting "a rising sense of East Asian identity".[119] The report of the East Asia Vision Group (EAVG), a semi-official group of eminent persons, set up at the behest of South Korean President Kim Dae Jung to prepare a blueprint for East Asian regionalism, stressed "fostering the identity of an East Asian community" as a key long-term objective.[120] The East Asia Study Group (EASG), an official group whose goal was to devise concrete measures of East Asian cooperation, also underscored the importance of "fostering a strong sense of East Asian identity".[121] What would the fate of the Southeast Asian regional idea be if an East Asian regional identity were to crystallize?

Yet the East Asian Community idea faces many of the same challenges that have plagued other frameworks of regionalism in Asia, including questions about geographical scope and membership, intraregional differences and the role of extraregional actors. The "historic" inaugural East Asia Summit (EAS), held in Kuala Lumpur on 14 December 2005, managed to rationalize the participation of India, Australia and New Zealand by professing a supposedly "functional", rather than geographical, view of the region. This underscores the problematic nature of regional construction. Speaking of the coherence of East Asia, T.J. Pempel has written, "East Asia today is a much more closely knit region than it was at the end of World War II or even a decade ago." Yet "no single map of East Asia is so inherently self-evident and logical as to preclude the consideration of equally plausible alternatives."[122] The problem of regional definition has generated conflicting pathways to the development of the East Asian Community. The decision to invite Australia, New Zealand and India to the summit was divisive. China would prefer the APT process, involving ASEAN and the three Northeast Asian states, to drive the East Asian Community process forward, while Japan would prefer to see the East Asian Summit, with the participation of India, Australia and New Zealand, and subsequently the U.S. and Russia, assume centre stage in regional community-building.

There are several other barriers to the realization of the East Asian Community idea. During the Koizumi era in Japan, Sino-Japanese mistrust, fuelled by the Japanese Prime Minister's visit to the Yasukuni Shrine, cast a shadow over prospects for East Asian regionalism. While the advent of a new Japanese Government under the Democratic Party of Japan (DPJ) led to an improvement in Sino-Japanese ties, Prime Minister Yukio Hatoyama's 2009 proposal for an East Asian Community received no support from China. In the meantime, the implications of the participation of the United States in East Asian regionalism, including President Barrack Obama's attendance at the EAS in Bali in November 2011, remain uncertain. While professing a lack of interest in EAS membership, Washington had at first remained wary of the possibility that the East Asian process could lead to its own marginalization and exclusion from regional interactions. In 2005, even so staunch a U.S. supporter as Singapore's former Prime Minister, Goh Chok Tong, had contended that "East Asia cannot be extending to countries in the Pacific, for then even the political definitions would get stretched beyond belief." In Goh's view, East Asia's "engagement with the US could be through the APEC and the ARF".[123] But with the Obama administration's decision to let the United States accede to

ASEAN's Treaty of Amity and Cooperation in 2009 and its greater engagement with regional multilateral institutions, political barriers to the United States joining the EAS eased substantially. Yet, while such a broadening of the EAS may have dispelled fears of possible Chinese dominance, this development may cause the Chinese to lose interest in the EAS as the basis for building a regional community. The key challenge for East Asian visionaries and leaders will be to find the balance between Chinese and U.S. dominance and Chinese and U.S. indifference.

Another question about the EAC is how it would relate to wider Asia-Pacific organizations such as the ARF and APEC. These organizations have stalled. The ARF has encountered difficulties in moving from rudimentary confidence-building measures to preventive diplomacy. APEC never recovered from the loss of credibility it suffered in the wake of the 1997 regional financial crisis. The U.S. push for a Trans-Pacific Partnership (TPP) also undermines APEC. Yet, these two institutions remain in place, and the fortunes of the ARF could still be revived. Presumably, East Asian institutions could focus on financial cooperation, as the APT has done through the Chiang Mai Initiative and the system of currency swaps, while APEC could usefully take up trade facilitation. The ARF is developing cooperation against transnational dangers such as terrorism and nature disasters. But such a neat division of labour among the wider Asian regional institutions will not be easily accomplished. Against this backdrop, and in view of the lingering Sino-Japanese rivalry, ASEAN is actually in the "driver's seat" of both the East Asian and Asia-Pacific institutions, since it is the only politically acceptable entity to anchor regional cooperation in the absence of credible alternatives.

Conclusion

Post-1997 developments presented major challenges to the regional coherence of Southeast Asia. The Asian economic crisis exacerbated intraregional tensions and widened differences among Southeast Asian countries over political and strategic issues. The crisis demonstrated the vulnerability of the region to the forces of globalization, and the dependence of Southeast Asian countries on external forces, thereby calling into question the Southeast Asian elites' professed aspirations for regional autonomy. Other challenges have come from Southeast Asia's closer interdependence and integration with East Asian powers and institutions. The rise of China presents Southeast Asia not only with a powerful economic challenge, especially in terms of the diversion of investments, but also raises the danger (though exaggerated) of Southeast Asia being absorbed into a Chinese sphere of influence. The rise of India compounds the challenge to the Southeast Asian identity, as India, like China, has historically been a major source of ideational, cultural, economic and political influence in the region. The emergence of the idea for an East Asian Community, which could potentially still be dominated by China, also challenges Southeast Asian regionalism. Furthermore, transnational dangers that go beyond the region in terms of their origin and impact and whose management would require wider regional mechanisms raise fresh questions about the "regionness" of Southeast Asia. Transnational civil society elements, empowered by democratic transitions in the region, question the legitimacy of ASEAN's state-centric project. Nonetheless, for better or for worse, regional responses to these dangers have to be coordinated through ASEAN's official regional regionalism. ASEAN is after all the longest- standing regional institution, and its members have shown a greater measure of readiness to deal multilaterally with transnational dangers than with traditional interstate conflicts. The ability of Southeast Asian states to build upon these responses and redefine their regionalism will make the crucial difference between the permanence and transience of Southeast Asia as a region in the twenty-first century.

NOTES

[1]   For general discussions of development strategies in Southeast Asia, see Richard F. Doner, "Approaches to the Politics of Economic Growth in Southeast Asia", *Journal of Asian Studies* 50, no. 4 (1991): 818–49; K. Hay, "ASEAN and the Shifting Tides of Economic Power at the End of the 1980s", *International Journal* 44, no. 3 (1989): 640–59; James Clad, *Behind the Myth: Business, Money and Power in Southeast Asia* (London: Hyman Press, 1989); Walden Bello and Stephanie Rosenfeld, *Dragons in Distress: Asia's Miracle Economies in Crisis* (San Francisco: Institute for Food and Development Policy, 1990); Kunio Yoshihara, *Philippine Industrialization: Foreign and Domestic Capital* (New York: Oxford University Press, 1985); and Akira Suehiro, *Capital Accumulation and Industrial Development in Thailand* (Bangkok: Social Research Institute, 1985).

[2]   "Weathering the Storm: ASEAN's Response to Crisis", address by Rodolfo Severino, ASEAN Secretary-General, to the conference sponsored by the

Far Eastern Economic Review on "Weathering the Storm: Hong Kong and the Asian Financial Crisis", Hong Kong, 11 June 1998.

[3]   Suthad Setboonsarng, "ASEAN Economic Cooperation: Adjusting to the Crisis", in *Southeast Asian Affairs 1998* (Singapore: Institute of Southeast Asian Studies, 1999).

[4]   Kerstin Marx, "Asia: Crisis causes massive unemployment", Third World Network <http://www.twnside.org.sg/title/mass-cn.htm>. See also Chalongphob Sussangkarn, Frank Flatters and Sauwalak Kittiprapas, "Comparative Social Impacts of the Asian Economic Crisis in Thailand, Indonesia, Malaysia and the Philippines: A Preliminary Report", *TDRI Quarterly Review* 14, no. 1 (1999): 3–9.

[5]   Asian Development Bank, *Asian Development Outlook*, various years.

[6]   Frank Ching, "Social Impact of the Regional Financial Crisis", in *Policy Choices, Social Consequences and the Philippine Case*, three essays for the Asia Society's Asian Update series <http://www.asiasociety.org/publications/update_crisis_ching.html> (accessed 26 June 2006).

[7]   "The Asian Crisis: A View from the IMF", address by Stanley Fischer, first deputy managing director of the IMF at the midwinter conference of the Bankers' Association for Foreign Trade, Washington, D.C., 22 January 1998.

[8]   Ibid.

[9]   Setboonsarng, "ASEAN Economic Cooperation: Adjusting to the Crisis". The author was then the Deputy Secretary-General of ASEAN.

[10]   *Straits Times*, 5 August 1998, p. 16.

[11]   *Straits Times*, 1 March 1998.

[12]   Text of speech at the fifth symposium of the Institute for International Monetary Affairs, Tokyo, Japan, reproduced in the *New Straits Times*, 4 June 1998, p. 12.

[13]   "Singapore Urges No Retreat From Globalization", Xinhua News Agency Dispatch, 3 September 1998 (obtained from LexisNexis).

[14]   Lee Hsien Loong, "Whither Globalism — A World In Crisis", speech at the Economic Strategy Conference, Washington, D.C., 6 May 1998, cited in Chin Kin Wah, "Globalization and Its Challenges to ASEAN Political Participation", paper presented to the ISEAS 30th anniversary conference, "Southeast Asia in the 21st Century: Challenges of Globalization", Singapore, Institute of Southeast Asian Studies, 30 July–1 August 1998, p. 3.

[15]   *Straits Times*, 28 August 1998, p. 2.

[16]   "Singapore-KL Problems 'Not Alarming'", *Straits Times*, 21 September 1998 <http://ftdasia.ft.com/info-api/sh>.

[17]   For an overview of the impact of the Asian economic crisis in fostering divisions as well as unity in ASEAN see Derek da Cunha, "Division and Unity: ASEAN During the Asian Crisis", paper presented to the 1998 international

conference of The Korean Association of International Studies, Seoul, 13–14 November 1998.

[18] "Out of Its Depth", *Far Eastern Economic Review*, 19 February 1998, p. 25.

[19] "ASEAN's Failure: The Limits of Politeness", *The Economist*, 28 February 1998, p. 29.

[20] Ibid.

[21] "Thais Retract Call for ASEAN Intervention", *Straits Times Interactive*, 27 June 1998.

[22] Ibid.

[23] "ASEAN Loses Critic Anwar", *Asiaweek*, 18 September 1998, p. 54.

[24] Tommy Koh, "What E. Asia Can Learn from the EU", *Straits Times*, 10 July 1998, p. 48.

[25] "EU-Style Asean Possible", *Straits Times*, 19 August 1998, p. 21.

[26] "Think About Pax-Pacifica, Says Ramos", *Straits Times*, 4 March 2000.

[27] Sanchita Basu Das, "What ASEAN Must Do to Cope With the Crisis", in *Global Financial Crisis: Implications for ASEAN* (Singapore: Institute of Southeast Asian Studies, 2008), p. 35.

[28] Masahiro Kawai, "Global Financial Crisis and Implications for ASEAN", in *Global Financial Crisis: Implications for ASEAN* (Singapore: Institute of Southeast Asian Studies, 2008), p. 5.

[29] Hal Hill, "The Financial Crisis and What's in Store for Southeast Asia", East Asia Forum, 18 April 2009 <http://www.eastasiaforum.org/2009/04/18/the-financial-crisis-and-whats-in-store-for-southeast-asia> (accessed 5 March 2010).

[30] *Pedoman Umum Perjuangan Al-Jama'ah Al-Islamiyyah* (or PUPJI, "General Guide for the Struggle of Jemaah Islamiyah"), released by the Central Leadership Council, Jemaah Islamiyah, translated by the International Center for Political Violence and Terrorism Research, Institute of Defence and Strategic Studies, Nanyang Technological University, Singapore, 2004.

[31] Ahmed Rashid, *Taliban* (New Haven, CT: Yale University Press, 2001), chaps. 12 and 13.

[32] "SARS in Singapore--predictors of disease severity", <http://www.ncbi.nlm.nih.gov/pubmed/16829999>. A BBC report on 31 May 2009 put the world total of SARS-induced deaths at 812, of which 348 were in mainland China, 298 in Hong Kong, 84 in Taiwan, 32 in Singapore and 38 in Canada. "Singapore Success Against SARS", <http://news.bbc.co.uk/2/hi/americas/2951508.stm>. The WHO's own estimate was 774 deaths (out of 8,096 cases), with 349 of these being in mainland China. WHO, "Summary of Probable SARS Cases with Onset of Illness from 1 November 2002 to 31 July 2003", <http://www.who.int/csr/sars/country/table2004_04_21/en/index.html> (accessed 26 June 2006).

[33] World Health Organization, "Viet Nam SARS-Free", <http://www.who.int/mediacentre/news/releases/2003/pr_sars/en/>.

[34] "SARS in Singapore — Predictors of Disease Severity", <http://www.ncbi.
      nlm.nih.gov/pubmed/16829999>.

[35] Jahyeong Koo and Dong Fu, "The Effects of SARS on East Asian Economies",
      Expand Your Insight, Federal Reserve Bank of Dallas, 1 July 2003, <http://
      www.dallasfed.org/eyi/global/0307sars.html>.

[36] "The Impact of SARS on Asian Economy and ASEAN's Leaders' Response",
      address by H.E. Ong Keng Yong, Secretary-General of ASEAN, Beijing, 13
      May 2003, <http://www.aseansec.org/14787.htm>.

[37] The World Bank, "Tsunami Recovery in Indonesia", March 2006, available
      at <http://web.worldbank.org/WBSITE/EXTERNAL/COUNTRIES/
      EASTASIAPACIFICEXT/0,,contentMDK:20738359~pagePK:146736~piPK:
      146830~theSitePK:226301,00.html> (accessed 26 June 2006); EM-DAT Emergency
      Disasters Database, <http://www.em-dat.net/disasters/Visualisation/
      profiles/natural-table-emdat_disasters.php?dis_type=Wave+%2F+Surge&Su
      bmit=Display+Disaster+Profile> (accessed 26 June 2006).

[38] This paragraph draws from Amitav Acharya, "Securing a More United World",
      Straits Times, 10 January 2005.

[39] "Lessons from the Tsunami for Regional Cooperation: The Importance of
      Prevention and Early Responses", panel discussion, Singapore Institute of
      International Affairs, 16 February 2005.

[40] Singapore Government Information, "Aceh Quake and Tsunami Disaster",
      <http://www.gov.sg/tsunami.htm> (accessed 26 June 2006).

[41] "ASEAN's Response to the Tsunami Disaster — Issues and Concerns: A Special
      Report", Virtual Information Center, <http://www.vic-info.org/…/$FILE/
      050509-SR-IssuesAndConcernsOnASEANSpecialReport.doc>.

[42] For an overview, see Lye Tuck-Po, Wil de Jong, and Abe Ken-ichi, *The Political
      Ecology of Tropical Forests in Southeast Asia*, Kyoto Area Studies on Asia,
      vol. 6 (Kyoto: Kyoto University Press, 2003).

[43] Blue Planet Biomes, "Southeast Asian Rainforest", <http://www.blueplanet
      biomes.org/se_asian_rnfrst.htm> (accessed 8 March 2010).

[44] Navjot S. Sodhi, Lian Pin Koh, Barry W. Brook and Peter K.L. Ng, "Southeast
      Asian Biodiversity: An Impending Disaster", *Trends in Ecology and Evolution*
      19, no. 12 (2004), p. 654.

[45] Rainforest Relief, "Malaysia", <http://www.rainforestrelief.org/What_to_
      Avoid_and_Alternatives/Rainforest_Wood/What_to_Avoid_What_to_Choose/
      By_Country/Asia/Malaysia.html> (accessed 25 May 2010).

[46] Sodhi et al., "Southeast Asian Biodiversity", pp. 655–56.

[47] Thomas R. Leinbach and Richard Ulak, *Southeast Asia's Diversity and
      Development* (Upper Saddle River, NJ: Prentice Hall, 2000), p. 136.

[48] Maria Seda, "Global Environmental Concerns and Priorities: Implications
      for ASEAN", in *Environmental Management in ASEAN: Perspectives on Critical*

Regional Issues, edited by Maria Seda (Singapore: Institute of Southeast Asian Studies, 1993), p. 24.

49 "Fires Again Ravage Indonesia's Forests", *Los Angeles Times,* 23 March 1998.

50 Murray Hiebert and John McBeth, "Trial by Fire: Smog Crisis Tests Asean's Vaunted Cooperation", *Far Eastern Economic Review,* 16 October 1997.

51 "Its Mood Dark as the Haze, Southeast Asia Aches", *New York Times,* 26 October 1997.

52 Ibid.

53 "Suharto Says Indonesia Doing its Best to Combat Fires", *Agence France-Presse,* 4 October 1997. Officials in Indonesia said that six people in total died from respiratory diseases. In March 1998, the *Suara Pembaruan* newspaper in the capital, Jakarta, reported that smoke from the fires had caused 297 cases of pneumonia and that two people had died.

54 "Environment Minister to Make Fighting Fires a Priority", *Straits Times Interactive,* 18 March 1998.

55 David Glover and Timothy Jessup, eds., *Indonesia's Fires and Haze: The Cost of Catastrophe* (Ottawa: International Development Research Centre/Singapore, Institute of Southeast Asian Studies, 1999).

56 Rhett A. Butler, "Drought and Deforestation in Southeast Asia to Contribute to Climate Change", Mongabay.com, 9 December 2008, <http://news.mongabay.com/2008/1209-forests_drought.html>.

57 Channel News Asia (Singapore), 11 October 2006.

58 "Telephone call between Prime Minister Lee Hsien Loong and President Susilo Bambang Yudhoyono on Transboundary Haze Pollution", Ministry of Foreign Affairs, Singapore, 12 October 2006, <http://app.mfa.gov.sg/2006/press/view_press_print.asp?post_id=1856> (accessed 14 June 2008).

59 Gerald Giam, "Haze Problem: Bilateral Pressure on Indonesia Works Best", *Singapore Angle,* 13 October 2006 <http://www.singaporeangle.com/2006/10/haze-problem-bilateral-pressure-on.html> (accessed 14 June 2008).

60 Personal interview with Surin Pitsuwan, former Thai Foreign Minister, Bangkok, 23 October 2005.

61 ASEAN Vision 2020, <http://www.aseansec.org/5228.htm>.

62 "Declaration of ASEAN Concord II (Bali Concord II)", 7 October 2003, <http://www.aseansec.org/15159.htm>

63 Ibid.

64 Ministry of Foreign Affairs, Indonesia, *Deplu Paper on ASEAN Security Community,* tabled at the ASEAN ministerial meeting in Cambodia, 16–18 June 2003, p. 5. Deplu stands for Departemen Luar Negeri, which is the Ministry of Foreign Affairs in Indonesia. Many of these proposals drew upon a concept paper by Indonesian scholar Rizal Sukma. See Rizal Sukma, "The Future of ASEAN: Towards a Security Community", paper presented at the

seminar on "ASEAN Cooperation: Challenges and Prospects in the Current International Situation", Permanent Mission of the Republic of Indonesia to the United Nations, New York, 3 June 2003, pp. 8–9.

[65] Declaration of ASEAN Concord II (Bali Concord II), 7 October 2003, <http:// www.aseansec.org/15159.htm>.

[66] Ibid.

[67] The ASEAN Socio-Cultural Community (ASCC) Plan of Action, <http://www. aseansec.org/16832.htm>.

[68] Vitit Muntabhorn, "Charter Can Build an Asean Architecture", *Bangkok Post*, 1 December 2008.

[69] The role of such networks has been well captured by Diane Stone:

> Think tanks perform three important tasks in agenda setting efforts. Firstly, think tanks act as "innovators". Through think tanks, Asian intellectuals have generated new cognitive structures or causal frames of reference around which ideas about region are constructed. Secondly, think tanks diffuse these norms and understandings. They can start the ball rolling for a "habit of dialogue". Thirdly, through their networking and collaborative ventures intra-regionally, and for some through their involvement in the political processes of their home states, institutes can help shape the political choices made by states. They are proactive in the internalization of regionally developed understandings into domestic political thinking, policies and legal systems.

Diane Stone, "Networks, Second Track Diplomacy and Regional Cooperation: The Role of Southeast Asian Think Tanks", paper presented to the 38th annual International Studies Association Convention, Toronto, Canada, 22–26 March 1997, p. 3.

[70] Stuart Harris, "Policy Networks and Economic Cooperation in the Asia Pacific", *Pacific Review* 7, no. 4 (1994), p. 390.

[71] According to Jusuf Wanandi, Track-II networking "is basically a nongovernmental academic activity, where government officials also participate in private capacity. This brings official input but also flexible and free discussion in the networking." Jusuf Wanandi, "The Regional Role of 'Track-Two' Diplomacy: ASEAN, ARF, and CSCAP", in *The Role of Security and Economic Cooperation Structures in the Asia Pacific Region*, edited by Hadi Soesastro and Anthony Bergin (Jakarta: Centre for Strategic and International Studies, 1996), p. 152. Note that this definition overstates the "academic" nature of the discussions and does not mention the involvement of the private sector, which has been crucial to Track-II processes such as PECC (Pacific Economic Cooperation Council) in dealing with regional economic cooperation.

[72] The material on the ASEAN Tourism Association is taken from its official website, <http://www.aseanta.org>.

[73] Based on information from the website of the ASEAN Secretariat, <http:// www.aseansec.org>, and the official website of the ASEAN Foundation, <http://www.aseanfoundation.org>.

[74] This section draws mainly from Amitav Acharya, "Democratisation and the Prospects for Participatory Regionalism in Southeast Asia", *Third World Quarterly* 24, no. 2 (2003): 375–90.

[75] Information on APCET taken primarily from the following two websites, <http://www.asianexchange.org/Movements/94109509476240.php> and <http://www.iidnet.org/adv/timor/overview.htm>.

[76] Information on ALTSEAN-Myanmar is drawn from <http://www.asian exchange.org/Movements/94109392248271.php>.

[77] Forum-Asia official brochure, undated.

[78] Forum-Asia, *Human Rights in Asia* (Bangkok: Asian Forum for Human Rights and Development, 2001); Forum Asia, *Creating Asia: Flags of Human Rights, Seeds of Freedom* (Bangkok: Asian Forum for Human Rights and Development, 2000).

[79] Forum-Asia, *The Security Syndrome: Politics of National Security in Asia* (Bangkok: Asian Forum for Human Rights and Development, 1997).

[80] Manila People's Forum on APEC, *APEC: Four Objectives in Search of a Noun* (Manila: Focus on the Global South and Institute of Popular Democracy, 1996).

[81] Amitav Acharya and Arabinda Acharya, "Human Security in the Asia Pacific: Puzzle, Panacea or Peril?", *CANCAPS Bulletin*, November 2000.

[82] Personal interview, Forum-Asia, 21 June 2002.

[83] Pierre P. Lizee, "Civil Society and Regional Security: Tensions and Potentials in Post-Crisis Southeast Asia", *Contemporary Southeast Asia* 22, no. 3 (2000): 551–70.

[84] Acharya, "Democratisation and the Prospects for Participatory Regionalism in Southeast Asia".

[85] The ASEAN People's Assembly included plenary sessions on "Setting ASEAN's Agenda: The Role of the People"; "Towards Open Societies in ASEAN: The Issues; ASEAN and Regional Community Building"; "Reflections on ASEAN"; and panel discussions on "Critical Assessment of the ASEAN 2020 Vision"; "Globalization and Human Security"; "The Power of Women and Their Empowerment"; "The Media: Informer, Educator and Reformer?"; "Towards a Regional Human Rights Mechanism"; "The Role of Civil Society in Good Governance"; "Poverty in ASEAN: What More to be Done?"; "Limits and Opportunities of Resources and Environmental Management"; "Enhanced Interaction: Case Studies of Myanmar and East Timor"; and "Towards a Revolution in ASEAN's Education Systems".

[86] "Memorandum to the High Level Panel (HLP) on the establishment of the ASEAN Human Rights Body", by Forum-Asia and the SAPA Task Force on ASEAN and Human Rights (SAPA TFAHR), 22 June 2009. Correspondence from SAPA-Forum Asia to the author requesting signing the Open Letter to the HLP on the Memorandum, 19 June 2009, which the author did, and from SAPA-Forum-Asia to the author on 23 July 2009 outlining "improvements

in the text of the TOR (terms of reference) from the previous versions". It argued, "Our advocacy work managed to influence the modification and additional weight to the text of TOR."

[87] Focus on the Global South, "ASEAN Peoples' Forum", <http://focusweb.org/asean-peoples-forum.html?Itemid=1> (accessed 8 March 2010).

[88] Ibid.

[89] Forum-Asia, "ASEAN Peoples' Forum 'disappointed' over snub from government officials", 22 October 2009, <http://www.forum-asia.org/index.php?option=com_content&task=view&id=2360&Itemid=49> (accessed 8 March 2010).

[90] Amitav Acharya, "State-Society Relations: Asian and World Order after September 11", in *Worlds in Collision: Terror and the Future of Global Order*, edited by Ken Booth and Tim Dunne (London: Palgrave, 2002), pp. 194–204; Amitav Acharya, "The Retreat of Liberal Democracy", *International Herald Tribune*, 17 September 2002, p. 5.

[91] "Repositioning Asean for a New World", *World Security Network*, 12 September 2005, <http://www.globalsecuritynews.com/showArticle3.cfm?article_id=11907> (accessed 5 November 2009).

[92] Ibid.

[93] "China Snuggles Up to South-Asian Neighbors [*sic*]", *Taipei Times*, 10 October 2003, p. 5, <http://www.taipeitimes.com/News/world/archives/2003/10/10/2003071108> (accessed 20 June 2006).

[94] UNCTAD, *World Investment Report*, various issues, cited in Thitapha Wattanapruttipaisan, "Watching Brief on China and ASEAN Part One: The Rise of China as an Economic Power", BEI Studies Unit, Paper no. 05/2005, <http://www.aseansec.org/Watching_Brief_on_China_-_Thitapha.pdf> (accessed 26 June 2006).

[95] Nicholas Lardy, "China as Awakened Giant", *The Nation*, 18 October 2002.

[96] "ASEAN's Investment in China Totals 38.22 Billion Dollars", *People's Daily Online*, 10 January 2006, <http://english.people.com.cn/200601/10/eng20060110_234130.html> (accessed 20 June 2006).

[97] United Nations Public Administration Network (UNPAN), "Foreign Direct Investments to China and Southeast Asia: Has ASEAN Been Losing Out?", *Economic Survey of Singapore (Third Quarter)* 2002, <http://unpan1.un.org/intradoc/groups/public/documents/APCITY/UNPAN010347.pdf> (accessed 20 June 2006).

[98] "Backgrounder: Development of China-ASEAN Trade Relations", *People's Daily Online*, 31 December 2009, <http://english.people.com.cn/90001/90776/90883/6857416.html>.

[99] "The China-ASEAN Free Trade Agreement: Ajar for Business", *The Economist*, 7 January 2010, <http://www.economist.com/world/asia/displaystory.cfm?story_id=15211682>.

[100] John Wong and Sarah Chan, "China-ASEAN Free Trade Agreement: Shaping Future Economic Relations", *Asian Survey* 43, no. 3 (2003): 507–26.

[101] Michael Vatikiotis, "A Too Friendly Embrace", *Far Eastern Economic Review*, 17 June 2004, pp. 20–22.

[102] ASEAN Secretariat, "Declaration on the Conduct of Parties in the South China Sea", 4 November 2002, <http://www.aseansec.org/13163.htm> (accessed 20 June 2006).

[103] Ron Moreau and Richard Ernsberger Jr., "Strangling the Mekong", *Newsweek*, Atlantic edition, 19 March 2001, p. 26; for details of the Chinese dams, see S.D. Muni, *China's Strategic Engagement with the New ASEAN*, IDSS Monographs no. 2 (Singapore: Institute of Defence and Strategic Studies, 2002), p. 84.

[104] Andrew Selth, "The Burmese Army", *Jane's Intelligence Review* 7, no. 11 (1995), p. 515.

[105] Andrew Selth, "Burma: A Strategic Perspective", Asia Foundation Working Paper no. 13, May 2001, originally presented at the conference on "Strategic Rivalries in the Bay of Bengal: The Burma/Myanmar Nexus", Washington, D.C., 1 February 2001, <http://www.asiafoundation.org/pdf/WorkPap13.pdf>.

[10] David C. Kang, "Getting Asia Wrong: The Need for New Analytical Frameworks", *International Security* 27, no. 4 (2003), p. 66.

[107] ASEAN Secretariat, "ASEAN-China Dialogue Relations", <http://www.aseansec.org/5874.htm>; India Brand Equity Foundation, "India & ASEAN", <http://www.ibef.org/india/indiaasean.aspx> (accessed 6 January 2010).

[108] Zhao Hong, "India's Changing Relationship with ASEAN in China's Perspective", EAI Background Brief no. 313 (Singapore: East Asian Institute, 2006), p. 10, <http://www.eai.nus.edu.sg/BB313.pdf>.

[109] Ibid., p. 14.

[110] David Kihara, "A Naturally [*sic*] Ally", *Cambodia Daily*, <http://www.camnet.com.kh/cambodia.daily/asean/13.htm> (accessed 6 November 2009).

[111] Cited in ibid.

[112] Ibid.

[113] "India and ASEAN: Shared Perspectives", Prime Minister Vajpayee's address to the Institute of Diplomatic and Foreign Relations, Kuala Lumpur, 16 May 2001, <http://www.indianembassy.org/special/cabinet/Primeminister/pm_may_16_2001.htm> (accessed 6 November 2009).

[114] Asia Regional Integration Center, "Chiang Mai Initiative (CMI): Current Status and Future Directions", <http://aric.adb.org/pdf/cmi_currentstatus.pdf> (accessed 20 June 2006).

[115] Bank of Japan, "The Agreement on the Swap Arrangement under the Chiang Mai Initiative (as of May 4, 2006)", <http://www.boj.or.jp/en/type/release/zuiji_new/data/un0605a.pdf> (accessed 20 June 2006).

[116] Cited in Ted Bardacke, "East Asian Nations Reach Accords", *Financial Times* website <www.ft.com>, 29 November 1999, p. 1.

[117] "We Should've Done It My Way", *Asiaweek*, 29 October 1999.

[118] Ali Alatas, "ASEAN Plus Three Equals Peace Plus Prosperity", *Trends in Southeast Asia*, no. 2 (Singapore: Institute of Southeast Asian Studies, January 2001), pp. 2–3.

[119] Simon Tay, "Asean Plus Three: Challenges and a Caution About A New Regionalism", in *Asia Pacific Security: Challenges and Opportunities in the 21st Century*, edited by Mohamed Jawahar Hassan, Stephen Leong and Vincent Lim (Kuala Lumpur: Institute of Strategic and Insternational Studies, 2002), pp. 99–117.

[120] East Asia Vision Group, "Towards an East Asian Community: Region of Peace, Prosperity and Progress", Report, 2001, pp. 1–6, <http://www.mofa.go.jp/region/asia-paci/report2001.pdf> (accessed 26 June 2006).

[121] East Asia Study Group, "Final Report of the East Asia Study Group", ASEAN+3 Summit, Phnom Penh, Cambodia, 4 November 2002, <http://www.mofa.go.jp/region/asia-paci/asean/pmv0211/report.pdf> (accessed 26 June 2006).

[122] T.J. Pempel, "Introduction: Emerging Webs of Regional Connectedness", in *Remapping East Asia: The Construction of a Region*, edited by T.J. Pempel (Ithaca, NY: Cornell University Press, 2005), pp. 24–25.

[123] "High stakes at the Kuala Lumpur Summit", *Financial Express*, 9 November 2005.

Section C

1. Vietnam Joins ASEAN

Brunei's ruler Sultan Hassanal Bolkiah (R) shakes hands with Vietnam's Foreign Minister Nguyen Manh Camh at the 28th ASEAN Ministerial Meeting in Bandar Seri Begawan, Brunei Darussalam, 29 July 1995. Vietnam officially became the seventh member of ASEAN, a dramatic diplomatic breakthrough given Hanoi's steadfast hostility towards the grouping since its inception.

Source: Photo by Romeo Gacad/AFP/ Getty Images.

2. Asia Pacific Economic Cooperation (APEC)
First Informal Meeting of Ministers, Canberra, November 1989.

Source: Courtesy of the APEC Secretariat.

3. ASEAN Regional Forum
Delegates at the Inaugural Meeting of ASEAN Regional Forum, Bangkok, 25 July 1994.

Source: Courtesy of the ASEAN Secretariat.

4. ASEAN Plus Three

Chinese Premier Wen Jiabao (2nd L) asks Indonesian President Megawati Sukarnoputri (2nd R) to lead down the stage while Japanese Prime Minister Junichiro Koizumi (R) and South Korean President Roh Moo-Hyun (L) look on after a group photo of ASEAN+3 meeting in Nusa Dua, Bali, 7 October 2003. ASEAN's policy is to engage the three East Asian countries, despite the risk of being caught in the rivalry between China and Japan.

Source: Photo by Roslan Rahman/ AFP/Getty Images.

5. East Asia Summit

U.S. President Barack Obama (2nd R) waves with Indonesian President Susilo Bambang Yudhoyono (L), Myanmar President Thein Sein (R) and Brunei Sultan Hassanal Bolkiah (2nd L) at the East Asia Summit in Nusa Dua on Indonesia's resort island of Bali on 19 November 2011. Obama sent Hillary Clinton to Myanmar in December, the first visit there by a US Secretary of State in fifty years, to encourage democratic reform. The U.S. entry into the EAS countered potential Chinese dominance of East Asian regionalism.

Source: Photo by Saul Loeb/AFP/Getty Images.

6. Ali Alatas

Indonesia's longest serving foreign minister (1988–98) spanning Presidents Soeharto and Habibie. Alatas played a key part in the negotiations to end the Cambodia conflict leading to the 1991 Paris Peace Agreement, and in ASEAN's post-Cold War development, during which time he represented the traditional ASEAN approach to regionalism, including the non-interference doctrine.

Source: Photo by Torsten Blackwood/Getty Images.

7. Surin Pitsuwan

As Thailand's Foreign Minister in the aftermath of the Asian Financial Crisis in 1997, Pitsuwan, a Muslim (seen here at a Islamic school, Pondok Pesantren, Pabelan near Yogyakarta, Indonesia), became known for his advocacy of "flexible engagement", which called for reforming ASEAN's non-interference doctrine to deal with human rights issues in Myanmar and transnational challenges facing the region. He went on to become ASEAN's Secretary-General for a five-year term starting in 2008.

Source: Photo taken by the author.

8. The Fall of Soeharto

Indonesian President Soeharto signs an agreement in Jakarta, Indonesia on 15 January 1998 with the International Monetary Fund (IMF) as its Director-General Michel Camdessus watches. The letter outlined major reforms and austerity measures linked to a massive bailout led by the IMF. A vivid symbol of the political consequences of the 1997 Asian financial crisis, the image was widely seen as the ultimate humiliation of the Indonesian president who had provided ASEAN with leadership and direction while ruling with an iron fist over Southeast Asia's most populous nation for thirty-two years.

Source: Photo by Agus Lolong/AFP/Getty Images

9. Terrorist Attack in Bali

A view of the bomb blast site at Legian area on 16 October 2002 in Denpasar, Bali, Indonesia. The blast occurred in the popular tourist area of Kuta on 12 October, leaving 180 people dead and 132 injured. The attacks, known as Southeast Asia's 9/11, underscored the threat posed by transnational terrorism to the region. It led to counter-terrorism cooperation among the ASEAN countries, and between individual ASEAN countries and Western nations such as the United States and Australia.

Source: Photo by Edy Purnomo/Getty Images.

10. Haze: Singapore Out

Tourists take photos of the haze-shrouded Singapore skyline (compare with Photo 17, Section B) on 21 October 2010 as smoke from forest fires in nearby Sumatra caused serious pollution in Singapore and Malaysia. Singapore's National Environment Agency said the air quality in the city-state reached "unhealthy" levels, advising people with heart or respiratory ailments to reduce physical exertion and outdoor activities until the pollution levels eased. The recurring haze problem led to unprecedented criticism of Indonesia from Singapore and Malaysia, thereby denting ASEAN's non-interference doctrine.

Source: Photo by Aziz Hussin/AFP/Getty Images.

11. Severe Acute Respiratory Syndrome (SARS)

A traveller wears a mask to protect against the Severe Acute Respiratory Syndrome (SARS) virus as she checks her flight departure time at Changi International Airport on 30 April 2003 in Singapore. The SARS crisis prompted a united and ultimately successful response from Southeast Asian countries in cooperation with China and Western nations.

Source: Photo by Paula Bronstein/Getty Images.

12. Banda Aceh, Sumatra before the Indian Ocean tsunami, 26 December 2004

Source: IKONOS Satellite Image © CRISP 2003–2004.

13. Banda Aceh, Sumatra after the tsunami
The tsunami prompted an outpouring of international aid and alerted Southeast Asia to the need for cooperation in disaster prevention management.

Source: IKONOS Satellite Image © CRISP 2003–2004.

14. Making Mischief in the South China Sea?
This photo dated 20 March 1999 shows the newly built four-level Chinese fort at the Mischief Reef, an area claimed by the Philippines located in the disputed Spratly islands in the South China Sea. China, Brunei, Malaysia, the Philippines, Taiwan and Vietnam have claims in the Spratlys. China became more assertive in pursuing its claim a decade later, ending its "charm offensive" and stoking fear and mistrust among its Southeast Asian neighbours.

Source: Photo by Romeo Gacad/AFP/Getty Images.

15. Two Faces of the Asian Values Debate

Deputy Prime Minister Anwar Ibrahim (L) greets Prime Minister Mahathir Mohamad (R) after the opening of the United Malays National Organisation (UMNO) general assembly in Kuala Lumpur, 5 September 1997. At the centre is Abdul Hamid Othman, Minister in the Prime Minister's department. The two leaders, which were to fall out dramatically in September 1998, when Anwar was arrested on charges of corruption and sodomy, also symbolized the divergent political views within Southeast Asia. Mahathir championed "Asian values" and cultural relativism in human rights, which many saw as a justification of his authoritarianism, while Anwar called for more liberal values in Asia and was among the first leaders to call for a more interventionist approach by ASEAN in promoting human rights and democracy in Southeast Asia.

Source: Photo by Francis Silvan/AFP/Getty Images.

16. The Strongmen of Myanmar

Military rulers Than Shwe (L), Maung Aye (C) and Khin Nyunt (R) stand with State Law and Order Restoration Council (SLORC) members in this photo taken in Yangon, Myanmar on 21 February 1997. For over two decades, Myanmar provided the key test of human rights and democracy in Southeast Asia. ASEAN initially favoured "constructive engagement" and opposed sanctions against the regime, but gradually changed its stance in the 2000s to more diplomatic pressure and criticism after realizing that the old policy harmed its international standing.

Source: Photo by Emmanuel Dunand/AFP/Getty Images.

17. Hope for East Timor

Large crowds gather at Dili, East Timor on 25 August 1999 during the last day of campaigning for a referendum to decide the future of East Timor. The majority (78.5 per cent) of East Timorese chose independence, rather than autonomy within the Indonesian Republic. Brutal violence and massacres, carried out by pro-integration militias backed by the Indonesian armed forces, broke out soon after the voting, leading to intervention by an Australian-led force. Indonesia's Southeast Asian neighbours initially did not participate in the operation due to a lack of capacity to intervene and out of deference to the principle of sovereignty and non-interference.

Source: Photo by Paula Bronstein/Getty Images.

18. Democracy in Indonesia

Indonesian Muslim women queue to vote on 5 April 2004 in Jakarta, Indonesia in the country's second parliamentary elections since the fall of the long-serving Soeharto in 1998. The government and civil society of the newly democratic Indonesia supported the cause of human rights and democracy in the region, including in Myanmar.

Source: Photo by Dimas Ardian/Getty Images.

19. Support Democracy in Myanmar

An Indonesian activist holds a painting of pro-democracy Aung San Suu Kyi during a protest in Jakarta on 28 July 2003. Scores of activists showed their support for Suu Kyi as Myanmar Foreign Minister Win Aung met Indonesian President Megawati Sukarnoputri. Indonesian democratization saw support for Myanmar's democratization from civil society groups, even as the governments of ASEAN countries were reluctant to pressure the regime.

Source: Photo by Inoong/AFP/Getty Images.

20. A Sense of Cultural Identity

Thai dancers perform a traditional dance during the opening ceremony of the 15th ASEAN Summit at the elite beach resort of Hua Hin, Thailand on 23 October 2009. Developing a regional identity through cultural exchanges and "peoples' engagement" is a key purpose of ASEAN's Socio-Cultural Community, which complements the ASEAN Economic Community and ASEAN Political-Security Community.

Source: Photo by Christophe Archambault/AFP/Getty Images.

9

Whither Southeast Asia?

"Asean's Quest for an Identity Gains Urgency" — thus read the headline of a story in the *Straits Times* of Singapore on 5 December 2005.[1] The story reported the results of a survey conducted among a thousand English-speaking urban residents in Indonesia, Malaysia, Singapore, the Philippines, Thailand and Vietnam on, among other things, whether "people in ASEAN identified with one another". Although the survey found doubts and scepticism about the pace of regional integration in ASEAN, it also revealed that six out of ten polled agreed that "people in ASEAN identified with one another". Perhaps what is really important about this survey is not the numbers that did not agree with the question, but the numbers that did.

The year 2005 was the first in which the members of ASEAN celebrated "ASEAN Day" on 8 August. Three years later, in 2008, a different survey, this time of 2,170 students in all ten ASEAN countries (including both arts and social sciences as well as science and technology students), conducted by the Institute of Southeast Asian Studies, found that "over 75 per cent agreed that they felt themselves to be citizens of ASEAN. Nearly 90 per cent felt that membership in ASEAN was beneficial to their nation and nearly 70 per cent felt that it was beneficial to them personally."[2]

These surveys came at a time of increasing reference to the regional idea and identity in ASEAN official statements and the speeches of leaders of Southeast Asian countries. For example, ASEAN's 2020 vision, issued in 1997, aims at developing "an ASEAN community conscious of its ties of history, aware of its cultural heritage and bound by a common regional identity".[3] More eloquently, Singapore's then Foreign Minister George Yeo argued in 2005 that:

> there is a coherence in Southeast Asia which we know exists and grows stronger by the day. ... Because Southeast Asia was never united as one political entity, there is tolerance for diversity, a willingness to syncretize, a cosmopolitan spirit which welcomes foreigners in our midst and the mixing of blood, especially among members of the elite.[4]

Others have spoken of the need for a sense of regional identity as a prerequisite for more effective regional cooperation. Thus, "an Asean identity [elsewhere in the article, "a rising awareness of being 'citizens of Asean'"] would provide a sense of belonging among member states and hopefully encourage them to coordinate their policies in regard to external powers".[5] Against this backdrop, we return to an argument, originally presented by this author in a separate essay, but which underpins the central thesis of this book:

> Southeast Asia is a region built on shared human and physical characteristics and endeavours, external geopolitical and economic currents, and collective social imagination. But its claim to be a region should be seen as being based as much on the construction of a regional identity as on the sum total of shared physical attributes and functional interactions among its units. The development of a regional identity may not necessarily conform to the "facts" of geography, history, culture, or politics. The notion of Southeast Asia as a homogenous cultural or geographic entity can indeed be overstated. But its social and political identity, derived from the conscious promotion of the regional concept by its states, societies, and peoples, is what makes it a distinct idea in the latter part of the 20th century.[6]

The construction of Southeast Asia's regional identity rests on the close interaction between the ideas of region and regionalism. The two are closely linked and mutually reinforcing. The notion of Southeast Asia as a region — based on such traditional attributes of "regionness" as proximity, shared history, similarities in culture and heritage, as well as more dynamic variables such as commercial, strategic and political interactions before and after the colonial period — has been a central basis of regionalism in Southeast Asia. At the same time, regional cooperation, including the development of norms and institutions, has been crucial to the development of Southeast Asia's regional identity.

Of course, region and regionalism are both relatively new ideas, much more recent than the concepts of nationalism and the nation-state. But as historians of Southeast Asia tell us, before regionalism in its modern, institutional sense had made its mark on the area east of India and south of China, "regionwide" patterns of interstate relations and a degree of interaction and interdependence did exist among the political units inhabiting that area. Any serious study of Southeast Asia's international relations and its claim to be a region must, therefore, begin with a historical framework that includes the interstate system during the pre-colonial period. Drawing upon the work of a variety of scholars, I have looked at the role of traditional cultural-political frameworks and commercial interactions in creating the basis for the idea of Southeast Asia. These frameworks also included the overlapping (in both time and space) system of *mandalas* (a term of reference for loosely territorialized and hierarchical polities in classical Southeast Asia based on the Indic model) such as Funan, Champa, Srivijaya, Pagan, Angkor, Ayutthaya, Ava, Majapahit and Malacca (which started as a Hindu polity and which, even after its rulers embraced Islam, remained true to the idea of an Indic *mandala*). Moreover, Southeast Asia was the hub of a regional commercial system. These interactions were not casual or intermittent, but long-term and continuous, until they were decisively disrupted by colonial intrusion. They featured both conflict and cooperation. Moreover, the cultural (including artistic), commercial and political concepts and institutions underpinning these interactions were not separable, but closely intertwined.

It must not be forgotten that the *mandala* system, or the "galactic polity", is a historical reconstruction; it is not likely that ancient Southeast Asians saw their polities in this way, or considered themselves to be part of a region. Even so, the study of the pre-colonial state system should occupy an important place in Southeast Asia's claim to be a region, because its constituent units shared important characteristics as well as a degree of interaction and interdependence that served to reduce, if not eliminate, the diversity of Southeast Asia.

Moreover, the pre-colonial regional pattern does provide a framework for studying the political impact of colonialism in fragmenting the region. It also reinforces the claim of latter-day nationalists and regionalists, that Southeast Asia's claim to be a region was not simply a figment of Western imagination or an accidental by-product of Western geopolitics, as exemplified by the Southeast Asia Command (SEAC). The relationship between nationalism and regionalism, one of the key determinants of the modern Southeast Asian identity, was not always easy or complementary. Initially, nationalism undermined the prospects for regionalism. This was certainly the case with Indonesia's Sukarno, whose brand of nationalism threatened his Southeast Asian neighbours and left little scope for the idea of Southeast Asian (as opposed to Afro-Asian) regionalism to flourish. Nationalism and nation-building also undercut regionalism in another way. Preoccupied with domestic nation-building issues, and facing historical, political and economic conditions that varied widely from country to country, Southeast Asia's early post-colonial leaders were not only prevented from paying sufficient attention to regionalism, but these conditions also produced conflicting responses. While some nationalists saw regionalism as helpful for their cause, it was not necessarily a regionalism framed within a Southeast Asian context. In fact, in some cases, wider regionalist concepts conflicted with incipient ideas about Southeast Asian regionalism. And both were overwhelmed by the great-power geopolitics of the early Cold War period.

Indeed, during the first two decades of the post-World War II period, Southeast Asia's international relations were determined by a struggle between continued Western dominance (including competitive great-power interactions) on the one hand and nationalism on the other. Regionalism played a marginal role in this contestation. Southeast Asia as a region was defined not just by geopolitical currents in which external powers were the central actors, but also by academic writings and policy debates in which Westerners played a dominant role. The situation during the next twenty years was dramatically different, however. During this period, Southeast Asian regionalism came into its own. After a shaky start, Southeast Asian regionalists who espoused the cause of "moderate nationalism" (to borrow Wang Gungwu's term as discussed in Chapter 4) succeeded in creating and sustaining a regionalist framework, which proved effective in containing intraregional conflicts and projecting a collective regional identity. These leaders recognized a sufficient congruence between the nationalist and regionalist projects, despite significant cultural, linguistic, political and economic differences among the regionalist-minded nations themselves.

It was during the 1960s that the moderate nationalist leaders of Southeast Asia saw regionalism as a way of preserving their state security and regime survival, not from neo-colonial pressures, but from the twin dangers of Cold War superpower rivalry and domestic insurrections. Thus, the Cold War, while helping to polarize Southeast Asia into two ideologically hostile segments, might have inadvertently contributed to the regionalist cause by promoting solidarity among like-minded regimes, despite their recognition that such a regionalism would be less than fully Southeast Asian in scope and would be greeted by the excluded actors (the Indochinese countries) with open hostility.

At its origin, regionalism in Southeast Asia was limited in scope and objective. It comprised the anti-communist states of the region and was ostensibly geared to the fulfilment of vague economic and political objectives. It was geared as much to the maintenance of peaceful relations among the participants themselves as to the creation of a common front against potential adversaries both within and outside the region. But even this limited framework of regionalism made an important contribution to the idea of the region.

Southeast Asian regionalists contributed to the idea of region in two distinct ways. The first was by maintaining regional unity and preventing any serious escalation of intramural conflicts. This was done, among other things, through an effort to adhere to certain norms of interstate behaviour as well as through the development of bilateral and multilateral mechanisms for consultation and consensus-building. Moreover, even in conflicts that involved non-regionalists such as the Indochinese states led by Vietnam, the regionalists pursued a moderate path and left the door open to negotiations and the eventual incorporation of the latter states into their regionalist vision and framework.

A second way in which regionalism might have contributed to the regional idea of Southeast Asia was in the pursuit of what could be called regional autonomy and self-reliance. The regionalists developed a *modus vivendi* with larger, more powerful external players through collective bargaining without seeking their complete exclusion from regional affairs. Through proposals for regional self-reliance and autonomy, as manifested in the idea of neutralization and the Zone of Peace, Freedom and Neutrality (ZOPFAN), Southeast Asian regionalists articulated a common stance *vis-à-vis* the outside world that reinforced Southeast Asia's claim to be a region. What is striking is that, during these years, Southeast Asia's regional identity was indigenously constructed, rather than exogenously determined.

ASEAN's region-building project should not, however, be seen simply as an example of newly liberated Third World states attempting to exert control over affairs within their own region by means of a communal organization. The project served a purpose that independent nationalisms were not able to, that is, the reclamation of a regional identity whose historical foundations had been severely disrupted by colonialism.

To be sure, regionalism has had a mixed impact on the regional identity of Southeast Asia. On the one hand, ASEAN reflected the polarization of Southeast Asia. Discourses on regionalism and competing visions of regionalism before and after the formation of ASEAN highlighted the problematic nature of Southeast Asia as a region. But despite its mixed impact, regionalism played a central role in making Southeast Asia an even more distinct region in external perceptions. In 1966, a year before ASEAN's birth, Kenneth T. Young, a former U.S. ambassador to Thailand, observed about Southeast Asia: "This is a so-called region without any feeling for community, without much sense of shared values and with few common institutions."[7] Yet D.G.E. Hall, a doyen of Southeast Asian studies, would write in 1973 that "to all its component parts, Southeast Asia has become a meaningful term ... the integrity of Southeast Asian history is every bit as real as that of European ..."[8] And in 1984, Russell Fifield would reach the conclusion that "the regional concept of Southeast Asia, as perceived by decision makers in and outside the area, is a living reality".[9]

What makes the region of Southeast Asia possible? Notwithstanding the divergent views it has generated, there seems to be a surprising degree of agreement among Southeast Asian specialists on the central role of regionalism, especially as embodied by ASEAN.[10] In 1984, Donald Emmerson would call ASEAN an "international regime", reflecting perhaps the dominant theoretical framework of the day — neoliberal institutionalism. In 1985, Donald Weatherbee would note that "there is now in the Southeast Asian area an ASEAN spirit, a sense of belonging and real sense of achievement. One of the major components of this ASEAN spirit is perhaps mythical, but very symbolic — that is the effort to replicate in ASEAN what they consider to be the traditional patterns of Asian behavior."[11] Leonard Andaya would be even more forceful, relating the rediscovery of a regional identity, specifically to the major project of regionalism in Southeast Asia:

> In participating in ASEAN activities and using the term "Asean", these nation-states are reaffirming the existence of Southeast Asia. Southeast Asia is being reborn by means of a solid core consisting of the ASEAN nations. Through participation in ASEAN, the ASEAN Business Forum, cooperative academic ventures among ASEAN universities ... the peoples of Southeast Asia have come to accept as a matter of course their identification as "Southeast Asians".[12]

In an essay published in 1995, Michael Leifer would "claim quite categorically that ASEAN has become an institutionalized vehicle for intra-mural conflict avoidance and management ... ASEAN has been able to prevent disputes from escalating and getting out of hand through containing and managing contentious issues."[13] This was also the time when the idea of an ASEAN as a security community came to be aired.[14] All these amounted to a powerful endorsement of the role of ASEAN and the impact of regionalism in the making of Southeast Asia as a region. It also suggests that the development of the regional concept should be seen as a social process of identity-building. While the pre-colonial interstate system had a regional scope, albeit a weak and impermanent one, it was the regionalism of the 1970s and 1980s that gave Southeast Asia a regional identity. Similarly, while the recognition of Southeast Asia as a political region during the Cold War was the result of global geopolitical currents and outside perceptions and influences, genuine and lasting recognition came only in the course of the efforts by Southeast Asian regionalists to manage regional conflicts (such as the Cambodian conflict) and seek out collective positions *vis-à-vis* outside powers. While the very idea of the nation-state as an "imagined community" came into prominence in Southeast Asia (as in other areas under colonial rule) through the adaptation of a somewhat alien concept by the local elite, region-building in Southeast Asia was based primarily, but not exclusively, on indigenous frameworks of socialization. While the main forces shaping the recognition of Southeast Asia during the early post-World War II period were the "Orientalist" scholarship on the region and great-power geopolitics, in the 1970s and 1980s, an inward-looking and exclusionary concept of regionalism developed by ASEAN proved crucial to developing a sense of regional destiny and identity.

Will this unravel? The international relations of Southeast Asia have been transformed as the result of developments in the global arena. While several of these changes have been positive, new sources of conflict and tension have emerged. Unless carefully managed, these could seriously undermine prospects for regional unity and the very idea of Southeast Asia as a region. In the post-Cold War era, the international relations of Southeast Asia have been increasingly linked to developments in the wider Asia-Pacific region, especially relations among the major powers such as the United States, China, Japan, Russia and India. While a new regional order might emerge, based on the foundations laid by ASEAN, such an order would have clear limitations in ensuring a balance of power that would preserve stability. Issues related to the role of the major powers, such as the U.S. military presence in the region, the power projection potential of China, India and Japan, will have a major bearing on the security milieu of Southeast Asian states in the twenty-first century. This could challenge the concept of Southeast Asia as a distinct security region.

On the economic front, the regional concept of Southeast Asia is being challenged by the forces of globalization. For some, Southeast Asia has already been too closely integrated into Northeast Asia and the Western countries to be considered a distinct economic region. Efforts to develop a pan-Asia-Pacific economic institution, later joined by efforts to develop an East Asian grouping (ASEAN plus China, Japan and South Korea), recognize this reality. But the contagion effect of the Asian economic crisis during the 1997–99 period, encompassing South Korea, Russia, Thailand, Brazil and Indonesia, underscored this point in a much more powerful way.

Moreover, the view of ASEAN as an organization "of and for the region" must be seen against the backdrop of lingering tensions and animosities that have surfaced with alarming regularity among its original core members — Indonesia, Malaysia, the Philippines, Singapore and Thailand. The Asian economic crisis provided some of the most dramatic illustrations of this. The fact that some of these quarrels are about questions of ethnicity (as between Singapore and Malaysia) while others are about colonial territorial allocations is particularly troubling to those who have come to expect that a nascent regional identity might replace particular national ones. While regionalism has given an additional measure of clout to Southeast Asian countries in dealing with the outside world, the limits of such clout must not be overlooked. In dealing with the larger powers in security, economic or political matters (such as human rights), Southeast Asian countries have found themselves suffering as much from a lack of resources as of resolve. The record of ASEAN in dealing with the 1997 economic crisis or the rise of Chinese power attests to this.

The confidence that marked the entry of Southeast Asian regionalists into the post-Cold War period led them not only to embark on a project of regionalist expansion ("One Southeast Asia"), but also to aspire to a "leadership" role in wider Asia-Pacific regional institutions. This is a striking feature of modern Southeast Asian history. Not long ago, these states were considered "objects" rather than leaders of international relations in the Asia-Pacific, not to mention the larger international system. But the euphoria of the early 1990s proved to have been somewhat unwarranted. Since the 1997 Asian financial crisis, there has been a more realistic assessment of the limits and possibilities of collective Southeast Asian regional clout. The "One Southeast Asia" project had run into considerable trouble, especially with the issue of the accession by Myanmar and Cambodia into ASEAN. Expansion, while diluting the decision-making homogeneity of regionalism, also presented the regionalist project with new economic and security burdens that had not been fully anticipated.

These difficulties notwithstanding, there is little question that regionalism has been the key anchor of the idea of Southeast Asia as a region. Weatherbee argues that "in order to study Southeast Asia as a region, it will be necessary to identify unifying transnational or institutional patterns."[15] If so, then since 1967, ASEAN has provided such unifying patterns. What began as a straightforward case of intergovernmental cooperation has now acquired a complexity that would be difficult to analyse from a nation-state perspective.

Southeast Asian regionalism has not only encouraged the study of Southeast Asia as a region holistically, it has also broadened and enriched Southeast Asian studies as a field. In Chapter 3, I briefly discussed the contribution of Southeast Asian studies to regional identity. It now appears that the study of regionalism, regional identity and a regional perspective on Southeast Asian international relations has in turn contributed to the growth of Southeast Asian studies. It seems useful to reflect on this theme for a moment.

As in the past, the state of Southeast Asian studies continues to evoke strong language and lively debate. For some, Southeast Asian studies deserves the same scepticism as the claim of Southeast Asia be a region. Thus, Charles Keyes contends that "Southeast Asia does not exist as a place" and "Southeast Asian studies does not exist as a distinctive field of study."[16] Others have been less negative: "Whether Southeast Asia will acquire greater coherence in the future, or become increasingly irrelevant, is a question that cannot be answered."[17] Benedict Anderson maintained his earlier critique of Southeast Asian studies in the United States by arguing in 1992 that "no very convincing intellectual case has been made for the field, which continues to rest on visibly shaky foundations".[18] Southeast Asian studies has also been caught up in the general sense of uncertainty and scepticism about area studies in an era of globalization.[19] Yet, for Donald Emmerson, "at least for the time being, enough people speak, teach, learn and write as though 'Southeast Asia' did exist for us to give them the benefit of the doubt."[20] In his view, trends in Southeast Asian studies neither vindicate Anderson's pessimism about Southeast Asian studies in America nor prove his optimism about "indigenization".[21]

At the same time, however, Reid and Diokono suggest that one cannot ignore significant progress on indigenization, especially with the emergence of programmes and centres on the region within the region, in Singapore, Thailand and nearby places like Australia, which is close enough by to sustain a significant two-way traffic of Australian and Southeast Asian students of the region.[22] Sketching an indigenous history of Southeast Asian studies, they contend: "The study of Southeast Asia begins and ends in the region that gave rise to it."[23] To be sure, studies that take Southeast Asia as a region continue to lag. Emmerson argues that in order to be considered as a "scholarly enterprise", "the first and highest threshold" should be that the members of a scholarly community "in their own *research* must occupy themselves with all of it. Among Southeast Asianists, that is not the case."[24] But a cultural historian of the region argues that "thanks to a fruitful half century, we now know enough about Southeast Asia's pieces to return to questions of the whole ... Either that, or the field dies."[25]

Emmerson also points out that Southeast Asian studies has been strengthened by the "rising visibility of human rights" in Indonesia and elsewhere, as well as the issue of democratization.[26] One might add that not just human rights but a whole range of transnational issues — including the Asian financial crisis of 1997, pandemics (for example, the SARS crisis of 2003), terrorism (the Bali and Jakarta bombings), migration, natural disasters (the tsunami of 2004 and Cyclone Nargis of 2008) and environmental degradation (haze from Indonesia) — have highlighted Southeast Asia's place and role in the world in the era of globalization, because these challenges happened in the region and attracted global attention. Although the publicity surrounding these events was mostly unflattering, they nonetheless attracted the attention of both policy-makers and scholars on regional issues, and this helped to reinforce the perception of Southeast Asia as a region. ASEAN also played its part. Back in 1984, Leonard Unger had recognized not only that ASEAN was one of "the most interesting and promising institutions" that "looms large in the region" but also that it was clearly among the "many questions concerning the *whole of Southeast Asia* which need to be more thoroughly investigated"[27] (emphasis added). Moreover, a significant rise in networking among Southeast Asian NGOs, in connection with regionalism-related issues such as the ASEAN Charter and the ASEAN human rights mechanism, also contribute to the growth of a regional perspective.

In passing judgement on the subject, Emmerson concludes unequivocally that Southeast Asian studies "do exist" because:

> the following conditions are met. (1) There are specialists who study, on a more than casual basis, at least some part(s) or aspect(s) of the area that 'Southeast Asian studies' claims to span. (2) There are not so few of these specialists – teachers, students, researchers, writers — as to belie the plural noun 'studies.' (3) There studies are comprehensive in the additive sense that taken together, they cover enough of the region and its phenomena — history, politics, culture, language, and so on — to warrant the adjective 'Southeast Asian.' And (4) most of them are willing to identify themselves as "specialists" of that area, to allow deans and donors to do so, and to speak, write, meet, and raise money as if there were something called Southeast Asia out there after all.[28]

Although Emmerson does not frame his arguments in terms of international relations theory, social constructivist perspectives on regions would readily recognize these arguments as their own. The last point is especially important: the identity of Southeast Asia as a region is inextricably linked to the self-identification of those who study it. In his account, the region of Southeast Asia comes through as more of an *imagined community* than in the perspective of the man who famously coined the term to describe nation-states.

In 1995, Ruth McVey, mindful of the origins of the field in the World War II era South East Asia Command, feared that the "so shallow genealogy of the field only emphasized the field's insecurity, threatening it with absorption into more established academic empires".[29] But the field had survived and in some ways strengthened, and contributed in a major way to the popularization of the regional concept of Southeast Asia. McVey had noted: "The study of Southeast Asia was conceived in a powerful but narrow ideological framework that was of foreign origin but has been strongly internalized by the region's postcolonial ruling elites ... Nonetheless, global and regional forces, and the corrosive power of time, are looking to loosen its grip."[30] To me, among those forces were not only the processes of "diversification" or "indigenization" that Donald Emmerson and Benedict Anderson would respectively speak of in 1984, but also the stirrings of Southeast Asian regionalism and region-building that this book has highlighted. To be sure, the study of Southeast Asian regionalism is not always interesting and sophisticated, and there is a great deal of policy-oriented or polemical writings that would surely fail Anderson's standard for scholarly contribution.[31] But the study of regionalization, regionalism, regional identity and regional patterns of international relations — pioneered by scholars like Michael Leifer, Don Emmerson and others, and continued by a subsequent generation, first at the level of the state and increasingly with attention to the level of culture and civil society, and within the context of disciplinary approaches (comparative regionalism and international relations) — has become increasingly diverse and sophisticated. It enriches the field of Southeast Asian studies and validates Southeast Asia's claim to be a region.[32]

At the dawn of a new millennium, Southeast Asia as a region (and Southeast Asian studies as a field of study) has witnessed the emergence of new challenges to its regional coherence, especially the simultaneous rise of China and India in the immediate neighbourhood, transnational dangers that cut across not just national, but also regional boundaries, and new regionalist ideas and frameworks (such as the East Asia Community concept). Against this backdrop, it may be too optimistic to argue that the regional concept of Southeast Asia will become a permanent reality or endure indefinitely into the future. Some of the economic and strategic forces affecting Southeast Asia, such as globalization and great-power relations, are beyond the control of Southeast Asian countries. But as a new book, *Locating Southeast Asia*, argues: "The likelihood that the future will bring a common Southeast Asian currency, or that the people of the region will one day call themselves 'ASEANs', seems remote, but at the start of the twentieth century it would have seemed equally unlikely that 100 years later France and Spain would have a common currency and be part of a single market, or the Germans and Italians would be using 'European' as an identity rather than a geographic expression."[33] For much of the post-World War II period, the idea of Southeast Asia has been invented, kept alive and promoted by an unlikely combination of Western powers, historians of the region and, especially, a section of the region's elite, which is now selling regional identity to the peoples of the region. Southeast Asia at its origin as a regional concept has been an imagined community. It may well continue to be so into the future.

NOTES

[1]   *Straits Times*, 5 December 2005.

[2]   Eric C. Thompson and Chulanee Thianthai, *Attitudes and Awareness Towards ASEAN: Findings of a Ten-Nation Survey* (Singapore: Institute of Southeast Asian Studies, ASEAN Studies Centre, 2008).

[3]   ASEAN, "ASEAN Vision 2020", <http://www.aseansec.org/1814.htm> (accessed 11 June 2006).

[4]   George Yeo, speech to the Global Leadership Forum, Kuala Lumpur, 6 September 2005, <http://www.mfa.gov.sg/internet/> (accessed 24 June 2006).

[5]   Pavin Chachavalpongpun, "In Search of an Asean Identity", *The Nation*, 4 May 2006, <http://www.nationmultimedia.com/2006/05/04/opinion/opinion_30003161.php> (accessed 21 June 2006).

[6]   Amitav Acharya, "Imagined Proximities: The Making and Unmaking of Southeast Asia as a Region", *Southeast Asian Journal of Social Science* 27, no. 1 (1999), p. 73.

[7]   Kenneth T. Young, *The Southeast Asia Crisis* (New York: The Association of the Bar of the City of New York, 1966), p. 5.

[8]   D.G.E. Hall, "The Integrity of Southeast Asian History", *Journal of Southeast Asian History* 4, no. 2 (1973), p. 168.

[9]   Russell Fifield, "'Southeast Asia' and 'ASEAN' as Regional Concepts", in *Southeast Asian Studies: Options for the Future*, edited by Ronald A. Morse (Lanham, MD: University Press of America, 1984), p. 128.

[10] Donald K. Emmerson, "ASEAN as an International Regime", *Journal of International Affairs* 41, no. 4 (1987): 1–16.

[11] Donald Weatherbee, "An Overview of Cultural and Historical Roots of Contemporary Southeast Asia", Proceedings of a Study Group Series and Symposium presented in cooperation with the Asia Society in Atlanta, 1985, p. 9.

[12] Leonard Y. Andaya, "Ethnonation, Nation-State and Regionalism in Southeast Asia", in Proceedings of the International Symposium, "Southeast Asia: Global Area Studies for the 21st Century", organized by Project Team: An Integrated

Approach to Global Area Studies (funded by Monbusho Grant-in-Aid for Scientific Research on Priority Areas) and Center for Southeast Asian Studies, Kyoto University, Kyoto International Community House, 18–22 October 1996, p. 135.

[13] Michael Leifer, "ASEAN as a Model of a Security Community", in *ASEAN in a Changed Regional and International Political Economy*, edited by Hadi Soesastro (Jakarta: Centre of Strategic and International Studies, 1995), p. 132.

[14] Among those who used the term "security community" to describe ASEAN were Richard Mansbach, Noordin Sopiee, Sheldon Simon, Donald Weatherbee, David Martin Jones and this writer. For a discussion of these different formulations of ASEAN as a security community, see Amitav Acharya, *Constructing a Security Community in Southeast Asia: ASEAN and the Problem of Regional Order* (London: Routledge, 2001), pp. 127 and 128; of the writers mentioned, David M. Jones, who in 1997 argued that ASEAN "might at best be considered a security community", would subsequently change his views. David Martin Jones, *Political Development in Pacific Asi* (Cambridge: Polity Press, 1997), p. 185.

[15] Donald K. Weatherbee, "Introduction: The What and Why of Southeast Asia", in *International Relations in Southeast Asia: The Struggle for Autonomy*, edited by Donald K. Weatherbee et al. (Lanham, MD: Rowman and Littlefield, 2005), p. 15.

[16] Charles F. Keys, "A Conference at Wingspread and Rethinking Southeast Asian Studies", in *Southeast Asian Studies in the Balance: Reflections from America*, edited by Charles Hirschman, Charles F. Keyes, and Karl Hutterer (Ann Arbor, MI: Association for Asian Studies, 1992), p. 9; cited in Donald K. Emmerson, "Situating Southeast Asian Studies: Realm, Guild, and Home", in *Southeast Asian Studies: Pacific Perspectives*, edited by Anthony Reid (Tempe: Arizona State University, Program for Southeast Asian Studies, 2003), pp. 47–48.

[17] Paul Kratoska, Remeo Raben, and Henk Schulte Nordholt, "Locating Southeast Asia", in *Locating Southeast Asia: Geographies of Knowledge and Politics of Space*, edited by Paul Kratoska, Remeo Raben, and Henk Schulte Nordholt (Singapore: Singapore University Press/Athens: Ohio University Press, 2005), p. 14.

[18] Cited in Anthony Reid, "Southeast Asian Studies: Decline or Rebirth?" in Reid, *Southeast Asian Studies: Pacific Perspectives*, p. 4.

[19] Ruth T. McVey, "Globalization, Marginalization and the Study of Southeast Asia", in *Southeast Asian Studies: Reorientations*, edited by C.J. Reynolds and R. McVey (Ithaca, NY: Cornell University, 1998), pp. 37–64.

[20] Emmerson, "Situating Southeast Asian Studies", p. 48.

[21] Ibid., pp. 32–33.

22 Anthony Reid and Maria Serena Diokno, "Completing the Circle: Southeast Asian Studies in Southeast Asia", in Reid, *Southeast Asian Studies: Pacific Perspectives*, pp. 93–107.

23 Ibid., p. 93.

24 Emmerson, "Situating Southeast Asian Studies", p. 49.

25 Richard A. O'Connor, "Critiquing the Critique of Southeast Asia: Beyond Texts and States to Culture History", in Reid, *Southeast Asian Studies: Pacific Perspectives*, p. 80.

26 Emmerson, "Situating Southeast Asian Studies", pp. 42–47.

27 Leonard Unger, "A Practitioner's Perspective on Southeast Asian Studies", in Morse, *Southeast Asian Studies: Options for the Future*, p. 22.

28 Ibid., p. 49.

29 Ruth McVey, "Change and Continuity in Southeast Asian Studies", *Journal of Southeast Asian Studies* 26, no. 1 (1995), p. 1.

30 Ibid., p. 8.

31 To him, the criteria for "distinguished" scholarship in Southeast Asian studies are two: first "one would recommend such a book to someone not particularly involved with the country concerned", and second "one would read it a second time, all the way through, oneself". Benedict Anderson, "Politics and their Study in Southeast Asia", in Morse, *Southeast Asian Studies: Options for the Future*, p. 51.

32 Amitav Acharya and Richard Stubbs, "Theorising Southeast Asian Relations: An Introduction", in *Theorising Southeast Asian Relations: Emerging Debates*, edited by Amitav Acharya and Richard Stubbs (London: Routledge, 2009): 1–9.

33 Kratoska, Raben and Nordholt, "Locating Southeast Asia", p. 15.

Bibliography

Acharya, Amitav. "An Arms Race in Post-Cold War Southeast Asia? Prospects for Control". Pacific Strategic Paper no. 8. Singapore: Institute of Southeast Asian Studies, 1994.

————. "The Asia-Pacific Region: Cockpit for Superpower Rivalry". *The World Today* 43, nos. 8–9 (1987): 155–59.

————. "Democratisation and the Prospects for Participatory Regionalism in Southeast Asia". *Third World Quarterly* 24, no. 2 (2003): 375–90.

————. "Do Norms and Identity Matter? Community and Power in Southeast Asia's Regional Order". *Pacific Review* 18, no. 1 (2005): 95–118.

————. "How Ideas Spread: Whose Norms Matter? Norm Localization and Institutional Change in Asian Regionalism". *International Organization* 58, no. 2 (2004): 239–75.

————. "Human Rights and Regional Order: ASEAN and Human Rights Management in Post-Cold War Southeast Asia". In *Human Rights and International Relations in the Asia-Pacific*, edited by James T.H. Tang. London: Pinter, 1995.

————. "Human Rights in Southeast Asia: Dilemmas of Foreign Policy". Eastern Asia Policy Paper no. 11. Toronto: University of Toronto – York University Joint Centre for Asia Pacific Studies, 1995.

————. "Ideas, Identity, and Institution-Building: From the 'ASEAN Way' to the 'Asia-Pacific Way'?" *The Pacific Review* 10, no. 3 (1997): 319–46.

————. "Identity without Exceptionalism: Challenges for Asian Political and International Studies". Keynote address to the inaugural workshop of the Asian Political and International Studies Association (APISA), Kuala Lumpur, Malaysia, 1–2 November 2001.

————. "Imagined Proximities: The Making and Unmaking of Southeast Asia as a Region". *Southeast Asian Journal of Social Science* 27, no. 1 (1999): 55–76.

————. "A New Regional Order in Southeast Asia: ASEAN in the Post-Cold War Era". Adelphi Paper no. 279. London: International Institute for Strategic Studies, 1993.

————. *The Quest for Identity: International Relations of Southeast Asia*. Oxford: Oxford University Press, 2000.

————. "Regional Military-Security Cooperation in the Third World: A Conceptual Analysis of the Association of Southeast Asian Nations". *Journal of Peace Research* 29, no. 1 (1991): 7–21.

————. "State-Society Relations: Asian and World Order after September 11". In *Worlds in Collision: Terror and the Future of Global Order*, edited by Ken Booth and Tim Dunne. London: Palgrave, 2002.

————. "Transnational Production and Security: Southeast Asia's Growth Triangles". *Contemporary Southeast Asia* 17, no. 2 (1995): 173–85.

————. "The United States versus the U.S.S.R. in the Pacific: Trends in the Military Balance". *Contemporary Southeast Asia* 9, no. 4 (1988): 282–99.

Acharya, Amitav and Ananda Rajah. "Introduction: Reconceptualising Southeast Asia". *Southeast Asian Journal of Social Science* 27, no. 1 (1999): 1–6.

————, eds. "Reconceptualising Southeast Asia". *Southeast Asian Journal of Social Science* 27, no. 1 (1999): 7–24.

Acharya, Amitav and Arabinda Acharya. "Human Security in the Asia Pacific: Puzzle, Panacea or Peril?" *CANCAPS Bulletin* no. 27, November 2000, pp. 2–3.

Acharya, Amitav and Richard Stubbs. "Theorising Southeast Asian Relations: An Introduction". In *Theorising Southeast Asian Relations: Emerging Debates*, edited by Amitav Acharya and Richard Stubbs. London: Routledge, 2009.

Acharya, Amitav and See Seng Tan. "Betwixt Balance and Community: America, ASEAN, and the Security of Southeast Asia". *International Relations of the Asia-Pacific* 6, no. 1 (2005): 37–59.

Adler, Emanuel. "Imagined (Security) Communities: Cognitive Regions in International Relations". *Millennium: Journal of International Studies* 26, no. 2 (1997): 249–77.

Adler, Emanuel and Beverly Crawford. "Constructing a Mediterranean Region: A Cultural Approach". Paper presented at the conference on "The Convergence of Civilizations? Constructing a Mediterranean Region". Lisbon, Portugal, 6–9 June 2002.

Adler, Emanuel and Michael Barnett, eds. *Security Communities*. Cambridge: Cambridge University Press, 1998.

Alagappa, Muthiah. "Regional Arrangements and International Security in Southeast Asia: Going Beyond ZOPFAN". *Contemporary Southeast Asia* 12, no. 4 (1991): 269–305.

―――. "Bringing Indochina into Asean". *Far Eastern Economic Review*, 29 June 1989, pp. 21–22.

Alatas, Ali. Text of Statement as Co-Chair of the Paris Peace Conference on Cambodia, 23 October 1991.

―――. "ASEAN Plus Three Equals Peace Plus Prosperity". *Trends in Southeast Asia*, no. 2. Singapore: Institute of Southeast Asian Studies, January 2001.

Anand, R.P. and P.V. Quisumbing, eds. *ASEAN: Identity, Development and Culture*. Quezon City: University of the Philippines Law Center/Honolulu: East-West Center, Culture Learning Institute, 1981.

Andaya, Barbara W. and Leonard Y. Andaya. *A History of Malaysia*. London: Macmillan, 1982.

Andaya, Leonard Y. "Ethnonation, Nation-State and Regionalism in Southeast Asia". In Proceedings of the International Symposium, "Southeast Asia: Global Area Studies for the 21st Century", organized by Project Team: An Integrated Approach to Global Area Studies and Center for Southeast Asian Studies, Kyoto University, 18–22 October 1996, pp. 131–49.

Andaya, Leonard Y. and Barbara W. Andaya. "Southeast Asia in the Early Modern Period: Twenty-Five Years on". *Journal of Southeast Asian Studies* 26, no. 1 (1995): 92–98.

Anderson, Benedict. "The Idea of Power in Javanese Culture". In *Culture and Politics in Indonesia*, edited by Claire Holt. Ithaca, NY: Cornell University Press, 1972.

―――. *Imagined Communities: Reflections on the Origin and Spread of Nationalism*. Rev. ed. London: Verso, 1991.

―――. "Politics and their Study in Southeast Asia". In *Southeast Asian Studies: Options for the Future*, edited by Ronald A. Morse. Lanham, MD: University Press of America, 1984.

―――. *The Spectre of Comparisons: Nationalism, Southeast Asia, and the World*. New York: Verso, 1998.

ASEAN. "ASEAN-China Dialogue Relations", August 2009. <http://www.aseansec.org/5874.htm>.

―――. *The ASEAN Declaration*. Bangkok: Association of Southeast Asian Nations, 1967.

―――. "The ASEAN Regional Forum: A Concept Paper". Jakarta: ASEAN Secretariat, 1995.

————. "ASEAN's Response to the Tsunami Disaster—Issues and Concerns: A Special Report". Virtual Information Center. <http://www.vic-info.org/.../ $FILE/ 050509-SR-IssuesAndConcernsOnASEANSpecialReport.doc>.

————. "The ASEAN Socio-Cultural Community (ASCC) Plan of Action". <http://www.aseansec.org/16832.htm> (accessed 26 June 2006).

————. "ASEAN Vision 2020", 15 December 1997. <http://www.aseansec. org/5228.htm> (accessed 26 June 2006).

————. "China-ASEAN Trade Soars 25 percent in First Half of 2005", 30 September 2005. <http://www.aseansec.org/afp/134.htm> (accessed 20 June 2006).

————. "Declaration of ASEAN Concord II (Bali Concord II)", 7 October 2003. <http://www.aseansec.org/15159.htm> (accessed 20 June 2006).

————. "Declaration on the Conduct of Parties in the South China Sea", 4 November 2002. <http://www.aseansec.org/13163.htm> (accessed 20 June 2006).

————. "Joint Communiqué of the Twenty-Sixth ASEAN Ministerial Meeting, Singapore, 23–24 July 1993". Jakarta: ASEAN Secretariat, 1993.

————. "Singapore Declaration of 1992, ASEAN Heads of Government Meeting, 27–28 January 1992". Jakarta: ASEAN Secretariat, 1992.

————. "Summary Record: New Directions for ASEAN Economic Cooperation". Proceedings of the Second ASEAN Roundtable, Kuala Lumpur, Institute of Strategic and International Studies, 20–21 July 1987.

Asian Defence Journal. "A New Era of Cooperation", March–April 1977, pp. 14–20.

————. "Operation Cooperation: The Malaysian-Thai Joint Border Operations", October 1977, pp. 18–21.

Asian Development Bank. "Chiang Mai Initiative (CMI): Current Status and Future Directions. <http://aric.adb.org/pdf/cmi_currentstatus.pdf> (accessed 20 June 2006).

Asia-Pacific Conference on East Timor (APCET). <http://www.asianexchange. org/Movements/94109509476240.php> (accessed 20 June 2006).

Asiaweek. "We Should've Done It My Way", 29 October 1999.

Association of Asian Studies. "The Future of Asian Studies". *Viewpoints.* Contributions from Jim Scott, Bruce Cumings, Elizabeth Perry, Harry Harootunian, Arjun Appadurai, Andrew Gordon, Thongchai Winichakul, 1997.

Association of Southeast Asia. *Report of the Special Session of Foreign Ministers of ASA.* Kuala Lumpur/Cameron Highlands: Federation of Malaya, 1962.

Aung San. *Burma's Challenge.* South Okklapa, Myanmar: U Aung Gyi, 1974.

————. *Bogyoke Aung San Maint-Khun-Myar, 1945–1947* [General Aung San's speeches]. Rangoon: Sarpay Bait Man Press, 1971.

————. "Problem for Burma's Freedom" [General Aung San's speeches]. Rangoon: Sarpay Bait Man Press, 1971.

Aung-Thwin, Michael. "Spirals in Early Southeast Asian and Burmese History". *Journal of Interdisciplinary History* 21, no. 4 (1991): 575–602.

————. "The 'Classical' in Southeast Asia: The Present in the Past". *Journal of Southeast Asian Studies* 26, no. 1 (1995): 75–91.

Australia, Department of Foreign Affairs and Trade. *The New ASEANs: Vietnam, Burma, Cambodia and Laos*. Canberra: Department of Foreign Affairs and Trade, 1997.

Australia, Joint Committee on Foreign Affairs and Defence. *Power in Indochina Since 1975*. Canberra: Australian Government Publishing Service, 1981.

Awanohara, Susumu. "'Look East'—The Japan Model". *Asia-Pacific Economic Literature* 1, no. 1 (1987): 75–89.

Ayoob, Mohammed, ed. *Regional Security in the Third World*. London: Croom Helm, 1986.

Bank of Japan. "The Agreement on the Swap Arrangement under the Chiang Mai Initiative (as of 4 May 2006)". <http://www.boj.or.jp/en/type/release/zuiji_new/data/un0605a.pdf> (accessed 20 June 2006).

Banks, Michael. "Systems Analysis and the Study of Regions". *International Studies Quarterly* 13, no. 4 (1969): 335–60.

Bastin, John and Harry J. Benda. *A History of Modern Southeast Asia: Colonialism, Nationalism and Decolonization*. Englewood Cliffs, NJ: Prentice Hall, 1968.

Bastin, John and R. Roolvink, eds. *Malayan and Indonesian Studies*. Oxford: Clarendon Press, 1964.

Bates, Robert H. "Area Studies and the Discipline: A Useful Controversy?" *PS: Political Science and Politics* 30, no. 2 (1997): 166–69.

Becker, Elizabeth. "Stalemate in Cambodia". *Current History* 86, no. 519 (1987): 156–59.

Bekker, Konrad. "Historical Patterns of Cultural Contact in Southeast Asia". *Far Eastern Quarterly* 9, no. 1 (1951): 3–15.

Bellamy, Alex J. *Security Communities and their Neighbours: Regional Fortresses or Global Integrators?* London: Palgrave Macmillan, 2004.

Bello, Walden and S. Rosenfeld. *Dragons in Distress: Asia's Miracle Economies in Crisis*. San Francisco: Institute for Food and Development Policy, 1990.

Benda, Harry J. "The Structure of Southeast Asian History: Some Preliminary Observations". *Journal of Southeast Asian History* 3, no. 1 (1962): 106–38.

Bentley, G.C. "Indigenous States of Southeast Asia". *Annual Review of Anthropology* 76 (1985): 275–305.

Bernard, Mitchell. "Regions in the Global Political Economy: Beyond the Local-Global Divide in the Formation of the Eastern Asian Region". *New Political Economy* 1, no. 3 (1996): 335–53.

Bernard, Mitchell and J. Ravenhill. "Beyond Product Cycles and Flying Geese: Regionalization, Hierarchy, and Industrialization of East Asia". *World Politics* 47, no. 2 (1995): 171–209.

Boeke, J.H. *Economics and Economic Policy of Dual Societies as Exemplified by Indonesia*. New York: Institute of Pacific Relations, 1953.

Booth, Ken and Tim Dunne, eds. *Worlds in Collision: Terror and the Future of Global Order*. London: Palgrave Macmillan, 2002.

Bowles, Paul. "ASEAN, AFTA and the New Regionalism". *Pacific Affairs* 70, no. 2 (1997): 219–33.

Braudel, Fernand. *The Mediterranean and the Mediterranean World in the Age of Philip II*. Vols. 1 and 2. Berkeley: University of California Press, 1995.

Breslin, Shaun, Christopher W. Hughes, Nicola Phillips, and Ben Rosamond, eds. *New Regionalisms in the Global Political Economy*. London and New York: Routledge, 2002.

Bresnan, John. *From Dominos to Dynamos: The Transformation of Southeast Asia*. New York: Council on Foreign Relations Press, 1994.

Briggs, Lawrence Palmer. "The Hinduized States of Southeast Asia: A Review". *Far Eastern Quarterly* 7, no. 4 (1951): 376–93.

Broinowski, Alison, ed. *Understanding ASEAN*. London: Macmillan, 1982.

Bull, Hedley, ed. *Asia and the Western Pacific: Towards a New International Order*. Melbourne and Sydney: Thomas Nelson, 1975.

Buszynski, Leszek. "Declining Superpowers: The Impact on ASEAN". *Pacific Review* 3, no. 3 (1990): 257–61.

Butler, Rhett A. "Drought and Deforestation in Southeast Asia to Contribute to Climate Change". *Mongabay.com*, 9 December 2008. <http://news.mongabay.com/2008/1209-forests_drought.html>.

Buzan, Barry. *People, States, and Fear: An Agenda for International Security Studies in the Post-Cold War Era*. Boulder, CO: Lynne Rienner, 1990.

Buzan, Barry and Gowher Rizvi, eds. *South Asian Insecurity and the Great Powers*. London: Croom Helm, 1986.

Buzan, Barry and Ole Wæver. *Regions and Powers: The Structure of International Security*. Cambridge: Cambridge University Press, 2003.

Cady, John F. *Southeast Asia: Its Historical Development*. New York: McGraw-Hill, 1964.

Caldwell, J.A. *American Economic Aid to Thailand*. Lexington, MA: D.C. Heath, 1974.

Cameron, A.W. *Indochina: Prospects After "the End"*. Washington, D.C.: American Enterprise Institute for Public Policy Research, 1976.

Cantori, L.J., and S.L. Spiegel, eds. *The International Politics of Regions: A Comparative Approach*. Englewood Cliffs, NJ: Prentice Hall, 1970.

Chachavalpongpun, Pavin. "In Search of an Asean Identity". *The Nation*, 4 May 2006. <http://www.nationmultimedia.com/2006/05/04/opinion/opinion_30003161.php> (accessed 21 June 2006).

Chan, H.C. "Political Stability in Southeast Asia". Paper presented to the seminar on "Trends and Perspectives in ASEAN". Institute of Southeast Asian Studies, Singapore, 1–3 February 1982.

———. "The Interests and Role of ASEAN in the Indochina Conflict". Paper presented to the international conference on "Indochina and Problems of Security and Stability in Southeast Asia". Chulalongkorn University, Bangkok, 19–21 June 1980.

Cheung Tai Ming. "China's Regional Military Posture". *International Defense Review* 24, no. 6 (1991): 618–22.

Chin Kin Wah. "The Five Power Defence Arrangement and AMDA: Some Observations on the Nature of an Evolving Partnership". Occasional Paper no. 23. Singapore: Institute of Southeast Asian Studies, 1974.

———. "Globalization and Its Challenges to ASEAN Political Participation". Paper presented to the ISEAS 30th anniversary conference "Southeast Asia in the 21st Century: Challenges of Globalization". Institute of Southeast Asian Studies, Singapore, 30 July–1 August 1998.

Ching, Frank. "Social Impact of the Regional Financial Crisis". In *Policy Choices, Social Consequences and the Philippine Case*. Three essays for the Asia Society's Asian Update Series. <http://www.asiasociety.org/publications/update_crisis_ching.html> (accessed 26 June 2006).

Chng, M.K. "ASEAN Economic Cooperation: The Current Status". In *Southeast Asian Affairs 1985*. Singapore: Institute of Southeast Asian Studies, 1985.

Christie, J.W. "Negara, Mandala, and Despotic State: Images of Early Java". In *Southeast Asia in the 9th to 14th Centuries*, edited by David G. Marr and A.C. Milner. Singapore: Institute of Southeast Asian Studies/Canberra: Australian National University, Research School of Pacific Studies, 1990.

Christie, Ken. "Review of *The Quest for Identity: International Relations of Southeast Asia*". *International Affairs*, 2001.

Chutintaranond, Sunait. "*Mandala*, Segmentary State and Politics of Centralization in Medieval Ayudhya". *Journal of the Siam Society* 78, no. 1 (1990): 80–100.

Clad, J. *Behind the Myth: Business, Money and Power in Southeast Asia*. London: Hyman Press, 1989.

Coedès, G. *The Indianized States of Southeast Asia*, edited by Walter Vella and translated by Susan Brown. Honolulu: University of Hawaii Press, 1968.

———. "Some Problems in the Ancient History of the Hinduized States of South-East Asia". *Journal of Southeast Asian History* 5 (1964): 1–14.

Cotton, James. "APEC: Australia Hosts Another Pacific Acronym". *The Pacific Review* 3, no. 2 (1990): 171–73.

Crone, Donald. Review of *The Quest for Identity: International Relations of Southeast Asia*. *Pacific Affairs* 75, no. 2 (2002): 319–21.

Das, Sanchita Basu. "What ASEAN Must Do to Cope With the Crisis". In *Global Financial Crisis: Implications for ASEAN*. Singapore: Institute of Southeast Asian Studies, 2008.

Datta-Ray, Sunanda K. "Tying Together a Rope of Sand". *Times Higher Education Supplement*, 16 February 2001.

Davis, M. Jane, ed. *Security Issues in the Post-Cold War World*. London: Edward Elgar, 1995.

Day, Anthony. *Fluid Iron: State Formation in Southeast Asia*. Honolulu: University of Hawaii Press, 2002.

Deyo, F.C., ed. *The Political Economy of New Asian Industrialism*. Ithaca, NY: Cornell University Press, 1987.

Dirlik, A. "The Asia-Pacific Region: Reality and Representation in the Invention of the Regional Structure". *Journal of World History* 3, no. 1 (1992): 55–79.

Dixon, C. *South East Asia in the World-Economy: A Regional Geography*. London: Cambridge University Press, 1991.

Djiwandono, J. Soedjati. "The Political and Security Aspects of ASEAN: Its Principal Achievements". *Indonesian Quarterly* 11, no. 3 (1983): 19–26.

Doner, R.F. "Approaches to the Politics of Economic Growth in Southeast Asia". *Journal of Asian Studies* 50, no. 4 (1991): 818–49.

East Asia Study Group. "Final Report of the East Asia Study Group". ASEAN+3 Summit, Phnom Penh, Cambodia, 4 November 2002. <http://www.mofa.go.jp/region/asia-paci/asean/pmv0211/report.pdf> (accessed 26 June 2006).

East Asia Vision Group. "Towards an East Asian Community: Region of Peace, Prosperity and Progress". Report, 2001. <http://www.mofa.go.jp/region/asia-paci/report2001.pdf> (accessed 26 June 2006).

Economist Intelligence Unit. *The Economic Effects of the Vietnam War in East and Southeast Asia*. QER Special, no. 3. London: Economist Intelligence Unit, November 1968.

EM-DAT Emergency Disasters Database. <http://www.em-dat.net/disasters/Visualisation/ profiles/natural-table-emdat_disasters.php?dis_type=Wave+%2F+Surge&Submit =Display+Disaster+Profile> (accessed 26 June 2006).

Emmerson, Donald K. "Beyond Western Surprise: Thoughts on the Evolution of Southeast Asian Studies". In *Southeast Asian Studies: Options for the Future*, edited by Ronald A. Morse. Singapore: Institute of Southeast Asian Studies/ Canberra: Australian National University, Research School of Pacific Studies, 1990.

———. "Situating Southeast Asian Studies: Realm, Guild, and Home". In *Southeast Asian Studies: Pacific Perspectives*, edited by Anthony Reid. Tempe: Arizona State University, Program for Southeast Asian Studies, 2003.

———. "Southeast Asia: What's in a Name?". *Journal of Southeast Asian Studies* 15, no. 1 (1984): 1–21.

Evans, Grant. "Between the Global and the Local There are Regions, Cultural Areas, and National States". Review of *History, Culture and Region in Southeast Asian Perspectives*, by O.W. Wolters. *Journal of Southeast Asian Studies* 33, no. 1 (2002): 147–61.

Evans, Paul. "The Changing Context of Security Relations in Eastern Asia". Paper prepared for the workshop on "Korea and the Changing Asia-Pacific Region", 8–9 February 1990.

Evers, Hans-Dieter. "Review of 'Reconceptualizing Southeast Asia'". *International Quarterly for Asian Studies* 30, nos. 3–4 (1999): 414

――――, ed. *Sociology of South-East Asia*. Kuala Lumpur: Oxford University Press, 1980.

Fairclough, Gordon. "Standing Firm". *Far Eastern Economic Review*, 15 April 1993.

Fawcett, Louise and Andrew Hurrell, eds. *Regionalism in World Politics: Regional Organization and International Order*. Oxford: Oxford University Press, 1995.

Federspiel, H.M. and K.E. Rafferty. *Prospects for Regional Military Cooperation in Southeast Asia*. McLean, VA: Research Analysis Corporation, 1969.

Fifield, Russell H. "The Southeast Asia Command". In *The ASEAN Reader*, edited by Kernial S. Sandhu. Singapore: Institute of Southeast Asian Studies, 1992.

――――. "Southeast Asian Studies: Origins, Development, Future". *Journal of Southeast Asian Studies* 7, no. 2 (1976): 151–61.

Fischer, Stanley. "The Asian Crisis: A View from the IMF". Address to the Midwinter Conference of the Bankers' Association for Foreign Trade, Washington, D.C., 22 January 1998. <http://www.imf.org/external/np/speeches/1998/012298.htm>.

Fisher, Charles A. "Southeast Asia: The Balkans of the Orient? A Study in Continuity and Change". *Geography* 47 (1962): 347–67.

――――. *South-East Asia: A Social, Economic and Political Geography*. London: Methuen, 1964.

Forum-Asia. *Creating Asia: Flags of Human Rights, Seeds of Freedom*. Bangkok: Asian Forum for Human Rights and Development, 2000.

――――. *Human Rights in Asia*. Bangkok: Asian Forum for Human Rights and Development, 2001.

――――. *The Security Syndrome: Politics of National Security in Asia*. Bangkok: Asian Forum for Human Rights and Development, 1997.

Frost, Frank. "The Origins and Evolution of ASEAN". *World Review* 19, no. 3 (1980): 5–16.

――――. "Vietnam and ASEAN: From Enmity to Cooperation". *Trends*, 29 December 1991.

Furnivall, J.S. *Colonial Policy and Practice: A Comparative Study of Burma and Netherlands India*. New York: New York University Press, 1956.

Gainsborough, Martin. "Vietnam II: A Turbulent Normalisation with China". *The World Today* 48, no. 11 (1992): 205–7.

Geertz, Clifford. *Negara: The Theatre State in Nineteenth-Century Bali*. Princeton, NJ: Princeton University Press, 1980.

Ghai, Yash. *Human Rights and Governance: The Asia Debate*. San Francisco: The Asia Foundation, Center for Asian Pacific Affairs, 1994.

Giam, Gerald. "Haze Problem: Bilateral Pressure on Indonesia Works Best". *Singapore Angle*, 13 October 2006. <http://www.singaporeangle.com/2006/10/haze-problem-bilateral-pressure-on.html> (accessed 14 June 2008).

Gill, Ranjit. *ASEAN: Coming of Age*. Singapore: Sterling Corporate Services, 1987.

Girling, J.L.S. *Thailand: Society and Politics*. Ithaca, NY: Cornell University Press, 1981.

Glover, David and Timothy Jessup, eds. *Indonesia's Fires and Haze: The Cost of Catastrophe*. Ottawa: International Development Research Centre/Singapore, Institute of Southeast Asian Studies, 1999.

Goh Chok Tong. "Towards a Positive Relationship with Vietnam". *Speeches*, vol. 15, no. 5 (September–October 1991).

Golay, F.H., R. Anspach, M.R. Pfanner, and B.A. Eliezer. *Underdevelopment and Economic Nationalism in Southeast Asia*. Ithaca, NY: Cornell University Press, 1969.

Gordon, Bernard K. *The Dimensions of Conflict in Southeast Asia*. Englewood Cliffs, NJ: Prentice Hall, 1966.

Goscha, C.E. *Thailand and the Southeast Asian Networks of the Vietnamese Revolution, 1885–1954*. Richmond, Surrey: Curzon Press, 1999.

Grant, Margaret, ed. *South Asia Pacific Crisis: National Development and World Community*. New York: Dodd, Mead and Company, 1964.

Haas, E.B. "Regime Decay: Conflict Management and International Organizations, 1945–1981". *International Organization* 37, no. 2 (1983): 189–256.

————. *Why We Still Need the United Nations: The Collective Management of International Conflict*. Berkeley: University of California, Institute of International Relations, 1986.

Halib, Mohammed and Tim Huxley, eds. *An Introduction to Southeast Asian Studies*. London: I.B. Tauris, 1996.

Hall, D.G.E. *A History of South East Asia*. London: Macmillan, 1968; 4th ed., 1981.

————. "The Integrity of Southeast Asian History". *Journal of Southeast Asian History* 4, no. 2 (1973): 159–68.

————. "Looking at Southeast Asian History". *Journal of Asian Studies* 19, no. 3 (1960): 243–53.

Hall, K.R. *Maritime Trade and State Development in Early Southeast Asia*. Honolulu: University of Hawaii Press, 1985.

Hanggi, Heiner. "ASEAN and the ZOPFAN Concept". Pacific Strategic Paper no. 4. Singapore: Institute of Southeast Asian Studies, 1991.

Harris, Stuart. "Policy Networks and Economic Cooperation in the Asia Pacific". *Pacific Review* 7, no. 4 (1994): 381–95.

Harrison, Brian. *South East Asia: A Short History*. London: Macmillan, 1963.

Hassan, Mohamed Jawahar, Stephen Leong, and Vincent Lim, eds. *Asia Pacific Security: Challenges and Opportunities in the 21st Century*. Kuala Lumpur: Institute of Strategic and International Studies, 2002.

Hatch, W. and K. Yamamura. *Asia in Japan's Embrace: Building a Regional Production Alliance*. New York: Cambridge University Press, 1996.

Hay, K. "ASEAN and the Shifting Tides of Economic Power at the End of the 1980s". *International Journal* 44, no. 3 (1989): 640–59.

Henderson, W. "The Development of Regionalism in Southeast Asia". *International Organization* 9, no. 4 (1955): 462–76.

Hernandez, Carolina. "ASEAN Perspectives on Human Rights and Democracy in International Relations: Problems and Prospects". Working Paper 1995–1. Toronto: Centre for International Studies, University of Toronto, 1995.

————. "One Southeast Asia in the 21st Century: Opportunities and Challenges". Paper presented to the 1995 convention of the Canadian Council for Southeast Asian Studies on "The Dynamism of Southeast Asia". Université Laval, Quebec City, 27–29 October 1995.

Hervouet, Gerard. "The Return of Vietnam to the International System". Occasional Paper no. 6. Ottawa: Canadian Institute for International Peace and Security, 1988.

Hettne, Bjorn and Andras Inotai. *The New Regionalism*. Tokyo: United Nations University, World Institute for Developmental Economics Research, 1994.

Hettne, Bjorn and Frederik Soderbaum. "Theorising the Rise of Regionness". In *New Regionalisms in the Global Political Economy*, edited by Shaun Breslin et al. London and New York: Routledge, 2002.

Hiebert Murray and J. McBeth. "Trial by Fire: Smog Crisis Tests Asean's Vaunted Cooperation". *Far Eastern Economic Review*, 16 October 1997. <http://www.singapore-window.org/1016feer.htm>.

Higham, Charles. *The Archeology of Mainland Southeast Asia from 10,000 B.C. to the Fall of Angkor*. Cambridge: Cambridge University Press, 1989.

Hill, Hal. "The Financial Crisis and What's in Store for Southeast Asia". East Asia Forum, 18 April 2009. <http://www.eastasiaforum.org/2009/04/18/the-financial-crisis-and-whats-in-store-for-southeast-asia> (accessed 5 March 2010).

Hirono, Ryokichi. "Japan: Model for East Asia Industrialization?" In *Achieving Industrialization in East Asia*, edited by Helen Hughes. Cambridge: Cambridge University Press, 1988.

Holt, Claire, ed. *Culture and Politics in Indonesia*. Ithaca, NY: Cornell University Press, 1972.

Hughes, Helen, ed. *Achieving Industrialization in East Asia*. Cambridge: Cambridge University Press, 1988.

Hurrell, Andrew. "Regionalism in Theoretical Perspective". *Review of International Studies* 21, 1995.

Huxley, Tim. "The ASEAN States' Defence Policies, 1975–81: Military Response to Indochina?" Working Paper no. 88. Canberra: Australian National University, Strategic and Defence Studies Centre, 1986.

————. "Indochina as a Security Concern of the ASEAN States 1975–81". Ph.D. dissertation, Australian National University, 1986.

————. "South-East Asia's Arms Race: Some Notes on Recent Developments". *Arms Control* 11, no. 1 (1990): 69–76.

India Brand Equity Foundation. "India & ASEAN". <http://www.ibef.org/india/indiaasean.aspx> (accessed 6 January 2010).

Indonesia, Ministry of Foreign Affairs. *Deplu Paper on ASEAN Security Community*. Tabled at the ASEAN Ministerial Meeting in Cambodia, 16–18 June 2003.

Institute of Southeast Asian Studies. *Regional Outlook 1991*. Singapore: Institute of Southeast Asian Studies, 1991.

Institute of Strategic and International Studies. *Proceedings of the Second ASEAN Roundtable, Kuala Lumpur, 20–21 July 1987*. Kuala Lumpur: Institute of Strategic and International Studies, 1987.

International Institute for Strategic Studies. "Vietnam Joins ASEAN". *Strategic Comments*, no. 5, 8 June 1995.

————. *Strategic Survey 1982–1983*. London: International Institute for Strategic Studies, 1983.

Irvine, David. "Making Haste Less Slowly: ASEAN from 1975". In *Understanding ASEAN*, edited by Alison Broinowski. London: Macmillan, 1982.

Ispahani, M.Z. "Alone Together: Regional Security Arrangements in Southern Africa and the Arabian Gulf". *International Security* 8, no. 4 (1984): 152–75.

Jackson, Karl D. and M. Hadi Soesastro, eds. *ASEAN Security and Economic Development*. Research Papers and Policy Studies no. 11. Berkeley: Institute of East Asian Studies, University of California, 1984.

Japan Economic Institute. *JEI Reports*. Washington, D.C.: Japan Economic Institute, various dates.

Jayasuriya, Kanishka. "Singapore: The Politics of Regional Definition". *The Pacific Review* 7, no. 4 (1994): 411–20.

Jemaah Islamiyah. *Pedoman Umum Perjuangan Al-Jama'ah Al-Islamiyyah (PUPJI)* [General guide for the struggle of Jemaah Islamiyah]. Released by the Central Leadership Council, Jemaah Islamiyah. Translated by the International Center for Political Violence and Terrorism Research, Institute of Defence and Strategic Studies, Nanyang Technological University, Singapore, n.d.

Joenniemi, Pertti, ed. *Cooperation in the Baltic Sea Region*. London: Taylor and Francis, 1993.

Johnson, Chalmers. "Political Institutions and Economic Performance: The Government-Business Relationship in Japan, South Korea, and Taiwan". In *The Political Economy of New Asian Industrialism*, edited by F.C. Deyo. Ithaca, NY: Cornell University Press, 1987.

Jones, David Martin. *Political Development in Pacific Asia*. Cambridge: Polity Press, 1997.

Jones, Sidney. *The Impact of Asian Economic Growth on Human Rights*. Asia Project Working Paper. New York: Council on Foreign Relations, 1995.

————. "The Organic Growth". *Far Eastern Economic Review*, 17 June 1993

Jorgensen-Dahl, A. *Regional Organization and Order in Southeast Asia*. London: Macmillan, 1982.

Kahin, George M. *Governments and Politics of Southeast Asia*. Ithaca, NY: Cornell University Press, 1964.

———. "The Role of the United States in Southeast Asia". In *New Directions in the International Relations of Southeast Asia: The Great Powers and Southeast Asia*, edited by T.S. Lau. Singapore: Singapore University Press, 1973.

Kang, David C. "Getting Asia Wrong: The Need for New Analytical Frameworks". *International Security* 27, no. 4 (2003): 57–85.

Karunan, Victor P. *The Security Syndrome: Politics of National Security in Asia*. Bangkok: Asian Forum for Human Rights and Development, 1997.

Katzenstein, Peter J., ed. *The Culture of National Security: Norms and Identity in World Politics*. New York: Columbia University Press, 1996.

———. *A World of Regions: Asia and Europe in the American Imperium*. Ithaca, NY: Cornell University Press, 2005.

Kawai, Masahiro. "Global Financial Crisis and Implications for ASEAN". In *Global Financial Crisis: Implications for ASEAN*. Singapore: Institute of Southeast Asian Studies, 2008.

Keys, Charles F. "A Conference at Wingspread and Rethinking Southeast Asian Studies". In *Southeast Asian Studies in the Balance: Reflections from America*, edited by Charles Hirschman, Charles F. Keyes, and Karl Hutterer. Ann Arbor, MI: Association for Asian Studies, 1992.

Kitamura, Hiroshi and A.N. Bhagat. "Aspects of Regional Harmonization of National Development Plans". In *Economic Interdependence in Southeast Asia*, edited by T. Morgan and N. Spoelstra. Madison: University of Wisconsin Press, 1969.

Kondo, Shigekatsu. "The Evolving Security Environment: Political". Paper presented to the workshop on "Arms Control and Confidence-Building in the Asia-Pacific Region". Organized by the Canadian Institute for International Peace and Security, Ottawa, 22–23 May 1992.

Koo, Jahyeong and Dong Fu. "The Effects of SARS on East Asian Economies". *Expand Your Insight*, Federal Reserve Bank of Dallas, 1 July 2003. <http://www.dallasfed.org/eyi/global/0307sars.html>.

Kratoska, Paul, Remeo Raben and Henk Schulte Nordholt, eds. *Locating Southeast Asia: Geographies of Knowledge and Politics of Space*. Singapore: Singapore University Press/Athens: Ohio University Press, 2005.

Kroef, J.M. Van Der. "ASEAN, Hanoi, and the Kampuchean Conflict: Between Kuantan and a Third Alternative". *Asian Survey* 21, no. 5 (1981): 515–35.

———. "The Hinduization of Indonesia Reconsidered". *Far Eastern Quarterly* 9, no. 1 (1951): 17–30.

Kulke, Hermann. "The Early and Imperial Kingdoms in Southeast Asian History". In *Southeast Asia in the 9th and 14th Centuries*, edited by David G. Marr and A.C.

Milner. Singapore: Institute of Southeast Asian Studies/Canberra: Australian National University, Research School of Pacific Studies, 1990.

Lake, David A. and Patrick M. Morgan, eds. *Regional Orders: Building Security in a New World*. Philadelphia: Pennsylvania State University Press, 1997.

Lau, T.S. "Conflict-Resolution in ASEAN: The Sabah Issue". Department of Political Science, University of Singapore, n.d.

————, ed. *New Directions in the International Relations of Southeast Asia: The Great Powers and Southeast Asia*. Singapore: Singapore University Press, 1973.

————. "The Role of Singapore in Southeast Asia". *World Review* 19, no. 3 (1980): 36–44.

Lee, Hsien Loong. Text of speech to the Indonesia Forum as Singapore Minister for Trade and Industry. Jakarta, 11 July 1990.

————. Speech to the ASEAN 100 Leadership Forum. Singapore, 28 September 2005. <http://www.mfa.gov.sg/internet/> (accessed 24 June 2006).

Legge, John D. "The Writing of Southeast Asian History". In *The Cambridge History of Southeast Asia*, vol. 1, edited by Nicholas Tarling. Cambridge: Cambridge University Press, 1992.

Leifer, Michael. "ASEAN as a Model of a Security Community". In *ASEAN in a Changed Regional and International Political Economy*, edited by Hadi Soesastro. Jakarta: Centre for Strategic and International Studies, 1995.

————. *Conflict and Regional Order in Southeast Asia*. Adelphi Paper no. 162. London: International Institute for Strategic Studies, 1980.

————. "Debating Asian Security: Michael Leifer Responds to Geoffrey Wiseman". *Pacific Review* 5, no. 2 (1992): 167–69.

————. *Indonesia's Foreign Policy*. London: Allen and Unwin, 1983.

————. "International Dynamics of One Southeast Asia: Political and Security Contexts". In *One Southeast Asia: In a New Regional and International Setting*, edited by Hadi Soesastro. Jakarta: Centre for Strategic and International Studies, 1997.

————. "The Paradox of ASEAN: A Security Organisation Without the Structure of an Alliance". *The Round Table* 68, no. 271 (1978): 261–68.

————. "Power-Sharing and Peacemaking in Cambodia". *SAIS Review* 12, no. 1 (1992): 139–53.

————. Review of *The Quest for Identity: International Relations of Southeast Asia*. *Pacific Review*, 2001.

Leinbach, T.R. and R. Ulak. *Southeast Asia's Diversity and Development*. Upper Saddle River, NJ: Prentice Hall, 2000.

Leur, J.C. van. *Indonesian Trade and Society: Essays in Asian Social and Economic History*. The Hague: W. Van Hoeve, 1955.

Lieberman, Victor. "An Age of Commerce in Southeast Asia? Problems of Regional Coherence". *Journal of Asian Studies* 54, no. 3 (1995): 796–807.

————. "Local Integration and Euroasian Analogies: Structuring Southeast Asian History, c. 1350–c. 1830". *Modern Asian Studies* 27, no. 3 (1993): 475–572.

————. *Strange Parallels: Southeast Asia in Global Context, c. 800–1830*. Cambridge: Cambridge University Press, 2003.

Lim, J. and S. Vani, eds. *Armed Communist Movements in Southeast Asia*. Aldershot, Hants: Gower, 1984.

Lizee, Pierre P. "Civil Society and Regional Security: Tensions and Potentials in Post-Crisis Southeast Asia". *Contemporary Southeast Asia* 22, no. 3 (2000): 551–70.

Lockard, Craig A. "Integrating Southeast Asia into the Framework of World History: The Period before 1500". *The History Teacher* 29, no. 1 (1995): 7–35.

Ludden, David. "Area Studies in the Age of Globalization". University of Pennsylvania. 25 January 1998. <http://www.sas.upenn.edu/~dludden/areast2.htm>.

Luhulima, C.P.F. "ASEAN's Security Framework". CAPA Reports no. 22. San Francisco: Center for Asia Pacific Affairs, The Asia Foundation, 1995.

Lye Tuck-Po, Wil de Jong, and Abe Ken-ichi. *The Political Ecology of Tropical Forests in Southeast Asia*. Kyoto Area Studies on Asia, vol. 6. Kyoto: Kyoto University Press, 2003.

Mabbett, I.W. "The 'Indianization' of Southeast Asia: Reflections on the Historical Sources". *Journal of Southeast Asian Studies* 8, no. 2 (1976): 143–61.

————. "The 'Indianization' of Southeast Asia: Reflections on the Prehistoric Sources". *Journal of Southeast Asian Studies* 8, no. 1 (1976): 1–14.

Mack, Andrew. "Asia's New Military Build-Up". *Pacific Research* 4, no. 1 (1991): 12 –13.

Mahapatra, Chintamani. *American Role in the Origin and Growth of ASEAN*. New Delhi: ABC Publishing House, 1990.

Mahbubani, Kishore. "New Areas of Asean Reaction: Environment, Human Rights and Democracy". *Asean-ISIS Monitor* 5 (1992): 13–17.

Majumdar, R.C. *Greater India*. 2nd ed. Bombay: National Information and Publications, 1948.

Majumdar, R.C., H.C. Raychaudhuri, and Kalikinkar Datta. *An Advanced History of India*. London: Macmillan, 1948.

Mak, J.N. "The ASEAN Process ('Way') of Multilateral Cooperation and Cooperative Security: The Road to a Regional Arms Register?" Paper presented to the MIMA-SIPRI workshop on "An ASEAN Arms Register: Developing Transparency". Kuala Lumpur, 2–3 October 1995.

Malik, Adam. "Djakarta Conference and Asia's Political Future". *Pacific Community* 2, no. 1 (1970): 66–76.

————. "Regional Cooperation in International Politics". In *Regionalism in Southeast Asia*. Jakarta: Centre for Strategic and International Studies, 1975.

Manila People's Forum on APEC. *APEC: Four Objectives in Search of a Noun*. Manila: MPFA/Bangkok: Focus on the Global South and Institute of Popular Democracy, 1996.

Marr, David G. and A.C. Milner, eds. *Southeast Asia in the 9th to 14th Centuries*. Singapore: Institute of Southeast Asian Studies/Canberra: Australian National University, Research School of Pacific Studies, 1990.

Mason, M. "Foreign Direct Investment in East Asia: Trends and Critical Issues". CFR Asia Project Working Paper. New York: Council on Foreign Relations Press, 1994.

Mauzy, Diane. Review of *The Quest for Identity: International Relations of Southeast Asia*. *Contemporary Southeast Asia* 22, no. 3 (2000): 613–15.

McCloud, Donald G. *Southeast Asia: Tradition and Modernity in the Contemporary World*. Boulder, CO: Westview Press, 1995.

———. *System and Process in Southeast Asia: The Evolution of a Region*. Boulder, CO: Westview Press, 1986.

McVey, Ruth T. "Globalization, Marginalization and the Study of Southeast Asia". In *Southeast Asian Studies: Reorientations*, edited by C.J. Reynolds and R. McVey. Ithaca, NY: Cornell University, 1998.

———. "Change and Continuity in Southeast Asian Studies". *Journal of Southeast Asian Studies* 26, no. 1 (1995): 1–9.

Melchor, A. Jr. "Security Issues in Southeast Asia". In *Regionalism in Southeast Asia*. Jakarta: Centre for Strategic and International Studies, 1975.

Milivojevic, M. "The Spratly and Paracel Islands Conflict". *Survival* 31, no. 1 (1989): 70–78.

Miller, L.B. "Regional Organization and the Regulation of Internal Conflict". *World Politics* 19, no. 4 (1967): 582–600.

Moreau, Ron and Richard Ernsberger Jr. "Strangling the Mekong". *Newsweek*, Atlantic edition, 19 March 2001.

Morgan, T. and N. Spoelstra, eds. *Economic Interdependence in Southeast Asia*. Madison: University of Wisconsin Press, 1969.

Morse, Ronald A., ed. *Southeast Asian Studies: Options for the Future*. Lanham, MD: University Press of America, 1984.

Morse, Ronald A. and David B.J. Adams. "Establishing a New Agenda for Southeast Asian Studies in America". In *Southeast Asian Studies: Options for the Future*, edited by Ronald A. Morse. Lanham, MD: University Press of America, 1984.

Muni, S.D. *China's Strategic Engagement with the New ASEAN*. IDSS Monographs no. 2. Singapore: Institute of Defence and Strategic Studies, 2002.

Munslow, Alun. *The Routledge Companion to Historical Studies*. London: Routledge, 2000.

Murphy, Alexander B. "Regions as Social Constructs: The Gap Between Theory and Practice". *Progress in Human Geography* 15, no. 1 (1991): 23–35.

Murray, M.J. *The Development of Capitalism in Colonial Indochina, 1870–1940*. Los Angeles: University of California Press, 1980.

Muscat, R.J. *Thailand and the United States: Development, Security, and Foreign Aid*. New York: Columbia University Press, 1990.

Myint, Hla. *Southeast Asia's Economy: Development Policies in the 1970s*. New York: Praeger, 1972.

Nair, K.K. "ASEAN-Indochina Relations Since 1975: The Politics of Accommodation". Canberra Papers on Strategy and Defence no. 30. Canberra: Australian National University, Strategic and Defence Studies Centre, 1984.

———. "Defence and Security in Southeast Asia: The Urgency of Self-Reliance". *Asian Defence Journal* 1 (1975): 9–17.

Neher, Clark. Review of *The Quest for Identity: International Relations of Southeast Asia*. *Journal of Asian Studies* 61, no. 3 (2002): 1101–3.

———. "The Social Sciences". In *Southeast Asian Studies: Options for the Future*, edited by Ronald A. Morse. Lanham, MD: University Press of America, 1984.

Neil, Robert Van. "Southeast Asian Studies in the U.S.A.". *Journal of Southeast Asian History* 5, no. 1 (1964): 188–94.

Ness, Garry and Martha Morrow. "Assessing U.S. Scholarly Resources on Southeast Asia". In *Southeast Asian Studies: Options for the Future*, edited by Ronald A. Morse. Lanham, MD: University Press of America, 1984.

Neumann, Iver B. "A Region-Building Approach to Northern Europe". *Review of International Studies* 20, no. 1 (1994): 53–74.

Nor, Commodore A. Ramli. "ASEAN Maritime Cooperation". Paper presented to the Defence Asia '89 conference on "Towards Greater ASEAN Military and Security Cooperation: Issues and Prospects". Singapore, 22–25 March 1989.

Nuechterlein, Donald E. "Thailand: Another Vietnam?". *Asian Survey* 7, no. 2 (1967): 126–30.

O'Connor, Richard A. "Critiquing the Critique of Southeast Asia: Beyond Texts and States to Culture History". In *Southeast Asian Studies: Pacific Perspectives*, edited by Anthony Reid. Tempe: Arizona State University, Program for Southeast Asian Studies, 2003.

O'Reilly, Dougald J.W. *Early Civilizations of Southeast Asia*. Lanham, MD: Rowman and Littlefield, 2007.

Osborne, Milton. *Region of Revolt: Focus on Southeast Asia*. Rushcutters Bay, NSW: Pergamon Australia, 1970.

———. *Southeast Asia: An Illustrated Introductory History*. 5th ed. St. Leonards, NSW: Allen and Unwin, 1990.

Owen, Norman. "Economic and Social Change". In *Cambridge History of Southeast Asia*. Vol. 2, *The Nineteenth and Twentieth Centuries*, edited by Nicholas Tarling. Cambridge: Cambridge University Press, 1992.

Owen, Sarah, ed. *The State and Identity Construction in International Relations*. London: Macmillan, 1999.

Pace, B. et al. *Regional Cooperation in Southeast Asia: The First Two Years of ASEAN–1967–1969*. McLean, VA: Research Analysis Corporation, 1970.

Palmer, Ronald D. *Building ASEAN: 20 Years of Southeast Asian Cooperation*. The Washington Papers no. 127. New York: Praeger/Center for Strategic and International Studies, 1987.

Panorama. "No Alternative to Regionalism". Interview with Rodolfo C. Severino, Jr., August 1999. <http://www.aseansec.org/2829.htm>.

Paribatra, Sukhumbhand. "ASEAN Ten and Its Role in the Asia Pacific". Paper prepared for the conference "Asia in the XXI Century", organized by the Institute for International Relations, Hanoi, 28–29 April 1997.

Paribatra, Sukhumbhand and Chai-Anan Samudavanija. "Internal Dimensions of Regional Security in Southeast Asia". In *Regional Security in the Third World*, edited by Mohammed Ayoob. London: Croom Helm, 1986.

Pempel, T.J., ed. *Remapping East Asia: The Construction of a Region*. Ithaca, NY: Cornell University Press, 2005.

Pentland, Charles. "The Regionalization of World Politics: Concepts and Evidence". *International Journal* 30, no. 4 (1975): 599–630.

Peou, Sorpong. "Realism and Constructivism in Southeast Asian Security Studies Today". *The Pacific Review* 15, no. 1 (2002): 119–38.

Peterson, Erik. *The Gulf Cooperation Council: Search for Unity in a Dynamic Region*. Boulder, CO: Westview Press, 1988.

Phanit, Thakur. "Regional Integration Attempts in Southeast Asia: A Study of ASEAN's Problems and Progress". Ph.D. dissertation. Pennsylvania State University, 1980.

Popper, Karl. *The Poverty of Historicism*. Boston: The Beacon Press, 1957.

Ptak, Roderich. "In Memoriam: Denys Lombard (1938–1998)". *IIAS Newsletter* 16, Summer 1998. <http://www.iias.nl/iiasn/16/general/gen11.html> (accessed 12 March 2010).

———. "International Symposium on the 'Asian Mediterranean' (Paris, 3–5 March, 1997)". *Archipel* 55 (1998): 11–14.

Pye, Lucian W. *International Relations in Asia: Culture, Nation and State*. Sigur Center Asia Papers no. 1. Washington, D.C.: Sigur Center for Asian Studies, George Washington University, 1998.

———. *Southeast Asia's Political Systems*. 2nd ed. Englewood Cliffs, NJ: Prentice Hall, 1974.

Rajanubhab, Damrong. *The Chronicle of Our Wars with the Burmese: Hostilities Between Siamese and Burmese When Ayutthaya was the Capital of Siam*. Bangkok: White Lotus Press, 2001.

Rajaratnam, Sinnathamby. "Riding the Vietnamese Tiger". *Contemporary Southeast Asia* 10, no. 4 (1989): 343–61.

Rashid, Ahmed. *Taliban*. New Haven, CT: Yale University Press, 2001.

Ravenholt, Albert. *Maphilindo: Dream or Achievable Reality*. American University Field Staff Reports. Southeast Asia Series 12, no. 1 (1964): 1–14.

Reid, Anthony. *Charting the Shape of Early Modern Southeast Asia*. Chiang Mai: Silkworm Books, 1999.

———. "A Saucer Model of Southeast Asian Identity". *Southeast Asian Journal of Social Science* 27, no. 1 (1999): 7–23.

———. *Southeast Asia in the Age of Commerce 1450–1680*. Vol. 1, *The Lands Below the Winds*. New Haven, CT: Yale University Press, 1988.

———. *Southeast Asia in the Age of Commerce 1450–1680*. Vol. 2, *Expansion and Crisis*. New Haven, CT: Yale University Press, 1993.

———. "Southeast Asian Studies: Decline or Rebirth?". In *Southeast Asian Studies: Pacific Perspectives*, edited by Anthony Reid. Tempe: Arizona State University, Program for Southeast Asian Studies, 2003.

———, ed. *Southeast Asian Studies: Pacific Perspectives*. Tempe: Arizona State University, Program for Southeast Asian Studies, 2003.

Reid, Anthony and Maria Serena Diokno. "Completing the Circle: Southeast Asian Studies in Southeast Asia". In *Southeast Asian Studies: Pacific Perspectives*, edited by Anthony Reid. Tempe: Arizona State University, Program for Southeast Asian Studies, 2003.

Reynolds, Craig J. "A New Look at Old Southeast Asia". *Journal of Asian Studies* 54, no. 2 (1995): 419–46.

———. *Seditious Histories: Contesting Thai and Southeast Asian Pasts*. Seattle: University of Washington Press, 2006.

Ricklefs, Merle C. *A History of Modern Indonesia Since c.1300*. 2nd ed. Stanford, CA: Stanford University Press, 1993.

Rieger, H.C. "Regional Economic Cooperation in the Asia-Pacific Region". *Asia-Pacific Economic Literature* 3, no. 2 (1989): 5–33.

Robison, Richard, Richard Higgott, and K. Hewison, eds. *South East Asia in the 1980s: The Politics of Economic Crisis*. Sydney: Allen and Unwin, 1987.

Russett, Bruce M. *International Regions and the International System: A Study in Political Ecology*. Chicago: Rand McNally, 1967.

Sandhu, Kernial S. et al., ed. *The ASEAN Reader*. Singapore: Institute of Southeast Asian Studies, 1992.

———. "Comment". In *Southeast Asian Studies: Options for the Future*, edited by Ronald A. Morse. Lanham, MD: University Press of America, 1984.

Sardesai, D.R. *Southeast Asia: Past and Present*. Boulder, CO: Westview Press, 1994.

Seah, C.M. "Singapore's Position in ASEAN Cooperation". Occasional Paper no. 38. Department of Political Science, National University of Singapore, 1979.

SEATO. *The History of SEATO*. Bangkok: Public Information Office, SEATO Headquarters, n.d.

Seda, Maria, ed. *Environmental Management in ASEAN: Perspectives on Critical Regional Issues*. Singapore: Institute of Southeast Asian Studies, 1993.

Selth, Andrew. "Burma: A Strategic Perspective". Asia Foundation Working Paper no. 13, May 2001. Originally presented at the conference on "Strategic Rivalries in the Bay of Bengal: The Burma/Myanmar Nexus". Washington, D.C., 1 February 2001. <http://www.asiafoundation.org/pdf/WorkPap13.pdf> (accessed 26 June 2006).

————. "The Burmese Army". *Jane's Intelligence Review* 7, no. 11 (1 November 1995).

Setboonsarng, Suthad. "ASEAN Economic Cooperation: Adjusting to the Crisis". In *Southeast Asian Affairs 1998*. Singapore: Institute of Southeast Asian Studies, 1999.

Severino, Rodolfo C. "Weathering the Storm: ASEAN's Response to Crisis". Address to the conference sponsored by the *Far Eastern Economic Review*, "Weathering the Storm: Hong Kong and the Asian Financial Crisis". Hong Kong, 11 June 1998.

Shafie, Mohammed Ghazali bin. "ASEAN's Response to Security Issues in Southeast Asia". In *Regionalism in Southeast Asia*. Jakarta: Centre for Strategic and International Studies, 1975.

————. "Confrontation Leads to ASEAN". *Asian Defence Journal*, February 1982, pp. 30–35.

————. "The Neutralisation of Southeast Asia". *Pacific Community* 3, no. 1 (1971): 110–17.

Shea, Christopher. "Political Scientists Clash Over Value of Area Studies". *Chronicle of Higher Education*, January 1997.

Sheng, Lijun. "China-ASEAN Free Trade Area: Origins, Developments and Strategic Motivations". ISEAS Working Paper, International Politics and Security Issues Series no. 1. Singapore: Institute of Southeast Asian Studies, 2003.

Sidel, John T. Review of *The Quest for Identity: International Relations of Southeast Asia. Survival*, 2002.

Silverstein, Josef. "The Political Legacy of Aung San". Data Paper no. 86. Ithaca, NY: Department of Asian Studies, Southeast Asian Program, Cornell University, 1972.

Simon, Sheldon N. *ASEAN States and Regional Security*. Stanford, CA: Hoover Institution Press, 1982.

————. "The ASEAN States: Obstacles to Security Cooperation". *Orbis* 22, no. 2 (1978): 415–34.

————. "United States Security Policy and ASEAN". *Current History* 89, no. 545 (1990): 97–132.

Singapore Government Information. "Aceh Quake and Tsunami Disaster". <http://www.gov.sg/tsunami.htm> (accessed 26 June 2006).

Singapore Institute of International Affairs. "Lessons from the Tsunami for Regional Cooperation: The Importance of Prevention and Early Responses". Panel discussion. Singapore Institute of International Affairs, Singapore, 16 February 2005.

Singer, J.D., ed. *Quantitative International Politics: Insights and Evidence*. New York: Free Press, 1968.

Singh, Hari. "Hegemonic Construction of Regions: Southeast Asia as a Case Study". In *State and Identity Construction in International Relations*, edited by Sarah Owen. London: Macmillan, 1999.

———. "Prospects for Regional Stability in Southeast Asia in the Post-Cold War Era". *Millennium* 22, no. 2 (1993): 279–300.

———. "Understanding Conflict Resolution in Cambodia: A Neorealist Perspective". *Asian Journal of Political Science* 7, no. 1 (1999): 41–59.

———. "Vietnam and ASEAN: The Politics of Accommodation". *Australian Journal of International Affairs* 51, no. 2 (1997): 215–29.

Smail, John R. "On the Possibility of an Autonomous History of Modern Southeast Asia". *Journal of Southeast Asian History* 2, no. 2 (1961): 72–102.

Sodhi, Navjot S., Lian Pin Koh, Barry W. Brook, and Peter K.L. Ng. "Southeast Asian Biodiversity: An Impending Disaster". *Trends in Ecology and Evolution* 19, no. 12 (2004): 654–60.

Soesastro, Hadi. "ASEAN's Participation in the GATT". *Indonesian Quarterly* 15, no. 1 (1987): 107–27.

———, ed. *One Southeast Asia: In a New Regional and International Setting*. Jakarta: Centre for Strategic and International Studies, 1997.

———. "Prospects for Pacific-Asian Regional Trade Structures". In *Regional Dynamics: Security, Political and Economic Issues in the Asia-Pacific Region*, edited by Robert Scalapino et al. Jakarta: Centre for Strategic and International Studies, 1990.

Soesastro, Hadi and Anthony Bergin, eds. *The Role of Security and Economic Cooperation Structures in the Asia Pacific Region*. Jakarta: Centre for Strategic and International Studies, 1996.

Solidum, Estrella D. *Towards a Southeast Asian Community*. Quezon City: University of the Philippines Press, 1974.

Sopiee, Noordin. "ASEAN and Regional Security". In *Regional Security in the Third World*, edited by Mohammed Ayoob. London: Croom Helm, 1986.

———. "The Neutralisation of Southeast Asia". In *Asia and the Western Pacific: Towards a New International Order*, edited by Hedley Bull. Melbourne and Sydney: Thomas Nelson, 1975.

South-East Asia Treaty Organization. *History of SEATO*. Bangkok: Public Information Office, SEATO Headquarters, n.d.

Spencer, Joseph E. *Oriental Asia: Themes Toward a Geography*. Englewood Cliffs, NJ: Prentice Hall, 1973.

Sricharatchanya, P. "Wait and See". *Far Eastern Economic Review*, 11 May 1989, pp. 21–24.

Steinberg, David J., ed. *In Search of Southeast Asia: A Modern History*. Rev. ed. Honolulu: University of Hawaii Press, 1987.

Stockwell, Anthony John. "Southeast Asia in War and Peace: The End of European Colonial Empires". In *Cambridge History of Southeast Asia*. Vol. 2, *The Nineteenth and Twentieth Centuries*, edited by Nicholas Tarling. Cambridge: Cambridge University Press, 1992.

Stone, Diane. "Networks, Second Track Diplomacy and Regional Cooperation: The Role of Southeast Asian Think Tanks". Paper presented to the 38th Annual International Studies Association Convention, Toronto, Canada, 22–26 March 1997.

Stubbs, Richard. "Geopolitics and the Political Economy of Southeast Asia". *International Journal* 44, no. 3 (1989): 517–40.

—————. "The Political Economy of the Asia-Pacific Region". In *Political Economy and the Changing Global Order*, edited by Richard Stubbs and G.R.D. Underhill. 2nd ed. Toronto: Oxford University Press, 1999.

—————. "Regionalization and Globalization". In *Political Economy and the Changing Global Order*, edited by Richard Stubbs and G.R.D. Underhill. 2nd ed. Toronto: Oxford University Press, 1999.

—————. "Signing on to Liberalization: AFTA and the Politics of Regional Economic Cooperation". *The Pacific Review* 13, no. 2 (2000): 297–318.

Stubbs, Richard and G.R.D. Underhill, eds. *Political Economy and the Changing Global Order*. 2nd ed. Toronto: Oxford University Press, 1999.

Subrahmanyam, Sanjay. "Connected Histories: Notes Towards A Reconfiguration of Early Modern Eurasia". *Modern Asian Studies* 31, no. 3 (1997): 735–62.

—————. "Notes on Circulation and Asymmetry in Two Mediterraneans". In *From the Mediterranean to the China Sea: Miscellaneous Notes*, edited by Claude Guillot et al. Wiesbaden: Harrassowitz, 1998.

Suehiro, Akira. *Capital Accumulation and Industrial Development in Thailand*. Bangkok: Social Research Institute, 1985.

Sukma, Rizal. "The Future of ASEAN: Towards a Security Community". Paper presented at the seminar on "ASEAN Cooperation: Challenges and Prospects in the Current International Situation". Permanent Mission of the Republic of Indonesia to the United Nations, New York, 3 June 2003.

Suriyamongkol, M.L. *Politics of ASEAN Economic Co-operation*. Singapore: Oxford University Press, 1988.

—————. "The Politics of Economic Cooperation in the Association of Southeast Asian Nations". Ph.D. dissertation. University of Illinois at Urbana-Champaign, 1982.

Sussangkarn, Chalongphob, Frank Flatters, and Sauwalak Kittiprapas. "Comparative Social Impacts of the Asian Economic Crisis in Thailand, Indonesia,

Malaysia and the Philippines: A Preliminary Report". *TDRI Quarterly Review* 14, no. 1 (1999): 3–9.

Sutherland, Heather. "Contingent Devices". In *Locating Southeast Asia: Geographies of Knowledge and Politics of Space*, edited by Paul Kratoska, Remeo Raben, and Henk Schulte Nordholt. Singapore: Singapore University Press/Athens: Ohio University Press, 2005.

———. "Southeast Asian History and the Mediterranean Analogy". *Journal of Southeast Asian Studies* 34, no. 1 (2003): 1–20.

Tambiah, Stanley J. *Culture, Thought, and Social Action: An Anthropological Perspective.* Cambridge: Harvard University Press, 1985.

———. *World Conqueror and World Renouncer: A Study of Buddhism and Polity in Thailand Against a Historical Background.* Cambridge: Cambridge University Press, 1976.

Tarling, Nicholas, ed. *The Cambridge History of Southeast Asia*, vol. 1. Cambridge: Cambridge University Press, 1992.

———, ed. *The Cambridge History of Southeast Asia.* Vol. 2, *The Nineteenth and Twentieth Centuries.* Cambridge: Cambridge University Press, 1992.

———. *Nations and States in Southeast Asia.* Cambridge: Cambridge University Press, 1998.

Tay, Simon. "Asean Plus Three: Challenges and a Caution About A New Regionalism". In *Asia Pacific Security: Challenges and Opportunities in the 21st Century*, edited by Mohamed Jawahar Hassan, Stephen Leong, and Vincent Lim. Kuala Lumpur: Institute of Strategic and Insternational Studies, 2002.

Than Han, Daw. "Common Vision: Burma's Regional Outlook". Occasional Paper. Washington, D.C.: Institute for the Study of Diplomacy, Georgetown University, 1988.

Than, M. "ASEAN, Indochina and Myanmar: Towards Economic Cooperation". *ASEAN Economic Bulletin* 8, no. 2 (1991): 173–93.

Thayer, Carlyle A. "The Challenges Facing Vietnamese Communism". *Southeast Asian Affairs 1992*. Singapore: Institute of Southeast Asian Studies, 1992.

Thompson, Eric C. "Southeast Asia". In *International Encyclopedia of Human Geography*, vol. 1, edited by R. Kitchin and N. Thrift. Oxford: Elsevier, 2009.

Thompson, William R. "The Regional Subsystem: A Conceptual Explication and a Propositional Inventory". *International Studies Quarterly* 17, no. 1 (1973): 89–117.

Thongswasdi, Tarnthong. "ASEAN after the Vietnam War: Stability and Development through Regional Cooperation". Ph.D dissertation. Claremont Graduate School, 1979.

Thu, My. "Renovation in Vietnam and Its Effects on Peace, Friendship and Cooperation in Southeast Asia". In *Unity in Diversity: Cooperation Between Vietnam and Other Southeast Asian Countries*, edited by Duy Quy Nguyen. Hanoi: Social Science Publishing House, 1992.

Tilly, Charles. *Coercion, Capital, and European States: AD 990–1990*. Cambridge: Cambridge University Press, 1990.

Tilman, Robert O., ed. *Man, State, and Society in Contemporary Southeast Asia*. London: Pall Mall Press, 1969.

————. *Southeast Asia and the Enemy Beyond: ASEAN Perceptions of External Threats*. Boulder, CO: Westview Press, 1987.

Trocki, Carl A. "Political Structures in the Nineteenth and Early Twentieth Centuries". In *Cambridge History of Southeast Asia*. Vol. 2, *The Nineteenth and Twentieth Centuries*, edited by Nicholas Tarling. Cambridge: Cambridge University Press, 1992.

Turnbull, C.M. "Regionalism and Nationalism". In *Cambridge History of Southeast Asia*. Vol. 2, *The Nineteenth and Twentieth Centuries*, edited by Nicholas Tarling. Cambridge: Cambridge University Press, 1992.

UNDP Programme Thailand. <http://www.undp.or.th/tsunami/tsunami.htm> (accessed 26 June 2006).

Unger, Leonard. "A Practitioner's Perspective on Southeast Asian Studies". In *Southeast Asian Studies: Options for the Future*, edited by Ronald A. Morse. Lanham, MD: University Press of America, 1984.

United Nations Public Administration Network (UNPAN). "Foreign Direct Investments to China and Southeast Asia: Has ASEAN Been Losing Out?". *Economic Survey of Singapore (Third Quarter) 2002*. <http://unpan1.un.org/intradoc/groups/public/documents/APCITY/UNPAN010347.pdf> (accessed 20 June 2006).

Vandenbosch, Amry and R. Butwell. *The Changing Face of Southeast Asia*. Lexington: University of Kentucky Press, 1966.

Vatikiotis, Michael. "Going Regional". *Far Eastern Economic Review*, 20 October 1994, p. 16.

————. "Measure for Measure: Malaysia, Singapore Poised to Acquire New Arms". *Far Eastern Economic Review*, 30 April 1992, p. 18.

————. "A Too Friendly Embrace". *Far Eastern Economic Review*, 17 June 2004, pp. 20–22.

————. "Signing on to Liberalization: AFTA and the Politics of Regional Economic Cooperation". *The Pacific Review* 13, no. 2 (2000): 297–318.

Wæver, O. "Culture and Identity in the Baltic Sea Region". In *Cooperation in the Baltic Sea Region*, edited by Pertti Joenniemi. London: Taylor and Francis, 1993.

Wales, H.G. Quaritch. *The Making of Greater India*. 2nd ed. London: Bernard Quaritch, 1951.

Walton, J. "Economics". In *An Introduction to Southeast Asian Studies*, edited by Mohammed Halib and Tim Huxley. London: I.B. Tauris, 1996.

Wanandi, Jusuf. "The Regional Role of 'Track-Two' Diplomacy: ASEAN, ARF, and CSCAP". In *The Role of Security and Economic Cooperation Structures in the*

Asia Pacific Region, edited by Hadi Soesastro and Anthony Bergin. Jakarta: Centre for Strategic and International Studies, 1996.

————. "Security Issues in the ASEAN Region". In *ASEAN Security and Economic Development*, edited by Karl D. Jackson and M. Hadi Soesastro. Research Papers and Policy Studies no. 11. Berkeley: Institute of East Asian Studies, University of California, 1984.

Wang Gungwu. "Introduction". In *Southeast Asia in the 9th to the 14th Centuries*, edited by David G. Marr and A.C. Milner. Singapore: Institute of Southeast Asian Studies/Canberra: Australian National University, Research School of Pacific Studies, 1990.

————. "Nation Formation and Regionalism in Southeast Asia". In *South Asia Pacific Crisis: National Development and World Community*, edited by M. Grant. New York: Dodd, Mead and Company, 1964.

————. "The Universal and the Historical: My Faith in History". Fourth Daisaku Ikeda Annual Lecture, Singapore Soka Association, 2005.

Wattanapruttipaisan, Thitapha. "Watching Brief on China and ASEAN Part One: The Rise of China as an Economic Power". BEI Studies Unit, Paper no. 05/2005. <http://www.aseansec.org/Watching_Brief_on_China_-_Thitapha.pdf> (accessed 26 June 2006).

Weatherbee, Donald E. "An Overview of Cultural and Historical Roots of Contemporary Southeast Asia". Proceedings of a Study Group Series and Symposium presented in cooperation with the Asia Society, Atlanta, 1985, pp. 6–11.

————. et al. *International Relations in Southeast Asia: The Struggle for Autonomy*. Lanham, MD: Rowman and Littlefield, 2005.

Weinstein, Franklin B. "Indonesia Abandons Confrontation". Interim Report Series, Modern Indonesia Project, Southeast Asia Program, Department of Asian Studies, Cornell University, 1969.

Wendt, Alexander. "Collective Identity and the International State". *American Political Science Review* 88 (1994): 384–96.

————. *Social Theory of International Politics*. Cambridge: Cambridge University Press, 1999.

Wertheim, W.F. "Early Asian Trade: An Appreciation of J.C. van Leur". *Far Eastern Quarterly* 3, no. 2 (1954): 167–73.

Wheatley, Paul. "Comments on the Dynamics of the Process of Indianization". In *Early Malaysia*, edited by Kernial Singh Sandhu. Singapore: Singapore Education Press, 1973.

————. "Desultory Remarks on the Ancient History of the Malay Peninsula". In *Malayan and Indonesian Studies*, edited by John Bastin and R. Roolvink. Oxford: Clarendon Press, 1964.

————. "Presidential Address: India Beyond the Ganges — Desultory Reflections on the Origins of Civilization in Southeast Asia". *Journal of Asian Studies* 42, no. 1 (1982): 13–28.

Wolters, O.W. "Culture, History and Region in Southeast Asian Perspectives". In *ASEAN: Identity, Development and Culture*, edited by R.P. Anand and P.V. Quisumbing. Quezon City: University of the Philippines Law Center/ Honolulu: East-West Center, Culture Learning Institute, 1981.

————. *History, Culture and Region in Southeast Asian Perspectives*. Rev. ed. Ithaca, NY: Cornell University Southeast Asia Program/Singapore: Institute of Southeast Asian Studies, 1999.

Wong, John and Sarah Chan. "China-ASEAN Free Trade Agreement: Shaping Future Economic Relations". *Asian Survey* 43, no. 3 (2003): 507–26.

World Bank. "Tsunami Recovery in Indonesia", March 2006. <http://web. worldbank.org/ WBSITE/EXTERNAL/COUNTRIES/EASTASIAPACIFICEXT/ 0,,contentMDK:20738359~pagePK:146736~piPK:146830~theSitePK:226301,00. html> (accessed 26 June 2006).

World Health Organization. "Summary of Probable SARS Cases with Onset of Illness from 1 November 2002 to 31 July 2003". <http://www.who.int/csr/ sars/country/ table2004_04_21/en/index.html> (accessed 26 June 2006).

Yeo, George. Speech to the Global Leadership Forum, Kuala Lumpur, 6 September 2005. <http://www.mfa.gov.sg/internet/> (accessed 24 June 2006).

Yoshihara, Kunio. *Philippine Industrialization: Foreign and Domestic Capital*. New York: Oxford University Press, 1985.

Young, Evans. "Development Cooperation in ASEAN: Balancing Free Trade and Regional Planning". Ph.D. dissertation. University of Michigan, Ann Arbor, 1981.

Young, K.T. *The Southeast Asia Crisis*. New York: The Association of the Bar of the City of New York, 1966.

Zacher, M.W. *International Conflicts and Collective Security, 1946–1977*. New York: Praeger, 1979.

Zarkovic, M. "The Revival of ASEAN". *Review of International Affairs* (Belgrade) 28, no. 5 (1977): 29–31.

Zhao Hong. "India's Changing Relationship with ASEAN in China's Perspective". EAI Background Brief no. 313. Singapore: East Asian Institute, 2006. <http:// www.eai.nus.edu.sg/BB313.pdf>.

Index

About the Author

AMITAV ACHARYA is Professor of International Relations at the School of International Service, American University, Washington, D.C. He is also the UNESCO Chair in Transnational Challenges and Governance and Chair of the University's ASEAN Studies Center at the American University. Previously, he was Professor of Global Governance at the University of Bristol; Professor, Deputy Director and Head of Research of the Institute of Defence and Strategic Studies (now the S. Rajaratnam School of International Studies), Nanyang Technological University, Singapore; Professor of Political Science at York University, Toronto; Fellow of the Asia Center, Harvard University, and Fellow of the Center for Business and Government at Harvard's John F. Kennedy School of Government.

He has held several visiting professorships and fellowships, including the Direk Jayanama Visiting Professorship in Political Science at Thammasat University, Thailand; ASEM (Asia-Europe Meeting) Chair in Regional Integration at the University of Malaya; Visiting Professorial Fellow, Institute of Southeast Asian Studies, Singapore; Senior Fellow, Asia Pacific Foundation of Canada, Vancouver; Visiting Professor, Lee Kuan Yew School for Public Policy, Singapore; and the Nelson Mandela Visiting Professorship in International Relations at Rhodes University, South Africa.

Professor Acharya's other books include: *Constructing a Security Community in Southeast Asia* (2nd edition, 2009); *Crafting Cooperation: Regional International Institutions in Comparative Politics* (co-edited, 2007); *Whose Ideas Matter: Agency and Power in Asian Regionalism* (2010). The latter was one of the five books shortlisted by the Asia Society for their "exceptional contributions to the understanding of contemporary Asia or US-Asia relations" for its Bernard Schwartz Book Award in 2010. His essays have appeared in the world's top academic and policy journals such as *International Organization, International Security, International Studies Quarterly, World Politics, Foreign Affairs, Journal of Peace Research, Journal of Asian Studies, Survival*, and *Washington Quarterly*. He has appeared on a wide variety of international media, including CNN International, BBC World Service, Al-Jazeera TV, CNBC, CTV (Canada) Canadian Broadcasting Corporation, Radio Australia, and Channel News Asia. His current affairs commentaries have appeared in *Financial Times, International Herald Tribune, Australian Financial Review, Times of India, Indian Express, Straits Times, Jakarta Post, Bangkok Post, Far Eastern Economic Review, Japan Times, South China Morning Post*, and *YaleGlobal Online* covering topics in international and Asian security and regionalism.

www.ingramcontent.com/pod-product-compliance
Ingram Content Group UK Ltd.
Pitfield, Milton Keynes, MK11 3LW, UK
UKHW041955260225
455627UK00002B/10